THE BIBLE
THROUGHOUT THE AGES

THE BIBLE THROUGHOUT THE AGES

ITS NATURE, INTERPRETATION, AND RELEVANCE FOR TODAY

THE SCRIPTURE COLLECTIVE SERIES

LYDIA JAEGER AND
CRAIG G. BARTHOLOMEW, EDITORS

ZONDERVAN
ACADEMIC

ZONDERVAN ACADEMIC

The Bible throughout the Ages

Published in Grand Rapids, Michigan, by Zondervan. Zondervan is a registered trademark of The Zondervan Corporation, L.L.C., a wholly owned subsidiary of HarperCollins Christian Publishing, Inc.

Requests for information should be addressed to customercare@harpercollins.com.

Zondervan titles may be purchased in bulk for educational, business, fundraising, or sales promotional use. For information, please email SpecialMarkets@Zondervan.com.

Library of Congress Cataloging-in-Publication Data

Names: Jaeger, Lydia, editor. | Bartholomew, Craig G., 1961-, editor.
Title: The Bible throughout the Ages : its nature, interpretation, and relevance for today / Lydia Jaeger and Craig Bartholomew, editors.
Description: Grand Rapids, Michigan : Zondervan Academic, [2024] | Series: The scripture collective series | Includes bibliographical references and index.
Identifiers: LCCN 2024013161 | ISBN 9780310139232 (softcover) | ISBN 9780310139249 (ebook)
Subjects: LCSH: Bible—Criticism, interpretation, etc. | Bible—Study and teaching—History. | BISAC: RELIGION / Biblical Criticism & Interpretation / General | RELIGION / Christian Church / History
Classification: LCC BS500 .B5488 2024 | DDC 220.609—dc23/eng/20240529
LC record available at https://lccn.loc.gov/2024013161

Cover design: Tammy Johnson
Cover image: The Met Museum
Interior design: Kait Lamphere

Printed in the United States of America

---

24 25 26 27 28 29 30 31 32 33 34 /TRM/ 15 14 13 12 11 10 9 8 7 6 5 4 3 2 1

Contents

PREFACE

Reading the Bible Today

Lydia Jaeger

The Bible is a unique landmark in the world's literary heritage. Written in three different languages (Hebrew, Aramaic, and Greek), amidst diverse cultures, and during a period of over a thousand years, it displays both a remarkable diversity (the literary genres, the themes touched on, and the styles of writing) and a profound unity in the vision it sets forth. This vision can be summarized in three words: creation, fall, redemption. Everything that exists has come into being through the one creator God – evil is a painful perversion brought into the world by the abuse of created freedom – and the creator God entered into the history of his creation to vanquish every form of evil.

Completed almost two thousand years ago, the Bible is still the most widely read book in the world and the one that has been translated into the most languages. According to the statistics provided by *Wycliffe Global Alliance*, the complete Bible is available in 736 languages (which are used by 6 billion people). A further 1,658 languages (spoken by 824 million people) have versions of the New Testament. Shorter extracts exist for another 1,264 languages (spoken by 449 million people).[1] The Bible is by far the most widely distributed book in the world.

In addition, it has had an unparalleled impact on societies and on individuals. I have an unforgettable memory of the radiant face of a lorry driver from Brittany (France) when he took from his trouser pocket the New Testament

1. Figures are given for 2023: Wycliffe Global Alliance, "2023 Scripture Access Statistics," https://www.wycliffe.net/resources/statistics/. Wycliffe Global Alliance is an alliance of over one hundred organizations in the world with the common objective of translating the Bible for every language group which needs it.

that he carried with him everywhere he went. He had discovered the Christian faith late in life, and this portion of the Bible was the only book he ever read. Today many languages are being put into writing for the first time to publish biblical texts.

The importance of the Bible can also be measured by the number of books written about it – so many in fact that the question can be asked whether it is appropriate to add yet another one to the list. The first response to this question is to note the fascination with the Scriptures felt by a wide range of generations and groups of human beings. Everyone needs to make this book (or to be more accurate this library of books) their own. The hallmark of great texts is their ability to generate extended interaction.

But a second response to this question is that the present book is justified by several original features. First and foremost, there is the emphasis on epistemological questions (meaning "methodological" ones). This book not only deals with questions relating to the reading of the Bible but also to its status concerning truth and revelation, and it does so by insisting on epistemological problems: reading methods, hermeneutic principles according to different religious traditions, the reception of the text, whether we should hold what is said as true or merely a "signifier," literal or metaphorical reading, the contribution of doctrine in reading the Bible, devotional or academic reading, the role of textual history, and the influence of changes in the contemporary world in the way the meaning of the Bible can be grasped.

In addition, as a third response, the present book stands out through the diversity of the cultural areas, religious traditions, and academic disciplines represented by the authors. In terms of geography, the authors come from the English-speaking world on both sides of the Atlantic, continental Europe (Belgium, France, Germany, Netherlands), Israel, and the African continent (one author is originally from South Africa and another has been immersed for eight years in theological education under indigenous leadership in one of the poorest countries of French-speaking sub-Saharan Africa). In terms of religious background, the authors represent various traditions of Christianity (Reformed, Lutheran, Baptist, and Roman Catholic) and Judaism. In terms of academic disciplines, from biblical exegesis and systematic theology through to literary studies. What unites the authors is, on the one hand, their recognized expertise in the field of their contribution and, on the other, their passion for the Scriptures. This passion leads them to sharpen and defend vigorously their positions while at the same time entering into dialogue with differing options.

Other features contribute to the originality of the present book. In addition to providing extensive treatment of exegetical and doctrinal matters with regard to biblical interpretation, this book engages with the wider cultural context in which the Bible is read today, as for example in the developments revolving around the increased availability of the printed Bible at the onset of modernity and the rise of the modern subject (ch. 11), challenges posed by changing reading habits in the West and digital media (ch. 12), and the changes in understanding the Bible that are brought about by new fruitful insights from the global South (ch. 13). Although they are at the cutting edge of research, the authors have attempted to make their contributions accessible to a wide nonspecialist audience. In particular, students and people interested in the Bible will find that this book is a convenient introduction to a variety of questions asked today. A bibliography at the end of each chapter will suggest ways of exploring the themes under discussion further. And even the reader who is a specialist in biblical exegesis and theology will find that this book offers a wealth of information because of the vast range of issues covered.

The book is the result of a bilingual project. It brings together English- and French-speaking authors and is published both in French and in English.[2] Thus it makes research available across borders, providing the French-speaking public with access to the expertise of some of the world leaders in the field of biblical hermeneutics, and allowing non-French readers to discover the major trends in biblical scholarship on the European Continent. In particular, North American readers will benefit from reading authors from diverse sociocultural backgrounds, as many Western European countries, and in particular France, are strongly secularized. Although the American context is still very religious, it might well follow this trend. As we have seen with postmodernism, what develops in France often takes off in the United States. Thus there is a great benefit to this sort of work, which will enable American readers to discover the main issues from Western European scholars' point of view and for French readers to learn from English and American expertise.

Before inviting the reader to set out on this journey, a brief synopsis will provide an orientation. This publication can be broken down into three sections: the Bible as revelation, biblical interpretation, and reading the Bible in the contemporary world.

The first major section on the Bible as revelation comprises five chapters. Kevin Vanhoozer gets the ball rolling by examining the meaning of the assertion that the Bible is the Word of God. What can be the meaning of such a statement? The conviction that the Bible is the word of God must be understood

2. The French edition was published in 2022 by Bibli'O, the publishing house of the *Alliance biblique française* (the French Bible society) under the title *Lire la Bible aujourd'hui: Perspectives croisées sur les défis contemporains*.

against the background of other Christian beliefs about the manner of divine revelation and redemption. Christians maintain that saving knowledge of God depends on God's self-communication in the histories of Israel and of Jesus Christ. Special attention is therefore given to the word of God as a divine speech act that occurs "behind," "in," and "in front of" the biblical texts associated with these twin histories. The Bible is divine and human discourse: the human discourse is testimony to divine speech acts, in particular, the covenants that lie at the heart of the two testaments. The various elements in a doctrine of Scripture (e.g., inspiration, infallibility, illumination) only come into proper focus against this backdrop. The chapter concludes with reflections on how viewing the Bible as divine discourse affects its reading.

Next comes Henri Blocher's study on the notion of inerrancy: What exactly do we mean when we say that the Bible is without error? Too often misrepresentations have obscured the real issues in the ongoing debate on the topic. We should strive toward analytical clarity. Defining what should count as *error* (in Scripture) is a delicate matter, and this essay shows both that drawing boundary lines can be done consistently and that one may legitimately hesitate at some places. It investigates the authority of historical continuity, the notion of truth, conclusions in the field of textual and literary criticism, the place of phenomena and presuppositions, and the relationship to hermeneutics and other doctrines in the "body" of Christian teaching. A sound method will consider such matters to ground a wise decision for or against inerrancy.

Henk van den Belt examines, under the title of "Holy Resonance," the role that the Holy Spirit plays in the process of revelation through the Bible. The chapter starts with an analysis of the way Scripture speaks about the work of the Spirit in its relationship to revelation and to the authority of Scripture. It then focuses on several key concepts for understanding the relationship between the Spirit and the text: the spiritual unity of Scripture by which the apostolic and early Church received the Hebrew Bible as authoritative, the spiritual acceptance of the Bible as the principle of our knowledge of God, and the inner witness of the Spirit as understood in the Protestant Reformation. The chapter concludes reflecting on the work of the Spirit today in the context of the Christian community and how it bridges the historical gap between the original revelation and the present reception of Scripture as the Word of God.

Then, in a chapter entitled "The Bible Is Not an Image," Olivier Riaudel examines the relationship between Scripture, tradition, and reason. After clarifying the meaning of *sola scriptura* in Protestant theology, he endeavours to show that this statement is not absent from Roman Catholic theology, even in the Middle Ages, using the example of Thomas Aquinas. Then he suggests a theoretical framework derived from a contextualist, pragmatic approach to the philosophy of language in order to understand the place and role of different ecclesiastical traditions in reading the Bible.

Karsten Lehmkühler concludes the section with the question: How can we use the Bible in Christian ethics? This question is one of the most important issues in theological ethics today. After some remarks on the present state of research on the subject, the chapter discusses, with the help of concrete examples, the question of *hermeneutical rules* in connection with the use of the Bible for Christian ethics. How can we avoid literalism that does not respect the cultural gulf between a text from biblical times and our age? On the other hand, how can we go beyond very general principles such as love for our neighbour? Then the chapter addresses the *three moral theories* under discussion today, namely deontological ethics, consequentialist ethics, and virtue ethics. It considers whether the Bible enriches and shapes each of these ethical approaches.

The second main section of the book is dedicated to methodological issues raised by biblical interpretation. It opens with a masterful historical overview presented by Anthony Thiselton. All reading is interpretation, but it is not arbitrary because a text has contextual, historical, and theological constraints. Even the early church found this issue to be a problem. The Alexandrian thinkers extended meanings through the use of allegory and typology. However, others (primarily the Antiochene School) preferred to emphasize the literal meaning. The Reformation, particularly Luther, brought with it a desire to affirm the clarity of Scripture. Luther linked this "clarity" with practical reliance on God and the Bible, with which he compared Erasmus's tendency to hesitate until having reached complete certainty. The second half of the chapter presents and evaluates the contributions made by modern authors to biblical hermeneutics: Schleiermacher and his lasting influence on modern Bible reading, Dilthey with his stress on "life" and social science, Heidegger and Bultmann ushering in an era of existential interpretation, Gadamer's ontological hermeneutics, and the balancing and creative work of Paul Ricœur, who stressed both diversity and constraint in biblical interpretation.

Next, Craig Bartholomew examines the relationship between the Bible and history. Prior to the rise of modernity, the historical narratives were treated virtually unanimously as history telling. It is with the rise of modernity, and figures like Spinoza, Kant, Wilhelm de Wette and Julius Wellhausen, that history has become one of the most contested areas of biblical studies. The Radical Enlightenment was determined to eliminate or marginalize religion from the great public spheres of life. In its wake, biblical studies were secularized, and two opposing pictures of biblical history emerged: the confessional version enshrined in the Bible and those of modern critical scholarship. In the last quarter of the twentieth century, the historical emphasis in biblical studies experienced some major challenges. From the 1970s onwards, biblical studies experienced a literary turn, with the rediscovery of the Bible as literature. Postmodernism opened the door for a reengagement with religion, but at its extreme it virtually erased the distinction between fiction and history. The most recent ongoing "theological turn" argues that we need a theology of history (and literature, etc.) to inform biblical interpretation. The Bible developed a unique view of history that increases one's interest in the historicity of the Bible and orients one towards history in a particular way so that one can take the historical aspect of the Bible with full seriousness. The Bible is awash with historical narratives about divine action in history, but in so much modern biblical interpretation the one issue excluded is one's view of God. Affirm the biblical view of God as creator and redeemer – the God who sustains, governs, and acts in history – and then one is far more positively oriented towards the Bible and history. This does not solve all the many, many historical issues that emerge in biblical studies, but it creates a border within which solutions may be found.

Jeremiah Unterman undertakes the daunting task of presenting the multimillennial history of Jewish biblical interpretation. This history is the history of Jewish religious civilisation for the better part of the past three thousand years. Jewish exegesis has had as its main goals the understanding of the formative Holy Scriptures of the Jewish people – both as comprehending God's will and making it comprehensible and meaningful to the contemporary Jew – in both law and spirit. Such exegesis first occurred within the Jewish Bible and then in the extrabiblical Jewish literature of the late Second Temple period. Ancient rabbinic literature focused on legal and midrashic interpretation. The primary influences upon medieval rabbinic interpretation within the Muslim orbit (stretching from Babylonia – modern-day Iraq – to Spain) were Islamic philosophy, linguistics, grammar, and rhetoric. These developments were passed on by rabbinic scholars to their colleagues in Christian Europe. The development of the *peshat* approach independently in Sephardic and Ashkenazic Judiasm brought a greater emphasis on the plain meaning of the text as understandable to every Jew who knew Hebrew. Esoteric understandings remained mostly in obscurity. The Enlightenment in the modern period gave rise to more of a historical and academic approach, which eventually brought the systematic method of the New Criticism into literary analysis of the Bible. That method has been supplemented by archaeological discoveries and a greater dedication to Jewish interpretation as illustrating the history of Jewish ideas, ritual, and ethics.

Next comes a study by Emmanuel Durand of two giants of Christian theology, Augustine of Hippo and Thomas Aquinas. To present their biblical exegesis, Durand considers their respective ways of describing the functions of Scripture and the correct way to use it, the resources and textual tools available to them, and the reading methods that they preferred. After providing some essential bearings in these areas, a case study compares the exegesis by Augustine and Thomas of the words of Jesus: "My soul is overwhelmed with sorrow to the point of death" (Matt 26:38; Mark 14:34).

The section on biblical interpretation concludes with a presentation by Armin D. Baum on the so-called historical-critical method, which is the dominant method applied in modern biblical studies. Its roots go back to antiquity. The "historical-critical" method encompasses both an exegetical and a historical approach of the texts. The exegetical method consists of synchronic and diachronic text analysis. However, even if the exegetical method is applied carefully, it cannot offer existential access to the biblical texts. This can only be achieved by spiritual experience, which must never restrict the exegetical method, but complement it. The historical method consists primarily of external and internal source criticism. The historian must beware of methodical suspicion and the hypercritical evaluation of his sources that results from it. However, even if the historical method is applied perfectly, it cannot produce absolute certainty, only probability. But for Christians, the inner testimony of the Holy Spirit, which presupposes the strong historical evidence of the New Testament sources, reaches beyond the limited possibilities of historical research. Through the Holy Spirit a person can respond in faith to the biblical texts. After having presented the historical-critical method, Baum focuses on one aspect of it that has become an important ingredient since the nineteenth century: the adjective *critical* is often used in the sense of *a priori* rejection of the possibility of miracles. Therefore *historical-critical* has also come to mean *historical-and-miracle-critical*. The criterion of philosophical miracle criticism was promoted successfully in biblical scholarship by Ernst Troeltsch. However, this kind of criticism is not without its own critics, who regard a methodical openness as more appropriate, allowing for the possibility of supernatural acts of God in history.

The third and final section of the book moves on to the reading of the Bible in the context of contemporary society (or, in fact, societies). It opens with a chapter specifically commissioned for the English-language edition. The French edition contains a rare study of biblical references in contemporary fiction in the French language written by Dominique Ranaivoson-Hecht.[3] For the English

3. Dominique Ranaivoson-Hecht, "La Bible entre les lignes de la littérature contemporaine: Comment lire la Bible en laïcité," in *Lire la Bible aujourd'hui: Perspectives croisées sur les défis contemporains*, ed. Lydia Jaeger (Paris: Bibli'O, 2022), 329–57.

edition, we rather decided to include a chapter focusing on English literature: Karen Swallow Prior describes the way the Bible as a printed text contributed to the rise of modernity, modern literature, and the modern subject. The modern age saw a shift in authority from the objective and external world towards the inner world of self-consciousness, experience, and agency. In addition to these larger epistemological developments, the newly accessible ability to read the Bible (or any text) conferred validity upon the authority of that reading self. The validation, first, of the subjective authority of the self grew over time into the privileging of inner, self-generated authority over external, objective authority. As reading and interpretation became increasingly individual, private acts, so too did the authority of the inner life increasingly shape the mode of being of subjects within the modern world. Modern literature in many ways both expressed and cultivated this mode of thinking and being, one increasingly skeptical of the authority or even the relevance of the Bible. Yet even a brief survey of a few key, but varied, modern literary texts demonstrates that in building on and evoking a rich tradition rooted in biblical narratives, images, and language and by demanding critical rather than naïve readings, modern literature, in its own way, has given us the Bible again.

Philippe De Pol examines the impact of new reading habits in the West on Bible reading. The digital revolution highlights the development of media and of immediacy, making some people fear that books will disappear. The media-saturated world, in which several generations have grown up, has shaped an information culture. How is the Bible – the book par excellence, handed down over centuries – read and interpreted today? The Scriptures require readers to interpret the text and make it their own. What chance is there for this approach in a society where each new thing drives out the last one and where everyone claims to have their own truth? The writer concludes on a confident note: the very history of the Bible (its writing and its transmission) leads us to think that the Word of God will continue to be heard for a long time yet.

The worldwide Christian community constitutes the appropriate horizon for the last chapter written by Benno van den Toren. Since the second half of the twentieth century, the "centre of gravity" of the church is increasingly moving southward. The majority of the world's Christians no longer live in the Middle East, Europe, or North America, but in Africa, Latin America, and Asia. This change has raised the awareness that the Bible is not a book that belongs to the West. It can be and is read from many cultural perspectives. The chapter explores how from the very beginning the Christian Bible has been translated in different languages as it successively crossed ever new cultural boundaries. This translation is itself an example of how Scripture is read in multiple cultures and can be used as a model for cross-cultural hermeneutics. After introducing the hermeneutical implications of the process of cross-cultural translation, the chapter outlines some of the main approaches to Bible reading that have been developed in the context of the globalization and southward movement of the church since the latter half of the twentieth century such as inculturation hermeneutics, liberation hermeneutics, postcolonial hermeneutics, and Pentecostal hermeneutics. These reflect the need to take into account the role of culture, religious plurality, social tensions, global power relations, and personal spiritual involvement for understanding how people groups read the Christian Scriptures. The author argues for the need for an intercultural reading of the Scriptures in which different contextual readings can critically enrich each other. Thus modern Western readings are challenged to reflect in new ways on the question whether some readings are more able to do justice to the nature and content of the Christian Scriptures than others.

"To the law and to the testimony" the prophet Isaiah exclaimed (8:20).[4] The various contributions to this book are intended to be a prism that enables a greater enjoyment of the rich diversity of Scripture. May the reader gain through them a deeper understanding of the epistemological issues raised by reading the Bible in order to have a renewed encounter with this ancient text, which has never ceased to fascinate – and to shape – each person who has come into contact with it.

4. Henri Blocher's translation from the original Hebrew.

PART 1

The Bible as Revelation

CHAPTER 1

The Bible – Word of God?

Kevin J. Vanhoozer

The conviction that the Bible is the word of God, far from being an arbitrary claim about the superiority of one's own Scripture over rival sacred texts, is in fact part of a larger pattern of beliefs distinct to Christianity. That claim has significant implications for reading the Bible. The present chapter describes the nature and purpose of the Bible in terms suggested by the Bible itself as developed theologically in the Christian tradition.[1]

The Christian statement, "the Bible is the word of God," is not the formal equivalent of "the Qur'an is the word of God," "the Vedas are the word of God," or "the Book of Mormon is the word of God," despite the surface syntactic similarities. Comparative religious phenomenology of sacred Scriptures will misconstrue what Christians mean by identifying the Bible as the word of God.[2] Rather, what is needed is a careful unpacking of the grammar of Christian faith and, in particular, a parsing of the place of the Bible and its claim to authority in the broader pattern of divine revelation – what we might call the "economy

1. The conviction that the Bible is the speech of God is shared by Protestants and Roman Catholics. The Westminster Larger Catechism (1648) is representative of many Protestant statements: "The Holy Scriptures of the Old and New Testament are the Word of God, the only rule of faith and obedience" (question 3). *Dei Verbum* (1965), the Dogmatic Constitution on Divine Revelation (one of the seminal documents of the Roman Catholic Vatican *II* consulation) says something similar: "Sacred Scripture is the speech of God (*locutio Dei*) as it is attested in writing under the inspiration of the divine Spirit" (DV 9).

2. For a phenomenological approach to these texts, see James Fieser and John Powers, eds., *Scriptures of the World's Religions*, 6th ed. (New York: McGraw-Hill, 2017).

of self-communication," namely, the way God shares his light and life with the world via the work of his "two hands," the Son and Spirit.[3]

Divine intervention – direct divine action in history that makes a difference to that history – occupies a central place in Christian Scripture and tradition alike.[4] Indeed, without the belief that God has at some place and time made himself concretely known in intelligible speech, it becomes implausible, even impossible, to say what God is up to in the world. Divine interjection alone clarifies divine intervention: "If God does not speak, then it is not clear how we can know in any substantial way His intentions and purposes."[5] If God has not spoken, then any claim about God's purposes becomes as weak as any other ungrounded human speculation: "Our reaching up to Him in thought and inference is possible only because He condescends to make Himself intelligible to us, to speak to us through work or word, to reveal Himself."[6] Absent divine speech, theology falls headlong into the open arms of Ludwig Feuerbach, the atheistic "master of suspicion," who insisted that the secret truth of theology is that it is always and only anthropology, a projection of human hopes and values.[7]

If God has not at some point communicated to human beings, we are unable to say what God is doing, and the basic plot of the biblical story is evacuated of substance. Indeed, as this chapter will argue, unless God speaks, God cannot perform certain actions (for example, covenanting) insofar as they require doing things with words. The Bible presents sustained historical testimony to God's communicative action in the histories of Israel and of Jesus Christ. In light of this testimony, is there a compelling reason to reject the consistent claim of the biblical authors, as well as the communities that adhere to these texts as sacred Scripture, that God has made promises, issued commands, foretold the future, and forgiven sinners? The present essay begins by examining the economy of divine communication, that is, the various ways the Bible depicts divine communicative action. We then turn to an analysis of what it means to construe the

---

3. Ephesians 1:10 and 3:9 speak of the "plan" or "economy" (Gk. *oikonomia*) of salvation fulfilled in Christ. In Christian tradition, the Greek patristic theologians distinguished between *theologia* (the mystery of God's inmost, inner-Trinitarian eternal life that he has within himself) and *oikonomia* (the external works of Father, Son, and Spirit by which he reveals and enacts his eternal purposes in time). For the Christian view of the one God as Father, Son, and Spirit, see Gilles Emery and Matthew Levering, eds., *The Oxford Handbook of the Trinity* (Oxford: Oxford University Press, 2011).

4. The outstanding examples would be the exodus (liberating Israel from slavery to Egypt) and the resurrection (raising Jesus from the dead).

5. William J. Abraham, *Divine Revelation and the Limits of Historical Criticism* (Oxford: Oxford University Press, 1982), 25.

6. B. B. Warfield, "The Idea of Systematic Theology," *The Presbyterian and Reformed Review* 7 (1896): 250.

7. Ludwig Feuerbach, *The Essence of Christianity* (Buffalo: Prometheus, 1989).

Bible itself as a species of that action (i.e., divine discourse), followed by some reflections on how to read the Bible as a text coauthored by human and divine communicative agents.

THE WORD OF GOD BEHIND, IN, AND IN FRONT OF THE BIBLICAL TEXT

The distinctiveness of the Christian claim that the Bible is the word of God comes into sharper focus in the important opening statement to the book of Hebrews: "Long ago God spoke to our ancestors in many and various ways by the prophets, but in these last days he has spoken to us by a Son" (Heb 1:1–2 NRSV).[8] The author cites various Old Testament texts as themselves instances of divine speech, which he variously ascribes to the Father (Heb 1:5–13; 8:8–12), Son (Heb 10:5–7), and Spirit (Heb 10:15–17). In at least one instance (Heb 3:7–4:11), the author implies that God the Spirit is *presently* speaking to his readers through the citation of Psalm 95:7–11. The author of Hebrews also refers to his own "word of exhortation" (Heb 13:22), his sermon sent as a letter, as part and parcel of the divine address (Heb 12:25).

The first task, therefore, is to clarify the relationship between divine speaking and the books of the Bible. It will be useful to appeal to the threefold distinction, drawn from Paul Ricœur's textual hermeneutics, between the worlds behind, in, and in front of the text, although for present purposes the focus will be on the *word* (of God) behind, in, and in front of the text.[9]

THE WORD OF GOD BEHIND THE TEXT

"Long ago God spoke to our ancestors in many and various ways" (Heb 1:1). The word behind the text refers to reported instances of God speaking before there was a Bible. One of the most frequent phrases in the Old Testament is "the word of the Lord came to." The word of God comes to Abram (Gen 15:1), Samuel (1 Sam 15:10), Nathan (2 Sam 7:4), Solomon (1 Kings 6:11), Elijah (1 Kings 18:1), Isaiah (Isa 38:4), Jeremiah (Jer 1:11), Ezekiel (Ezek 1:3), and others, usually with a commission to transmit a message to someone else: "Thus says the Lord" (Exod 4:22; Josh 24:2; 1 Sam 10:18; Isa 7:7, etc.). This word of

8. All biblical references are to the *New Revised Standard Version* (1989).

9. For Ricœur's treatment of the world of and in front of the text, see *Interpretation Theory: Discourse and the Surplus of Meaning* (Fort Worth: Texas Christian University Press, 1976), 37, 87–94. For an application of this threefold distinction to biblical hermeneutics, see W. Randolph Tate, *Biblical Interpretation: An Integrated Approach*, rev. ed. (Peabody, MA: Hendrickson, 1997).

the Lord behind the text is the main engine that drives forward the entire story of the Bible.

Among the most important things the Bible records God as saying are the Ten Commandments (Exod 20:1–17) or "ten words" (Heb. *dabar*; Exod 34:28; Deut 4:13; 10:4), the law that was to define and constitute the nation Israel. In Israel's history, the way her kings and people responded to the word of the Lord – in obedience or disobedience, trust or unbelief – determined their fate, for better or for ill. The unrighteous kings of Israel did not "follow the law of the LORD the God of Israel" (2 Kings 10:31) and were subsequently judged. Eventually, the whole nation was sent into exile because of their failure to hear and heed God's word. The primary vocation of the prophets was to urge Israel to obey God's word, to explain the consequences of disobedience, and to console the people with the assurance that God would ultimately prove faithful to his promise, even when the people proved unfaithful.

Prior to the giving of the law was an even more consequential divine speech act, behind the text, that arguably lies at the heart of Israel's history: God's promise to Abraham to make him a great nation (Gen 12:2–3; 17:4–8). Martin Luther, the great Protestant Reformer, declared that "the chief topic of all of Holy Scripture is to know and comprehend God as the one who promises."[10] Without this historical anchoring word, there would be no covenant between God and Abraham, no promise awaiting fulfillment in the history of Jesus Christ (Gen 15:18). For the only way to make a covenant is to covenant, which involves uttering an oath with self-involving obligations (Gen 26:3; cf. Heb 6:17). No covenanting speech act, no covenant. Without such divine speech acts, it would not be possible to identify God or discern his purposes in history. Significantly, God identifies himself to Abraham as the one "who brought you from Ur of the Chaldeans" (Gen 15:7), to Israel as the one "who brought you out of the land of Egypt" (Exod 20:2), and to Christians as the one "who brought back from the dead our Lord Jesus" (Heb 13:20). God's words explain God's acts.

It is striking how many mighty acts ascribed to God by the biblical authors are speech acts. In addition to commanding and promising – the speech acts that generate what Luther calls God's "two words," law and gospel – God creates, warns, curses, blesses, consoles, informs, rebukes, and questions, to name but a few of his characteristic speech acts. Although God's word is not as prominent a behind-the-text feature of the New Testament, God is said to *call* and *forgive* sinners and to justify or *declare* them righteous. In examining the word of God behind the text, then, we discover that "*God speaking and God acting*

10. *Luther's Works*, vol. 8, *Lectures on Genesis Chapters 45–50* (St. Louis: Concordia, 1968), 201.

are often one and the same thing."[11] Consider, for example, speech acts with declarative illocutionary force: declaratives uniquely bring about a state of affairs when uttered by someone with the appropriate authority (e.g., "I now pronounce you man and wife"). Divine declaratives are integral for calling and anointing prophets (Jer 1:5), priests (Num 3:10), and kings (1 Kings 1:35). One particular appointment, to priesthood after the order of Melchizedek, is particularly important, for according to the author of Hebrews this divine speech act uniquely qualified Jesus Christ as savior of the world (Heb 5:5–6; 7:11–22).

According to G. E. Wright and other mid-twentieth-century proponents of the biblical theology movement, the history behind the text is the proper place to locate God's mighty revelatory acts.[12] On this view, the Bible is not itself revelation but is a record of or response to God's revelation behind the text in history. This is perhaps the majority view of modern biblical scholarship: Israel and the early church experienced something they believed was a word of God, and the Old and New Testaments were attempts to capture that experience. The salient point is that for this historical-critical method, the word of God remains firmly ensconced behind the biblical text and, to that extent, is hidden rather than revealed. We may here speak of the *nonidentity* of the Bible with the word of God.

THE WORD OF GOD IN FRONT OF THE TEXT

In the context of hermeneutics, the world "in front of" the text refers to the reader's appropriation of the text's subject matter, a possible way of looking at or being in the world. The book of Hebrews is a sermon set in writing that offers God's living Word, the Son, for the reader's appropriation and edification: "In these last days he has spoken to us by a Son" (Heb 1:2). It is precisely this better way of union with Christ – being-in-the-*Word* – that the author of Hebrews holds out to the reader in front of his written sermon.

Jesus is explicitly called the Word (Gk. *logos*) of God in the prologue to John's gospel (John 1:1–14).[13] Karl Barth, the great Swiss theologian of the twentieth century, insisted that Jesus Christ alone is God's definitive revelation: "God's Word is God Himself in His revelation."[14] God's Word is not a set of

11. Timothy Ward, *Words of Life: Scripture as the Living and Active Word of God* (Downers Grove, IL: InterVarsity Press, 2009), 26, emphasis original.

12. G. E. Wright, *God Who Acts: Biblical Theology as Recital* (London: SCM, 1952).

13. John's gospel speaks of Jesus as God's Word made flesh and highlights the words that Jesus speaks. See further Robert H. Gundry, *Jesus the Word according to John the Sectarian* (Grand Rapids: Eerdmans, 2002). The present essay adopts the convention of using Word of God to refer to Jesus Christ, "word of God" for the message of Scripture, and "divine speech" to the activity of God speaking.

14. Karl Barth, *Church Dogmatics* I/1 (Edinburgh: T&T Clark, 1975), 295.

propositional truths, a "paper Pope," but a person: the "living and active" (Heb 4:12) voice of its speaking subject, Jesus Christ. The Bible itself is not the *Word* of God, yet insofar as it is about Jesus, it may become the *word* of God when its witness to Jesus Christ is received in faith. According to Barth, God is free to reveal or not reveal himself to particular readers on particular occasions: "We cannot regard the presence of God's Word in the Bible as an attribute inhering once for all in this book."[15]

For Barth, the Bible becomes divine communication when God freely and graciously uses its reading or hearing as an occasion on which to make himself known. When readers encounter the living Christ "in front of" the text's witness, then the biblical text becomes a form of the word of God.[16] Barth considers both the Bible and Christian proclamation as potential forms of the word of God. Strictly speaking, however, Barth holds to an *indirect* identity thesis: the Bible becomes the word of God only when its readers follow its indication and meet the risen Christ. John Barton speaks for those who locate the word of God in front of the text in this christological way: "Christians are not those who believe in the Bible, but those who believe in Christ."[17]

THE WORD OF GOD IN THE TEXT

The writer of Hebrews refers to God's speaking not only behind the text (in the past) and in front of the text (contemporaneously) but also *in* his text. For, in addition to using *logos* to refer to messages from God, the writer also uses the term to identify his own message (Heb 5:11–13; 13:22). God's voice and the writer's voice occasionally converge, especially at those points where the writer is citing Old Testament passages, such as Psalm 95, as the text of his exposition, where the writer says that God is addressing his readers "today" just as he addressed Israel in former times (Heb 3:7–15). Moreover, toward the end of the letter, the writer exhorts his audience, "do not refuse the one who is speaking" (Heb 12:25), the implication being that God is speaking via the writer of Hebrews: "The writer believes that through his discourse (a sermon comprised of a series of scriptural expositions), he himself communicates that divine word and effects an encounter between his hearers and the God who speaks."[18]

---

15. Barth, *CD* I/1, 530.

16. See further Bruce L. McCormack, "The Being of Holy Scripture Is in Becoming," in *Evangelicals and Scripture: Tradition, Authority and Hermeneutics*, ed. Vincent Bacote, Laura C. Miguélez, and Dennis L. Okholm (Downers Grove, IL: InterVarsity Press, 2004), 55–75.

17. John Barton, *People of the Book? The Authority of the Bible in Christianity* (London: SPCK, 1988), 83.

18. Jonathan I. Griffiths, *Hebrews and Divine Speech* (New York: Bloomsbury T&T Clark, 2014), 2. See also Madison N. Pierce, *Divine Discourse in the Epistle to the Hebrews: The Recontextualization of Spoken Quotations of Scripture* (Cambridge: Cambridge University Press, 2020).

The writer of Hebrews is not the only biblical author conscious that his words were the vehicle for communicating the word of God. Both the prophets of the Old Testament and the apostles of the New often acknowledge that they are declaring God-given words. The book of Jeremiah is a fascinating example of God putting his words in the mouth of a prophet (Jer 1:9). Jeremiah communicates God's word or message (singular) in Jeremiah's own words (plural): "When hearers in the book of Jeremiah refuse to hear, it is not the word they hear but words, as if some vital ingredient in the message has not got through."[19] What Jeremiah says, God says. "The ontology of the book of Jeremiah as simultaneously the words of Jeremiah and the words of God sets the text itself as a location of God's activity."[20] The word of God is *in* the text, as also evidenced by the frequency with which God's words are said to be written down: "Thus says the Lord, the God of Israel: 'Write in a book all the words that I have spoken to you'" (Jer 30:2; cf. 36:2, 4, 6, 8, 11, 13, 16).

The Ten Commandments, similarly, are said to be "written with the finger of God" (Exod 31:18). The point of this intriguing detail is not to encourage speculation about the mechanics of the writing. Rather, the point is to show that the law of Moses is actually the law of God. The written law is a permanent witness to the will of God. This is why the ancient scrolls were revered in ancient Israel. The Torah was Israel's constitution, and the book of Deuteronomy was to be written down to serve as an enduring witness that Israel enjoyed a special, albeit precarious, relationship with God: "You shall write on the stones all the words of this law very clearly" (Deut 27:8).

Jesus often introduced citations from the Old Testament with the formula "It is written" and at one point explicitly identifies these writings (*graphē*) with God's word (John 10:34–36). John Wenham argues that Christians should hold the same view of these writings that Jesus held, namely, that what the prophets spoke was God's word and that what the apostles will speak, assisted by the Holy Spirit, shares in Jesus' own prophetic authority (Matt 28:18–20; Luke 12:12; John 14:26).[21] Christians recognize certain books as "Scripture," first, because their authors have been appointed or commissioned by God to deliver his word and, second, because they are thereby "holy" – set aside by God for a divine purpose. There is a striking reference in 2 Peter to the apostle Paul's writings as

19. Andrew G. Shead, *A Mouth Full of Fire: The Word of God in the Words of Jeremiah* (Downers Grove, IL: InterVarsity Press, 2012), 62.

20. Shead, *A Mouth Full of Fire*, 284.

21. See further John Wenham, *Christ and the Bible* (Downers Grove, IL: InterVarsity Press, 1972); and Donald Macleod, "Jesus and Scripture," in *The Trustworthiness of God: Perspectives on the Nature of Scripture*, ed. Paul Helm and Carl R. Trueman (Grand Rapids: Eerdmans, 2002), 69–95.

being comparatively more difficult in places than "the other scriptures" (2 Pet 3:16). This suggests that the writings of the apostles began to be regarded by the first Christians as on a par with the Old Testament prophets. We see this in one of Paul's own letters: "We also constantly give thanks to God for this, that when you received the word of God that you heard from us, you accepted it not as a human word but as what it really is, God's word, which is also at work in you believers" (1 Thess 2:13).

Patristic theologians in both the Greek-speaking East and the Latin-speaking West held what we might term a *direct identity* thesis, equating the humans words of the Bible with the word of God: "All the Church Fathers, without exception, believed that the Bible was God's word written, and that it could therefore be fully trusted in everything that it affirmed to be true."[22] Church historian Jaroslav Pelikan defines Christian doctrine as "what the church of Jesus Christ believes, teaches, and confesses on the basis of the word of God."[23]

The Niceno-Constantinopolitan Creed (381) identifies the Holy Spirit as the one "who spoke through the prophets" (*quo locutus est per prophetas*). What was implicit in the early centuries became explicit in the Protestant Reformation. In 1541, Martin Luther wrote, "The Holy Scripture is God's Word, written and (in my way of speaking) spelled out, put down in letters."[24] The direct identity thesis is itself spelled out in the Reformation and post-Reformation confessions of various Protestant churches. The doctrine of Scripture enjoys pride of first place in several of these confessions, including the Geneva Confession (1536), the First (1536) and Second (1566) Helvetic Confessions, and the Westminster Confession (1647). The latter states that the authority of Scripture depends "wholly upon God (who is truth itself) the author thereof: and therefore it is to be received, because it is the Word of God."[25] The confession spells out the names of all sixty-six books of the Old Testament and New Testament, indicating those writings (i.e., "Scripture") set apart by God (i.e., "holy") to be the rule (i.e., "canon") of faith and life. The Bible is thus the collection of just those texts acknowledged to be ultimately the result of God's communicative activity.

22. Gerald Bray, "Church Fathers and Their Use of Scripture," in *The Trustworthiness of God*, 159.

23. Jaroslav Pelikan, *The Christian Tradition: A History of the Development of Doctrine*, vol. 1, *The Emergence of the Catholic Tradition (100–600)* (Chicago: University of Chicago Press, 1971), 1.

24. Cited in Robert Kolb, *Martin Luther and the Enduring Word of God* (Grand Rapids: Baker Academic, 2016), 76.

25. Westminster Confession of Faith I.4.

THE BIBLE AS DIVINE DISCOURSE

"DID GOD SAY?" THE CHALLENGE OF MODERNITY

James Barr is representative of many modern biblical scholars for whom the whole idea of supernatural revelation, and particularly a speaking God, has become inconceivable: "We do not have any idea of ways in which God might straight-forwardly communicate articulate thoughts or sentences to men; it just doesn't happen."[26] We can overlook for the moment Barr's too hasty move from ignorance to pontification. After all, "God is spirit" (John 4:24), and spirits don't have vocal cords. For Barr, the Bible is not the word of God but the human record of the human attempt to understand and pass on the religious experience and faith tradition of the people of God. This makes it possible to view the Bible as having a natural history, and cultural context, like any other document of the university.

The idea that God produces words has become a significant stumbling block for modern academics and others influenced by scientific naturalism: "Language . . . cannot be literally predicated of pure spirit."[27] That the Bible is the "word of God" is, for many scholars, a metaphor that must not be taken literally. Doing so leads, according to theologian Sandra Schneider, to "the absurdity of the truth claims that must be made for patent human errors in the text" and to "the insoluble problem of double causality at the same level. . . . The literalist must reduce the human author to a passive instrument, a scribe taking dictation from the divine speaker."[28]

Schneider says that the most serious deleterious effect of literalizing the metaphor "word of God" is that "it impoverishes and distorts the mystery of divine revelation."[29] Revelation on her view is not the verbal transmission of information but a symbolic expression of and means of encountering God. Strictly speaking, the Bible is not itself revelation but is potentially revelatory, which is to say that it may be the occasion for a personal encounter with God: "Sacred scripture is the sacrament of the word of God."[30] In sum: modern biblical scholars and theologians are open to the possibility of somehow experiencing God through Scripture, but not to literally hearing from him in Scripture.

---

26. James Barr, *The Bible in the Modern World* (London: SCM, 1973), 17.

27. Sandra Schneider, *The Revelatory Text: Interpreting the New Testament as Sacred Scripture* (Collegeville, MN: Liturgical, 1999), 28.

28. Schneider, *The Revelatory Text*, 33.

29. Schneider, *The Revelatory Text*, 33.

30. Schneider, *The Revelatory Text*, 41.

FROM HUMAN TESTIMONY TO DIVINE TESTAMENT

In the face of modern challenges in a scientific age that privileges this-worldly explanations, why would anyone believe that the Bible is God's word? Before giving a positive reason, it is worth recalling the cost of denying God's ability to make himself known in words. First and foremost, without a clear word from God, we would simply not know what God is up to. Only speech disambiguates behavior: "Without His word, the alternative is not just a tentative, carefully qualified guessing at what God is doing, but a radical agnosticism."[31] We could not reliably say that God is love apart from divine speech acts that clarify God's intentions and purposes. A stark choice confronts the would-be believer: either God has spoken or agnosticism. A "mystery" without speech is a revelation of nothing in particular. Second, denying God's communicative agency diminishes God, for it is a serious handicap if God, "having made a world of rational creatures able to love and worship him, did not in any way communicate with them."[32]

The most important warrant for believing that God has spoken behind, in, and through the biblical text is the testimony of the Bible's own authors and readers across cultures and down through the centuries. Testifying is a speech act that enables others to know something. The Bible is not only filled with examples of people giving testimony but, significantly, also stresses the importance of giving true testimony: "You shall not bear false witness against your neighbor" (Exod 20:16). As a further indication of the importance of truthfulness, testimony from at least two witnesses was required in cases involving capital punishment (Deut 17:6). Fittingly enough, the whole of John's gospel is structured as a kind of court testimony in a trial to determine Jesus' true identity.[33]

Richard Bauckham characterizes the Gospels as eyewitness testimony and, as such, a kind of historiography: "An irreducible feature of testimony as a form of human utterance is that it asks to be trusted."[34] A number of recent philosophers argued that believing something someone tells you is eminently rational: "Our trust in the word of others is fundamental to the very idea of serious cognitive activity."[35] Along with memory, testimony is now widely recognized as a

---

31. Abraham, *Divine Revelation*, 21.

32. Basil Mitchell, "Does Christianity Need a Revelation?," *Theology* 83 (1980): 108.

33. See further Andrew Lincoln, *Truth on Trial: The Lawsuit Motif in the Fourth Gospel* (Peabody, MA: Hendrickson, 2000).

34. Richard Bauckham, *Jesus and the Eyewitnesses: The Gospels as Eyewitness Testimony* (Grand Rapids: Eerdmans, 2006), 5.

35. C. A. J. Coady, *Testimony: A Philosophical Study* (Oxford: Clarendon, 1992), vii.

reliable belief-forming mechanism.[36] Furthermore, "The 'ground,' 'basis,' or 'reason' on which a piece of testimonial knowledge rests is . . . *the testimony itself*."[37] H. H. Price calls this "principle A": "Believe what you are told by others unless or until you have reason for doubting it."[38]

What Christians believe on the basis of the testimony of the prophets and apostles is that God himself has testified, in words, to his character, will, and purposes. The prophets contrast the true God of Israel with false gods precisely because the latter neither speak nor act: "Their idols are like scarecrows in a cucumber field, and they cannot speak; they have to be carried, for they cannot walk" (Jer 10:5). By way of contrast, the holy of holies, Israel's most sacred place, was designed to hold "the ark of the covenant" or testimony: what God spoke to Moses concerning his law and promises for Israel (Exod 25:22). The Bible is therefore testimony to God's last will and testament. *Testament* is arguably the best single term to describe the content of the Bible, composed as it is by the Old and New Testaments or covenants (the Vulgate uses the Latin *testamentum* to translate both the Hebrew *berit* and the Greek *diathēkē*, the two biblical terms for "covenant"). God's *covenanting* is central to the story line of the Bible. There are mentions of the new covenant even in the Old Testament (Jer 31:31), and the New Testament presents Jesus as both fulfilment of the old covenant and mediator of the new (Luke 22:20; 1 Cor 11:25; Heb 9:15; 12:24).

The Bible is human testimony to divine testament – to God's unilateral speech enactment of his covenant with Israel and of his new covenant with people of every nation. It is the contention of the present essay that there can be no covenant between God and humanity, no divine last will and testament, unless there is an anchoring divine speech act. We turn now to consider how the Bible itself is the divinely authored constitution of the covenant of grace.

DIVINE DISCOURSE: HOW GOD DOES THINGS WITH WORDS

Recent work in the philosophy of language affords a new perspective on what it means to call the Bible the "word" of God. The operative term is *act*: words are the means by which speakers and authors perform diverse communicative

36. See Alvin Plantinga, *Warranted Christian Belief* (Oxford: Oxford University Press, 2000), esp. chs. 8–9; Nicholas Wolterstorff, *Thomas Reid and the Story of Epistemology* (Cambridge: Cambridge University Press, 2001); Jennifer Lackey, "The Epistemology of Testimony and Religious Belief," in *The Oxford Handbook of the Epistemology of Theology*, ed. William Abraham and Frederick D. Aquino (Oxford: Oxford University Press, 2017), 203–20.

37. Mats Wahlberg, *Revelation as Testimony. A Philosophical-Theological Study* (Grand Rapids: Eerdmans, 2014), 233, emphasis original.

38. H. H. Price, *Belief* (London: Allen & Unwin, 1969), 124.

actions.[39] The Bible depicts God too as *doing things with words*, including the human words – the prophetic and apostolic testimony – that comprise the Bible itself. To encounter God's word in either speech or writing is thus to encounter God himself in communicative action, as the author of Hebrews sought to make clear when he cited Psalm 95: "Today, if you hear his voice, do not harden your hearts as in the rebellion" (Heb 3:15).

Christian believers consider the biblical texts as authoritative not simply because, as revealed, they contained a deposit of divine truth; rather, they "derived their authority from the fact that they are God's address."[40] The Bible is the word of God not simply because it contains supernaturally given information that could not be obtained from anywhere else (though it may include this), but primarily because these human writings are the vehicle for a variety of divine speech acts, all of which contribute to understanding the person and work of Jesus Christ. The language of the Bible functions to convey information, to establish relationships and, as we now see, to do things.

Several scholars have recently proposed viewing the Bible in terms of divine *discourse*: something someone says to someone about something at some time in some way for some purpose.[41] Nicholas Wolterstorff argues that God speaks by either deputizing or appropriating human discourse: "To authorize a text is in effect to declare: let this text serve as medium of my discoursing."[42] An immediate advantage of this proposal is that it accounts for the many different kinds of discourse in the Bible.[43] For example, God not only promises and commands, but also instructs, warns, consoles, tells stories, and so forth: "I the LORD have spoken; I will accomplish it" (Ezek 17:24).

To identify the Bible as divine discourse is to put the accent not simply on the locutions (i.e., uttering, writing) but the *illocutions*, that is, the action

---

39. The classic text is J. L. Austin, *How to Do Things with Words*, 2nd ed. (Oxford: Clarendon, 1975). See also John R. Searle, *Speech Acts: An Essay in the Philosophy of Language* (Cambridge: Cambridge University Press, 1969).

40. Michael Horton, "Theologies of Scripture in the Reformation and Counter-Reformation," in *Christian Theologies of Scripture: A Comparative Introduction*, ed. Justin S. Holcomb (New York: New York University Press, 2006), 84.

41. See the essays by Kevin Vanhoozer, Dan Stiver, Nicholas Wolterstorff, and Anthony Thiselton, in *After Pentecost: Language and Biblical Interpretation*, ed. Craig Bartholomew, Colin Greene, and Karl Möller (Grand Rapids: Zondervan, 2001).

42. Nicholas Wolterstorff, *Divine Discourse: Philosophical Reflections on the Claim that God Speaks* (Cambridge: Cambridge University Press, 1995), 41.

43. See further Kevin J. Vanhoozer, "The Apostolic Discourse and Its Developments," in *Scripture's Doctrine and Theology's Bible*, ed. Markus Bockmuehl and Alan Torrance (Grand Rapids: Baker Academic, 2008), 191–207; Kevin J. Vanhoozer, "Triune Discourse: Theological Reflections on the Claim that God Speaks, in Two Parts," in *Trinitarian Theology for the Church: Scripture, Community, Worship*, ed. Daniel J. Treier and David Lauber (Downers Grove, IL: InterVarsity, 2009), 25–78.

performed in speaking (e.g., commanding, promising, narrating, etc.). Whereas philosophers focus on what speakers do on the sentence level, reading the Bible as divine discourse requires readers to acknowledge what God is doing at higher levels of discourse as well, everything from individual sentences to literary wholes. For example, when Jesus teaches in parables, he is not simply stating facts: he is telling stories, subverting wrong ways of looking at the world, and helping his listeners to understand the nature of the kingdom of God. Because God is the ultimate author of the whole of Scripture, we can also speak of illocutions at the canonical level. What God is doing at the level of the whole canon is instructing the believing community in the ways of the covenant and testifying to Christ.[44]

The Bible thus depicts God as a speaker and an author: a communicative agent with communicative intentions. How can God, who is spirit, produce speech or writing if he has neither vocal cords nor hands? The question occurred to theologians long before modernity, as Luther notes: "Not that God actually spoke, for he has no mouth, tongue, teeth, or lips as we do. But he who created and formed the mouth of all men can also make speech and the voice."[45] The divine inspiration of Scripture will be discussed in what follows. It suffices here to mention William Alston's argument that we may ascribe literal speech acts to God if we grant, first, that "action can be thought of as a change that is brought about by a volition or intention"[46] and, second, that though human beings perform speech acts via bodily movements, the movement of vocal cords is not a necessary component of speech. God can communicate and bring about the understanding of a verbal message (that is, produce the same effect as human speaking) in some other way (we don't have to specify how).[47] Bodily movement is not a necessary component of promising, commanding, or forgiving.

ELABORATING THE DOCTRINE OF SCRIPTURE

We turn now to a description of some of the features associated in the Christian tradition with the belief that the human discourse of the Bible is mysteriously

44. On canonical illocutions, see Kit Barker, *Imprecation as Divine Discourse: Speech Act Theory, Dual Authorship, and Theological Interpretation*, Journal of Theological Interpretation Supplement 16 (Winona Lake, IN: Eisenbrauns, 2016), 95–98.

45. Timothy Lull, ed., *Martin Luther's Basic Theological Writings* (Minneapolis: Fortress, 1989), 136–37.

46. William Alston, *Divine Nature and Human Language: Essays in Philosophical Theology* (Ithaca, NY: Cornell University Press, 1989), 96.

47. See further William Alston, "How to Think about Divine Action," in *Divine Action: Studies Inspired by the Philosophical Theology of Austin Farrer*, ed. Brian Hebblethwaite and Edward Henderson (Edinburgh: T&T Clark, 1990), 51–70, esp. 66–69.

identified with God's word, understood as divine discourse (the "Scripture principle").

THE NATURE OF THE BIBLE AS DIVINE DISCOURSE: VERBAL INSPIRATION

What the Bible *is* has an important bearing on how it should be read. Modern biblical scholarship treats the Bible as having a natural history only, so to speak: it was written by human authors who may have had religious experiences, but express them in fallible and culturally conditioned ways. On this view, the Bible is a humanly produced text, just like any other historical text.

By way of contrast, Christians have traditionally affirmed the dual authorship of the Bible, again largely on the basis of its own testimony. The apostle Paul says, "All scripture is inspired by God and is useful for teaching, for reproof, for correction, and for training in righteousness" (2 Tim 3:16). The Greek for "inspired" is *theopneustos*, literally "God-breathed." The apostle Peter uses a different image: "No prophecy of scripture . . . ever came by human will, but men and women moved by the Holy Spirit spoke from God" (2 Pet 1:20–21). This notion that the very human words of the Bible are also God's words gave rise to the doctrine of biblical inspiration, the idea that God preserves his discourse in an accessible and permanent form: written texts.

The degrees to which God's spirit is thought to have influenced the biblical authors varies. The dictation view depicts the biblical authors as mere mouthpieces for God. One church father described the Spirit playing passive prophets "as a flute-player breathed into a flute."[48] Contemporary biblical scholars, aware of the diversity of literary styles, cultural conditioning, and the importance of historical context, have swung to the other extreme and are willing to accept a sort of divine involvement, but one that stops well short of authorship. Keith Ward maintains that God guided the writing of the Bible so that it would communicate the main gist of his saving purpose, though it must be read with care and discrimination, because God "has not overruled the diverse and developing human perspectives that have gone to form it over a long period of time."[49] The difficulty with this view is that it leaves unclear which parts of the Bible are or are not to be trusted adequately to communicate the divine intent. Ward is confident that readers can trust those parts that promote social justice and the love of the good, but why privilege God's love over his holiness (and holy war)?

To affirm the Bible as God-breathed is to put the accent on the ultimate

48. Athenagoras, *Legatio pro Christianis* 7,9.

49. Keith Ward, *The Word of God? The Bible after Modern Scholarship* (London: SPCK, 2010), 30.

origin of the text and the result (the nature of the product) rather than the mechanics (the nature of the process). It is one thing to say *that* the Bible is inspired, quite another to say *how*. Some things must be said, however, to ensure understanding and prevent misunderstanding. Most importantly, what is divine about the Bible is not its words – there is nothing exceptional about the Hebrew or Greek terms themselves – but its discourse. Verbal inspiration does not mean that every individual word of the Bible is somehow filled with divine content. It means, rather, that the authorial speech acts expressed in words – the illocutions (that is, what is being *done* in saying just these words) – are divine. What is said and done is thus the product of two authorial agencies, human and divine: "God so acts as to make the text capable, fitting and fruitful in the publication of his Word."[50] Divine and human agency overlap but do not compete. As Creator (the infinite cause of finite causes), God's causality works on an entirely different level than other space-time agents. The Spirit gives human authors an impulse to write, an impulse that operates "intrinsically, as an augmentation of creaturely powers, and not merely as an extrinsic efficient cause."[51]

B. B. Warfield's definition is instructive: "Inspiration is that extraordinary, supernatural influence . . . exerted by the Holy Ghost on the writers of our Sacred Books, by which their words were rendered also the words of God."[52] John Webster likens inspiration to sanctification: "not a unilateral cognitive force but a compound act in which the creator and reconciler takes creatures and their powers, acts and products into his service."[53] According to Augustine, "God speaks in a human manner through a human being."[54] Affirming dual authorship does not eclipse the agency of the human author but locates it in a larger divine purpose. Herman Bavinck therefore speaks of inspiration as "organic": "The Spirit of the Lord entered into the prophets and apostles themselves and so employed and led them that they themselves examined and reflected, spoke

---

50. John Webster, *The Domain of the Word* (New York: T&T Clark International, 2012), 10.

51. John Webster, "On the Inspiration of Holy Scripture," in *Conception, Reception, and the Spirit: Essays in Honor of Andrew T. Lincoln*, ed. J. G. McConville and L. K. Pietersen (Eugene, OR: Cascade, 2015), 246. This crucial point is often missed. God sustains and cooperates with creaturely reality *as Creator*, not as a rival creaturely cause. See further Henri Blocher, "God and the Scripture Writers: The Question of Double Authorship," in *The Enduring Authority of the Christian Scriptures*, ed. D. A. Carson (Grand Rapids: Eerdmans, 2016), 497–541.

52. B. B. Warfield, *The Inspiration and Authority of the Bible* (Phillipsburg, NJ: P&R, 1970), 420. Cf. Gerald O'Collins: "'In-spiration,' understood broadly, describes a double agency, a 'spiritual' influence from God that empowers human beings to think, speak, or act in ways which go beyond their normal capacity" (*Inspiration: Towards a Christian Interpretation of Biblical Inspiration* [Oxford: Oxford University Press, 2018], 108).

53. Webster, *Domain of the Word*, ix.

54. Augustine, *City of God*, 17.6.

and wrote as they did. It is God who speaks through them; at the same time, it is they themselves who speak and write."[55]

As we have seen, Jesus is the Word of God made flesh, and according to his own testimony, both Old Testament and New Testament ultimately bear witness to his person and work (Luke 24:27). The distinctive Christian claim is not that the Bible is a Scripture like the sacred texts of other religions but that the Bible stands in unique relationship to Jesus Christ. For, while Scripture may be breathed out or superintended by the Spirit of God, it ultimately is part of the Son's prophetic office: "Scripture is a creaturely reality that is assembled, sanctified, requisitioned and employed by the risen Christ in his work of self-communication."[56] The divine Word made flesh speaks through the human words made text that he both commissions and ultimately authors.

THE AUTHORITY OF THE BIBLE AS DIVINE DISCOURSE: *SOLA SCRIPTURA*

It should by now be clear that Christians mean something very specific when they confess the Bible to be the word of God. There is nothing magical about the biblical texts; they are rather the ordinary, creaturely means God uses to say and do extraordinary things, such as making covenants, teaching wisdom, and testifying to salvation in Jesus Christ. Still, because these texts are set apart for a divine purpose, they are "holy" – and authoritative. Biblical authority is shorthand for "the Holy Spirit speaking in the Scriptures."[57] Authority is rightful say-so, and the Bible is a key ingredient in a broader pattern of authority that centers on Jesus Christ, God's say-so made flesh: "Christ is the supreme object of the witness of the Spirit, and Christ is the supreme content of the Scriptures."[58]

Sola scriptura ("Scripture alone") means that the Bible is the supreme and singular (though not the only) authority for understanding the person and work of Jesus Christ and for ruling the Christian life.[59] Creedal statements and

55. Herman Bavinck, *Reformed Dogmatics*, vol. 1, *Prolegomena*, trans. John Vriend (Grand Rapids: Baker Academic, 2003), 432.

56. Fred Sanders, "Holy Scripture under the Auspices of the Holy Trinity: On John Webster's Trinitarian Doctrine of Scripture," *International Journal of Systematic Theology* 21 (2019): 17. See also Timothy J. Harmon, "Biblical Inspiration and the Doctrine of God, With Attention to the Example of John Webster," in *God of Our Fathers: Classical Theism for the Contemporary Church*, ed. Bradford Littlejohn (Moscow, ID: Davenant Institute, 2018), 159–86.

57. Westminster Confession of Faith, I.10.

58. Bernard Ramm, *The Pattern of Religious Authority* (Grand Rapids: Eerdmans, 1959), 37. For more on the principle and pattern of authority, see my *Biblical Authority after Babel: Retrieving the Solas in the Spirit of Mere Protestant Christianity* (Grand Rapids: Brazos, 2016), 83–85, 123–38.

59. See further my "*Sola Scriptura* Means Scripture First! A 'Mere Protestant' Dogmatic Account (and Response)," in *Sola Scriptura: Biblical and Theological Perspectives on Scripture, Authority, and Hermeneutics*, ed. Hans Burger, Arnold Huijgen, Eric Peels (Leiden: Brill, 2018), 335–58.

confessions of faith (that is, tradition) have derivative authority to the extent they rightly interpret the biblical texts (see what follows on reading). The divine discourse of the Bible can be authoritative, however, only if what it says and does is intelligible (i.e., clear) and trustworthy (i.e., infallible).

God speaks clearly in the Scriptures, for God is light (1 John 1:5) and his word is a light to our path (Ps 119:105). It does not follow, however, that the meaning of every passage is transparent or simple. Recall Peter's caution about Paul's epistles that they include "some things in them hard to understand" (2 Pet 3:16). By *clarity* the Protestant Reformers meant, first, that Scripture interprets Scripture (that is, the difficult portions are to be read in light of the clearer portions) and, second, that readers do not need experts to follow the main story line of the Bible or to grasp its central truths, but only the illumination of the Spirit, who enables readers to grasp its subject matter (Jesus Christ).[60]

God speaks truth in the Scriptures, for his word is truth: "The saying is sure and worthy of full acceptance: that Christ Jesus came into the world to save sinners" (1 Tim 1:15; cf. 1 Tim 4:9; 2 Tim 2:11; Titus 1:9; 3:8). The risen Christ addresses the author of Revelation and says, "Write this, for these words are trustworthy and true" (Rev 21:5). This does not mean that God intended people to use the Bible as a textual talisman that provides insights into molecular biology or unerring advice on the stock market. That kind of simplistic biblicism has been roundly criticized.[61] Biblical infallibility means that the Bible will not fail to achieve the purpose(s) that God has for it (Isa 55:11), whether that involves stating facts, issuing warnings, telling stories, or offering consolation. The Bible is true and trustworthy because its author is the God who proves himself true and reliable (Rom 3:4). The Bible is infallible because its divine author stands by his words. Yet readers must correctly *understand* them too.

THE PURPOSE OF THE BIBLE AS DIVINE DISCOURSE: ECCLESIAL EDIFICATION

The sufficiency of Scripture refers to its providing everything needed to accomplish its purpose. This purpose is a function of its author's intention, not of the use to which readers might like to put it. The Bible may not answer every question that readers put to it: it does not tell us our fortunes or whom to marry. Yet it says enough to accomplish its intended purpose, which is to direct readers to Jesus Christ and to serve as the constitution for God's covenant community:

---

60. See further Mark D. Thompson, *A Clear and Present Word: The Clarity of Scripture* (Downers Grove, IL: InterVarsity Press, 2006).

61. See, e.g., Christian Smith, *The Bible Made Impossible: Why Biblicism Is Not a Truly Evangelical Reading of Scripture* (Grand Rapids: Brazos, 2012).

"*Theologically* Scripture is the means by which the Father presents his covenant to us, and therefore the means by which he presents himself to us as the faithful God of the covenant. It is also in the words of Scripture that the Word of God, Jesus Christ, comes to us so that we may know him and remain in him."[62]

Why did God speak instead of remain silent? God speaks in order to proclaim salvation in Christ: "So faith comes from what is heard, and what is heard comes through the word of Christ" (Rom 10:17). The ultimate purpose of the Bible is not merely to inform but to transform readers – to form the mind of Christ in us (Phil 2:5) – and then to form those who have the mind of Christ into the one body of Christ (1 Cor 12:27): "The Bible is canon precisely because of the indispensable, formative tasks it performs as an auxiliary of the Spirit in directing the church's life towards God."[63] The Bible exists to proclaim truth and serve as a means of grace: "Holy Scripture is *sufficient* for the instruction of the saints as they are conveyed by God towards eternal fellowship with himself."[64]

READING THE BIBLE AS THE WORD OF GOD

HISTORICAL CRITICISM AND THEOLOGY: TWO LOCATIONS; TWO INTERPRETIVE INTERESTS?

What one thinks about the nature of the Bible decisively influences the way one reads it. Modern biblical scholarship worked a Copernican revolution when it transformed the church's Scripture (the word of an infallible God) into the academy's Bible (the words of fallible men). The primary interest of modern academic scholars is to read the Bible "like any other book," to be explained in terms of its original historical context and means of cultural production. In contrast, when believing Christians read the Bible, their primary interest is to attend to God's word to come to know God and be formed as citizens of the city of God.

Undergirding the academic, historical-critical approach to biblical interpretation is a methodological assumption, often unspoken, that only natural causes and factors are relevant, and that history is a this-worldly, horizontal causal continuum, sealed off from outside influence (i.e., transcendence). The issue is not that scholars attend to history while people of faith do not, but that

62. Ward, *Words of Life*, 177.

63. Daniel Castelo and Robert W. Wall, *The Marks of Scripture: Rethinking the Nature of the Bible* (Grand Rapids: Baker Academic, 2019), 4.

64. Webster, *Domain of the Word*, 18.

they disagree about what history is.[65] Modern biblical scholars typically bracket out any thought of God literally speaking through the text and read it simply to determine what the human authors thought about God in their ancient contexts. This leaves the contemporary believer with thin gruel only, not the kind of reading that nourishes faith: "The historical-critical reconstruction of the text cannot speak to the present, since today's reader cannot by definition be its addressee."[66]

Many modern scholars are, of course, also confessing Christians. They may feel as though they are being asked, "Choose this day whose interpretive interests you will serve," the academy's or the church's (cf. Josh 24:15). A case can also be made for lining up one's interpretive interests with the interests of the text themselves, though this again raises the question, whose interests: the divine or human authors? However, as stated previously, this may be a false choice, for divine authorship is not in competition with human authorship. Neither should theology be in competition with exegesis.

In 1943, Pope Pius XII released an encyclical, *Divino Afflante Spiritu*, permitting Roman Catholic exegetes to employ the critical tools and methods of modern scholars. Cardinal Ratzinger (later Pope Benedict XVI) led the way in seeking a synthesis between faith-based and academic modes of reading the Bible as the word of God. Ratzinger criticized historical-critical scholarship only when it was unnecessarily reductionist, excluding the possibility that God was revealing himself in human words: "Faith itself is not a component of this method, nor is God a factor to be dealt with in historical events."[67] The way forward is, first, to confess that the events behind the text may themselves be part of a redemptive history whose meaning is revealed only in the event of Jesus Christ and, second, to see the church, not the academy, as the "primary setting" for biblical interpretation, that is, for reading the Bible to hear God's word.[68]

Reading the Bible theologically, and not just historically, involves acknowledging divine authorship of redemptive-history in general and the biblical text in particular. That means a willingness to read the two-Testament Bible together as a unified story about God's project to form a set-apart people to

65. For a theological account of history, as having ontological depth as well as temporal length, see Matthew Levering, *Participatory Biblical Exegesis: A Theology of Biblical Interpretation* (Notre Dame, IN: University of Notre Dame Press, 2008).

66. Ulrich Luz, "Reflections on the Appropriate Interpretation of New Testament Texts," in *Theology, History, and Biblical Interpretation: Modern Readings*, ed. Darren Sarisky (New York: Bloomsbury, 2015), 283.

67. Joseph Ratzinger, "Biblical Interpretation in Crisis: On the Question of the Foundations and Approaches of Exegesis Today," in *Biblical Interpretation in Crisis*, ed. Richard John Neuhaus (Grand Rapids: Eerdmans, 1989), 2.

68. See Benedict XVI, *The Word of the Lord* (Boston: Pauline, 2010), 45–48.

be salt and light for the world. Reading the Bible therefore requires attention not only to the original historical context of the human authors but also to the canonical context of each passage, which is to say, its place in the broader unified redemptive-historical context. Interestingly enough, reading the Bible theologically is slowly becoming acceptable, even in the academy: "The return of biblical scholars to the theological reading of the Scriptures, and the return of systematic theologians to sustained engagement with the scriptural texts – in a phrase, the return of both to theological readings of the Bible – is the most significant theological development in the last two decades."[69]

READING THE BIBLE AS SCRIPTURE WITH THE HELP OF THE SPIRIT: ILLUMINATION

"Indeed, the word of God is living and active, sharper than any two-edged sword . . . able to judge the thoughts and intentions of the heart" (Heb 4:12). Viewing the Bible as divine discourse accentuates the idea that God's voice in the human words of Scripture is living and active, not dead and passive. From a faith perspective, the Bible reads readers even as readers interpret the Bible. Stated differently: the Bible examines readers to see if they are in the faith and encourages them to be right-minded and right-hearted readers, people of interpretive virtue. Virtues like honesty, patience, diligence, and, above all, humility are needed to read the Bible as the word of God, for doing so requires bringing the right sort of attention to the words of the text: "To read the Bible, at least if one is properly prepared and disposed towards the task, is, on this view, to be addressed by God."[70]

Whereas inspiration pertains to the Spirit's role in guiding human authors, illumination refers to something that happens to readers in the present, a result of the Spirit's action "in front of the text." Earlier we saw that Barth identified Jesus Christ as the Word "in front of" the biblical text, that is, the subject matter to which the text bears witness. We also saw that the book of Hebrews raises the possibility that God is still speaking through (i.e., in front of) the text: "Today, if you hear his voice, do not harden your hearts as in the rebellion" (Heb 3:15). If we combine these insights about illumination in front of the text, about hearing God's voice today, and about Jesus being that Word, we arrive at the following

---

69. Miroslav Volf, "Reading the Bible Theologically," in *Captive to the Word: Engaging the Scriptures for Contemporary Reflection* (Grand Rapids: Eerdmans, 2010), 14. See also Andrew T. Abernethy, ed., *Interpreting the Old Testament Theologically* (Grand Rapids: Zondervan, 2018).

70. Charles Wood, *The Formation of Christian Understanding: Theological Hermeneutics* (Eugene, OR: Wipf & Stock, 2000), 39. Cf. Craig Bartholomew, who devotes a whole chapter to "Listening and Biblical Interpretation," in *Introducing Biblical Hermeneutics: A Comprehensive Framework for Hearing God in Scripture?* (Grand Rapids: Baker Academic, 2015), 17–47.

question: Does illumination mean that God says something *new* "in front of" the biblical text?

The problem with suggesting that God says something new in or through the text is that it wreaks havoc with biblical interpretation. It is as hard to interpret a text whose meaning changes as it is to put its authority into practice: What exactly is being required of readers? If God says new things through old words, interpreters are cast adrift on a sea of semantic relativity.

The way forward is to see inspiration and illumination as two aspects of a single communicative process. In inspiring, the Spirit guarantees that the human locutions (the words that express speech acts) are adequate to the divine illocutions, to what the divine author wants to say and do in and through the text. In illumining, the Spirit acts as Lord of the perlocution (that is, the effect of a speech act, what is brought about *by* locuting). Promises remain promises, commands remain commands, and gospel remains gospel whether or not readers or hearers rightly understand them. Illumination is the idea not that God is saying something new in the sense of producing new locutions or illocutions but rather that he is actively bringing about understanding (that is, the right perlocutionary effect) of what he has said and continues to say.[71]

The apostle Paul states, "Those who are unspiritual do not receive the gifts of God's Spirit, . . . they are unable to understand them because they are spiritually discerned" (1 Cor 2:14). It is not enough, then, simply to require readers to approach the biblical text with the right exegetical tools. Rather, the same Spirit who inspires the texts regenerates the hearts and illumines the minds of their readers. This requires a certain mortification of the reader – dying to one's self-centered interpretive interests; assuming a humble and repentant posture – as well as a certain vivification, namely, the Spirit's communication of light that enables readers to grasp not simply the meaning of individual terms but also "that we might understand the gifts bestowed on us by God" (1 Cor 2:12). Inspiration ensures that the divine discourse is preserved in writing; illumination ensures that the divine discourse is grasped in reading. God's Spirit superintends both the objective giving (the writing) and the subjective reception (the hearing), both the genesis and the revelation, as it were, of God's word.[72]

71. See further Kevin J. Vanhoozer, "The Spirit of Light after the Age of Enlightenment, Renewing/Reforming Pneumatic Hermeneutics via the Economy of Illumination," in *Spirit of God: Christian Renewal in the Community of Faith*, ed. Jeffrey Barbeau and Beth Felker Jones (Downers Grove, IL: IVP Academic, 2015), 149–67.

72. See further Webster, "Illumination," in *Domain of the Word*, 50–64; Bernard Ramm, *The Witness of the Spirit* (Grand Rapids: Eerdmans, 1960).

CONCLUSION: THE DOMAIN OF THE WORD

This essay has set forth what Christians mean when they call the Bible the word of God. It is neither an arbitrary or generic appeal to divine authority. It is rather a claim that the composition and the interpretation of the Bible – the before and after of the text, as well as the text itself – may rightly be described as elements in what Webster terms the "domain of the Word": "The Bible, its readers and their work of interpretation have their place in the domain of the Word of God, the sphere of reality in which Christ glorified is present and speaks with unrivaled clarity."[73] To identify the Bible as the word of God, then, is to situate it within the economies of revelation and redemption, a creaturely means of advancing the Creator's project of forming a people marked by the knowledge and love of God. That the Bible is the word of God is part and parcel of what Christianity is all about. Moreover, that the ultimate author and subject matter of the Bible is the Word made flesh, Jesus Christ, sets the Christian claim about its Scripture apart from those of all other religions.

As testimony to God's plan of salvation, the Bible is the covenant constitution for a holy nation, the word of an all-wise God, which no amount of biblical scholarship can ever hope to master. As God's word, the Bible is not simply a collection of revealed propositions (divine truth), but holy Scripture: a set-apart collection of diverse texts through which divine discourse shapes a community of readers into a holy nation. The Bible, says B. B. Warfield, is not merely "the record of the redemptive acts by which God is saving the world, but [*is*] *itself one of these redemptive acts*, having its own part to play in the great work of establishing and building up the kingdom of God."[74] Because the domain of the word is God's revelation of his own light and life, "we can never encompass or summarize it, but can only be *inside* it."[75]

Theology has been described as "faith seeking understanding" (Anselm). Similarly, the Bible too is a word "from faith to faith" (Rom 1:17 NASB). The faith that rightly understands the Bible as God's word is not, however, unthinking gullibility. It is rather the rationally warranted reflex of one who humbly acknowledges, with Shakespeare's Hamlet,

> There are more things in heaven and earth, Horatio,
> Then are dreamt of in your philosophy.[76]

73. Webster, *The Domain of the Word*, viii.
74. Warfield, *Inspiration and Authority of the Bible*, 161 (emphasis mine).
75. Brian Brock, "The *Communio Sanctorum* as Scripture's Home," in *Sola Scriptura*, 129.
76. William Shakespeare, *Hamlet*, act 1, scene 5.

FOR FURTHER READING

Abraham, William J. *Divine Revelation and the Limits of Historical Criticism*. Oxford: Oxford University Press, 1982.

Carson, D. A., ed. *The Enduring Authority of the Christian Scriptures*. Grand Rapids: Eerdmans, 2016.

East, Brad. *The Doctrine of Scripture*. Eugene, OR: Cascade, 2021.

Gordon, Joseph K. *Divine Scripture in Human Understanding: A Systematic Theology of the Christian Bible*. Notre Dame, IN: University of Notre Dame Press, 2019.

O'Collins, Gerald. *Inspiration: Towards a Christian Interpretation of Biblical Inspiration*. Oxford: Oxford University Press, 2018.

Ramm, Bernard. *Special Revelation and the Word of God: An Essay on the Contemporary Problem of Revelation*. Grand Rapids: Eerdmans, 1961.

Schneiders, Sandra M. *The Revelatory Text: Interpreting the New Testament as Sacred Scripture*. Collegeville, MN: Liturgical, 1999.

Swain, Scott R. *Trinity, Revelation, and Reading: A Theological Introduction to the Bible and Its Interpretation*. London: T&T Clark, 2011.

Vanhoozer, Kevin J. *Mere Christian Hermeneutics: Transfiguring What It Means to Read the Bible Theologically*. Grand Rapids: Zondervan Academic, 2024.

Ward, Timothy. *Words of Life: Scripture as the Living and Active Word of God*. Downers Grove, IL: InterVarsity Press, 2009.

Warfield, B. B. *The Inspiration and Authority of the Bible*. Phillipsburg, NJ: P&R, 1970.

Webster, John. *Holy Scripture: A Dogmatic Sketch*. Cambridge: Cambridge University Press, 2003.

Wolterstorff, Nicholas. *Divine Discourse: Philosophical Reflections on the Claim That God Speaks*. Cambridge: Cambridge University Press, 1995.

CHAPTER 2

The Inerrancy of Scripture?

Henri Blocher[1]

INTRODUCTION

It would be unfortunate if the word *inerrancy* was to be used as a shibboleth (Judg 12:5–6) – in other words, a word that as soon as it was pronounced by someone made them promptly guilty or innocent for other Christians. The debate concerns the truth and the authority of Biblical affirmations: Are they really free from error? Tradition and a significant minority (as we shall see) answer yes; the "academic" majority answer no. The simple fact of pronouncing the word *inerrancy* puts you immediately into a category. If you refuse the term, you are shot down for being a liberal, who is surrendering to the spirit of the age. If you embrace the term, you are cast out into the gloom of sectarian obscurantism. But the word does have its importance. The bitter arguments may in fact show its usefulness, provided that we properly examine the subject, as was the case with the word *homoousios*, *consubstantial* (the adjective adopted to express the divine nature of Christ in relation to the Father) in the christological debates of the fourth century.

The etymology of *inerrancy* is not very helpful. But in confessional documents, "without error" and "free from error" are paraphrases for *inerrant*. Since the end of the nineteenth century, the word has tended to replace *infallible*, etymologically, that which cannot fail, which was more characteristic in Protestant wording. Paul Helm wonders if there is a distinction between these words:

1. This chapter was translated by David Brown.

some people think it is negligible; others blow up its importance.[2] In practice, the two terms overlap in their use as far as intention and reference are concerned. And that is our position. What we intend to try to clarify is what is included in this term. What are the "errors" involved?

What is the landscape in which these debates are taking place? The affirmation of inerrancy characterises the evangelical movement. It is its axial direction, the orientation of the Lausanne Movement flowing from the 1974 Congress under the leadership of Billy Graham and John Stott.[3] The Evangelical Theological Society (with thousands of members in North America) makes it a condition of membership.

However, there have been recent developments. Inerrancy has been disputed by a significant number of theologians from the English-speaking world, asserting that they are *evangelicals* and often that they are postconservative. The situation is becoming complicated. James Barr, the relentless critic of fundamentalism, considers that the affirmation of inerrancy is its defining feature but argues that the methodology of representative writers is not truly fundamentalist or inerrantist.[4] The Evangelical Theological Society includes postconservatives among its members.[5] But we can also find the opposite case: proponents of traditional bibliology, *against* the ordinary historicocritical method, avoid the word *inerrancy*. James Orr is a striking example.[6] I have also met people with an intermediate position: they wholeheartedly assent to the inerrancy clause of their doctrinal basis and sign it, but would prefer not to have to, either because they deem it inexpedient or because they fear that ideas would be imputed to them which they do not hold.

So how important is this debate? There is no unanimous answer. The "domino theory" whereby discarding the inerrancy of Scripture would sooner or later lead to the rejection of the major Christian doctrines does not always prove

2. Paul Helm, "The Idea of Inerrancy," in *The Enduring Authority of the Christian Scriptures*, ed. Donald A. Carson (Grand Rapids: Eerdmans, 2016), 900–901 (reference henceforth *EA*).

3. *Lausanne Covenant*, art. 2 on the Bible: "without error in all that it affirms." *The Cape Town Commitment* of the 3rd Congress, 2010, maintains this, I/§ 6.C.

4. James Barr, *Fundamentalism* (London: SCM, 1977), 40, 51, for the first affirmation; and 88, 124, for the second. He quotes the *New Bible Dictionary*.

5. R. Scott Smith notes this difficulty in "Non-Foundational Epistemologies and the Truth of Scripture," in *EA*, 849.

6. See James Orr, *The Problem of the Old Testament Considered with Reference to Recent Criticism* (London: Nisbet, 1909). David F. Wright, "Soundings in the Doctrine of Scripture in British Evangelicalism in the First Half of the Twentieth Century," *Tyndale Bulletin* 31 (1980): 87–106, shows that Orr is close to the inerrantist position, without entirely adopting it, as are several others such as H. McIntosh, J. Denney, M. Dods, and even G. T. Manley. (For Roger Nicole, "The Nature of Inerrancy," in *Standing Forth. Collected Writings of Roger Nicole* (Fearn: Mentor, 2002), 44; J. Orr "did not exclude the possibility of errors in details but affirmed he had never found in Scripture anything which forced him to say 'That's wrong.'"

to be true! In the institutions governed by the dictum *sola scriptura* ("by the Scriptures alone" which is taken to be the "formal principle" of the Protestant Reformation), to admit there is error would deprive them of the objective criterion for doctrinal discipline. As long as healthy doctrine is maintained, the affirmation of inerrancy plays little role in piety and the church. But it becomes determinant as soon as a dispute arises.

The *other* Protestants reject the idea of biblical inerrancy. The idea appears to be laughable to the most liberal ones. Debate between them and inerrantists seems to be hopeless since their points of reference and their criteria are light-years apart. With moderate liberals or "semi-liberals," however, dialogue can be useful.

With Catholic theologians, the situation is unclear. The word conveys the authority of a strong traditional declaration in the Dogmatic Constitution of the Vatican 1 Council (1870) and the Providentissimus Deus, Spiritus paraclitus, and Divino afflante encyclicals. But the deliberate ambiguity of Vatican II (1962–65) and the usage of biblical scholars would suggest a weakening of the meaning.[7]

This chapter hopes to dissipate misunderstandings and sharpen discernment. It will not be in a hurry to make known our preferences – but there is no intention to conceal them!

WHAT IS AFFIRMED OR DENIED

Inerrant means "without error," but what qualifies as an error? This clarification is all the more a priority when opponents of the doctrine of inerrancy are quick to accuse its proponents of sprinkling their definition with so many nuances and restrictions as to empty it of any real content: this definition allows them to recognize the presence of what everyone else would call an error (according to their critics), for example in chronologies, while refusing to use the term.[8]

CLARIFICATION ABOUT THE SUBJECT ASCRIBED: WHAT DO WE MEAN BY *SCRIPTURE*?

The declaration of inerrancy concerns the Bible, the *corpus* of which is sacred for Christians.

The question arises about its delineation, the *canon*. It is a legitimate question. If we neglect it, the position of Luther may be misrepresented, for example.

7. Henri Fesquet, correspondent of *Le Monde* at the council, reported this from the remarks of Cardinal Meyer, archbishop of Chicago, in the debates: "If we correctly understand the inerrancy of Scripture, he added, there is no difficulty in allowing there to be errors in the Bible" (October 7, 1964).

8. Helm, "The Idea of Inerrancy," 917, mentions this criticism.

Space does not permit us to deal with this subject. We take it that Scripture is composed of the canon of the Synagogue, the Tanakh,[9] and the canon of the New Testament received by (nearly) every church, in spite of their disagreement on many other subjects – we can see the hand of providence in this consensus.

The Original in the Linguistic Sense

Traduttore, traditore. The wisdom of every people recognizes the gap between an original text and its translation into another language. The proponents of inerrancy do not attribute this to translators of the Bible. The normative text is the original Hebrew, Greek, and, for a few chapters, Aramaic.

However, two debates have become attached to this reasonable distinction. In the early church through the influence of the Letter of Aristeas, several men held that the translation of the Septuagint (LXX) was inspired. Jerome's call to return to the *hebraica veritas* met with resistance, even by Augustine. That Jerome's *Vulgate*, in which he translated the Old Testament from the Hebrew, should prevail was a small miracle. A Greek Orthodox theologian may advocate the authority of the LXX. But Protestants will not go down that path.

The LXX is quoted in the New Testament, and a second debate springs from that fact. A good number of quotations are the same in the LXX, both in form and content (provided that the first century text is recovered) and in the Hebrew. But others modify the form. Some appear to correct the LXX in order to better translate the Hebrew. *Yet others follow the LXX and depart from the original.*[10] The latter are difficult for proponents of inerrancy – although it is an excessive generalisation to claim that the authors "habitually modify the text of the OT and find meanings which are not obviously present in the original, showing clearly that they do not consider the OT to be a document without error."[11]

Our response must be geared to particular cases. Inerrancy does not demand the reproduction of the form of the text that is quoted as opposed to what academic standards prescribe: abbreviations or clarifications are allowed.

---

9. Are the headings part of the Psalms? The uncertainty about this and the difference of ancient translations have led many inerrantists to reply in the negative.

10. This classification is based on Patrick Fairbairn's (1805–74) according to Roger Nicole, "Patrick Fairbairn and Biblical Hermeneutics as Related to the Quotations of the Old Testament in the New," expanded in "The New Testament Use of the Old Testament," in *Standing Forth*, 79–90, and 223–42. On this subject, more widely, the bibliography is most abundant; I would draw attention to Moisés Silva, "The New Testament Use of the Old Testament: Text Form and Authority," in *Scripture and Truth*, ed. D. A. Carson and John D. Woodbridge (Grand Rapids: Zondervan, 1983), 147–65; and Douglas J. Moo and Andrew D. Naselli, "The Problem of the New Testament Use of the Old Testament," in *EA*, 702–46.

11. Paul J. Achtemeier, *Inspiration and Authority. Nature and Function of Christian Scripture* (Peabody: Hendrickson, 1999), as summarized by Moo and Naselli, "The Problem of the New Testament Use of the Old Testament," 703.

The meaning is respected if typology is borne in mind, even *sensus plenior*: the language of type (Jerusalem) can be applied to the antitype (the church). Paul and the author of Hebrews quote the LXX as a widespread translation but do not guarantee its options in its translation. "A body you prepared for me" in Hebrews 10:5 renders the meaning of Psalm 40:7 "My ears you have pierced."[12] In Hebrews 11:21, the majority justify the reading of the Hebrew consonants by the LXX (compared with the Masoretes), or else, like Calvin, minimise the significance: "The Apostle had no difficulty in accommodating what was customarily received to his comments."[13]

The Original in the Autographic Sense

Translators make mistakes, as do copyists and printers. Inerrancy applies to texts *before* any deterioration due to the transmission process. Various confessions of faith attribute this to *autographs*. This word is not to be used literally. The authors were not all scribes. They used secretaries. What we have are the documents that the authors sanctioned, the original as it was first propounded and then reproduced by copyists.

This reasonable distinction has triggered two debates. Opponents of inerrancy object that to have recourse to autographs, *which we do not have*, empties the doctrine of all significance. *Our* Bible contains errors. Answer: transmission errors would be disastrous for the value of the text *if* they completely disfigured it, *if* the autographic text were lost. But this is not the case, even for the most "damaged" Old Testament books. (The Qumran manuscripts eased our fears: the differences with the Masoretic attested text are minimal.) The New Testament has more confirmation than any other work from antiquity. Inerrantists participate with their colleagues in "textual criticism" research, that is, seeking to deduce the most probable original text from existing copies without their theological difference impairing their collaboration.

Inerrancy is not affirmed in isolation or for its own sake. It is bound up with the *status* of the text. The qualitative difference is radical between a text that errs (in the same way that to err is human) and an inerrant text, *because it has been inspired by God*, even if it has been fallibly copied.[14]

---

12. Nicole, "The Nature of Inerrancy," 46n7.

13. Jean Calvin, *ad loc.*, *Commentaires sur le Nouveau Testament IV* (Paris: Meyrueis, 1854), 499. The Masoretes (i.e., the "traditionists") are the rabbis who fixed the text of the Hebrew Bible, read in the synagogues, by adding the vowels which were absent in the ancient manuscripts. In Genesis 47:31 the ancient manuscripts ancients have *MṬH*. The Masoretes vocalised *miṭṭâ*[*h*], "bed," but the translators of the LXX, following the writer to the Hebrews read *maṭṭè*[*h*], "staff."

14. Nicole, "The Nature of Inerrancy," 33, compares the duality to that of a text of Cicero, which was badly copied and a text of heavy and incorrect Latin impossible to attribute to the orator.

But then another objection arises. It questions the very notion of autograph. The understanding of many biblical scholars is that there is no single *author* but rather a collective piece of work over several generations. The legacy of a prophet, which is often meager, has been revised, amplified, and updated through a process of rereading and rewriting. What is the inspired text? Joseph Coppens presents two solutions: first, that of Franz Rosenzweig, who focuses on the final redactor – "R, i.e. the redactor who is our master, he is the Rabbenou, he is the sole inspired hagiographer" – and second, the opinion that all who took part in the process were inspired.[15]

However, the prevalent understanding is far from being proved. Does it not project modern expectations onto ancient texts? Parallels from that time are not in favour of this understanding: the sacred texts have scarcely been rewritten.[16] The principle of Deuteronomy 4:2 precludes adding to or subtracting from the text (cf. Rev 22:18ff and Flavius Josephus on the attitude of the Jews, *Against Apion*, 1,8). The Jewish scholar Y. Kaufmann stresses that we do not have the least proof of a redactional work by circles of disciples.[17]

Certain books, nevertheless, demonstrate a plurality of authors and gradual composition, such as Proverbs with "the men of Hezekiah." Some forthright proponents of inerrancy recognize editorial updates. Much depends on the amount of alterations, quantitatively and qualitatively. The tendency is to extend inspiration to revisions right through to the stabilized form of the text.[18]

What the Text Strictly Affirms

"Scripture is free of error" means: the content of the utterance whereby the author expresses what he believes to be true or good complies with what is true and good. In the vocabulary of the *speech act*, it is an *illocutionary* act.[19]

The content of an utterance that the author records or quotes does not necessarily comply in the same way. That seems self-evident. The Scripture

15. [J. Coppens], *Comment mieux concevoir et énoncer l'inspiration et l'inerrance des Saintes Ecritures?* (Louvain: Publications Universitaires de Louvain, 1964), 937 (on p. 938: Norbert Lohfink only attributes a limited, mediated, and nonthematic inerrancy to subsequent redactors).

16. Cf. the different writings Kenneth Kitchen, from *Ancient Orient and Old Testament* (London: Tyndale, 1966), to *On the Reliability of the Old Testament* (Grand Rapids: Eerdmans, 2003).

17. *The Religion of Israël*, trans. Moshe Greenberg (Chicago: University of Chicago Press, 1960), 355, quoted by Wayne Grudem, "Scripture's Self-Attestation and the Problem of Formulating a Doctrine of Scripture," in *Scripture and Truth*, 361n21.

18. Cf. Michael A. Grisanti, "Inspiration, Inerrancy, and the Old Testament Canon: The Place of Textual Updating in an Inerrant View of Scripture," *Journal of the Evangelical Theological Society* 44 (December 2001): 577–98; (henceforth *JETS*).

19. John L. Austin, *How to Do Things with Words*, 2nd ed. (Cambridge, MA: Harvard University Press, 1976), 109: "what one does when one says something (affirms, calls, describes, . . .)."

contains words of the Devil! However, a complication emerges. An author may quote without an introductory phrase: his readers will recognize as *implicit* quotations, the extraneous elements that the author has incorporated, and his own opinions. The evangelical commentator Gordon Fee attributes to Paul's adversaries the famous "Women should remain silent" (1 Cor 14:34), which the apostle is quoting. Is he *misusing* the idea? The Catholic magisterium condemned the excessive use of this procedure by the biblical scholar Ferdinand Prat: he removed problematic utterances far too easily by making them "implicit quotations" that do not imply the agreement of the Biblical author.[20] James Orr allowed himself this easy solution, allowing inspiration not to require any correction of the sources used.[21] Are we not close to reducing the effect of inspiration to the wise choice of fallible sources? Amusing inerrancy if it is limited to "the *divinely* certain judgement that these documents were *humanly* worthy of confidence"![22] "As a general rule, when an author borrows a text from his predecessors, he makes it his own."[23]

There is another restriction on the meaning formulated in the text: inerrancy does not cover the personal opinions of the authors. The prophet or the apostle transmit the Word of *God* as they exercise their mission. They do not speak as private individuals. The Holy Spirit protects them from error when they speak in the name of God, but they are not infallible in themselves.

This distinction can be seen in 1 Peter 1:10–12. The thoughts of the prophets and their message are not identical: we can suppose that their *minds* have the capacity for error. Consequently, inerrancy is not valid concerning the opinions that the inspired authors *may* hold or *probably* held or that we *guess* they held. Does the mention of the moon in Psalm 121:6 allude to the influence of the stars? In any case this belief is not part of the meaning of this expression.

Vowel Pointing in Hebrew

Ancient Hebrew was written only in consonants. The vowel sounds were reproduced intuitively or by memory. Around the eighth century, in order to fix

---

20. [G. Courtade], "Inspiration et inerrance," in *Supplément* au *Dictionnaire de la Bible*, ed. André Robert, vol. 4 (Paris: Letouzey & Ané, 1949), cols. 549 (unsigned article, the name of the author was revealed by A. Robert en V, 407).

21. Orr, *The Problem of the Old Testament Considered with Reference to Recent Criticism*, 486f. Orr quotes the old "pastoral" commentator Matthew Henry.

22. Jean Schildenberger, "Inspiration et inerrance de la Sainte Écriture. Ancien Testament," in *Questions théologiques aujourd'hui I. Problèmes fondamentaux*, trans. Yves Claude Gélébart (Paris: Desclée De Brouwer, 1964), 187.

23. Courtade, "Inspiration et inerrance," col. 549.

the way in which texts should be read in the synagogues, the Masoretes added signs called the Masoretic vowel points. Are they part of Scripture?

Elia Levita (1469–1549) demonstrated the late origin of the Masoretic fixation, and Christians, whether Catholic or Reformed, accepted this position, allowing other suitable vowels to be attached to the consonants. But interdenominational controversy changed the nature of the debate.[24] Catholics presented the Masoretic text as corrupted to promote the Vulgate. Most Lutheran and Reformed Christians followed the opinion of the Hebrew scholars Johannes Buxtorf, father and son (1564–1629 and 1599–1664), and in spite of Louis Cappel (1585–1658), defended the antiquity of the received vocalization in order to defend the authority of the Hebrew text which we possess. They were aware of the absurdity of saying that the consonants alone were inspired while holding to verbal inspiration.

Do the Masoretic vowel points belong to the authorized text of the writers? Are they therefore inspired? The controversy has been bitter. The *Consensus helveticus* (1675) has a clever conclusion. It affirms that inspiration extends "as far as vowel points," which satisfies the conservatives. *But* it adds: *sive punctorum saltem potestatem*, "or, at least, the capability of pointing." The ambiguity of this expression was no doubt deliberate. The more conservative people could think that it was the vowels of the inspired words that the vowel points are able to represent, so there would be no difference with the Masoretic text. But the word *potestas* ("capability") could also be interpreted as the capability of the consonants to bear the vowel points, producing words giving a better meaning. In this way, the text avoids affirming the historical indefensible idea of the ancient origin of the Masoretic vocalization and consequently it opens (or half opens) the door to assigning other vowels. R. Nicole borrows the words of James D. G. Dunn: the *Consensus* "carefully avoids taking sides between Buxtorf and Cappel."[25] It is subtle. The alternative "either-or" relaxes the Masoretic normativity. The flexibility of this wording allowed Geneva, after debate, to adhere to the *Consensus*.[26]

---

24. Robert D. Preus, *The Theology of Post-Reformation Lutheranism: A Study of Theological Prolegomena* (Saint Louis: Concordia, 1970), 307–9, rightly insists on historic conditioning.

25. R. Nicole, "The Inspiration and Authority of Scripture: J. D. G. Dunn versus B. B. Warfield," *Standing Forth*, 210n8. A detailed refutation, pp. 159–222, of the two-part treatment, by J. Dunn, "The Authority of Scripture according to Scripture," *Churchman* 96 (1982): 104–22, and 201–25. Two authoritative champions who take opposite sides on inerrancy.

26. See also Richard A. Muller, *Post-Reformation Reformed Dogmatics: The Rise and Development of Reformed Orthodoxy, ca. 1520 to ca. 1725*, vol. 2, *Holy Scripture: The Cognitive Foundation of Theology* (Grand Rapids: Baker Academic, 2003), 404–13.

CLARIFICATION ABOUT THE OBJECT ASCRIBED: WHAT DO WE MEAN BY *ERROR*?

Infringing Rules of Grammar

In daily conversation we speak of errors regarding forms of expression that do not obey the rules of syntax or conjugation or the choice of vocabulary. This category of error does not concern inerrancy. These rules, which are fluctuating human conventions, have a certain normativity but no relation to truth.[27]

Modes of Expression Linked to the Ruggedness of Common Speech

God, when he condescends to inspire his spokesmen, "takes on the whole of human speech." Luis Alonso-Schökel draws this consequence: "If we wish to understand what 'God speaks to us' means, it is best to accept at the outset our human language as it is, then to extend our study to the multifaceted complexity of this language, without prejudice or exclusions. Error alone is inadmissible, like sin."[28] Language is naturally elastic, imprecise, inventive. Moisés Silva warns: "A sense of the fluidity of language – or flexibility if you prefer – must be foremost in our minds from beginning to end."[29] I use the word *unsophisticated* to designate all these features. Scripture uses natural, unsophisticated language. Modern readers who are used to the "hard sciences" falter over these scriptural expressions.

There is no error when you say "everybody" for a large majority or "always" for a long time or when you use round numbers (absolute precision doesn't exist). In French people say "fifteen days" to mean a fortnight whereas in fact there are only fourteen days. This can be compared to the "three days and three nights in the heart of the earth" between the death and the resurrection of Jesus in Matthew 12:40. It would be foolish to think of this way of speaking as an error.

Modes of Expression Linked to the Point of View Adopted

The description of the sun and the moon as the "two great lights," and similar expressions are sometimes discussed in the same way. An analysis shows rather that the language is literally exact according *to the angle chosen*, that of our perception. Different authors speak of "a language according to appearances," or "phenomenal" language (*phainomenon*: what is apparent). This point of view is

---

27. An argument that can already be found in Augustine, *De doctrina christiana*, 13.19.

28. Luis Alonso-Schökel, *La Parole inspirée, l'Écriture sainte à la lumière du langage et de la littérature*, Lectio divina 64 (Paris: Cerf, 1971) p. 113 (henceforth PI).

29. Moisés Silva, *Biblical Words and Their Meaning: An Introduction to Lexical Semantics* (Grand Rapids: Zondervan Academic, 1983), 177.

quite legitimate, even fundamental. There is no error, even if modern man prefers another angle of reality.

Some people may retort: the authors believed that they were describing a cosmological, scientific truth (and so they are mistaken). The fact remains to be proved. But if it were true, it would not disprove inerrancy *as far as what is said*: it renders experience and not subsequent theorizing.

Abuse of the principle exists. This point of view does not justify distorting facts. Selectivity, shortcuts, techniques of emphasis, yes, as long as it remains under a threshold that would lead to a deformed description. Inerrant truth excludes bias.

Tropes and Figures of Speech

Flexibility allows a simple expression to be *bent*; the competent reader or listener compensates for this bend and grasps the meaning while different effects are added to the communication (colorfulness or complicity, etc.). We speak of "figures of speech" or "tropes" or "stylistic devices." Biblical language is full of tropes, and if the reader doesn't recognize them, he mistakenly calls an error what is in fact a rhetorical way to please, to move, or to give pause for thought. When the Scriptures speak of the arm or the hand of YHWH or describe him as "coming down" from heaven to see what is happening, as if he really needed to (Gen 11:5; 18:21), this is a colorful description, one that contributes to the narrative technique. It would be foolish to take it literally, inconsistent with other passages.

Two figures of speech are more frequently found in the Bible than in our habitual language (conditioned by the discipline of quantitative hard science): metaphors and hyperboles. The Scriptures are steeped with metaphors and symbols. If you misinterpret them, ignoring their cognitive significance,[30] then you will scream that there are contradictions. The Near East loves hyperbole; there is no breach of truth when a change of régime hyperbolically becomes a cosmic upheaval or Tyre becomes a bare rock in its humiliation (Ezek 26:14).

Poetry is at a different level than tropes and higher than the attribution of a *genre* (cf. *infra*). It is not easy to define.[31] Its affinity to metaphor is an open secret. Many of the objections to inerrancy come from overly mundane reading of poetic texts (the pillars of the earth, the floodgates of heaven).

---

30. Cf. my "Biblical Metaphors and the Doctrine of Atonement," *JETS* 47, no. 4 (December 2004): 629–45. I elaborate an interpretation of metaphor by interacting with authors such as M. Black, N. Goodman, P. Ricœur, H. Rikhof, J. Soskice, etc.

31. Cf. My introduction, "La poésie dans la Bible," *Fac-Réflexion* 38 (1997): 4–13.

The Effect of Literary Genres

The bend of language is also present in complex groupings. Literary genres are characterised by conventions which bear on the meaning of expressions. The obvious example are parables. This genre, used by Jesus, implies a fictional meaning for sentences that would otherwise refer to real events. In the apocalyptic genre, numbers are also symbols. Before speaking of error, the text must be read according to its genre.

However, the fluidity of genres makes this discernment more difficult. They do not have an immutably fixed form that can be unmistakably recognized. The author employing them can forge a new usage. Mergers, or "contaminations," can take place (such as allegorical parables). But within the genre, the potential for "bending" is not very great. As a result the ordinary meaning must be given priority. Catholic Bible scholars called on literary genres in the post-1945 "modernising" period; were they freeing themselves from the true meaning of certain texts, despite the warnings of the Pontifical Biblical Commission?[32] Their example has attracted more recent Evangelicals.

Dissent concerns the genre of Genesis 1–3 and the *historical* genre. Whereas the liberal interpretation sees fiction pretending to be history (the exploits of David or Esther as a "historical novel"), the dominant interpretation among evangelicals defends its historicity, but the interpretation of conservative Catholics is making concessions.[33] Everyone recognises that biblical historiography does not conform to modern practices: it modifies the chronological order, leaves out data that modern historians would consider important, and summarises long speeches.

Are some genres to be excluded *a priori*? Catholics have debated the question.[34] Unless one takes an abstract view, that would seem to be the case. Libertine fiction is assuredly a genre. *Myths* serve as a basis of inhabiting the *pagan* world.[35] The gospel genre is unique and serves the message of Christ; just as the Christ event is itself unique, the literary genre of the Gospels differs sufficiently from ancient biographies to be considered unique.

---

32. H. Höpfl, "Critique biblique. § V,B: Les genres littéraires," *Supplément au Dictionnaire de la Bible* 2 (1934), col. 207, quoting a response dating from 23rd June 1905. Col. 208: ancient historians clearly distinguished between proved events and fiction.

33. This is the impression given by Courtade, "Inspiration and inerrancy," col. 550–56: he refuses to state clearly whether the events related, commemorated at *Pourim*, really happened in the Persia of Ahasuerus/Xerxes.

34. Courtade, "Inspiration and inerrancy, col. 538.

35. See my contribution to the book H. Blocher and F. Lovsky, *Bible et histoire* (Lausanne: Presses Bibliques Universitaires, 1980), "L'Evangile, mythe ou histoire?," 31–57.

Restriction to Faith and Conduct

Certain writers confess inerrancy only as it regards statements of faith and conduct. Traditional inerrantists reject this limitation. For Catholics this feature distinguishes the infallibility of the Scriptures from ex cathedra pontifical promulgations: these are only infallible concerning faith and conduct (the *charisma* of the pope is to serve the Word of God) whereas the Scriptures are infallible in every area.[36]

Those who wish to limit the scope of inerrancy argue from the function of Scripture and divine intention. If the Bible has not been given to us to teach us how the heavens function but how to go to heaven (Galileo, quoted by Cardinal Baronius), why insist on the absence of error in astronomy?

The argument does not stand up to examination. The choice of a principal aim does not lead to indifference in adjacent areas. Our "human too human" measurements do not allow us to decree that what we consider as "details" are insignificant *for God*. Does not the Master require faithfulness in little things (cf. Luke 16:10)? If this Word is *God's*, is it not presumptuous to push *a priori* to the fringes what he has committed to his spokesmen? Recognising the *scopus* (the main purpose, the aim) helps in the interpretation of the text without disqualifying a part of it.

Nowhere does the Bible make this disconnection, which is not constrained by our experience. *Faith* is connected to history, that is what makes it distinctive among religions. As is well-known, the word *Gospel* (*euaggelion*) means "(good) news": it isn't first and foremost a doctrine, whether moral or spiritual, but news (i.e., a proclamation of what happened). The nature of faith is altered if it is uprooted from worldly reality, the object of human knowing.

HISTORICAL BEARINGS

IS INERRANCY AN INNOVATION?

Some people claim that the affirmation of inerrancy is an innovation dating from the nineteenth century and that it toughened up the common confession of the truth of Scripture, the Word of God – previously minor errors were accepted in areas extraneous to faith. The theologians of Princeton were seen to be the innovators: Charles Hodge (followed by his son A. A. Hodge) and Benjamin B. Warfield. They were supposed to have yielded to the influence of *modern* rationalist empiricism and of Scottish *common sense* realism. Some acknowledged

36. Cf. Courtade, "Inspiration et inerrance," col. 521.

that seventeenth-century orthodoxy professed the doctrine without the word *inerrancy*, but they thought that orthodoxy had diverged from the Reformers. The book written by Jack B. Rogers and Donald K. McKim,[37] coinciding with the critics of fundamentalism,[38] spread this portrayal of things.

INERRANCY, CONFESSED FROM THE BEGINNING

Other witnesses enable us to have another vision of history. "If the unanimous consent of the Fathers is not a delusion, if the constant, perpetual and universal nature of a doctrine is a rule of faith, then there is no dogma more solidly established than the inerrancy of Scripture."[39] The conviction of Biblical inerrancy can be found in every age of the Christian church. This chapter can but give a short overview.

The Conviction of Ancient Judaism

The church begins before its own beginning. Judaism affirms that the Scriptures are without error (there was no dispute with the church on this point). George F. Moore summarized this position: "It was an axiom that no-one disputed that every syllable of the Scriptures possesses the veracity and the authority of the Word of God."[40] In addition to the *Contra Apionem* of Josephus, other sources supply strong affirmations. A *baraitha* of the Sanhedrin 99b tract applies Numbers 15:31, "he has despised the word of YHWH," to the negation of a detail (*diqdouq*): even to suggest that there is one small error is to attack divine authority.[41] Today we see a convergence between the beacons of Jewish science (U. Cassuto on Genesis) and evangelical Bible scholars.

The Teaching of the Church Fathers

Among the orthodox, the conviction was not debated in the ancient church: the Scriptures could not contain falsehood. As early as the first century, Clement of Rome wrote to the Corinthians to this effect (45:2). Justin Martyr is clear in his *Dialogue with Trypho the Jew* (65). Several others could be quoted, in particular the church father Saint Augustine in his letter 82 (1.3) written to

37. Jack B. Rogers and Donald K. McKim, *The Authority and Interpretation of the Bible: A Historical Approach* (San Francisco: Harper & Row, 1979).

38. In particular as developed by George Marsden and Ernest Sandeen.

39. R. P. F. Prat, SJ, *La Bible et l'histoire* (Paris: Bloud, 1904), 15, as quoted by Courtade, "Inspiration et inerrance," col. 524.

40. George F. Moore, *Judaism in the First Centuries of the Christian Era* (Cambridge, MA: Harvard University Press, 1927) 1:239, as quoted by Grudem, "Scripture's Self-Attestation and the Problem of Formulating a Doctrine of Scripture," 36 and 363n42.

41. Quoted by Marc-Alain Ouaknin, *Le Livre brûlé. Philosophie du Talmud*, Points Sagesses 52 (Paris: Seuil, 1993), 31. Cf. le *Livre des Antiquités bibliques*, 25,13.

Jerome: "Towards the only books of Scripture which are called canonical I have learned to bear such respect and honour from my very strong belief that none of the authors erred (*errasse*) at any point in writing them; and if I come across anything which seems to be contrary to the truth, the only possibilities of what has happened are: either the manuscript (*codicem*) is wrong, or the interpreter hasn't grasped what has been said or else I haven't understood."[42] It is for good reason that he devoted a whole book, *De Consensu evangelistarum*, to finding a solution to the difficulties arising from a comparison of the Gospels.

Where the tradition of the church fathers has great weight, there was a reluctance to water down inerrancy. The Catholic Church officially maintained the affirmation, at least until the middle of the twentieth century.

The Orthodoxy of the Reformers and Their Successors

That the scholastics should have followed the conviction of Augustine is unsurprising. Thomas Aquinas quotes Letter 82 just as we have just done (*Summa theologica*, 1^{a}, qu. 1, art. 8, ad 2^{m}). That the Reformers should have maintained inerrancy in the same way has been disputed. Is it because the Lutheran or Reformed identity of certain liberals that makes it difficult for them to accept a reading of Luther or Calvin so far from their own conviction?

A common portrayal of Luther drags him away from inerrancy. The freedom of his eloquence and the subjectivity of his judgements have contributed to this misunderstanding. But the wires have gotten crossed. An image has been built on some of Luther's statements *which for him do not bear on books that are clearly canonical*, chiefly the epistle of James. His doctrine of Scripture has been deduced from his commentaries on texts that he believes do not belong to the Scriptures! Luther does not have a very clear-cut position on the canon; we can suppose that he didn't wish to upset his conservative followers, along with Melanchthon. As far as the canonical Scriptures are concerned (practically all the other books of the Bible), he wrote that they "have never been in error," unlike the Fathers, the councils, and the apocryphal writings.[43] "Not only the words," he dares to write, "but the style of speech (*phrasis*) is divine, which the Holy Spirit and the Scriptures use."[44] The case for Luther and inerrancy is strong.[45]

---

42. My translation. It is repeated a little later in the same letter (2.5). Compare *Confessiones* 12.23.32.

43. Luther, *D. Martin Luthers Werke: kritische Gesammtausgabe* (Weimar: Hermann Böhlau, 1883–2009), 7:315, and several times. Hereafter, *WA*.

44. *WA* 40:254.

45. I elaborated on this, in a study with a great many quotations, in which I refer to: "Luther et la Bible," in *Dieu parle! Études sur la Bible et son interprétation* (Aix-en-Provence: Kerygma, 1984), 127–41. In particular I was able to benefit from two overlooked syntheses made by the German Wilhelm M. Oesch in several articles in the review *Lutherischer Rundblick* and by the American Michael Reu.

That Calvin should be categorized as noninerrantist is even less comprehensible. Is it because of his daring freedom in his commentaries? From the outset he goes to the very limits of the doctrine of inerrancy – but *he never goes beyond them*. The accuracy of his observation and the consistency of his logic are remarkable.

It is surprising to note the negligent reading of some authors.[46] Otto Ritschl had to correct H. Heppe.[47] Kenneth S. Kantzer, after devoting his thesis to the bibliology of Calvin, has dealt with this subject several times.[48] R. Nicole's synthesis, typical of his meticulous thoroughness, reveals an unsurpassed mastery of the bibliography.[49] The opinion of a theologian who does not himself subscribe to inerrancy, Edward A. Dowey Jr., is just as definite: for Calvin, inspiration makes the Scriptures "a series of documents without error in their original form."[50] "For Calvin the theologian an error in Scripture is unthinkable. Thus the continual harmonization, explanation and interpretation of passages which seem contradictory or inexact."[51] Nobody has been able to cite a single passage where Calvin indisputably attributes an error to an original author.[52]

The work of Richard A. Muller has shown the continuity between Calvin and Protestant orthodoxy. The link is clear with contemporaries such as Peter Martyr Vermigli and Girolamo Zanchi, and especially with Théodore de Bèze, his assistant and successor. Admittedly a scholastic form of speech replaces popular speech: that is the natural evolution of a movement that is now becoming a lasting reality. We should avoid caricaturing these successors. Apart from their teaching activity, they were also vibrant "existential" preachers.

François Turretin (1623–87) represents the firmness of Reformed orthodox,

---

46. Rogers and McKim (*The Authority and Interpretation of the Bible*, 110) write: "In his Commentary on Acts 7:16, Calvin declares that Luke made an obvious mistake . . ." Now, as was brought out by W. Robert Godfrey, "A Question of Transition," in *Scripture and Truth*, 233, Calvin in fact carefully avoids saying this. Calvin wrote: "I think that this discrepancy [70/75] came from the mistake of those who were copying the books" (*Commentaires sur le Nouveau Testament II*, 553) in the LXX, and Luke, didn't correct it, but just used the current version. In his introduction to 2 Peter, Calvin specifically rejected pseudonymy.

47. Otto Ritschl, *Dogmengeschichte des Protestantismus*, vol. 1, *Prolegomena. Biblicismus und Traditionalismus in der altprotestantischen Theologie* (Leipzig: Hinrichs, 1908), 64.

48. Kenneth S. Kantzer, "Calvin and the Holy Scriptures," in *Inspiration and Interpretation*, ed. John Walvoord (Grand Rapids: Eerdmans, 1957), 115–55.

49. Roger Nicole, "John Calvin and Inerrancy," in *Standing Forth*, 103–49.

50. Edward A. Dowey Jr., *The Knowledge of God in Calvin's Theology* (Grand Rapids: Eerdmans, 1994), 102.

51. Dowey, *The Knowledge of God in Calvin's Theology*, 104.

52. J.-Marcel Nicole, "Calvin, homme de la Bible," *Revue de théologie et d'action évangéliques* 3, no. 4 (October 1943): 319, concludes, after extensive research: "Nothing allows us to allege that he allowed the possibility of errors in the original texts."

all the more so in that he is more flexible than some teachers of dogmatics. Contrary to a misguided understanding, he says that infallibility is necessary and does *not* impute to the inspired authors what he thinks to be error.[53] His conciliatory sensitivity can be seen in the debate about vowel points.[54]

The so-called Geneva *Revival* at the beginning of the nineteenth century, which has very much left its mark on French-speaking Protestantism, brought together pietist fervour and orthodoxy (with a reintroduction of the *Consensus Helveticus*). Its theologian, Louis Gaussen, restored seventeenth-century bibliology. He attracted both approval and opposition with his work *Théopneustie*, or *The Plenary Inspiration of the Holy Scriptures* (1st ed., 1840; 2nd ed., 1842). Through its translation into English, its influence was strong and long-lasting.[55]

And what about Princeton? Both before and after 1900, there have been scandalous caricatures of the teachers of this famous faculty. They were not rationalists. Would to God that theologians might imitate their piety and their spirited preaching of the gospel![56] Charles Hodge has been much criticised for using the methods of the natural sciences in theology. He has been made out to be a rationalist-empiricist, subjected to Scottish "common sense" philosophy. Admittedly, as an apologist, he made the most of the prestige of natural science and followed its method too closely for what is appropriate in theology. The few pages in which he indulges in following the spirit of the age should not be separated from the whole of his work with its vision and *practices*, which are far richer and more astute. The influence of Francis Bacon and Thomas Reid can be

53. François Turretin, *Institutio theologiae elencticae*, loc. secundus, qu. V, § 10. Cf. § 30 on Acts 7:14.

54. Turretin, *Institutio theologiae elencticae*, Loc. secundus, qu. XI, § 12 argues for the value of Masoretic points but § 13 concludes in a conciliatory way: "This question seems to be more grammatical than theological."

55. About Gaussen, see Jean D. P. Decorvet, "Every Scripture ΘΕΟΠΝΕΥΣΤΟΣ: An Assessment of Louis Gaussen's Case for Theopneustia within the Context of Geneva's Réveil" (PhD thesis, Wheaton College, December 2011).

56. Cf. Bradley N. Seeman, "The 'Old Princetonians' on Biblical Authority," in *EA*, 195–237, especially pp. 216, 229–35, and the entries "Hodge, Charles," by P. J. Wallace, and "Warfield, Benjamin Breckenridge," by B. J. Gundlach, in *Biographical Dictionary of Evangelicals*, ed. Timothy Larsen, David Bebbington, and Mark A. Noll (Downers Grove, IL: InterVarsity Press, 2003) 303b–307b and 698a–701b. The young Charles Hodge triggered a "revival" through his profession of faith at the college where he studied; in Germany he attended the lectures of famous pietists and maintained a warm relationship with them; he devoted his inaugural lesson to the importance of piety for the interpretation of the Bible. Benjamin Warfield published poems and hymns of his own composition. His sermon on "The Religious Life of the Theological Student" was a landmark. Francis Patton called his sermons "models": "the mature fruit of religious experience and careful exegesis, and in their meditative simplicity remind us of some of the best of the Puritan Doctors" (quoted by Samuel G. Craig, foreword to Warfield's edited volume of works, *The Person and Work of Christ* [Philadelphia: Presbyterian & Reformed, 1950], viii; the volume contains three sermons by Warfield, pp. 535–75).

detected in his teaching, but Francis Turretin, the great Reformed teacher of dogmatics from Geneva, is the man he most closely follows. Warfield, admittedly, considerably trusts scientific reason. He does not belong to Abraham Kuyper's *neo-Calvinist* school of thought, which makes reason depend on religious attitudes and on faith (biblical genuine or apostate). But he is mindful of the noetic effect of sin and of the need for regeneration in order for intelligence to comply with the truth. Although he is not a follower of Kuyper, he makes common cause with him and his colleague Herman Bavinck in maintaining inerrancy.[57] It was he who invited them to the United States to Princeton. Warfield did more than any other to defend the entire trustworthiness of Scripture. Warfield did more than any other to defend dogma "scientifically." This tradition remains active and fruitful.[58]

The Counterpoint of the Refusal of Inerrancy

The affirmation of biblical inerrancy has rarely been self-evident. From the time of the church fathers, sharp-eyed writers pointed to "errors" in the Scriptures, developing arguments that have been taken up ever since, such as the impossibility of accepting that the book of Daniel comes from him in the sixth century BC with such specific and detailed predictions. The philosopher Celsus was the first pagan thinker to have taken seriously the "threat" of Christianity, and it needed the intellectual might of Origen to respond to him. Porphyry, the secretary and editor of Plotinus, continued in the same vein. Celsus and Porphyry set themselves up as the sworn enemies of Christianity. Spinoza (whose *Tractatus theologico-politicus* laid the basis of the disconnection between the truth of facts and beliefs) was not a confessing Christian and thus remains outside of the scope of this study, as do the Socinians Lelio and Fausto Sozzini and their disciples – they considered themselves Christians, but theirs was a very different Christianity.

Erasmus appears to be the "father" of minimizing, moderate criticism. In his thinking, the Holy Spirit left the Evangelists to draw on their defective memory when they quoted the Old Testament. Criticized by Johannes Eck, attacked by

57. See Seeman "The 'Old Princetonians' on Biblical Authority," in *EA*, 195–237; John D. Woodbridge and Randall H. Balmer, "The Princetonians and Biblical Authority: An Assessment of the Ernest Sandeen Proposal," in *Scripture and Truth*, 251–79; Richard B. Gaffin Jr., *God's Word in Servant Form: Abraham Kuyper and Herman Bavinck on the Doctrine of Scripture* (Jackson, MS: Reformed Academic Press, 2009); James B. Hunt, "Bavinck and the Princetonians on Scripture: A Difference in Doctrine or Defense?," *JETS* 53, no. 2 (2010): 317–33.

58. See the work of the Anglican theologian James I. Packer or the many contributors to the book *The Enduring Authority of the Christian Scriptures*, edited by D. A. Carson, cited above.

Spanish monks, he drew back, but there is little doubt about his conviction.[59] "Some other scholars shared his opinion."[60]

Several other names could be mentioned over the next centuries. The spirit of Erasmus led Hugo Grotius in the same direction. He was a lawyer but also an exegete and a theologian with a wide influence.[61] Jean Le Clerc in the Netherlands generated lively debate and had a Catholic "counterpart," Richard Simon, who was vigorously opposed by Bossuet. They set in motion the so-called critical (historico-critical) approach to the sacred texts. On the sidelines of the so-called orthodox or Evangelical persuasion, in every generation through to the nineteenth century and beyond, thinkers can be found who consider themselves faithful but moderate, respectful of Biblical authority but unable to go as far as inerrancy.[62] Was a recognized evangelical author such as Andrew T. McGowan touched by this spirit?[63]

The originality of Karl Barth and the effect of his "revolution" demands a place in our study. He refers to the Scriptures as "the Word written by God."[64] He goes as far as to write: "The Bible 'is' the Word of God."[65] However, *we should not be misled*. Barth repudiates any return to "the Scriptural theory of the final era of the former Protestant orthodoxy."[66] For Barth, the word *is* here means that "the bible 'has been' and 'will be' the Word of God,"[67] whenever and wherever it has pleased or will please God. In this event, "we cannot negate the distinction, even the opposition, between form and content."[68] Barth tramples on the idea of inerrancy: "Duplicates and contradictions are abundant (between the law and the prophets, between John and the synoptic gospels, between Paul and James.)"

59. Courtade, "Inspiration et inerrance," col. 498; Woodbridge and Balmer, "The Princetonians and Biblical Authority," in *Scripture and Truth*, 398n34, and "German Pietism and Scriptural Authority," *EA*, 155.

60. Courtade, "Inspiration et inerrance," col. 498, who adds: "The bishop of Spalato, M.-A. de Dominis, accustomed to playing a double game, implies that Erasmus is correct, while still blaming his temerity."

61. On the eighteenth-century pietists, especially Bengel, whose adherence to inerrancy was put into question, see the refutation by Woodbridge, "German Pietism," in *EA*, 164.

62. Does Frederick F. Bruce subscribe to this line? I am undecided, the "spirit" is very different: F.F. Bruce resisted the pressure to conform to liberal academic conformity.

63. Andrew T. McGowan, *The Divine Inspiration of Scripture: Challenging Evangelical Perspectives* (Leicester: Apollos, 2007), neither affirms nor denies inerrancy but takes up a number of the arguments of opponents of inerrancy, Response of James W. Scott, "Reconsidering Inerrancy: A Response to A. T. B. McGowan's *The Divine Authenticity of Scripture*," *Westminster Theological Journal* 71 (2009): 185–209.

64. Karl Barth, title of section § 4.2, *Kirchliche Dogmatik*, I, 1 (Zollikon-Zürich: Evangelischer, 1932), 96–107. Hereafter, *KD*.

65. *KD*, I, 2, 557.

66. *KD*, I, 1, 139.

67. *KD*, I, 2, 557. Barth sometimes slightly varied his wording; the one from *Dogmatics* is authoritative to define his theology.

68. *KD*, I, 1, 180 (already 161ff).

That doesn't just concern the periphery: "The Bible is also vulnerable and fallible in its most specifically religious and theological structures."[69] "That the lame walk, that the blind see, that the dead are raised to life, that sinful and fallible men proclaim the Gospel, that is the miracle we are speaking of when we affirm that the Bible is the Word of God."[70] The analogy should lead him to indicate that the lame and the blind were not healed. Barthians do not have the aura of the great man of Basel, but they have not come back to inerrancy. Bruce L. McCormack is close to orthodox doctrine, yet he dismisses their theology of Scripture.[71]

The benevolent critic of Barth, that outstanding observer of the theological scene, the professor of systematic theology at the Free University of Amsterdam Gerrit C. Berkouwer (1903–96) went from Reformed orthodoxy to a rejection of the traditional position and of inerrancy.[72] He sets rational objectivity against faith commitment: he alleviates and softens tradition with a pastoral intent. This can be seen in his *magnum opus* on the subject (but the American translation should be handled with care[73]). His influence has impacted the recent development of one wing of evangelicalism.

On the Catholic side, some distinguished voices began to erode inerrancy in the nineteenth century. The rector of the Catholic Institute of Paris, Monseigneur d'Hulst, precipitated by his rash statements the warning of *Providentissimus Deus* (1893). John Henry Newman, the convert who eventually became a cardinal, introduced in 1884 the idea of *obiter dicta* ("by the way") in Scripture, "statements, clauses or phrases in Scripture on purely factual matters and which do not concern faith or conduct," which are purely human and are not "binding for our faith."[74] The suggestion is incompatible with the

69. *KD*, I, 2, 565.

70. *KD*, I, 2, 587.

71. McCormack, "The Actuality of God: Karl Barth in Conversation with Open Theism," in *Engaging the Doctrine of God: Contemporary Protestant Perspectives*, ed. Bruce L. McCormack (Grand Rapids: Baker Academic, 2008), 195.

72. On the way Berkouwer's thought evolved, Robert C. Sproul, "The Case for Inerrancy: A Methodological Approach," in *God's Inerrant Word: An International Symposium on the Trustworthiness of Scripture*, ed. John Warwick Montgomery (Minneapolis: Bethany Fellowship, 1974), 243–45.

73. G. C. Berkouwer, *De Heilige Schrift*, 2 vols. (Kampen: Kok, 1966–67), translated (and unfortunately abridged by one third) by Jack B. Rogers, under the title *Holy Scripture* (Grand Rapids: Eerdmans, 1975). The abbreviation omits some instructive historical developments, and the translation is not wholly reliable.

74. As quoted by Jaak Seynave, *Cardinal Newman's Doctrine on Holy Scripture according to His Published Works and Previously Unedited Manuscripts* (Louvain: Publications Universitaires de Louvain, Oxford: Blackwell, Tielt: Lannoo, 1953), 169, giving as a reference *Stray Essays II*, 51, 52. Cf. Courtade, "Inspiration et inerrance," col. 498.

recognition of God as the prime *author*.[75] Newman, an adversary of liberalism, also cried out in faith: "Ten thousand difficulties do not make a doubt."[76]

THE CONSTRUCTION OF THE DOCTRINE (DOGMATIC PERSPECTIVES)

THE METHOD: DEDUCTION OR INDUCTION?

Criticism of the Orthodox Inerrantist Elaboration

A debate on methodology has involved several writers: to determine the relationship between Biblical inspiration and the presence of errors, should one proceed by deduction or induction, from theological principles or from observed facts? (In point of fact, the simplicity of this alternative is deceiving as we shall see.) The adversaries of inerrantism criticise its use of the *deductive* method, which follows an all too human logic: the words of Scripture are pronounced by God; God cannot be in error or lead into error; therefore, the words of Scripture cannot be in error or lead into error. The flaw in this deduction isn't just because it overestimates the strength of the rational sequence (God is subjected to logic), but it takes no account of the complexity linked to the instrumental role of the human author (God cannot be in error but man can).

What does the combination of a divine author and a human author imply? The critics say: Do not start with an *a priori*. The safer way is *induction*. Does inspiration produce inerrancy? Let's examine the text to see if this is the case! J. Ramsay Michaels echoes this thought: Warfield only establishes inerrancy, complains Michaels, "by exercising arbitrary abstraction" and ignoring "the other phenomena of Scripture."[77]

Examining the "phenomena" will lead far away from Warfield, according to the critics. Sometimes, some of them add, the deductive process is excessively hardened: a principle with a judicial flavour is applied: "Wrong in one place,

75. Courtade, "Inspiration et inerrance," col. 498. Seynave, *Cardinal Newman's Doctrine on Holy Scripture*, 175, shows that Newman did not really understand the concept of instrumentality.

76. Newman, *Apologia pro vita sua: Being a History of his Religious Opinions* (London: Longmans, Green, 1893), 239. Newman speaks of the difficulties raised against religion. Against liberalism, "Note A," 285–97.

77. Michaels, "Inerrancy or Verbal Inspiration? An Evangelical Dilemma," in *Inerrancy and Common Sense*, edited by Roger R. Nicole and J. Ramsey Michaels (Grand Rapids: Baker, 1980), 69n29 (argument developed pp. 60–64). Michaels challenges the idea that the Bible presents teaching about itself. Similarly John Goldingay, *Models for Scripture* (Grand Rapids: Eerdmans, 1994). An examination of this book requires more space than this article can afford: his strategy consists of disconnecting the different intrabiblical genres to prevent any generalization of their characteristics.

unreliable everywhere." Inerrantists go as far as to say: if there is but one error in the Bible, I can no longer grant it my entire confidence.[78] To explain such extremism, critics suspect a neurotic need of security.[79]

The Suggested Response

Some inerrantists have made themselves susceptible to these criticisms. But not the most competent ones.[80] Their method is far from such caricatures, and the method of the critics then proves to be problematic.

The meaning of "Scripture is (the) Word of God" is not at all a postulate, an *a priori* on which one can merely deduce. The exegesis of a great many texts *on inspiration* is a foundation and a guide – induction, if you like (or adduction, where the thinker builds and tests models to see if they are appropriate). For any doctrine, this type of elaboration alone respects *sola scriptura*.[81]

Inerrancy depends on the *way* Scripture *is* the Word of God. The statement "The Bible *is* the Word of God" can be taken in a very strict way. Everything it says, God says, as clearly as if he had spoken from heaven with no intermediary – or in a looser and vaguer way – the Bible is the means God uses to communicate himself, despite different imperfections, and its overall message makes him known. No theologian allowing for errors has been able to hold on to the maximum force of *is* and tighten the link. To deny inerrancy is to begin to loosen its force. Do the texts on inspiration, and so on, allow this? What is the force of *is* according to the teaching of the Bible itself? The work of Warfield (who was primarily an exegete of the New Testament) on the texts draws the conclusion that *is* has the maximum force. To refute this assertion, it is necessary to refute not the theology but the exegesis of Warfield.

It isn't the word *inerrancy* that is decisive. The Scriptures express the concept in other language, in formulations that imply it. For example, the cleansing of the smelter's oven so that no impurity remains (Prov 30:5; Ps 18:30). The insistence that that commandments of YHWH as "truth" are righteous *altogether, as a whole* (Ps 19:9; cf. Ps 119:128). God will not allow *any* of the words of his prophet to "fall to the ground" (1 Sam 3:19). The perfection of his commands is boundless (Ps 119:96). This insistence makes the attribution of truth universal, for every part of the whole. The word in the prologue of Luke, *a/sphaleia* (Luke 1:4),

78. We are close to this in Turretin, *Institutio*, loc. secundus, qu. 5, § 7: "If we admit that things of lesser importance are corrupt, why not those of greater weight?"

79. Barr, *Fundamentalism*, 317, shows that he knows "his" evangelicals well enough to dismiss the idea (but 319, psychological *effects*).

80. Cf. R. Nicole, "Induction and Deduction with Reference to Inspiration," in *Standing Forth*, 151–58.

81. Cf. in this volume Vanhoozer, "The Bible – Word of God?"

is constructed on the same model as *in/fallibility*. When Jesus discussed the words of Psalm 82, he declared that no particular word of Scripture can be "unfastened" or "loosed" (from the verb *luein*, picturing authority; John 10:35).

The argument from silence and what is implicit are decisive here: the New Testament in its *use* of the Old Testament bears witness. To imagine that the apostles would never have had the opportunity to point this out, if they believed in the possible presence of errors, is implausible. If they had done so, it would have invalidated their appeal to scriptural texts as an authority to bring the debate to a close (as Jesus did with the story of David in Matthew 12:4). It would empty "It is written" of its force.

The inductive method based on the "phenomena" appraised by the reader gives him or her its final authority: I am the one who will draw the dogmatic conclusion on the degree of truthfulness of the inspired text from my assessment of Scriptural statements, whether they appear to me right or wrong, accurate or not. The issue is not only subjectivism. In reality, "my" evaluation relies on contemporary opinions: if I trust it, I run the high risk of being conformed to the "pattern of the world," to its Zeitgeist (Rom 12:2). Let us take note of the pattern of this issue. If the primacy is given to *my* assessment of the "phenomena," I am no longer following Jesus Christ and the apostles he trained. Instead, I am making an independent judgement apart from him. The specificity of a disciple is to trust his master more than his own understanding. Am I still a disciple?

THE METHOD: THE RELATIONSHIP WITH OTHER DOCTRINES

The Parallel with Christology

Doctrines are interdependent within the corpus of revealed truth. The link between bibliology and Christology is clearly enlightening. The Johannine writings use the title *Logos* three times for the person of Christ (John 1:1, 15, *Logos*; 1 John 1:1, *Logos* of life; Rev 19:13, *Logos* of God). The parallel is tempting between the incarnate Word and the inscripturated Word. Pius XII carries it through to inerrancy: "Just as the substantial Word of God came in every way like man 'except for sin' (Heb 4:15), in the same way the words of God, expressed in human languages, are similar in every way to human language, except for errors" (*Divino afflante* §37).

Some use the same relationship to draw the opposite conclusion. For Barth, "Word of God signified by the prophetic and apostolic word, the Holy Scripture, corresponds exactly (*genau*) to the unity of God and man in Jesus Christ."[82] But he continues: to deny that the Bible writers were liable to error (even in their

82. *KD* I, 2, 555. There is hyperbole here, since Barth emphasises shortly that identity is only indirect, etc.

wording) would be to "deprive them of their human condition and . . . fall into Docetism."[83] Since Docetism is a *christological* heresy which affirms that the human form of Jesus is just an appearance, the accusation only makes sense with the analogy Word / Person and Word / Book. The argument is strengthened by the emphasis on the kenosis of the Son in his incarnation: he renounced his prerogatives in order to share the condition of fallen mankind. The divine Word of the prophets and apostles also submits to the conditions of human communication. *Errare humanum est*, error is human. Kenosis in bibliology means assuming human error.

Defenders of inerrancy expose the inconsistency *if* Christology remains orthodox. Inerrancy and the impeccability of Christ (the fact that he is sinless) match each other "exactly" (Barth's word). There is condescendence, in the sense of the Greek fathers, in the merciful action of a God who comes down to us, but that does not imply error. Herman Bavinck puts it simply: "The writing down of the word, of the revelation forces us to recognise also in Scripture the weakness, the self-abasement, the nature of a servant. But just as the human in Christ, although weak and self-abased, remained free of sin, in the same way Scripture is *sine labe concepta* (conceived spotless)."[84]

To establish the accusation of Docetism, it would be necessary to show that it is *essentially* human to sin, for nature *as created* and in *every* word pronounced: for inerrancy supposes the preservation of just certain words (those of the inspired writers in their mission). We are far from this. Preservation restores the original integrity.

Kenosis needs to be handled with care. We must not stray far away from Philippians 2:7 from which the word is derived. Sober interpretation avoids "evacuating" the divinity of Christ[85] and does not justify, according to the parallel, rejecting inerrancy.

But is the parallel valid? *Grosso modo*, doubtlessly. If you look closely, the contrast emerges between the incarnation – one person (the Son) and two natures (divine and human) – and the production of the Scriptures – two persons (the divine and human authors) and one "nature," or one meaning. Rather than *parallel*, the relationship is *perpendicular*. Scripture is the Word *of Christ*: his memorised teaching is the heart of the New Testament; the rest comes from his ambassadors, through whom he speaks (2 Cor 13:3), led by his Spirit. This can be extended to the Old Testament: ahead of time, *his* Spirit spoke through

83. *KD* I, 2, 565.

84. Herman Bavinck, *Gereformeerde Dogmatiek*, vol. 1 (Kampen: Bos, 1906), 460 (§ 115), my translation.

85. Cf. my summary in *La Doctrine du Christ*, Didaskalia (Vaux-sur-Seine: Édifac, 2002), 115–17, 169–79.

the prophets (1 Peter 1:11). Scripture is the fruit of the prophetic ministry of Christ, in his person and through his associates, divine and human Word because Christ is God and man! The Son who has come in the flesh – that is inerrancy.

Accommodation

The condescension of God, of the Son, can be expressed in this way: he accommodated himself to our weakness. This is a classic theme. It agrees with the spirit of Calvin.[86] However, it is sometimes used to argue against inerrancy. It is asserted that the self-abasement of the Son and his entry into human solidarity led him to accommodate himself to *common errors*. And we find them in Scripture.

This understanding breaks with the classical notion which ruled out sharing in the errors of sinful humanity.[87] No clear biblical statement authorises it: the change of *requirements* according to different ages (Matt 19:8) does not put into question the *truth* of the statements. It conflicts with the attitude of Jesus towards many of the opinions around him, such as what is pure and impure: he doesn't prove to be very accommodating! It has great difficulty in avoiding arbitrary judgement, the enshrinement of the opinion of the reader, who is always keen to declare that what he doesn't like must be accommodation to the errors of another age.

The argument comes from a sharp awareness today that individual judgements are conditioned by the system of ideas of a culture. The response demands a closer analysis of culture. Accommodating errors is only required of Christ and the biblical authors when there is an unjustified overevaluation of the effect of the historical and cultural context.[88]

The Relationship with Other Doctrines

In a theological system, other doctrines have a relationship with the affirmation or the denial of inerrancy. The divine-human *concursus* of inspiration is one particular case of human causality wholly penetrated and driven by God's causality.[89] Without dualism or monism. Any *synergism* that bestows an

86. Emphasised by James I. Packer, "Calvin's View of Scripture," in *God's Inerrant Word*, 95–114, especially 102–6.

87. A strong demonstration by Glenn S. Sunshine, "Accommodation Historically Considered," in *EA*, 238–65.

88. I refer you to my essay "Permanent Validity and Contextual Relativity of Doctrinal Statements," in *The Task of Dogmatics. Explorations in Theological Method*, ed. Oliver D. Crisp and Fred Sanders (Grand Rapids: Zondervan, 2017), 107–30.

89. Cf. in this volume Vanhoozer, "The Bible – Word of God?"

irreducible independence on the human contribution stumbles over this difficulty. The doctrine of *creation* presents a structure contrary to both monism and dualism, as does the doctrine of the *Holy Spirit*, who works in us "to will and to act" (Phil 2:13).

Justification by faith alone is cited by some critics of the doctrine of inerrancy. To ask the believer to be subject to Scripture, they think, would be to demand a *work*. So the principle of pure grace "without works" would be undermined. But being subject to Scripture is not a work; it is a *liberation*, by grace, from the dehumanising tyranny of error (John 8:31–36; Rom 6:17–22). For the orthodox, indeed, to the extent to which this subjection is a different thing than adherence to Christ, it is not required for justification.

THE APPEAL TO TRUTH

Inerrancy Refused on the Grounds of Religious Truth

Advocates of inerrancy only reject the distortion of truth. Many critics therefore accuse them of remaining prisoners to a concept of truth tied to modern science, to rationalist empiricism. This means that they miss out on the religious, subjective, existential truth that come from faith. According to these critics, being interested only in truth as the correlation between facts and statements, as inerrantists generally do, is a fatal mistake. It would be the same as listening to a symphony to count the number of times a certain note is repeated or searching for the "historic" Hamlet! It is a category error, *metabasis eis allo genos* ("change to another sort")! Most of the critics consider the truth as a correlation to facts, similar to common sense, but reserve it for the hard natural sciences and deny it for the Bible.

The disconnexion between truths is nothing new. The "double truth" of medieval Averroism set the stage. Spinoza in his *Tractatus* led the fight by separating out revealed knowledge, which is only interested in our conduct, from natural knowledge coming from reason: "These two types of knowledge have nothing in common."[90] Most of all, we owe to Kant the split that characterised subsequent thought. He summarised it in this way: "I had to remove *knowledge* (for what lies beyond natural sciences) to make room for *belief*."[91] However, the truth of faith is rational (the necessary postulate of practical reason). Kierkegaard

---

90. Baruch Spinoza, *Tractatus theologico-politicus*, Gebhardt edition, 1925: http://www.philotextes.info/spip/IMG/pdf/gebhardt.pdf, Praefatio (iii–10 in margin): cognitio revelata "nihil cum hac [naturali cognitione] commune habere."

91. Immanuel Kant, preface to the 2nd ed. of *Kritik der reinen Vernunft* (1787), ed. Raymund Schmidt (Leipzig: Felix Meiner, 1926), xxx: "Ich mußte also das *Wissen* aufheben, um zum *Glauben* Platz zu bekommen."

radicalises this opposition to save faith from being engulfed by Hegel. Although the complexity of his thought is misrepresented by only quoting the paradoxical assertions in *Concluding Unscientific Postscript to Philosophical Fragments*, identifying truth with subjectivity (the passion of existential commitment) had a major cultural impact. Its prestige gave credence to the argument against inerrancy.

Protest about Truth

The philosophical tradition just mentioned is far from being unanimous. Realism, the idea of truth as corresponding to a reality regardless of the thinker, is in good health. The unity of one's personal life – in which biology and spirituality, history and transcendence, social and private, intertwine and interact – testifies against the split. Scripture itself supports a sufficiently unified notion of truth.

More thorough study illustrates this.[92] Nowhere does Scripture, which values personal commitment, devalue the objectivity of correspondence. I can build on solid ground! I will wholeheartedly submit to the doctrine endowed with normative force. The realist "moment" is undeniable (right from Gen 42:16): the other features of meaning do not have any negative repercussions.

Error, Mistake, and Sin

The parallel with Christology suggests an equivalence between inerrancy and the sinless nature of Christ. But we must scrutinize this. Everyone usually makes a distinction between an error and a mistake, to such an extent that a common excuse is "I didn't do it on purpose." He who commits an error does not feel guilty, but like a victim. Yet again a distinction is sometimes made between an error, which is an ethical issue, and sin, which is the opposite of faith (Rom 14:23) and is committed "before God." For such theologians, when this double distinction is taken into account, sin is indeed incompatible with the holiness of God, and it must be eliminated regarding a text written under the inspiration of a holy God, since it would be an unacceptable stain.

A first remark: the holiness of God being absolute, "a consuming fire," a polarizing distinction (i.e., relatively more or less) will not suffice. In order for error not to stain the holiness of the divine Word, it must be free of any trace of sin. The all-holy God will not overlook a "small" dose of sin. However venial

92. R. Nicole, "The Biblical Concept of Truth," in *Standing Forth*, 133–49; Anthony C. Thiselton, "Truth," in *The New International Dictionary of New Testament Theology*, ed. Colin Brown, vol. 3 (Grand Rapids: Zondervan, 1978), 874–902. I offered my synthesis in "Qu'est-ce que la vérité ? Orientations bibliques dans le débat," *Hokhma* 100 (2011): 54–79.

the sinful action might seem to *us*, the devastating reaction of his holiness is let loose (the breach of Uzzah; 2 Sam 6:7). Or a few dead flies . . . (Eccl 10:1). So in order for error to be compatible with the holiness that must be acknowledged for Scripture, the separation between error and sin must be absolute. However, it is difficult, indeed highly improbable, to prove this absolute separation.

Nothing in Scripture goes in this direction. Sin is committed "before God," admittedly, but also in the sight of everyone! There can be no independent ethics in a biblical perspective, and the God who reveals himself is intensely ethical: what he wants is the greatest good. When he imposed rituals and "carnal" prescriptions (as the book of Hebrews states) during the time of the Old Testament, it was to educate the people "until the time of reformation" (Heb 9:10). Henceforth, "to the pure, all things are pure" (Titus 1:15). Thus, error and sin are inseparable.

Biblical language treats error in the same way. A spirit of error wages war against God. A lack of clear-sightedness does not wholly acquit. One can sin unintentionally ("by error," Lev 4:2 and Num 15:24; the Septuagint translated "unintentionally") and unconsciously (Ps 19:13; 1 Cor 4:3ff); however, they are guilt-producing and must be atoned for. For any sin, the guilty person is at the same time the victim. Conversely, the analysis of error does not exonerate from moral blame. It amounts to foolhardiness that deserves condemnation. Descartes explained it in this way: the will, an infinite faculty, exceeds what finite understanding proffers; the responsibility of the thinker is to guard against this excess. Moreover errors cannot be isolated from the fabric of moral life: there is often a lack of foresight, sometimes an obstinate refusal of the evidence, before committing the error.

Error, mistake, and sin go together as do inerrancy and complete holiness!

NEIGHBOURING DEBATES

INERRANCY AND BIBLICAL CRITICISM

Proponents of inerrancy feel at home in historical and theological debate. But in fact their opponents base their opposite opinion on *other* grounds: they deem that scientific criticism has *proved* the presence of numerous errors in the canonical texts. This is the "certain conclusion" of the historical-critical method ("higher criticism," *Sachkritik*).[93]

93. Cf. in this volume Armin D. Baum, "The Historical-Critical Method in Biblical Scholarship: Its History, Potential, and Limitations."

The debate about critical methods is beyond the scope of the present article. However, the word is ambiguous. If by *criticism* we mean self-criticism, concerned with getting information and not "swallowing" uncritically received interpretations, many inerrantists wish to be critical and would use this adjective for themselves. It's the *ordinary* way this method is handled that they object to; they accept its contributions but think that the conclusion that there are errors is unjustified.

The "criticism of the criticism" is being fought on three fronts. First, it denounces a certain neglect of data from the ancient Near East: the Egyptologist Kenneth A. Kitchen, whose compilation is huge, has developed this argument.[94] Another approach brings out the conjectural nature of the elaboration. A symptom of this is the disagreement between critics according to their national traditions or schools of thought. Another symptom of this fragility is the upheaval caused by a new discovery. A historian at the Sorbonne, a former director of the French School in Rome, has well summarized this aspect of the criticism of criticisms.[95] The third front is epistemological, including research on paradigms (Thomas S. Kuhn), world visions and frameworks of faith (Michael Polanyi), and fundamental patterns (Herman Dooyeweerd).[96] The autonomy of scientific reason is rejected; the participation of dogmatics in the debate is rendered legitimate; the idea that "criticism" carried out in the faith does *not* lead to incompatible results has been demonstrated.

There remains a raft of unresolved difficulties (no more than our ignorance and the gaps in our material can generate). Representative inerrantists guard against forced harmonisations; the theoretical basis of their procedure seems sound.[97] Several recent contributions deserve to be mentioned to illustrate this assessment.[98]

---

94. Cf. Kitchen, *On the Reliability of the Old Testament.*

95. Charles Pietri, "De quelques paralogismes de la critique biblique. Questions d'un historien," *Les Quatre Fleuves* 7 (1977): 43–67.

96. On these concepts, see Lydia Jaeger, *Croire et connaître. Einstein, Polanyi et les lois de la nature* (Nogent-sur-Marne: Éditions de l'Institut Biblique; Cléon d'Andran: Excelsis, 1999), and her other books.

97. See Moisés Silva, "The Place of Historical Reconstruction in New Testament Criticism," and Craig L. Blomberg, "The Legitimacy and Limits of Harmonization," in *Hermeneutics, Authority, and Canon*, ed. D. A. Carson and John D. Woodbridge (Grand Rapids: Zondervan Academic, 1986), 109–33 (nn383–88) and 139–74 (nn388–97).

98. Noel K. Weeks, "Biblical Studies: The Ambiguity of Biblical 'Background,'" *Westminster Theological Journal* 72 (2010): 219–36, is perceptive on a very important methodological question. Peter Gentry and Andrew M. Fountain, "Reassessing Jude's Use of the Enochic Traditions (with Notes on their Later Reception History)," *Tyndale Bulletin* 68, no. 2 (2017): 261–86, is innovative on an old difficulty. Andrew Loke, "Does the Bible Affirm Scientific Errors? A Reply to Denis Lamoureux," *Science and Christian Belief* 30 (2018): 116–33, is well informed.

INERRANCY AND HERMENEUTICS

Our time is "the age of hermeneutics"! Work on this topic has taken front stage over the last few decades. Inerrant orthodoxy has been accused of *ignoring* hermeneutics. This charge seems incongruous when you think of the title of works from the seventeenth century, such as the *Hermeneutica sacra* of J. C. Dannhauer,[99] and the regular publication of manuals of biblical interpretation in evangelical circles. Recent research, however, is more philosophical and radical concerning meaning, as well as its relationship to the author and the reader, and this subject has hardly been explored by the inerrancy tradition. Is this weakness an insurmountable difficulty? Certain heirs of this tradition demonstrate a fine mastery of philosophies of language and other ingredients of this discussion: suffice it to mention Kevin Vanhoozer and Vern Poythress, who both subscribe to inerrancy.

How would the emphasis on hermeneutics interfere with the affirmation of inerrancy? Mainly by increasing the distance between the meaning of the text (according to the intention of its author) and what we can do with it today – reading it but *also interpreting it*. As seen by their critics, inerrantists naively believe they can reach the meaning intended by the author, which coincides with the Holy Spirit's, and which they can appropriate directly. Hermeneutic awareness recognizes a divide, which is in a certain way impossible to cross, and rejoices over it. This divide is understood in two ways, the divide between cultures and contexts *and* the qualitative divide between divine reality and its capture in human language, so that a statement about God cannot be understood as an ordinary statement but with a disparity, a shift, which everyone interprets for himself.

This rhetoric likes to think it is being modest, when it isn't being intimidating. But it cannot escape being challenged. Concerning the way Scripture is presented as being "cultural," my remarks above will suffice. The hypothesis of the second type of divide isn't really a hermeneutical issue: it raises questions of theological and metaphysical presuppositions that do not fit *easily* with Scripture. The topic is too vast and the debate too complex to deal with it in this article. We will limit ourselves to one remark: orthodoxy recognises the language used to describe God as being analogical without depriving the language of revelation of a more direct mode of operation.

The relationship between inerrancy and hermeneutics can be interpreted in the other direction: the affirmation of inerrancy generates a manner of interpretation; its rejection, another manner. According to the choice made, we would

99. See R. Preus, *Post-Reformation Lutheranism*, 389n178 (several titles).

or would not expect complementarity in face of difficulties, we would look for harmony or be suspicious of it, we would suspend our judgement or not when coming across apparent contradictions or inaccuracies. The weight of theological affirmation is revealed in hermeneutical practice. In light of this, the way texts are treated gives an operational definition.[100]

The concept of inerrancy that emerges from these different debates proves to be consistent, with boundaries drawn by common sense. If its application remains difficult at its borders, the concept is not disqualified. The length of time that this affirmation has been held and its embedding in the orthodox construction are assets. But in the system of modernity, you have to remain somewhat impervious to the influences of the environment in order to hold to it. All-conquering modernity, with its autonomous and critical reason originating from the Age of Enlightenment and its scientism, cannot bear any dogma hanging over it or the honour given to some old texts amongst others. This attitude retains a strong hold in our time, late modernity, and on the "scientific" treatment of biblical texts (and when reason falls into relativism, or even nihilism, it will suffer no norm impinging on individual choice). How can we decide between these two options? The decision seems to be taken at the root, taking into account the "grounds" that guide reason, that shape its outlook, that provide points of reference: either the grounds of secularizing humanism or the grounds of the God, who is our Creator and Redeemer revealed in Jesus Christ and known by the holy Scripture.

FOR FURTHER READING

"The Chicago Statement on Biblical Inerrancy." https://library.dts.edu/Pages/TL/Special/ICBI_1.pdf.

Barr, James. *Fundamentalism*. London: SCM, 1977.

Berkouwer, G. C. *Holy Scripture*. Grand Rapids: Eerdmans, 1975.

Carson, D. A. "Three More Books on the Bible: A Critical Review." *Trinity Journal* 27 (2006) p. 1–62.

Carson, D. A., ed. *The Enduring Authority of the Christian Scriptures*. Grand Rapids: Eerdmans, 2016.

Carson, D. A., and John D. Woodbridge, eds. *Scripture and Truth*. Grand Rapids: Zondervan, 1983.

100. Cf. my "Inerrance et herméneutique," in *Dieu parle* (n45 *supra*), 85–103.

[Courtade, G.] "Inspiration et inerrance." In *Supplément au Dictionnaire de la Bible*, edited by André Robert, vol. 4, col. 482–55. Paris: Letouzey & Ané, 1949.

Courthial, Pierre et al. *Dieu parle! Études sur la Bible et son interprétation*. Aix-en-Provence: Kerygma, 1984.

McGowan, Andrew T. *The Divine Spiration of Scripture: Challenging Evangelical Perspectives*. Leicester: Apollos, 2007.

Nicole, Roger. *Standing Forth: Collected Writings of Roger Nicole*. Fearn: Mentor, 2002.

CHAPTER 3

Holy Resonance

God's Spirit in the Scriptures and in Human Hearts

Henk van den Belt

The Bible starts by describing how the Holy Spirit hovers over the waters at creation (Gen 1:2), and it ends with the Spirit's and the bride's unified longing for Jesus' return (Rev 22:17). How are the Word of God and the Spirit of God related? How does this affect the lives of Christians, who live in many different contexts and still have their love for the Word of God in common? How does the Holy Spirit let the Word of God resound in all these different contexts? How does the work of the Spirit relate to the certainty of faith that God is really speaking through the words of Scripture?

This chapter seeks to answer these questions by starting with some basic clues from the Old and New Testaments, by listening to a few voices from the history of theology, and finally by discussing the systematic-theological question of how the authority of Scripture can be accepted today.

Genesis describes how the patriarchs heard the voice of God. We do not know how Abraham recognized the call to leave his country for the promised land as a divine command. Was he simply following his intuition? According to the French Reformer John Calvin, when God spoke to the patriarchs, "They were convinced and understood that what they had learned proceeded from God."[1]

1. John Calvin, *Institutes of the Christian Religion*, ed. John T. McNeill, trans. Ford Lewis Battles

This claim, however, is not without problems. Any claim of divine revelation can be defended by referring to a deep internal conviction. But not all these claims can be true at the same time.

As we will see, Calvin relates this certainty regarding God's revelation to the inner witness of the Holy Spirit. Divine revelation is a religious experience par excellence, but this does not imply that the certainty regarding divine revelation is something purely subjective. Later in this chapter, we will explore how Calvin develops his view of the authority of Scripture and the work of the Spirit, examine its relevance for today, and reflect on how revelation in Christianity relates to other religions and nonreligious positions. First, however, we will investigate how the Bible speaks about divine revelation in relationship to the Holy Spirit.

THE SPIRITUAL CHARACTER OF THE BIBLE

The first time in the Bible that the Word of God is pronounced with authority by a human being is when Moses and Aaron address the pharaoh of Egypt: "This is what the LORD, the God of Israel, says: 'Let my people go'" (Exod 5:1).[2] It is a word of liberation. It is pronounced with authority as it is rooted in the divine command to communicate it. The author of Exodus presumes that those who are called by God speak with authority. Furthermore, God is concerned with the response of those who hear the message. Although they have their doubts, the leaders of Israel responded with trust and faith. Pharaoh, on the other hand, rejected this divine revelation – "Who is the Lord, that I should obey him?" (Exod 5:2). According to Exodus, the Lord remained in control. Pharaoh hardened his heart, but even that response was governed and directed by God's will as Romans 9:18 teaches.

Pharaoh's example is just one of the many cases in the Old Testament where prophets are called to address people with a divine message and where the response depends on the softening or hardening of the heart by God. Obviously, there is a close relationship between divine revelation, the authoritative communication of that revelation, and the response to that revelation.

Throughout the Bible these three aspects of revelation (i.e., its original emergence, its proclamation, and the reaction to it) are ascribed to the Holy

(London: SCM, 1961), 1.6.2 (p. 71). For the Latin text, cf. John Calvin, *Opera Selecta*, 3rd ed., ed. Peter Barth and Wilhelm Niesel (Munich: Christian Kaiser, 1967), 3:62.

2. The fact that Moses was the first to address others with divine authority is highlighted by the medieval Jewish philosopher Moses Maimonides in *The Guide for the Perplexed*, ch. 63.

Spirit. In his "last words," King David claimed to be anointed by the God of Jacob: "The Spirit of the LORD spoke through me; his word was on my tongue" (2 Sam 23:2). The prophets spoke with authority, aware of their divine calling. Though they did not always mention the Spirit as the source of their authority as explicitly as Micah, who claimed to be filled with the Spirit of the Lord to confront the people of Israel with their transgressions and sins (Mic 3:8), nevertheless they were aware that their prophetic work was spiritual in nature.

The emergence of revelation is always a religious experience. The prophets and all those in the Bible who received and communicated divine revelation expressed a deep sense of being called by God to do so. At times they tried to avoid this calling, but it proved to be irresistible. While experiencing this to be true, not all expressed it in such existential words as Jeremiah, who complained that God overpowered him: "If I say, 'I will not mention his word or speak any more in his name,' his word is in my heart like a fire" (Jer 20:9).

This deep religious experience might not differ much (at least in a psychological sense) from the experiences of those adherents of other religions who feel that they are called to proclaim a divine message. Given the fact that the Spirit of God makes use of natural and human means, it would be surprising if there was a great difference in experience between the prophets of Israel and the prophets of other peoples.[3] Below we will discuss the work of the Spirit in revelation today and reflect on how our concept of revelation relates to other religions and nonreligious perspectives.

One of the most important differences historically, however, lies in the fact that in the ancient Near East most prophecies were not written down, whereas written texts became very important for the Israelites. Words became Scripture and were handed down from generation to generation. Revelation in this written form was respected and received as the very Word of God.[4] The most essential difference between revelation given to Israel and that received by other peoples, however, lies in the content of the message. As we will argue below, all alternative religions are "autosoteric" – humanity has to save itself – while the Bible teaches a God-given salvation.

---

3. Bavinck writes, "The divine descends so deeply into the human that the boundaries between special revelation and analogous phenomena are sometimes hard to draw." Herman Bavinck, *Prolegomena*, vol. 1 of *Reformed Dogmatics* (Grand Rapids: Baker Academic, 2003), 343.

4. "The 'scribal turn' can be seen in the increasing focus on the written text as a sign and a carrier of revelation." Martti Nissinen, *Ancient Prophecy. Near Eastern, Biblical, and Greek Perspectives* (New York: Oxford University Press, 2017), 352. We have other examples of written prophecies in the ANE, but no texts as long as those in the Bible. Cf., for example, John W. Hilber, *Cultic Prophecy in the Psalms*, Beihefte zur Zeitschrift für die Alttestamentliche Wissenschaft 352 (New York: De Gruyter, 2005).

THE TANAKH

There is a diversity of books in the Old Testament. The Jews divide them into the Law or Teaching (*Torah*), the Prophets (*Nevi'im*), and the Writings (*Ketuvim*), together commonly abbreviated as *Tanakh*. In each section divine revelation is presented as a spiritual process. The Law is the most basic part of divine revelation, the Prophets call Israel to repent and return to God and his revelation as found in the Law, and the Writings (such as the psalms or wisdom literature) reflect on the divine revelation given in the Law and the Prophets. Naturally, in the third part we do not often find the same authoritative tone (e.g., "This is what God says") because it is a different genre. It is especially in the Writings, however, that the divine authority of the Law and the Prophets is acknowledged.[5] The later recipients recognize the work of the Spirit as the basis of the authority with which the prophets spoke.

In the books of Chronicles – which belong to the Writings – it is even said of lesser-known prophets like Azariah, the son of Oded, and Jahaziel son of Zechariah, that the Spirit came on them (2 Chron 15:1; 20:14) when they spoke to Israel. From the way the major prophets are viewed by later generations, it is clear that, as Nehemiah says, God warned his people through them by his Spirit (Neh 9:30). This acknowledgement is an important aspect of the relationship between Word and Spirit. If God really speaks, the Word is recognized as divine revelation in the community of believers, even though the message is unpleasant for the addressees and at first meets resistance. False prophets tell things that the people want to hear and at first are praised and accepted, but in the end they are discovered as deceivers because their words are not proved by the course of history and by the reception by God's people. This is especially clear in the case of Jeremiah, whose message of the approaching deportation was rejected. The leaders of Israel preferred the attractive message of prophets like Hananiah, who told the people that God would break the yoke of the king of Babylon (Jer 28:12). Whereas the prophecies of Jeremiah were esteemed after the Babylonian exile, the words of Hananiah were not included in the canon. The unicity of true prophecy does not lie in the religious experience of the prophets but in their faithfulness to God and in the truth of their message.

Divine revelation often meets unbelief, but the prophets trust that the

---

5. In Judaism, the authority of the Writings is also related to their inspiration by the Holy Spirit, although their authority is lower than that of the Law and the Prophets. For a discussion of the role of the Holy Spirit in the Writings, see Alan Cooper, "Aspects of Jewish Reception of the Ketuvim (Writings)," in *The Oxford Handbook of the Writings of the Hebrew Bible*, ed. Donn F. Morgan (New York: Oxford University Press, 2018), 430–47, there: 432–33. Of course, in Judaism the term *holy Spirit* refers not to the third person of the Trinity but to the divine force and influence of God.

people of Israel will finally repent and believe their message. This hope rests in their confidence in the Spirit of God. The Lord will put his Law in the minds of his people and write it on their hearts, just as he wrote the Ten Commandments on tablets of stone (Jer 31:33). God's Spirit will no longer depart from them, and his words will always be on their lips and on those of their descendants (Isa 59:21). The prophets declare that God will give his people a new heart and a new spirit and, after removing their heart of stone, will put his Spirit in them and move them to follow his decrees (Ezek 36:26). He will let them know that he is the Lord their God by pouring out his Spirit on their sons and daughters who will prophesy (Joel 2:28). In all these cases, the original recognition of the divine message and its authoritative proclamation by the prophet, as well as the final acceptance by the people, are related to the work of the Holy Spirit.

The prospect of a glorious future in which the people of Israel will finally listen to the Word of God through the Spirit is intertwined with the messianic expectation of a prophet like Moses whom God will raise up, putting his words in his mouth (Deut. 18:18). Isaiah says concerning the Messiah from the house of David:

> The Spirit of the LORD will rest on him—
> the Spirit of wisdom and of understanding,
> the Spirit of counsel and of might,
> the Spirit of the knowledge and fear of the LORD. (Isa 11:2)

In the second part of the book, this is applied to the Servant of the Lord, who would be endowed with his Spirit (Isa 42:1).

THE SPIRIT OF TRUTH AND JESUS

Compared to the Old Testament, the New Testament is more explicit in describing the role of the Holy Spirit because the person and work of the Spirit are more clearly revealed in the ministry of Jesus Christ. According to the synoptic gospels, Jesus understands himself to be the Son of Man, promised by the prophets, who came into the world to fulfil all the demands of the divine law. He was the servant on whom God put his Spirit to proclaim justice to the nations (Matt 12:18). At Jesus' baptism the Holy Spirit descended on him in the form of a dove to mark the beginning of his public ministry (Matt 3:16; Mark 1:10; Luke 3:22).

The gospel of John specifically connects the Word of God with the Spirit of God. In the prologue, Jesus Christ is identified as the eternal Word who in the beginning was with God and was God and through whom all things were made

(John 1:1, 3). Jesus, who is the Word, also speaks the words of God because God has given him the Spirit without limit (John 3:34). As such, the words he has spoken are full of the Spirit and life (John 6:63) and have divine authority. Jesus promised that after his resurrection and return to heaven he would share this Spirit – and thus the authority of the Spirit – with his disciples. This is the special emphasis in Jesus' farewell speech. There he announced the coming of the Spirit, which he calls "the other *Paracletos*," or the other advocate; literally, "the One who is called upon to assist."[6] Just as the disciples could call upon the assistance of Jesus while he was with them, so too when he was gone, they would receive the assistance of the Lieutenant-Advocate.

Scripture declares that the Spirit of truth will teach Christ's disciples all things by reminding them of everything Jesus has taught them (John 14:17, 26). It is the work of the Spirit to assist the disciples in their witness of Christ (John 15:26). In this impossible task the Spirit will help them (1) by convincing the world – or by proving the world to be in the wrong – about sin, righteousness, and judgement; (2) by guiding the disciples into all truth; and (3) by glorifying Jesus (John 16:8, 13, 14). The work of the Spirit is a work of communication. The witness of the Spirit consists of words that he will make known; he will speak what he hears (John 16:13). The witness of the Spirit concerning Jesus Christ is both verbal and intimate.

According to Luke's account in the book of Acts, Jesus' promises were fulfilled after his resurrection and ascension when the disciples were together waiting in prayer and expectation of the fulfilment of Jesus' words. At Pentecost, all those who were gathered "were filled with the Holy Spirit and began to speak in other tongues as the Spirit enabled them" (Acts 2:4). People from a variety of countries heard them declaring the wonders of God. Peter interpreted this event as the fulfilment of Joel's prophecy that God would pour out his Spirit on all people so that sons and daughters would prophesy, young men see visions, and old men dream dreams. He proclaimed that those who would repent and be baptized in Jesus' name would also receive the gift of the Holy Spirit (Acts 2:38).

That the Spirit and the Word go together also becomes clear in those instances in which the Spirit is related to preaching. Lydia's heart is opened to respond to Paul's message (Acts 16:14), and although the Spirit is not explicitly mentioned in this story, the opening of the heart for the Word of God and through the Word of God is the work of the Holy Spirit. In the same way, the gift of the Spirit is mentioned as a result of preaching. At the house of Cornelius,

---

6. For an extensive discussion of the meaning and function of the *Paracletos*, see James M. Hamilton, *God's Indwelling Presence: The Holy Spirit in the Old and New Testaments* (Nashville: B&H, 2006), 75–91.

the apostle Peter shares the good news of peace through Jesus Christ, the Lord of all. While he was speaking these words, the Holy Spirit descended on all who heard the message and, to the astonishment of the Jewish believers, was even poured out on the gentiles (Acts 10:45). The apostle Paul also recalls that the Galatians received the Spirit by believing what they had heard (Gal 3:2). Those who are called to preach have to be aware of the fact that this is a spiritual task, for no one knows the thoughts of God except the Spirit. A preacher should therefore speak in words "taught by the Spirit, explaining spiritual realities with Spirit-taught words" (1 Cor 2:13).

To understand the power and the authority of the message of Scripture correctly, we need to consider the role of the Holy Spirit. Three words are important in this respect: truth, witness, and persuasion. The history of the world is characterized by an ongoing struggle between truth and falsehood. This is, at least, the perspective of Jesus, as he is presented to us in the fourth gospel. Jesus is sent by God his Father to tell people the truth, to witness to the truth, and thus to set them free (John 8:32). In this way he unmasks the opponent, the devil, who is a liar and the father of lies (John 8:44). Although Jesus' message meets resistance and unbelief, people continue to be persuaded that he really is the Son of God. The knowledge of the truth, the witness to the truth, and the persuasion of the truth are all the work of the Holy Spirit.

As we will see below, this opens a venue to explore and explain the similarities and differences between the message of the gospel and alternative religious or nonreligious truth claims. These competing claims can be interpreted as part of an ongoing spiritual struggle. Diverse religions witness to these truth claims, and people find these testimonies either persuasive enough to trust them or too unconvincing to believe them. That something is true or not in a religious or spiritual sense cannot be proven from the outset, as if there is some kind of isolated island of neutrality in the midst of the ocean of religiosity. The truth can only be discovered from the effects of a message, from the way it relates to the deepest questions and needs of human beings. It will be recognized from a persuasive testimony.

THE SPIRITUAL AUTHORITY OF THE NEW TESTAMENT

In Christianity, the work of the Spirit in and through the witness of Jesus and the apostles forms the foundation of the authority of the books of the New Testament. They contain the core of the message of Jesus and of his death and resurrection, as a summary of the apostolic testimony of the eyewitnesses of Christ.[7]

7. Cf. Richard Bauckham, *Jesus and the Eyewitnesses: The Gospels as Eyewitness Testimony* (Grand Rapids: Eerdmans, 2006). See also chapter 1 in this book, Kevin J. Vanhoozer, "The Bible – Word of God?"

This proclaimed testimony was written down in the period when Jesus' apostles and their immediate pupils grew old. The written testimony of the apostles has the same promise – that is, the advocacy of the Holy Spirit – connected to it as their oral witness in preaching. This is not stated explicitly in the New Testament, but it is clear from the authoritative claim on the reader with which they present themselves.

The author of Luke and Acts, for instance, says that he is writing an account of things handed down to him by eyewitnesses and servants of the word so that his addressee, Theophilus, will know the certainty of the things he has been taught (Luke 1:4). At the beginning of his second book, he refers to his gospel as a book in which he wrote "about all that Jesus began to do and to teach until the day he was taken up to heaven, after giving instructions through the Holy Spirit to the apostles he had chosen" (Acts 1:1–2). The word *began* implies that this new book, the so-called Acts of the Apostles, offers a record of what Jesus continues to do through pouring out his Spirit on his disciples. It might be more proper to call it the Acts of Jesus Christ through his Spirit.

In a similar vein, John ends his gospel with an authoritative call to believe. Jesus performed many other signs and wonders not recorded in this narrative, "but these are written that you may believe that Jesus is the Messiah, the Son of God, and that by believing you may have life in his name" (John 20:31). The claim of an authoritative message is clear. The Gospels are not biographies of Jesus that the reader can take for granted. The gospels lay hold of the reader by claiming that Jesus of Nazareth is the Son of God and that he is still alive and active today. The spiritual authority of the Gospels is implicit: they are a testimony or witness to Jesus and thus confront the reader with the message of Jesus himself as a witness of the truth.

The same can be said of the letters in the New Testament. They often originate in a specific situation and follow up on the apostolic preaching, going into specific details or answering concrete questions. Nevertheless, apostolic authority is always present right below the surface of the text. To give but one example, the first letter of the apostle Paul to the Thessalonians, probably the oldest book in the New Testament, opens with a word of thanks for the Thessalonians' faith. Paul recalls how his gospel came to them "not simply with words but also with power, with the Holy Spirit and deep conviction" (1 Thess 1:5). When he urges them to live a holy life, he refers to the previous instructions he gave them "by the authority of the Lord Jesus" (1 Thess 4:2).

The authority of the Gospels and other New Testament writings is founded on what is commonly called the *kerygma* (from the Greek verb for preaching, *kerusso,* which means to proclaim something with authority as a herald sent by a king). The apostolic proclamation of salvation through Christ carries on the witness of Jesus regarding the truth and the kingdom of God and consists of the apostolic witness regarding Christ's death and resurrection.

The spiritual character of the Bible's authority raises the question how this authoritative message – often met with unbelief and scorn – was still believed by so many in the first centuries that Christianity became a new world religion and is still accepted by so many people in different cultures today. The Bible's emphasis on the work of the Spirit suggests that the answer to this question might be found in the work of the Spirit as well. The Bible hints at the advocacy of the Spirit, who convinces the world that Jesus is the Messiah by leading the apostles into all truth and by glorifying Christ through this witness, making it effectual in the hearts of its recipients. Not only in the Bible but also throughout Christian history, we thus meet the triad of the truth, the witness to the truth, and the persuasion of the truth through the Spirit. Again, this raises the question of how this relates to alternative religious or secular positions.

THE SPIRITUAL UNITY OF THE BIBLE

According to the confessions of the early church, there is a spiritual unity between the Old and the New Testaments. The same Spirit who inspired the prophets of old to witness to Christ is given by the resurrected and exalted Christ to his church to lead them into all truth. The acceptance of the Bible as a unity is less self-evident than later history suggests. A strong undercurrent in early Christianity suggested that the God of the Jews was inferior to the Father of Jesus Christ, the God of love. Marcion of Sinope (c. AD 85–160) rejected the Old Testament and only saw a selection from the gospel of Luke and the Pauline letters as normative writings. He advocated for complete discontinuity between the Tanakh and the Gospels, claiming that the God of the Old Testament, the so-called Demiurge, was a jealous deity. Later Gnostics held similar views. They could only do so, however, by acknowledging a small selection of the New Testament as authoritative and by rejecting the Tanakh, which was, however, the only Bible the Christians had before the New Testament was written and completed.

THE AUTHORITY OF THE TANAKH IN THE NEW TESTAMENT

The way quotations from or references to the Old Testament are introduced in the New Testament reveals how the apostolic church regarded the authority of the Tanakh. According to Mark, Jesus refers to Psalm 110 by saying that David through the Holy Spirit called the coming Messiah his Lord (Mark 12:36). After the death of Judas Iscariot, the other apostles concluded that the Scripture was fulfilled "in which the Holy Spirit spoke long ago through David" (Acts 1:16 with references to Pss 69:25; 109:8). Quotations from Scripture can even be related to the Spirit in the present tense: "As the Holy Spirit says: 'Today, if you hear his voice, do not harden your hearts'" (Heb 3:7–8 quoting Ps 95:7–8).[8]

The Spirit of Christ was already revealing to the prophets the grace that was to come (1 Peter 1:11). They were led by the Spirit to foretell the sufferings and the resurrection of the Messiah, even though they still did not see everything clearly (when compared to the full light of the gospel). The prophets served the New Testament believers as they had been speaking of those things that were more fully proclaimed in the gospel of Christ by those who preached "by the Holy Spirit sent from heaven" (1 Peter 1:12). In other words, the same Spirit who witnessed in the Tanakh now speaks more clearly, using, applying, and reinterpreting the words revealed formerly to and through the prophets.

In his second letter, Peter explains where the power and authority of the Scriptures originate from. He compares the authority of Scripture with his own religious experience, when he saw Christ in his transfiguration and heard the voice of God himself saying, "This is my Son, whom I love; with him I am well pleased" (Matt 17:5; Mark 9:7; Luke 9:35). Indeed, Peter presents himself as an eyewitness to Christ's majesty. At the same time, he refers to the prophetic message as something completely reliable, or "something even more sure." This prophetic witness is so sure because it was given beforehand and is clearly fulfilled in the life and work of Christ. The prophecies concerning Jesus did not come about by the prophets' own interpretations, but the prophets, though mere human beings, "spoke from God as they were carried along by the Holy Spirit" (2 Peter 1:21).

The authority of the Tanakh appears most clearly in a text that is often quoted to prove the inspiration of the Bible. Writing to his spiritual son Timothy, the apostle Paul recalls how from infancy he knew the Holy Scriptures, which are able – have the intrinsic power – to make people wise for salvation through faith in Christ Jesus. Then Paul adds that "all Scripture is God-breathed and is useful" (2 Tim 3:16). This is the most important text for the inspiration in the whole Bible, at least of all the books of the Old Testament to which Paul is referring as "all Scripture." The Greek word *theopneustos* ("God-breathed") is an immediate reference to the role of the Spirit with respect to the Bible. The Spirit

---

8. For a discussion of the formulae introducing quotations from the Old Testament in the New Testament, see Benjamin B. Warfield, "'It Says:' 'Scripture Says:' 'God Says,'" in Warfield, *The Inspiration and Authority of the Bible* (Phillipsburg; P&R, 1948), 299–348.

not only took care of the original inspiration at the moment Scripture was written down but also now breathes through the Word when it is opened and read privately or interpreted and applied in preaching. Not only is the inspiration of the text a historical event, but the text, being inspired, has this dynamic power.

We do not know exactly how Timothy was convinced of the truth of the gospel, but when Paul travelled through Asia Minor on his second missionary journey with Silas, he met this young disciple in Derbe and Lystre (Acts 16:1) and asked him to join him as his assistant. His father was Greek and his mother Jewish. Maybe the tension can be seen in his name. *Timo-theos* is a Greek name without Hebrew or Jewish connotations, but it does say something: one who honors God. It is a name with a promise. Will Timothy choose a faith from a foreign country, derived from an old-fashioned book, or will he follow the more popular polytheism of Greek culture? Many years later, Paul recalls that there was something – a strange and convincing power – evidenced in the faith of his mother and grandmother (2 Tim 1:4–5) and found in that old book with stories about Abraham, Moses, and David.

This old book is what Paul refers his assistant to as the only norm and source for guiding the churches into all truth. Paul is worried because he foresees "terrible times in the last days" (2 Tim 3:1) and because there will be false teachers in the churches who deceive others with a form of godliness. Therefore, he urges Timothy to continue in what he has learned and refers him especially to all of the God-breathed Scriptures because they will help him to lead the churches in teaching, rebuking, correcting, and training its members (2 Tim 3:16).

THE NICENO-CONSTANTINOPOLITAN CREED: "WHO SPOKE THROUGH THE PROPHETS"

The church fathers likewise confessed the unity of the Scriptures. This is most clearly expressed by the Niceno-Constantinopolitan Creed, in which the phrase "and in the Holy Ghost" from the Nicene Creed (325) was replaced by the longer phrase at the council of Constantinople (381): "And in the Holy Ghost, the Lord and Giver of life, . . . who spoke through the prophets." The formula goes back to older sources.

In the *Ancoratus* (374), Epiphanius, bishop of Salamis, says, "And we believe in the Holy Spirit, who has spoken in the Law, preached in the Prophets, has come down to the Jordan, who speaks in the apostles and lives in the saints."[9] This extensive formulation shows that the continuity between the Old and the

---

9. H. Denzinger and A. Schönmetzer, *Enchiridion symbolorum, definitionum et declarationum de rebus fidei et morum* (Barcelona: Herder, 1963), 44. See also chap. 1 in this book, Vanhoozer, "The Bible – Word of God?"

New Testament is at stake. The same Spirit who descended on Jesus witnesses through the apostles, dwells in the saints, and spoke in the Law and the Prophets of old.

That the phrase intends to confess the unity of the old and new dispensations is confirmed by various quotations from church fathers. In his summary of the apostolic doctrine (in form a Trinitarian confession), Origen, for example, wrote that the Spirit inspired both the prophets and the apostles and that the old dispensation did not have a different Spirit.[10] Cyril of Jerusalem also said that the same Spirit present in the Law and the Prophets is present in the Gospels and the apostles.[11] In his polemic against the Gnostics, Irenaeus summarized the faith the church received from the apostles as obtained "in the Holy Spirit, who proclaimed through the prophets the dispensations of God, and the advents, and the birth from a virgin, and the passion, and the resurrection from the dead, and the ascension into heaven in the flesh of the beloved Christ Jesus, our Lord, and His future manifestation from heaven in the glory of the Father."[12] Apparently, the historical background of the phrase in the Niceno-Constantinopolitan Creed is grounded in the belief that the Old Testament is inspired by the Spirit to witness to the coming of Christ. Christianity is not new; it is rooted in the Old Testament. The Scriptures are perfect since they were spoken by God's Word and Spirit.[13]

The earliest precursor of the formula is probably Justin Martyr, who in his *First Apology* (155) wrote about "the prophetic Spirit" and taught that in baptism Christians are washed "in the name of the Holy Spirit, who foretold all things concerning Jesus through the prophets."[14] The opening verse of Hebrews – "God spoke to our ancestors through the prophets at many times and in various ways" – says the same, without mentioning the Spirit explicitly. The resurrected Jesus himself said that everything that was written about him in the Law of Moses, the Prophets, and the Psalms was fulfilled (Luke 24:44). This text shows that the Tanakh as a canon of divinely inspired books was already accepted at the time.

The use of the Tanakh as the authoritative source in the New Testament and by the confessions of the early church has far-reaching implications. (1) Difficult

10. Origen, *De principiis*, introduction, 4. Cf. J. Pelikan and V. Hotchkiss, *Creeds and Confessions of Faith in the Christian Tradition* (New Haven, CT: Yale University Press, 2003), 1–63.

11. Cyrill of Jerusalem, *Catechesis*, 17.5, cf. 16.3.

12. Irenaeus, *Adversus Haereses*, 1.10.1.

13. Irenaeus, *Adversus Haereses*, 2.28.2.

14. Justin Martyr, *First Apology*, 1.13, 1.61. Cf. Pelikan and Hotchkiss, *Creeds and Confessions*, 1:46–47. Cf. R. Staats, *Das Glaubensbekenntnis von Nizäa–Konstantinopel. Historische und theologische Grundlagen* (Darmstadt: Wissenschaftliche Buchgesellschaft, 1996), 93.

texts of the Old Testament, characterized by the ancient cultural context, are nevertheless inspired by the Spirit of grace that is revealed in the ministry of Jesus and promised by him to his disciples. (2) The texts of the Old Testament, though they have a specific first meaning in the original historical context, refer also to further fulfilment in Jesus Christ and can be interpreted legitimately from the perspective of that fulfilment. (3) The texts of the Tanakh (the Law, the Prophets, and the Writings) resonate in the hearts of believers in later contexts because the Spirit, who has spoken through the authors, still speaks to believers in their own contexts. The Spirit bridges historical and cultural gaps. A psalm of David sung in a situation of anxiety can still comfort the heart of the believer as if it were written exclusively for her or him.

THE SPIRITUAL ACKNOWLEDGMENT OF THE BIBLE

The spiritual character of scriptural authority evokes the question of how this authoritative message can be accepted by so many people. Over the course of the history of theology, the question regarding the acknowledgement of Scripture has been discussed, but only in the time of the Reformation, when the authority of the institutional church was questioned, did the work of the Holy Spirit come fully to the fore regarding the acknowledgement of and trust in Scripture as a witness to the work of Christ.

In the later medieval period, parts of the Bible were read even by many lay people, be it mostly within the liturgical context of fixed prayers and meditations on psalms and portions of the Gospels. The Bible had a high place within the medieval church. The question was not *if* the Bible had authority but *why* it had authority and *how* that authority related to the other authorities: church fathers and ecclesiastical decisions. Some Catholic theologians claimed that the church was entrusted with extrabiblical traditions that could be traced back to Jesus and the apostles through oral communication. They based some of the traditional aspects of Catholic doctrine or practice on this oral tradition. In general, however, the understanding of tradition in the Middle Ages was that it functioned as an instrument or medium to carry on from one generation to the other the message of the gospel contained in the Scriptures and summarized in the early creeds.

The early church held that the apostolic teaching, as embedded in Scripture, was mediated by tradition. During the Middle Ages a new understanding emerged that took tradition as an extrabiblical authority. Thus, two views of the relationship between Scripture and tradition developed during the Middle Ages.

The first view – sometimes called the one-source theory – saw tradition as the vehicle by which apostolic and scriptural truth was conveyed from generation to generation. The second view – the two-source theory – understood tradition as the authoritative transmission of teachings and practices of Jesus and the apostles preserved in the church as a complement to Scripture.[15] The Reformers embraced and developed the first, whereas Roman Catholics endorsed the second opinion.[16]

MARTIN LUTHER: SCRIPTURE IS CERTAIN, SIMPLE, AND INTELLIGIBLE

The Wittenberg Reformation did not originate from a new formal doctrine regarding the authority of Scripture. Instead, the Ninety-Five Theses emerged from a recovery of the Augustinian doctrine of grace. Only later, in discussion with Johann Eck, did Luther switch to appeal to biblical authority. Originally, he sought to reform the church from within by means of a church council, thereby showing a desire to connect with the conciliarism of the Middle Ages.

In their Leipzig debate (1519), Eck accused Luther of positions that coincided with Jan Hus, whose views had been judged as unorthodox by the Council of Constance in 1415. In confirming his agreement with Hus, however, Luther lost the possibility to appeal to the authority of a council. Therefore, Luther claimed that no Christian can be forced to recognize any authority beyond that of Scripture.[17] Luther's appeal to Scripture was a means to protect the doctrine of grace from the power of the church. Notwithstanding, Scripture was not understood as separated from the tradition or the confessions of the church. After all, Luther wanted to reform the church from inside, not start a new one. Thus, the Reformation moved from *sola gratia* to *sola scriptura*.[18]

This became clearer in Luther's *Defence of all the Articles* (1521), a reaction against the bull of excommunication. In it he wrote that the church still had the same Spirit of faith received at its beginning and that the church therefore should be able to study Scripture as the early church was permitted to do.

---

15. Heiko A. Oberman, *The Harvest of Medieval Theology: Gabriel Biel and Late Medieval Nominalism* (Cambridge, MA: Harvard University Press, 1963), 406.

16. For an in-depth discussion of the relationship between Scripture and tradition, see in this volume Olivier Riaudel, "The Bible Is Not an Image: Scriptures, Traditions, and Reasons."

17. Martin Luther, *Disputatio Ioannis Eccii et Martini Lutheri Lipsiae habita*, 1519, in Luther, *D. Martin Luthers Werke: Kritische Gesamtausgabe* (Weimar: Hermann Böhlaus Nachfolger 1883–2009), 2:279. Hereafter, *WA*.

18. See Henk van den Belt, "The Problematic Character of *Sola Scriptura*," in *Sola Scriptura: Biblical and Theological Perspectives on Scripture, Authority, and Hermeneutics*, ed. Hans Burger, Arnold Huijgen, and Eric Peels, Studies in Reformed Theology 32 (Leiden: Brill, 2018), 43.

Sometimes statements of the church are contradictory, so we need Scripture as the final judge, which would be impossible if Scripture does not have primacy. This also implies that Scripture must be "of itself certain, simple, and intelligible; it is its own interpreter, testing, judging, and illuminating everything else."[19] The well-known expression that Scripture is its own interpreter (*sui ipsius interpres*) does not refer to a hermeneutical rule in the original context. It is often explained in the sense that we should interpret Scripture from Scripture, especially the more difficult parts from the clearer ones. That is fine, but it is not what Luther says here. Luther means that if Scripture is to be its own interpreter or judge, its interpretation should not be bound to the external authority of the church. He refers to Psalm 119:130: "The unfolding of your words gives light." According to Luther, the Spirit teaches that understanding is given through God's Word alone as through a first principle from which we must start. He is referring to scholastic theology in which Scripture was seen as a first principle of knowledge. This means that God's words are a first principle for judging everything else.

The scholastic term *principium* stems from the introduction of Aristotelian philosophy into the prolegomena of theology. According to Aristotle, all sciences have their own self-evident or self-convincing principles (*principia per se nota*). Medieval theological surveys face the question whether theology is a science (*scientia*) and on which principles it rests. The second question in Thomas Aquinas's *Summa* deals with this issue: "Is sacred doctrine a science?" One should remember that science here refers to a specific kind of knowledge next to (for instance) wisdom (*sapientia*) and should not be understood in the modern sense of the word science. Still, theology does not seem to be an exact *science* because every science proceeds from self-evident principles; sacred doctrine, however, proceeds from the articles of faith. These are not self-evident but presuppose belief, which all do not have. Still Aquinas holds that theology or sacred doctrine is a science because not all sciences proceed from a principle known by natural light. Some sciences proceed from principles known by the light of a higher science, like music that depends on the principles of arithmetic. Aquinas concludes, "So it is that sacred doctrine is a science because it proceeds from principles established by the light of a higher science, namely, the science of God and the blessed. . . . Sacred science is established on principles revealed by God."[20]

---

19. Luther, *WA* 7:97. For the English translation, see Oswald Bayer, *Theology the Lutheran Way* (Grand Rapids, Eerdmans, 2007), 272n330.

20. Thomas Aquinas, *Summa Theologica*, 1.1.2. The English translation is from *Summa Theologica* (New York: Benziger Brothers, 1947–48).

JOHN CALVIN: THE *AUTOPISTIA* OF SCRIPTURE AND THE WITNESS OF THE SPIRIT

The French Reformer John Calvin took up this element of the Catholic understanding of Scripture as the final norm by using the Greek adjective *autopistos* when describing the Bible. The prefix *auto-* denotes "by itself" or "of itself," and the adjective *pistos* is derived from *pistis*, meaning "faith" or "trust." When something is *autopistos*, it is to be trusted or believed "because of itself" or "in itself." The term originates from ancient geometry used for the Euclidean axioms. In that original context, it referred to the fact that these statements were "self-convincing" because their demonstration was both unnecessary and impossible.

The *autopistia* of Scripture can easily be misunderstood as a form of circular reasoning, a reference to proof texts for divine inspiration, especially when it is translated as "self-authenticating." In that case, the authority of Scripture rests on claims in the New Testament – 2 Timothy 3:16 is a well-known example – that the Scriptures are inspired. The concept of *autopistia*, however, is not a reference to proof texts; on the contrary, it is triggered by the attempt to avoid circular reasoning by comparing the authority of Scripture with the first *principia* or axioms on which all knowledge rests. The authority of Scripture does not rest on a claim, but on the message in which the living voice of God is heard.

Calvin introduced the term in the final edition of the *Institutes* (1559): "Let this therefore stand: those whom the Holy Spirit has inwardly taught, truly find rest in Scripture. It is indeed *autopistos*; it should not be submitted to demonstration by proofs. Still, it owes the certainty that it deserves among us to the testimony of the Spirit."[21] Calvin discussed the nature of Scripture for the first time in the second edition of the *Institutes* (1539) in the context of the knowledge of God. The question of how we can be assured of the divine origin of Scripture without the authority of the church was very important for Calvin. He was afraid that miserable consciences would not be able to find solid assurance of eternal life if the promises ultimately depended on human authority. The only alternative for him was to seek the certainty of eternal life in Scripture itself. Calvin then answered the question of how we can know the divine origin of Scripture by confessing that Scripture itself gives a sense of its own truth, just like light and dark, white and black, sweet and bitter things.

It is a dangerous error, according to Calvin, to derive the authority of Scripture from the *consensus* of the church because this makes the truth of God

---

21. Calvin, *Institutes* 1.7.5. The translation is mine. Cf. Van den Belt, *The Authority of Scripture in Reformed Theology. Truth and Trust* (Leiden, Brill, 2008), 53. For the Latin text see Calvin, *Opera Selecta*, 3:70.

dependent on human arbitrariness, thus undermining the certainty of faith. The persuasion of the authority of Scripture must be sought in a higher place than in human beings, namely in the inner witness of the Spirit.[22] Scripture gains reverence for itself by its own majesty, but only affects us seriously when the Spirit seals it in our hearts. Arguments for Scripture can never persuade us in and of themselves since they can only be useful after we have embraced Scripture. Calvin, however, still mentions two arguments: first, the plain language in which Scripture clothes the truth, and second, that Scripture is confirmed by the consensus of the church. Thus, the authority of the church functions only *a posteriori* and is not a foundation for the authority of Scripture.

There is a reciprocal relationship between the self-convincing character of Scripture and the witness of the Holy Spirit. Scripture is only accepted as the Word of God through the witness of the Spirit, and the Spirit gives his testimony through the Word because Scripture deserves that certainty of itself since it is *autopistos*. The deepest motive for Calvin's emphasis on the independent authority of Scripture is his concern for the certainty of salvation. Our conscience cannot find rest if our salvation depends merely upon human opinion and not upon God. According to Calvin, faith can only rest in the witness of the Spirit and not on the human judgment of the church.

THE WORK OF THE SPIRIT IN REVELATION TODAY

Thus far we have discussed how the Bible speaks about divine revelation in relationship to the Holy Spirit and how the acceptance of the authoritative message of Scripture was interpreted. We will now turn to the contemporary relevance of this concept. What do we mean by the resonance of the Word in the hearts of the believers through the Spirit? First, we will ask how Christianity's views of revelation relate to other religious and nonreligious positions. Otherwise, all the claims made above might seem to hang in the air because they presuppose the faith that they seek to explain.

Much has been written about the relationship between Christianity and the other religions and about the character of revelation. Together with Judaism and Islam, Christianity is a religion of a book. The three Abrahamic religions are monotheistic. They each believe in a beginning and end of present history, that is in creation and in the *eschaton*, and that God has revealed himself through

22. Calvin, *Opera Selecta*, 3:69. In the final edition Calvin rephrases this into "from the hidden testimony of the Spirit" (*Institutes*, 1.7.4).

prophets whose teachings were written down resulting in Scripture. This implies that these religions have a very different concept of revelation than other religions. That makes it difficult to explain in short how the Christian view of revelation relates to all these other views, let alone how it relates to secular views that seemingly reject the whole concept of revelation.

It will be hard – if not impossible – to argue for the truth of the Christian faith convincingly by demonstrating that its view of revelation is the only plausible option. Moreover, we are not describing revelation from the perspective of comparative religious studies but from a theological perspective. From that perspective, the most important part of the answer with regards to the differences between Christianity and other religious and nonreligious positions lies in the content of Christianity's message of salvation.

THE GENERAL WORK OF THE SPIRIT

There are many different views among Christians about what revelation is. The Roman Catholic theologian Avery Dulles (1918–2008), for instance, distinguishes five alternative models: revelation as doctrine, as history, as inner experience, as dialectical presence, and as a new awareness.[23] According to Dulles, the first model is characteristic for conservative evangelicals. For them supernatural revelation is necessary because it is not sufficient that God makes himself known through nature. The supernatural or special revelation can be found in the written records of the prophetic and apostolic teaching in the Bible. Scripture is therefore understood as a set of propositional statements that are universally valid. In my view this is a caricature of what the evangelical position intends to be. I have argued for a view that also takes the historical development of revelation, Dulles's second model, and religious experience, his third model, into account. Nevertheless, he is right that evangelicals make a distinction between general and special revelation to cope with the question of revelation in other religions.[24]

We will use that distinction to assess the possible implications of our view for the similarities and differences between revelation in Christianity and in other religious or nonreligious positions. The triad of the truth, the witness to the truth, and the persuasion of the truth might be helpful. As we have seen from Scripture – and especially from John's account of Jesus' words about the Spirit – and from the history of Protestant Christianity, in the Christian view of revelation all three parts of the triad are connected to the work of the Holy

23. Avery Dulles, *Models of Revelation* (Garden City, NY: Doubleday, 1983).

24. For a brief discussion of general or universal revelation, see Cornelis van der Kooi and Gijsbert van den Brink, *Christian Dogmatics: An Introduction* (Grand Rapids: Eerdmans, 2017), 181–85.

Spirit. We can expand this idea in two ways: by explaining religious and secular convictions from the framework of competing truths, witnesses, and persuasions and by reflecting on the way the Spirit of truth might be actively present in this competition.

The fact that human beings are ineradicably religious can be explained from a desire or longing for truth and certainty about the truth. In order to give a meaningful interpretation to the world and our lives, men and women long for satisfying answers to their deepest questions. We will only be persuaded of the trustworthiness of certain interpretations of good and evil and of the ultimate goal of our lives if we find the witnesses to a certain comprehensive explanation convincing.

The message of Christianity, revealed in the Bible, meets the deepest needs of humanity. At the core of Christianity lies the gospel of the incarnation. The Son of God, who is one with the Father, becomes a human being to redeem the world by saving fallen human beings from their sins. Notwithstanding many differences among Christians, the answer to the problem of evil shared by them all points to God's sovereign initiative. As a human being, the Son of God took upon himself the consequences of sin to take sin away and offer forgiveness to all who trust in him. This is the unique selling point of the Christian faith, and although it is still foolishness and a stumbling block to many, the message of the crucified Saviour displays the power and wisdom of God (1 Cor 1:23).

Over against this "theosoteric" (God saves) message stands an "autosoteric" (save yourself) message according to which lost humanity has to rescue itself, either by fulfilling religious duties or by finding a secular way to cope with the power of evil, keeping it in balance as much as possible by choosing the good. Seen from the perspective of the gospel, in all the alternatives "humans are always their own savior: all religions other than the Christian religion are autosoteric."[25]

This fundamental difference between Christianity and the rest, of course, implies an inside perspective. The only way to see clearly that this message meets the deepest needs of human beings is by believing it. There is no neutral island from where we can judge the different claims of revelation by the methods of comparative religious studies. Therefore, in a sense, apologetics is always

25. Bavinck, *Reformed Dogmatics. Sin and Salvation in Christ*, vol. 3 of *Reformed Dogmatics* (Grand Rapids: Baker Academic, 2006), 492. The term stems from German philosophy and especially from Eduard von Hartmann (1842–1906), who used it to characterize his own position. Bavinck acknowledges that in religions help is sought from divine power but insists that the emphasis always falls on human action. Warfield applies the term to Pelagianism within Christianity. See Warfield, "Autosoterism," in *The Plan of Salvation* (Eugene: Wipf and Stock, 2000), 27–48.

presuppositional because any convincing explanation of Christianity presupposes that the soteriological claims of the gospel are taken into account. This also means that any explanation of the convincing character of the Christian faith remains vulnerable to the objection of subjectivity. This seeming weakness, however, may prove to be a strength once we acknowledge that faith is a matter of spiritual trust that cannot and should not be forced on free agents by threat or even by rational arguments. As a matter of fact, the gospel of God's saving work in Jesus Christ, witnessed to by prophets and apostles, has been so convincing in the arena of competing truths that many have put their trust in this message, accepting it as the truth, because it answered their most existential questions and met their deepest needs. The only way to discover this is by giving the gospel a real and honest try.

This, however, does not exclude, let alone disqualify, all other positions from the outset. Yes, there is a battle between truth and error in the arena of competing schemes of philosophical and religious worldviews. But the dividing line between truth and error does not run neatly between Christianity and the rest. There might be and has been much error in views that understood and presented themselves as Christian. That is the reason why the church needs continuous reformation and renewal. Christians do not possess the truth. They confess Jesus Christ as the truth, and he possesses them. That means that Christian views must be open to criticism and correction from the prophetic and apostolic witness to the truth by the ongoing persuading work of the Spirit.

On the other hand, there are many elements of truth outside of the Christian religion. These elements of truth are due to the general work of the Spirit of truth. Without claiming to offer a comprehensive "theology of religions" in this paragraph, one of the requirements for the ultimate truth should be a plausible answer to the question why there are so many other alternatives. To meet this requirement, Christian theology has developed a notion of a twofold revelation. Next to, or rather even before, God's revelation in Jesus Christ, God has spoken as the Creator of heaven and earth. In a missionary context it is very useful to appeal to this general or universal revelation. God, who has revealed himself as the God of Israel and the Father of Jesus, has not left himself without testimony to others (Acts 14:17). This testimony is the silent voice of God, who speaks without words in the creation and in his providential care.

In Athens the apostle Paul says that the "unknown God" he is introducing to them is the one they are seeking and trying to find. "He is not far from any one of us. 'For in him we live and move and have our being.' As some of your own poets have said, 'We are his offspring'" (Acts 17:28). Paul quotes the *Phaenomena* of Aratus, a Grecian poet who wrote this in a hymn to Zeus.

That does not mean that the God whom Paul is proclaiming is exactly the same as Zeus, for the concept of this highest god in the polytheistic pantheon differs radically from monotheism. Nevertheless, Paul believes that his God, the only true God, has not left himself without a witness or testimony to these people who, in his view, are worshipping idols. Even pagan thought contains some truth – namely, that the divine being does not consist of material, like gold, silver, or stone. That is what Paul argues from this quotation. Human beings are created in God's image and likeness, and therefore, God cannot be conceived of in likeness to material objects. Because we are his offspring, there is some relationship, some knowledge of God left in every human being.

God's revelation in creation and history is universal. The amazement one feels at a sunset on the beach, on a hike through the woods, or while looking through a microscope, has a "religious" character. The concept of general revelation is not unproblematic. In any case it is insufficient for salvation, due to the sinful character of fallen human nature. The resulting view of God will possibly portray him as the first of all causes, omniscient, and omnipotent, but it will not lead to the core of Christianity: a God who humbles himself assuming human nature to redeem a lost world. Still, from a Christian perspective, in all the elements of truth that are acknowledged in other religions and in nonreligious systems of thought, the Spirit of truth is actively present both by revealing the truth partially and by evoking a desire to know the truth.

There is a risk that general revelation is overvalued and replaces special revelation. For this reason, some theologians reject the whole notion of general revelation and claim that there is no revelation outside of Jesus Christ. These theologians, among whom Karl Barth (1886–1968) is the most famous, see revelation as God's dialectical presence, Dulles's fourth model. God's presence cannot be discovered in the realms of history or religious experience. God is present in his hiddenness, and this is a matter of faith. Although a complete denial of general revelation is problematic as well, because it severs the bond between the truth in Jesus Christ and truth in general, the concerns of dialectical theology about overestimating universal revelation make us cautious not to give general revelation an independent status.

A major problem with the emphasis on creation and history in general revelation is that it presupposes a certain view of the world as an orderly design and of history as a meaningful process. These notions were common in ancient philosophy and are still frequent among religious worldviews, but from the secular perspective nowadays common in Western philosophy and in science, the life results from the random process of evolution, and history as such is meaningless or multi-interpretable. What formerly was seen as God's general revelation in creation and history is no longer recognized as revelation. Perhaps God still speaks and still does not leave himself without testimony, but modern humanity has become deaf to this nonverbal communication. The secular and nonreligious perspective that has become dominant in the West is also part of the struggle of competitive worldviews in the arena of truth, where many witnesses compete to persuade us to put our final trust in them. In this arena other spiritual powers are also active next to and in opposition to the Spirit of truth. In the words of the New Testament, the evil prince of this present world is "the spirit who is now at work in those who are disobedient" (Eph 2:2). Nevertheless, the Spirit of truth is active even in a secular culture. Perhaps we can sense more of his presence in religious experience than in the field of rational apologetics that appeal to creation and history.

THE WORK OF THE SPIRIT IN RELIGIOUS EXPERIENCE

Christian theology connects the idea of general revelation in religious experience to the creation of human beings in the image and likeness of God. Because we are of divine descent, the human heart contains a kind of antenna for the divine. This awareness of the divine in the human consciousness – Calvin called it a *sensus divinitatis* – and the sense of good and evil in the human conscience witness to the existence of someone to whom we are related and who determines the moral rules. The antenna is broken due to the sinful condition of all human beings. That is the reason why no one is neutral regarding the truth and why everyone tends to oppose and suppress it. Humanity does not receive the divine signals correctly and makes the most of it. In this way religiosity can be connected to divine revelation. The fact that the result is distorted is the fault not of the divine transmitter but of the poor human receiver. John Calvin famously said that human nature "is a perpetual factory of idols."[26] The word *factory* is a bit anachronistic – Calvin was rather thinking of the forge of a smith than of a modern factory – but the picture is telling enough. Although the Spirit of truth witnesses to the human heart in religious experiences and evokes a desire for the divine, the result is so distorted that the true God is neither glorified nor thanked, and his glory is exchanged "for images made to look like a mortal human being and birds and animals and reptiles" (Rom 1:23).

For this reason, we should also be critical of Christian religiosity. There too distorted intellectual images of God and related wrong practices might occur. Calvin made a statement about idolatry to correct the veneration of images in churches. In any case, the spiritual struggle between the Spirit of truth and

26. Calvin, *Institutes*, 1.11.8.

competing spirits occurs not only in other religions but also in Christianity, not only in Athens on the Areopagus of philosophy but also in the church.

On the other hand, this critical approach of religious feeling has sometimes led to a one-sided view of other religions, as if they are only forms of devilish pseudoworship. According to Herman Bavinck, however, religiosity outside of Christianity also has "a revelation of God, an illumination by the Logos, a working of God's Spirit."[27] He explains this by the general activity of the Spirit. The founders of the religions were not deceived and deceptive instruments of Satan, but men with a religious calling for their time and people.

> The various religions, however mixed with error they may have been, to some extent have met people's religious needs and brought consolation amidst the pain and sorrow of life. What comes to us from the pagan world are not just cries of despair, but also expressions of confidence, hope, resignation, peace, submission, patience, etc. . . . Hence Christianity is not only positioned antithetically toward paganism; it is also the paganism's fulfilment. . . . What is sought there can be found here.[28]

His nephew, Johan Herman Bavinck (1895–1964), a prominent twentieth-century Dutch missiologist, is more critical of religious experience, partly influenced by the concerns of dialectical theology. He holds that religious experience comes from God's overwhelming deity and power, but "escaping from them and repressing them is the human answer to God's revelation, an answer that becomes evident in the history of religious man."[29] The religions arise from the human suppression of God's general revelation and its substitution with a surrogate.

However complicated and ambiguous religious experience may be from a Christian perspective, this mixed bag, in Christianity as well as in other religions, can be interpreted from the struggle in the spiritual arena between truth and error, between the Spirit of light and the power of darkness. Just as the Spirit of God testifies to the truth of the gospel in the hearts of every believer, so too the same Spirit witnesses through religious feelings in general to the existence of the true God and to his worthiness to be sought and praised. The question is

27. Bavinck, *Prolegomena*, 318.

28. Bavinck, *Prolegomena*, 319–20.

29. Johan Herman Bavinck, *The Church between Temple and Mosque: A Study of the Relationship between the Christian Faith and Other Religions* (Grand Rapids: Eerdmans, 1966), 124. For his work on religious experience, see Paul J. Visser, *Heart for the Gospel, Heart for the World: The Life and Thought of a Reformed Pioneer Missiologist Johan Herman Bavinck (1895–1964)* (Eugene: Wipf & Stock, 2003), especially ch. 4.

what people do with these experiences. By nature, they will suppress them and exchange the worship of God for idolatry. In a secular context this suppression takes the form of a psychological or even neurological explanation of religious experience and of the interpretation of all religions including Christianity as social constructs, functional in the evolution of the species of *homo sapiens* and helpful for the survival of the fittest. Happily, the gospel is a theosoteric message. Only God's grace can save from the errors that result from the fragments of divine revelation in religious experience and open the eyes of those who are blinded by secular prejudices.

The testimonies of outward universal revelation in nature and history and of inward universal revelation in religious consciousness and moral awareness all witness to the existence of God. Only when conjoined with the testimony of the Spirit will these universal witnesses lead to a longing for the true God. Just as we need the enlightenment of the Holy Spirit to see nature as God's creation, so also we need the special work of the Spirit to recognize religious experience as a reference to God in which he reveals something regarding himself. Many converts from a Muslim background testify that they were inspired by a dream or vision of Jesus to start searching for him. These religious experiences are extra-biblical references to the truth of the gospel.

The history of missions confirms that the message of the gospel in many cases meets the deepest needs of human beings who are all created in the image and likeness of God. At the same time, this function of general revelation as a preparation for the gospel might explain why missionary work or evangelism in secularized or post-Christian contexts is so difficult. The function of general revelation has been distorted by the cultural rejection of Christianity as an answer to the deepest human needs. The words of Augustine – "You have made us for Yourself, and our hearts are restless until they rest in You"[30] – convey a universal truth, but it is difficult for people in a modern Western context to believe that this rest can really be found in the God of Israel and the Father of Jesus Christ.

The testimony of universal revelation, even when conjoined with the general work of the Holy Spirit, does not suffice to know who our creator is. Only his verbal revelation meets this fundamental need. Therefore, religious experiences (such as the dreams that convert Muslims to Christianity) are lastingly effective only if they lead to the revelation of God as found in Jesus and in the Bible that tells us that he is the Messiah, the Son of God. Moreover, universal revelation does not have the same epistemic status as God's special revelation in

30. Augustine, *Confessions*, LCL (Cambridge, MA: Harvard University Press, 2014), 1.1.

the witness regarding Jesus Christ. The first is always a reference to the second and does not add new information about Christ. Religious experience is not a source of knowledge independent of Scripture. And yet there are psychological similarities between the event of God's revelation to the biblical prophets and religious experiences in general, even of prophets in other religions. The fact that human beings have these kinds of divine experiences is a general pointer to our fundamental relationship with God our creator. The truth of these experiences, however, depends on their conformity to God's special revelation in Jesus Christ and in the Scriptures that witness of him.

The Spirit of God makes use of natural human and psychological means. If any religious experience, even any Christian religious experience, can be equated with the revelation that took place at the moment of inspiration, then the Bible becomes open-ended. What makes special revelation so special is the divine authority of the prophetic and apostolic witnesses confirmed by the witness of the Holy Spirit.

THE SPIRIT AND THE MYSTERY OF THE GOSPEL

What do we mean by the resonance of the Word through the Spirit? Revelation is an ongoing process that cannot be fixed at a certain moment. It implies that something is hidden or unknown, which makes us curious to know the secret of God. In a certain sense the acceptance of Scripture by the believer also can be called "revelation." What happens at the moment of faithful acceptance of Jesus Christ as Lord and Saviour is so new and so powerful that it is likened to the opening of the heart or as scales falling from one's eyes (Acts 9:18; 16:14). Still, it is more proper to reserve the word *revelation* for the *kerygma* of Jesus Christ and the prophetic and apostolic witness to him. Christ is the core of God's revealed secret. What happens at the acceptance of Christ as Saviour is an illumination of the Spirit, who sheds light on the revelation in the Word.

The word *mysterion* in the New Testament generally refers to a mystery and as such underlines the hiddenness of the message, although the New Testament often stresses that this mystery has now been revealed in the gospel through the cross and resurrection of Jesus Christ. Thus, Paul writes about the mystery that has been so hidden that no eye has seen, and no ear has heard it, but these "things God has revealed to us by his Spirit" (1 Cor 2:10). He relates the revelation of this mystery to the written Word of God, which is placed in a new perspective through its fulfilment in the coming of Jesus Christ. The message he proclaims about Jesus Christ is in full accordance with "the revelation of the mystery hidden for long ages past, but now revealed and made known through the prophetic writings" (Rom 16:25–26). These references illustrate how close even the apostles related the revelation of God's mystery to God's written Word and to the illuminating work of the Spirit. The gospel is not something new; it is the Word of God in its fulfilment in Jesus Christ.

As we have seen, this revealed mystery or testimony regarding Jesus Christ is accepted by the Christian through the witness of the Holy Spirit. He or she believes the Bible because it is the Word of God. He or she believes it is the Word of God because of its witness regarding Christ. Ultimately, he or she believes that this witness, and Scripture as the medium of this witness, is trustworthy through the inner witness of the Holy Spirit.

It is very important not to isolate this witness from the witness of the church of all ages and places, even though the certainty with which the Christian embraces the Scriptures is not based on the external authority of the church. But we need to recognize that this witness generally takes place within the context of the Christian community. In other words, the witness of the Spirit is never a merely individual feeling or certainty, but it resonates within the context of the community and is confirmed by the witness of many others. This is especially important in the context of postmodernity, where the reference to the internal witness of the Spirit easily leads to the conclusion that revelation is arbitrary and that every authentic religious experience stands on the same level. If the *autopistia* of Scripture and the witness of the Spirit are interpreted starting from the autonomy of the individual believer, it too easily becomes an *autopistia* of oneself.[31] In that case Scripture loses its critical character and becomes the self-confirming echo of one's own religious feelings. The authority of Scripture will evaporate in the postmodern context if it is interpreted as a matter of individualistic and relativistic choice. The authority of Scripture, however, always functions within a covenantal relationship; Scripture is the living voice of God.

THE SPIRIT IN THE TRANSMISSION OF THE TEXTS

It is also important not to isolate this witness from the historical process of textual transmission in which there are at least five layers. The first or historical layer consists of the deeds done by the God of Israel and the Father of Jesus Christ, such as the exodus and the resurrection. The second or oral layer is the proclamation of these deeds by prophets and apostles. This proclamation has, in the third place, been written down in original documents. This scriptural layer has, fourthly, been collected, edited, copied, and transmitted by the church from generation to generation; we may call this fourth element the layer of tradition.

31. See Van den Belt, "Scripture as the Voice of God: The Continuing Importance of *Autopistia*," *International Journal of Systematic Theology* 13, no. 4 (2011): 445.

Finally, the message of these texts is translated, interpreted, and proclaimed in the present context.

The most important moments of "revelation" are at the beginning and at the end of the process: the moment when the prophet realizes that God has something to say through her or him and the moment when the believer on the other side of the process of transmission understands and hears the voice of the living God. Nevertheless, you cannot say that only one aspect is real revelation. The content of the revelation is given to the prophet through the Spirit. The transmission of this divine message is also the work of the Spirit. The final acceptance of the message is likewise the Spirit's work. To bridge the gap between the original moment of revelation and the moment of the acceptance or application of revelation in the present time, all the other parts of the chain are necessary.

What holds these historical, oral, scriptural, traditional, and interpretational layers together in a real unity is the ongoing work of the Holy Spirit. The whole process is vulnerable, but the Spirit rules over it from beginning to end. The same Spirit who inspired the original witnesses to speak and write about the mighty deeds of God and who safeguarded the transmission of the texts dwells also in the hearts of Christians today. When the witness of the Spirit makes the witness of Scripture resonate in the heart, the living voice of God – this holy resonance – renews those who hear the Word and makes them witnesses of what he has done for them. An African American spiritual says, "Were you there when they crucified my Lord?" and Rembrandt painted a self-portrait in his *Raising of the Cross*. Perhaps artists and poets can express the relationship between Word and Spirit in a way that theologians should take careful note of.

FOR FURTHER READING

Bauckham, Richard. *Jesus and the Eyewitnesses: The Gospels as Eyewitness Testimony*. Grand Rapids: Eerdmans, 2006.

Bavinck, Herman. *Reformed Dogmatics*. 4 vols. Translated by John Vriend. Edited by John Bolt. Grand Rapids: Baker, 2003–2008.

Bavinck, Johan Herman. *The Church between Temple and Mosque: A Study of the Relationship between the Christian Faith and Other Religions*. Grand Rapids: Eerdmans, 1966.

Bayer, Oswald. *Theology the Lutheran Way*. Grand Rapids, Eerdmans, 2007.

Calvin, John. *Institutes of the Christian Religion*. Edited by John T. McNeill. Translated by Ford Lewis Battles. London: SCM, 1961.

Cooper, Alan. "Aspects of Jewish Reception of the Ketuvim (Writings)." In *The Oxford Handbook of the Writings of the Hebrew Bible*, edited by Donn F. Morgan, 430–47. New York: Oxford University Press, 2018.

Dulles, Avery. *Models of Revelation*. Garden City: Doubleday, 1983.

Hamilton, James M. *God's Indwelling Presence: The Holy Spirit in the Old and New Testaments*. Nashville: B&H, 2006.

Kolb, Robert. *Martin Luther and the Enduring Word of God: The Wittenberg School and Its Scripture-Centered Proclamation*. Grand Rapids: Baker Academic, 2016.

Muller, Richard A. *Holy Scripture*. Vol. 2 of *Post-Reformation Reformed Dogmatics: The Rise and Development of Reformed Orthodoxy*. Grand Rapids: Baker, 2003.

Oberman, Heiko A. *The Harvest of Medieval Theology: Gabriel Biel and Late Medieval Nominalism*. Cambridge: Harvard University Press, 1963.

Preiss, Théo. *Le temoignage interieur du Saint-Esprit, Cahiers theologiques de l'actualite protestante*. Vol. 13. Neuchâtel: Delachaux et Niestle, 1946.

Staats, R. *Das Glaubensbekenntnis von Nizäa-Konstantinopel: Historische und theologische Grundlagen*. Darmstadt: Wissenschaftliche Buchgesellschaft, 1996.

Van den Belt, Henk. *The Authority of Scripture in Reformed Theology: Truth and Trust*. Leiden: Brill, 2008.

Van den Belt, Henk. "The Problematic Character of *Sola Scriptura*." In *Sola Scriptura: Biblical and Theological Perspectives on Scripture, Authority, and Hermeneutics*, edited by Hans Burger, Arnold Huijgen, and Eric Peels, Studies in Reformed Theology 32, 38–55. Leiden: Brill, 2018.

Van der Kooi, Cornelis, and Gijsbert van den Brink. *Christian Dogmatics: An Introduction*. Grand Rapids: Eerdmans, 2017.

Visser, Paul J. *Heart for the Gospel, Heart for the World: The Life and Thought of a Reformed Pioneer Missiologist Johan Herman Bavinck (1895–1964)*. Eugene, OR: Wipf & Stock, 2003.

Warfield, Benjamin B. *The Works of Benjamin B. Warfield*. Edited by E. D. Warfield, W. P. Armstrong, and C. W. Hodge. New York: Oxford University Press, 1927–32. Reprint, Grand Rapids, Baker, 1981.

CHAPTER 4

The Bible Is Not an Image

Scriptures, Traditions, and Reasons

Olivier Riaudel

When it comes to reflecting on the respective roles of Scripture and ecclesial traditions in a book devoted to the reading of the Bible and its principles, it is tempting to take up the controversy at the point where the last Protestant or Catholic author thought the debate had ended. In this case, depending on one's tastes, more or less conciliatory positions will be defended, but the discussion will remain on topic. We will not do this for two reasons, which will form the first two points of our presentation: first, because *sola scriptura* in the Reformation is less a principle of Bible reading than an ecclesiological thesis (a very important question but not immediately our subject), and second, because *sola scriptura* is a principle defended by an author typically claimed by Catholics, Thomas Aquinas.

SOLA SCRIPTURA: THE MEANING OF THIS THESIS

When it comes to the relationship between Scripture and the traditions of the churches, the most problematic point seems to be summed up by the Protestant thesis of *sola scriptura*. To begin with, it is important to clarify two features of this "exclusive particle."

The first is this: the *sola scriptura* thesis is not primarily a thesis on the interpretation of the Bible or on the relationship between the Bible and theology. Positively, it's a thesis about the power of God's Word and its clarity, and negatively, it's a thesis that contests that, as far as faith is concerned, Scripture must be supplemented by something else, and in this sense the criticism underlying the *sola scriptura* formula has above all an ecclesiological bearing.

This can be seen more clearly in an opposing example. In the official Catholic theology of the nineteenth century, as formulated in the constitution *Dei Filius* of the first Vatican Council, "all that is contained in the Holy Scriptures and in tradition, and all that is proposed by the Church as divinely revealed truth, either by solemn judgment or by her ordinary and universal magisterium, must be believed with divine and Catholic faith. But because it is impossible without faith to please God and to be numbered among his children, no one is justified without it, and no one attains eternal life unless he has persevered to the end."[1]

Two aspects of this proposition are eminently questionable from the point of view of *sola scriptura*. Firstly, only Holy Scripture should be binding on faith, and secondly, the unique norm of Scripture cannot and must not play its role as a storehouse of theoretical instructions, as dogmatic propositions can. *Scriptura sola* thus states that Scripture alone is the norm of faith and that this norm does not operate as a conciliar definition, still less as the anathemas that sometimes end conciliar texts, and this above all for the simple reason that Scripture is the living Word of God, which as a promise is addressed to faith, and not a series of dogmatic propositions. Putting one's trust in the Word of God cannot be replaced by holding a doctrine to be true, be it that of a book or an ecclesiastical institution.

However, it seems to me that this *scriptura sola formula*, formulated in such a clear-cut way, for a Catholic theologian at least, could well have a Catholic meaning, and that it is *Dei Filius*, making salvation dependent on belief in magisterial definitions, that could well be problematic. We will return to this point, although the ecclesial consequences of *scriptura sola* will not be the main focus of our interest.

The second particular feature of this "exclusive particle" is that, unlike the other *solas*, it does not enter *directly*[2] into the expression of the event of justification,[3] according to which God offers human beings justification for Christ's

---

1. H. Denzinger, *Enchiridion Simbolorum, definitionum et declarationum de rebus fidei et morum*, ed. P. Hünermann (Freiburg: Herder, 1991), DH 3011–12.

2. It is right to recall, as K. J. Vanhoozer points out, that *sola scriptura* only makes sense with the other exclusive particles. Cf. K. J. Vanhoozer, *Biblical Authority after Babel. Retrieving the Solas in the Spirit of Mere Protestant Christianity* (Grand Rapids: Brazos, 2016), 109–46.

3. It is therefore highly questionable to treat it as a *formal principle* of the Reformation (justification by grace being the material principle), as some German Protestant theology has done since the nineteenth

sake alone (*solo Christo*), by grace alone (*sola gratia)*, through faith alone (*sola fide*), by listening to God's Word alone (*solo verbo*). As we can see, *sola scriptura* is of a different order: it can be described as metadiscourse.[4]

This is borne out by Luther's use of the expression. It has been shown that Luther uses the expression *sola gratia* 200 times in his works, *sola fide* 1,200 times, and *sola scriptura* only 20 times.[5]

As Volker Leppin clearly shows,[6] it was the discussion in Leipzig in 1519 with Johannes Eck and Eck's insistence on proving that certain Lutheran theses were identical to those of John Hus, already condemned by the Council of Constance, that forced Luther to draw out the consequences of his doctrine. In fact, as Leppin shows, Melanchthon was the first to formulate twenty-four theses for the degree of *baccalaureus biblicus*, some of which stemmed directly from the Leipzig *Disputatio*: "for a Catholic,[7] it is not necessary to believe other things in addition to what is attested in Scripture"[8] (thesis 16), and "the authority of councils is subject to the authority of Scripture"[9] (thesis 17).

Sola scriptura sets limits: not everything in the teaching of the faith must be imposed, not everything is indisputable, not everything must be believed by everyone, and only Scripture is binding on believers in these matters. The rest is human tradition, and this not only must not be imposed but can be harmful and even oppose God.

A further consequence was drawn in 1520 in his manifesto "To the Christian Nobility of the German Nation." The papacy opposes the "Christian condition," common to all believers, based on the universal priesthood of believers, with three walls that must be torn down: Roman immunity from secular power, Roman primacy over councils, and the wall that seals off the possibility of interpretation of Scripture by all believers. And if the interpretation of Scripture can be opened to all believers, the clarity of Scripture is to thank.

---

century. M. Kähler, *Zur Lehre von der Versöhnung*, Leipzig, 1898, is often quoted on this point, but the authorship of this distinction could be traced back to the rationalist theologian Karl Gottlieb Bretschneider, *Handbuch der Dogmatik der evangelisch-lutherischen Kirche* (Leipzig: Johann Ambrosius Barth, 1828), 1:46–47. This is the third edition of a book first published in 1814. See also Jan Rohls, *Protestantische Theologie der Neuzeit* (Tübingen: Mohr Siebeck, 1997), 1:390–91.

4. M. Leiner and O. Riaudel, "Sola scriptura et solo verbo." *RTL* 48, no. 3 (2017): 307–24. In the following, we take up some of the elements developed in this article.

5. Timothy J. Wengert, *Reading the Bible with Martin Luther* (Grand Rapids: Baker, 2013), 16; see also by the same author "A Note on 'Sola Scriptura' in Martin Luther's Writings," in *Luther-Bulletin Tijdschrift voor interconfessioneel Lutheronderzoek* 20 (2011): 21–31.

6. M. Leppin, *Martin Luther* (Darmstadt: WBG, 2006), 144–51.

7. A term by which Melanchthon obviously still understood all Christians at the time.

8. *Melanchtons Werke*, l.31–32, p. 24: "Conciliorum auctoritas est infra scripturae auctoritatem."

9. Martin Luther, *Assertio omnium articulorum M. Lutheri per bullam Leonis X novissimam damnatorum* (1521), WA 7, 98.

The link between *sola scriptura* and the clarity of Scripture is explicit in Luther's response to Pope Leo X's bull of excommunication: his assertion that "Scripture alone reigns (*solam scripturam regnare*[10])" is linked to the fact that, in his view, Scripture is "by itself the most certain, the clearest, and its own interpreter" (*per se certissima, apertissima, sui ipsius interpres*).[11]

Transforming *scriptura sola*, which is both a thesis on the intrinsic power of the Word of God and an ecclesiological thesis, into an epistemological thesis, according to which we should only consider what is expressed in what we consider to be the literal meaning of the Bible, is a relatively modern operation, typical of Protestant fundamentalism.

SCRIPTURA SOLA: A THESIS DEFENDED BY THOMAS AQUINAS

It cannot be denied that the recurring temptation of the Catholic Church was to give more space to its magisterial teaching than to the Word of God: for this, we need only look at the debates surrounding the writing of the dogmatic constitution *Dei Verbum* at the Second Vatican Council,[12] as well as the considerable effect on the Second Vatican Council of Geiselmann's study, published in 1957,[13] on the text of the Council of Trent: "*hanc veritatem et disciplinam contineri in libris scriptis et sine scripto traditionibus*" ("this truth and these rules are contained in written books and in unwritten traditions"). Geiselmann showed that the text of the Council of Trent, "*in libris scriptis et sine scripto traditionibus*" ("in written books and in unwritten traditions"), had been retained in place of a preparatory text which read "*hanc veritatem partim contineri in libris scriptis, partim sine scripto traditionibus*" ("partly in written books and partly in unwritten traditions"). It should also be pointed out that, although the "two sources" theory, which saw divine revelation as contained partly in Scripture and partly in tradition, was explicitly challenged by the text of *Dei Verbum*,[14] the idea is still

10. *Melanchtons Werke*, l.31–32, p. 24: "Conciliorum auctoritas est infra scripturae auctoritatem."

11. *Melanchtons Werke*, l.31–32, p. 24: "Conciliorum auctoritas est infra scripturae auctoritatem."

12. Luther, *Assertio omnium articulorum M. Lutheri*, 98.

13. In its dogmatic constitution *Dei Verbum*, the Second Vatican Council deliberately moved away from the "two sources" issue, emphasizing that both biblical texts and the transmission of church practices have their source in the one Word of God made flesh.

14. We are indebted for our knowledge of some of these texts to Bruno Decker, "Sola Scriptura bei Thomas von Aquino," in *Universitas: Dienst an Wahrheit und Leben (Festschrift für Bischof Dr. Albert Stohr)* (Mainz: Matthias Grünewald, 1960), 3:117–29.

alive and well in Catholic writers, who regularly write "Scripture and Tradition," as if they were two autonomous and equivalent entities.

Nevertheless, Catholic theology is not reducible to its post-Reformation developments, and patristic and medieval theological practice was not theorized around the idea of the inadequacy of Scripture, to be supplemented by tradition. A very clear illustration of this can be found in Thomas's commentary[15] on Pseudo Denys's *Book of the Divine Names*, where Thomas develops a precise definition of the relationship of "sacred science" to the Scriptures:

> Thus, the principles from which sacred science proceeds are those received through the revelation of the Holy Spirit and contained in the Holy Scriptures. He concludes, therefore, that in no way should anyone dare to say from his mouth or even think anything concerning the hidden and supra-substantial Deity, which surpasses all substance and because of this remains hidden from us, as opposed to the created substances whose knowledge and expression are proportionate to us, which is opposed to the truths that have been divinely expressed to us from the holy prophets, i.e. which are expressed by the sacred writers. And it is significant that he did not say: in the holy prophets [*in sanctis eloquiis*], but rather from the holy prophets [*ex sanctis eloquiis*], for the conclusions that can be drawn from what is contained in the holy Scriptures are not foreign to this doctrine, even though they themselves are not contained in it.[16]

A few lines further down, the formula is even briefer: "*Quae quidem divina revelatio in Scripturis sacris continetur*" ("This Revelation is contained in the sacred Scriptures"). There is no question here of a *scriptura sola*, any more than there is of a necessary complementation of Scripture by anything else. The exclusive particle *sola* is not necessary precisely because no one is putting forward the idea of any complement whatsoever to Scripture. In this context, Thomas's sentence cites only Scripture as the source of supernatural knowledge of God.

The same applies to the revelation of the divine will. Would the Word have become incarnate if Adam had not sinned? In his commentary on the *Sentences*, Thomas answers negatively, "*quia in canone Scripturae et dictis sanctorum expositorum, haec sola assignatur causa incarnationis*"[17] ("because in the

15. Luther, *Assertio omnium articulorum M. Lutheri*, 98.

16. See in particular R. Burigana, *La Bibbia nel concilio. La redazione della costitutione* Dei Verbum *del Vaticano II* (Bologna: Il Mulino, 1998); and Ch. Theobald, *Histoire du Concile Vatican II*, tome 5 (Paris: Cerf, 2005).

17. For the acts of the council, see *Concilium Tridentinum diariorum, actorum, epistularum, tractatuum nova collection*, ed. Societas Goerriesiana, 13 vols. (Freiburg: Herder, 1901–2001), here vol. 5. For

canonical Scriptures and the words of the saints no other cause is given for the incarnation")—namely, man's redemption and liberation from his sins. But in the mature *Summa Theologica*, Thomas writes: "Indeed, what depends on God's will alone, and to which the creature has no right, can only be known to us insofar as it is taught in Sacred Scripture, which has made God's will known to us."[18] In the *Summa*, where Thomas distinguishes more clearly between the force of scriptural arguments and those drawn from the exegesis of the fathers (since it is to the latter that reference is made to the word of the saints in the commentary on the *Sentences*), Thomas cannot cite these two sources on the same level: Scripture is therefore presented as *the* source that reveals God's will to us.

This hypothesis is reinforced by a reading of Ia, q. 1, a. 8, ad 2um. In this article, Thomas asks whether sacred doctrine argues, whether it is capable of putting forward demonstrations, capable of assuring conclusions in a certain way. In his reply to the second objection, Thomas states that sacred doctrine may well use arguments drawn from human reason or invoke the authority of philosophers, but "we must beware, however, that sacred doctrine employs these authorities only as arguments foreign to its nature, and having only a value of probability." He immediately continues: "On the contrary, it makes its own use of the authorities of canonical Scripture." What then of the reference to the doctors of the church? "It also uses them as its own arguments, but only in a probable way. And Thomas concludes his argument with a quotation from Augustine in support of the inerrancy of the canonical Scriptures: "The books of the canonical Scriptures are the only ones to which I grant the honor of believing very firmly their authors incapable of erring in what they write. The others, if I read them, it is not because they have thought a thing or written it that I consider it true, however eminent they may be in holiness and doctrine."[19] The fathers can therefore be used as arguments but only as probable arguments. Scripture alone is a proper and certain authority. We can see why Thomas, in the previous quotation, could no longer cite the authority of Scripture and references to the fathers in the same breath.

Just before quoting Augustine, Thomas sums up his thinking in a striking formulation: "*Innititur enim fides nostra revelationi apostolis et prophetis factae,*

Geiselmann's texts: Joseph R. Geiselmann, "Das Konzil von Trient über das Verhältnis der Heiligen Schrift und der nicht geschrieben Traditionen," in *Die mündliche Überlieferung*, ed. Michael Schmaus (Munich: Hüber, 1957), 123–206; see also Joseph R. Geiselmann, *Die Heilige Schrift und die Tradition: zu den neueren Kontroversen über das Verhältnis der Heiligen Schrift zu den nichtgeschriebenen Traditionen* (Fribourg en B.: Herder, 1962).

18. Thomas, *Summa Theologica* III, q. 1, a. 3. Author's translation.

19. Decker, "Sola Scriptura bei Thomas von Aquino," 120.

qui canonicos libros scripserunt, non autem revelationi, si qua fuit aliis doctoribus facta" ("Our faith rests on the revelation made to the apostles and prophets, not on other revelations, if any, made to other doctors"). In this response, Thomas clearly identifies "the revelation made to the apostles and prophets" and "canonical Scripture" without any need to mention oral tradition. There is no question of a revelation witnessed by the fathers and not recorded in Scripture. The fathers do not intervene here as witnesses to an unwritten revelation, but as commentators on Scripture, theologians who seek to understand the revelation transmitted by Scripture alone.[20]

A final text on the Thomistic meaning of *scriptura sola*. In the questions disputées *De Veritate*, Thomas asks whether it is necessary to have faith.[21] The eleventh objection argues that the things of faith have come to us through many intermediaries, whether prophets or apostles, or their successors. But it is impossible to be sure that all these intermediaries were infallible. We can therefore have no certainty whatsoever about the things of faith, and it therefore seems foolish (*stultum*) to assent to them.

To this objection, Thomas responds as follows: "The means by which faith comes to us are all beyond suspicion. Indeed, we believe in the prophets and apostles because God testified to them by working miracles, as it says in Mk 16:20: 'confirming their word by the miracles that accompanied it.' And we believe in the successors of the apostles and prophets only insofar as they announce to us the things they left in their writings."[22] The answer, then, is clear in principle, even if it may seem very strange to a Catholic reader after the Reformation: while Scripture is beyond suspicion, we give credence to the teaching of the successors of the prophets and apostles "only insofar as they announce to us the things they have left in their writings" (*nisi in quantum nobis ea annuntiant quae illi in scriptis reliquerunt*). Expressed from a Catholic perspective: we obey Church teaching only insofar as it agrees with Scripture.

One is tempted to wonder whether this demonstration is not some ruse since it seems to draw Thomas towards typically Protestant positions! We may then be tempted to invoke numerous other quotations from Thomas, such as this one, "The primary truth is proposed to us in the Scriptures soundly understood according to the doctrine of the Church,"[23] to immediately reinstate the role of ecclesial mediation.

---

20. Thomas Aquinas, *Questions disputées: De Veritate* (Le Barroux: Sainte-Madeleine, 2011), t. II, q. 14–29.
21. Aquinas, *Questions disputées*, t. II, q. 14, art. 10.
22. Aquinas, *Questiones disputatae*, q. 14, a. 10, ad. 11um.
23. Aquinas, *Summa Theologica*, IIa-IIae, q. 5, a. 3, sol. 2.

First, let's ask: Would Thomas ignore all oral tradition? Would he ignore the *sine scripto traditionibus* referred to by the Council of Trent? The answer, of course, is no. Thomas cites such traditions, for example, in connection with the veneration (the cult of lâtrie) of the images of Christ[24] or for the constitutive words of the sacraments.[25] Thus, for example, concerning the words on the cup in the Catholic liturgy, Thomas writes: "The words added: 'eternal' and 'mystery of faith,' come from the Lord's tradition, which reached the Church through the Apostles, according to what St. Paul says (1 Cor 11:23): 'I have received from the Lord what I have passed on to you.'"[26]

Is not there a contradiction with Thomas's very clear statements on Scripture, which make no mention of these oral traditions that he nonetheless knows about and receives? Note that the passages in which Thomas expresses himself so decisively on revelation through Scripture alone are texts in which he asks what is to be believed.[27] He is not asking whether the Scriptures contain all that God has *revealed*, but whether they contain all that must be *believed*. The examples we have cited in which Thomas refers to an unwritten tradition concern worship, that is, what is there *in the service of faith*, not the definition of the mystery itself.[28] In short, it is by no means a question of tradition supplementing a revelation transmitted by Scripture.

This idea of a complement is totally foreign to Thomas when it comes to conciliar or magisterial definitions. We can illustrate this with an article from II-IIae of the *Summa*. In question 1 (the object of faith), Thomas asks in article 9 about the transmission of the articles of faith through the symbol of faith, the Christian profession of faith.

The first objection states, "It seems unfortunate to put the articles of faith in a symbol. For Holy Scripture is the rule of faith, a rule to which it is not permitted to add or subtract: 'To the word that I speak to you,' says Deuteronomy (4:2), 'you shall neither add nor take away.' It was therefore no longer permissible to create a symbol that would be a rule of faith, after Sacred Scripture had been published."

Thomas's response to this objection is as follows:

---

24. We are indebted for our knowledge of some of these texts to Decker, "Sola Scriptura bei Thomas von Aquino," 117–29.

25. Thomas Aquinas, *In librum B. Dionysii De divinis nominibus expositio* (Turin, 1950), caput 1, lectio 1. Slightly modified translation from Serge Pronovost, published on http://docteurangelique.free.fr.

26. Thomas Aquinas, *Scriptum super Sententiis*, bk 3, dis. 1, q. 3. Here we follow the text of the Parma edition (1858).

27. Letter LXXXII, *Patrologiae Cursus Completus*, Series Latina (PL), 33, 277.

28. Decker, "Sola Scriptura bei Thomas von Aquino," 120.

> The truth of faith is contained in Sacred Scripture in a diffuse manner, in very different ways, and in obscure places, so that much study and effort are needed to bring it out. Not everyone who needs to know the truth of faith can do so, because most of them are busy with other matters and cannot devote themselves to study. This is why it has been necessary to draw from the sayings of Sacred Scripture a concise and clear compendium that could be offered to the faith of all. This is not adding, but rather extracting.

Two things should be noted in this response to the first objection. First, the response to the objection in no way calls into question the principle invoked by the objection: "Sacred Scripture is the rule of faith." Second, in Thomas's perspective, doctrinal statements are not *added* to Sacred Scripture, nor are they the result of a reading operation "in the light of tradition." No, they are *taken* purely and simply from Scripture.

For the latter, only the literal meaning is "contained" in Scripture, while the spiritual meanings are the result of interpretation by the reader.[29] It's easy to see why the Reformation refused to see human, ecclesiastical mediation in this hermeneutical operation, while Catholics strove to justify it, arguing (in the words of two authors who were hardly suspected of traditionalism at the time) that "Scripture does not contain all the *veritas evangelii*."[30]

The fact that this was not the case for the medievalists is best illustrated by this quotation from St. Thomas: "Every truth that can be reconciled with divine Scripture in respect of its letter is its meaning."[31] In other words, not only the literal sense but also the various spiritual senses, and even the propositions of the symbols of faith, are according to him the senses of Scripture and not the result of interpretation. This is obviously no longer the case for Luther, or for the Counter-Reformation.

---

29. Aquinas, *Questions disputées: De Veritate*, t. II, Q. 14–29.

30. *Summa Theologica*, III, q. 25, a. 3, ad 4: "The Apostles, guided by the inner impulse of the Holy Spirit, transmitted to the Churches certain traditions which they had not left in their writings, but in the practice of the Church, which the faithful passed on to one another. This is how St Paul tells the Thessalonians (2 Thess 2:14): 'Stand firm and hold on to the traditions you have received from us, whether by word of mouth or by letter'. And among these traditions is the adoration of the images of Christ." The translations of the *Summa Theologica* are those of Paris: Cerf, 1985.

31. For example *Summa Theologica*, III, q. 64, a. 2, ad 1: "The elements of the sacramental rite which are of human institution are not necessary to the sacrament, but contribute to the solemnity with which it is surrounded in order to excite devotion and respect in those who receive them. As for the elements necessary for the sacrament, they were instituted by Christ himself, who is both God and man; and if they are not all revealed to us in the Scriptures, the Church has nevertheless received them from the ordinary teaching of the Apostles; thus St. Paul writes (1 Cor 11:34): 'As for the other points, I will settle them when I come.'" Thomas refers to the same passage from the 1 Corinthians in III, q. 72, a. 4, ad 1.

Gilbert Dahan, in several studies, in particular in his collection *Lire la Bible au Moyen-Âge*,[32] stresses the plurality of meanings of Scripture for medieval authors: not only are the literal and spiritual meanings the meanings of the text itself, but – and this is a specificity of the Bible for them – not only the words but also the things (*res*) designated by these words carry inspired meanings.[33]

It would make no sense to promote a return to medieval hermeneutics today. But recent studies on this hermeneutic help us to avoid absolutizing our current relationship with the text, or with modern and contemporary hermeneutics. It is very likely that we no longer share some of the hermeneutical self-evidence of Luther and his contemporaries. So instead of returning to the question as it arose in the controversy between Catholics and Protestants in the sixteenth century, it might be interesting to turn for a moment to contemporary reflections on the question of meaning and its relationship to language.

A CONTEXTUALIST THESIS: MEANING IS IN USE

Our insistence on the pragmatic dimension of language calls into question many theses that are often taken for granted: the priority of the representative use of language, the priority of system over use, and more generally the priority of language over speech. Indeed, since Ferdinard de Saussure (1857–1913), a whole strand of linguistics has been based on the epistemological choice to exclude speech as an individual act from its analysis (although it is true that Émile Benveniste's [1902–76] analysis of enunciation helped to replace the distinction between language and speech with one between utterance and enunciation).

Much of the thinking on the inspiration of the Bible has been limited to considering only two aspects of language:

1. a *syntactic* aspect, according to which language is constituted by signs, by the relationships between signs in the sentence or between groups of sentences in sequences of sentences; we question the construction of relationships, in particular grammatical rules; and
2. a *semantic* aspect, according to which language as signs, words, and phrases relates to things or states of affairs; under this aspect we most often approach the question of the reference or truth of language.

32. *Summa Theologica*, III, q. 78, a. 3, ad 9.

33. Decker, "Sola Scriptura bei Thomas von Aquino," 122.

With syntax and semantics, we felt we had dealt with the question of meaning. In a biblical context, it was necessary to have studied the biblical languages to question the meaning of biblical texts, through a study of the relationships between words or sentences (syntax), and through a study of their possible historicity, or their truth (semantics).

And yet a whole section of the philosophy of language of recent decades has developed from the observation of an absence: the *pragmatic* aspect of language. This involves questioning the relations between speakers and signs and between speakers and the world or each other through these signs. By emphasizing this pragmatic aspect, which is not evaluated in the same way by all theories, we see the emergence (or reappearance) of a number of essential notions when it comes to language.

First, language is an *act*. Its main function is not to represent the world but to perform actions. To speak is to act, not only to act on the world or on others but above all to act by producing meaning. Second, language occurs in a *context*: concrete situations in which we speak, listen to someone, or read something. And finally, language implies *performance*: it is a question of carrying out an act in a context, which implies a certain number of skills on the part of speakers.

In my view, the most decisive effect of studying language in terms of pragmatics is to challenge, at the very least, the priority of the descriptive and representative function of language or, more radically, to challenge this representative function itself. This will be discussed according to the theoretical choices that are made between a minimalist option that will make pragmatics an empirical component of linguistic theory and a more radical option that conceives pragmatics as the basis of this theory, an option we'll call "contextualist."[34] We will focus here on the second.[35]

According to a widespread conception theorized by Frege in particular,[36] the meaning of an assertion corresponds to a thought, a proposition, which can be true if it has a reference in reality. This (Platonic) conception of the proposition makes its meaning stable, which does not vary in the different forms of its expression and therefore in the uses to which it is put. What contextualism criticizes, and more generally a whole school of thought from Wittgenstein[37] to

34. See an illuminating example confirming this hypothesis, in a commentary on Pseudo-Denys by Thomas in Decker, "Sola Scriptura bei Thomas von Aquino," 122.

35. Cf. on the different meanings of scriptural texts Anthony Thiselton, "Biblical Hermeneutics and Meaning," in this volume.

36. K. Rahner and J. Ratzinger, *Révélation et Tradition* (Paris: Desclée de Brouwer, 1972), 49.

37. "Omnis veritas quae, salva litterae circumstantia, potest divinae scripturae aptari, est ejus sensus" (Thomas Aquinas, *De Potentia*, q. 4, a. 1, sol.).

Charles Travis,[38] via Austin,[39] Searle,[40] or Putnam,[41] is the existence of a proposition that remains stable within or beyond its uses, a philosophy of language understood as a representation of the world.

This conception of representation is linked intimately to a conception of truth: to signify the world in language would be to represent something as being such and such (e.g., "There's coffee on the table"), and the question of truth would be to ask: Is this the case? For each state of affairs, there would be one and only one true representation, even if it could be expressed in different ways.

In such a theory, the uncertainty of the sentence, "There's coffee on the table," which can just as easily mean that there are bags of coffee on the table, or a thermos of coffee on the table (in which case it is an invitation to help oneself), or ground coffee on the table that has not been cleaned up (in which case it could be a reproach), is treated as an ambiguity linked to the fact that the same expression can correspond to several propositions. To treat this phenomenon as an ambiguity is to consider that there are propositions that are beyond or below language, "ideas," and to remove the ambiguity would be to reduce the correspondence between expression and proposition to a single one. And yet for every singular state of affairs, there should be an equally singular representation. As Travis puts it: "The idea that drives the mechanism here is that the difference in ways of representing things that never counts as making for two different things to think always does so. Independent of circumstances, there is just one right way of classifying cases as ones of thinking, or saying, the same thing, or

---

38. G. Dahan, *Lire la Bible au Moyen-Âge: Essais d'herméneutique médiévale* (Geneva: Droz, 2009); and *L'Exégèse chrétienne de la Bible en Occident médiéval, XIIe–XIVe siècles* (Paris: Cerf, 1999).

39. "In fact, whereas in other texts only words are found to have meanings, in this one not only words [*voces*] but also realities [*res*] signify. Just as in the sense between words and realities, knowledge of words is necessary, so in the sense between realities and mystical events, present or future, knowledge of realities is necessary. Knowledge of words is concerned with two things: elocution and signification; to elocution alone is devoted grammar, to signification, dialectics, rhetoric concerns both at once. Knowledge of realities consists of two things: form and nature. Form is found in outward disposition, nature in inner quality. The form of realities is considered in number, to which arithmetic is dedicated, in proportion, to which music is dedicated, in dimension, to which geometry is dedicated, or in movement, to which geometry is dedicated. Physics, on the other hand, studies the inner nature of realities." Hugues de Saint Victor, *De sacramentis*, prol. § 5, *PL* 176, 185 (quoted by G. Dahan, *Lire la Bible au Moyen-Âge*, 16–17). This example clearly shows how far the deepening of the meaning of a biblical text goes, extending beyond the words to the study of the realities the text designates.

40. A clear and detailed account can be found in, among others, Cl. Bianchi, "Contextualism," in *Handbook of Pragmatics*, ed. J.-O. Östman and J. Verschueren, vol. 14 (Amsterdam: Benjamins, 2010), 2–22.

41. An excellent French presentation can be found in: Bruno Ambroise, "Pragmatiques de la vérité: sens, représentation et contexte, de G. Frege à Ch. Travis," *Corela* [Online], HS-14 (2013), online June 25, 2014, https://doi.org/10.4000/corela.3082.

different things, or as saying just that which, or something other than, what someone thinks, or thinking what someone said."[42]

However, this way of thinking is not at all necessary. According to Travis, it's perfectly possible to deal with this phenomenon of ambiguity, as in the example, "There's coffee on the table," in terms of context sensitivity, or more precisely, *occasion sensitivity*. It's unlikely that if I have just arrived for a morning meeting, someone will inform me that there are bags of coffee on the table or reproach me for not having cleaned the table. The context here determines not only the meaning of the assertion but the meaning of the words themselves.

What's more, not only is the hypothesis of these propositions not indispensable, but it also does not ensure what this hypothesis is supposed to ensure, namely the absence of ambiguity. Hence the conditions for the truth of the proposition:

> To show that a structure of this type doesn't work, it's enough to show that, for any signifying sentence likely to be true, and therefore supposedly having a representational structure to be expressed enabling it to be true, it's possible for this sentence to be true about one thing, on one occasion of saying it, and to be false about the same thing (or the same state of affairs) on another occasion of saying it. In other words, the point is to show that, for any assertion, the predicate or concept we wish to apply admits of several understandings, not necessarily compatible.[43]

Perhaps the most famous biblical example of this are the demons who say that Jesus is the Christ. Or Mark's so-called messianic secret. Whatever the reasons, there are occasions when it is possible to say that Jesus is the Christ, and others when it is not. In much more everyday situations, it's not uncommon for the same perfectly clear assertion to be received in two completely different ways by two individuals, each of whom has perfectly legitimate reasons for doing so. Pragmatics, to put it *mildly*, does play a part in the constitution of meaning.

This is not to deny that propositions exist, in Frege's sense, but simply to assert that they are constituted by the use of an assertion in a given context. This context can be very broad historically and culturally (e.g., a South African comedian saying in the United States that "Africa won the World Cup" does not expect his words to be understood in the same way as they were in France),

---

42. Ch. Travis, *Unshadowed Thought* (Cambridge, MA: Harvard University Press, 2001), 70.

43. Ch. Travis, *Les liaisons ordinaires: Wittgenstein sur la pensée et le monde; leçons au Collège de France, juin 2002* (Vrin, Paris, 2003), 202.

but it can also be much more specific (who is speaking, on what occasion, in what tone, to whom, and so on).

Nor is it a question of denying that an assertion can be true. But it is a question of involving not just two but three elements in the definition of truth: the meaning of words, the state of things, and the circumstances of enunciation. We cannot reduce truth to expressions that set aside all consideration of enunciation and focus solely on the statement. And enunciation, according to Travis, means commitment on the part of the speaker: "Let us be deprived of the role we play in determining what it means for a judgment to be true, and at the same time true responsibility – an intelligible distinction between being right and merely appearing to be right – disappears. It is thus the removal of this role from us that at the same time causes us to lose judgment."[44]

It's not a question of relativizing any conception of truth but of thinking truth outside the representationalist paradigm and without the mentalist myth of a mirror-of-nature mind. To put it positively, it is a question of thinking about truth with language, and this can only be of interest to believers for whom truth was precisely spoken in a Word, and this Word was revealed both in the flesh of Jesus and in the letter of Scripture.

SCRIPTURE AND THE WORD OF GOD

Christian theologians are faced with many major questions concerning the status of Scripture. These questions include its relationship to history – the role of historical criticism and the status of the gap between the biblical narrative and historians' assumptions about the historical reality that may underlie it[45] – and the status of the Old Testament in Christianity. There's also the question of the normative status of Scripture in the face of contextual and actualizing readings, and many others. I'm not sure that the divergences that might arise in the answers to these questions correspond exactly to denominational differences.

Let's pause for a moment to consider the status of Scripture as *writing*. It is legitimate to insist on the difference between Luther's position, through *scriptura sola*, and fundamentalism or literalism. It is also important to insist on the role of Scripture vis-à-vis the church, a role that is underemphasized in Catholic theology, which sometimes tends to *include* Scripture within the church as a

44. *Melanchtons Werke*, l.31–32, p. 24: "Conciliorum auctoritas est infra scripturae auctoritatem."

45. L. Wittgenstein, *Philosophical Investigations*, trans.lated by G. E. M. Anscombe (London: Blackwell, 2001); trans. and ed. by E. Rigal, *Recherches philosophiques* (Paris: Gallimard, 2004).

particular crystallization of a wider process of transmission, of tradition, willingly leaving aside the fact that the church in its history comments on but does not extend the Bible (this is the basic principle of the closure of the canon).

In the face of modern criticism, whether historical, philological, or scientific, modern Protestantism has sought, in many ways, to think of a distinction between the Bible and the Word of God. But what has been called the "crisis of the scriptural principle"[46] has sometimes led some Protestant theologians to formulate the distinction between the Bible and the Word of God, or between Scripture and revelation,[47] taking up distinctions that are too clear-cut (and above all very logocentric, and therefore metaphysical, *volens nolens*) between the liveliness of the word and the supposed inertia of the letter.

The principle of *sola scriptura*, as well as the concern not to separate truth from the language that expresses it, invites us, on the contrary, to return to the priority of the text over its commentary,[48] for we never have direct access to the "Word of God," but only to books, which must be read and understood. These books are inspired,[49] and written by the hands of men (no one will dispute this point), which means that they are necessarily subject to different readings: historical, literary, philological, and, although more rarely today, *theological*.[50] More rarely, because, as Pierre Gisel writes, in modernity,

> The exegete-historian is always given the possibility and the task of telling the truth of the text, or at least its meaning or message; and this is always done in opposition to theological readings that are suspected of being ideological or

---

46. Of particular importance here is W. Herrmann's 1882 lecture *Die Bedeutung der Inspirationslehre für die evangelische Kirche* (Halle: Niemeyer, 1882). Here we see the deliberate shift from reflection on Scripture to reflection on revelation, which would also characterize Catholic theology after *Dei Verbum*. The concept of revelation becomes the principle for clarifying the Bible: "Revelation is more definite and more graspable than the New Testament, and that is why it alone is able to give the Christian community a stable existence and form. [This revelation . . . is the person of Christ, in the work of his life, in whom God makes known to humanity his eternal will, and in whom he has realized the specific act of the remission of our sins. . . . We must . . . seek nothing more in Scripture than a deeper understanding of the acts of God from which the Gospel is born]" (p. 27, my translation). On the evolution of Protestant theology on the scriptural principle, see J. Lauster, *Prinzip und Methode. Die Transformation des Protestantischen Schriftsprinzips durch die historische Kritik von Schleiermacher bis zur Gegenwart*, Hermeneutische Untersuchungen 46 (Tübingen: Mohr Siebeck, 2004).

47. "Commentary is our drug. Like sleepwalkers, we are protected from the often harsh and imperious radiance of naked presence by the soporific drone of the journalist or theorist." G. Steiner, *Réelles présences. Les arts du sens* (Folio Essais, Paris: Gallimard, 1994), 73.

48. Luther, *Assertio omnium articulorum M. Lutheri*, 98.

49. J. L. Austin, "The Meaning of a Word" (1940), and "Truth" (1950), in *Philosophical Papers* (Oxford: Oxford University Press, 1979), 55–75, 117–33.

50. J. Searle, *Sens et expression: Études de théorie des actes du langage* (Paris: Éditions de Minuit, 1982).

> ecclesiastical, and which are moreover seen – the two points are spontaneously linked here – as coming under the heading of addition, distortion, undue appropriation, intellectual or doctrinal overloading. . . . This posture is widely shared by secular modernity; it is also shared within the churches.[51]

Two principles are at work in this posture, both equally contestable: the primacy of an original meaning taken as a foundation, separated from the processes of reading biblical texts, and the exclusion of the possible *truth* of a theological reading. This posture can be prepared for by the division of roles sometimes validated within the churches: dogma belongs to theologians, history to exegetes. Once the identification between the theological truth of the biblical text and dogmatic constructs is challenged, we see the unenviable fate that awaits the claim to a theological truth of the biblical text.

Taking into account the historical dimension of the Christian faith requires not only a division of domains, but also a shift in the way we look at the Bible, its truth, theology, and Christianity as an established religion.[52] Our relationship with the Word of God is always mediated by a book, the Bible – in other words, by a historical reality, with its irreducible otherness (as writing and as history), by rules of reading (to which we shall return), and by everything that constitutes the reception and understanding of this text as the Word of God.

The written word, with its signifier, just like history, is always a sign of the gap with the origin,[53] and this gap is particularly important in Christianity: Jesus is not the founder of Christianity but its center, and the Holy Scriptures are not the immediate presence of the Word of God but testimonies of faith (Jewish, then Christian) *through which* God speaks, because his Spirit *inspires* these texts, because these texts are "filled with his Spirit." Reading the Scriptures as the Word of God can never be separated from meditation on what these texts are saying *here and now*:

> That Jesus spoke such and such a word, and that the exegete-historian can demonstrate this, has its own order of relevance, argumentation and contestation, but this in *no way* says in what way this word is humanly and theologically *true*, nor therefore *what we have to do with it*. This is indeed a

51. H. Putnam, "Is Semantics Possible?," in *Language, Belief, and Metaphysics* (Albany, NY: UNY Press, 1970), 50–63; and Putnam, "The Meaning of 'Meaning,'" in *Mind, Language and Reality, Philosophical Papers*, vol. 2 (Cambridge: Cambridge University Press, 1975), 215–71.

52. Ch. Travis, *Unshadowed Thought* (Cambridge, MA: Harvard University Press, 2000), 70. We follow Bruno Ambroise's translation in "Pragmatiques de la verité."

53. Ambroise, "Pragmatiques de la verité," § 30.

> theological question, even if it can only be developed in the context of history, or even by interweaving with what constitutes it, with what makes life, both individual and social.[54]

What we receive as the Word of God are not the ideas, proposals, beliefs, projects, and intentions that (perhaps) animated the hagiographers, but the Bible, read and proclaimed by believers who share the same Spirit that breathed life into these texts.

THE BIBLE IS NOT AN IMAGE

What happens to reading the Bible as the Word of God when we abandon the idea that the essence of the linguistic phenomenon lies not in the perceptible signifier, the sentence (*sentence*), but in the extra-linguistic signified, the proposition (*proposition*) it expresses?[55] What becomes of reading the Bible when we stop seeing it as the material support of a series of ideal propositions, but as literature, in the sense of writing driven by stylistic and aesthetic research, by poetics? What happens to the Bible when we see it as an act of speech, and not as a representation?

To develop all the consequences would take more space than we have here. But we can provide a few hints, in the form of brief theses.

THESIS 1: THE BIBLE IS NOT THE MIRROR OF A WORLD

Christian readings of the Bible are inseparable from pragmatics, from reflection on what we "do" when we read, proclaim, or meditate on Scripture. This is what ancient rhetoric did more than some modern authors, who are obsessed with the text's referential dimension alone, particularly in its historical aspect: "Did it happen like this?" Some forms of Christian fundamentalism share this same referential obsession with historical-critical approaches, but to defend the reality of the reference. It is possible to give a very strong meaning to Ricœur's expression "world of the text" to rediscover ancient exegetical practices, whether Jewish or Christian, for which the whole text, down to its very details, could produce meaning.

54. Ch. Travis, *Les liaisons ordinaires*, 202.

55. Cf. in this volume Craig Bartholomew, "The Bible and History," and Armin D. Baum, "The Historical-Critical Method in Biblical Scholarship: Its History, Potential, and Limitations."

THESIS 2: THE BIBLE IS NOT THE WRITTEN SUPPORT OF A FEW GREAT IDEAS

The biblical text is not a vehicle for propositions, whether analyzed as the author's intention or as the product of a historical-religious context. On the Protestant side,[56] this idea undoubtedly reached its apogee in the thesis of "limited inspiration," restricted to questions of faith or morals or to the great truths of revelation, and on the Catholic side in a limitation of inerrancy to the truths of faith alone.[57]

THESIS 3: MEANING IS INSEPARABLE FROM ITS EXPRESSION AND THEREFORE FROM THE LETTER OF THE TEXT

Attention to the meaning should not detract from attention to the letter. It is true that there is no such thing as a "single text" of the Bible, that there are only manuscripts that differ from one another, and that the text has constantly been translated. The fact remains, however, that Christian communities read a Bible, not a collection of manuscripts, and that Christian practice of the Bible constantly seeks to return to the Greek or Hebrew texts. The variety and lateness of the Iliad and Odyssey manuscripts and the existence of translations have never been obstacles to literary studies.

THESIS 4: INSPIRATION IS INSPIRATION OF TEXT, NOT OF MEANING

Whatever the variations in manuscripts, and whatever the practice of translation, the insistence on the letter must direct a theology of inspiration. The biblical text is inspired, not the representations it is supposed to carry. This should lead us to reconsider the distinction too often made between the Bible and the Word of God, the Bible being the text, the Word of God the word preached, "the event of the Word of God." If this distinction can make sense, it is a distinction between several *uses*: reading the text as a historical document, as a philosophical reflection, or as the Word of God. Recalling the preeminence of the text would allow us to revisit the notion of verbal inspiration.

THESIS 5: CHRISTIAN BIBLE READINGS ARE PRACTICES

The relationship between Christians and the Bible is structured by the life of Christian communities, by their faith, and by their liturgies. These forms of

56. W. Pannenberg, "Die Krise des Schriftprinzips," in *Grundfragen systematischer Theologie*, t. 1, (Göttingen, 1962), 11–21.

57. See Herrmann, *Die Bedeutung der Inspirationslehre für die evangelische Kirche*; and Lauster, *Prinzip und Methode*.

life determine the use we make of biblical texts, the type of reading we favor, and the rules we apply (if only the distinction between a New Testament and an Old Testament). Christian readings of the Bible are inseparable from these contexts. The role of tradition deserves to be reconsidered in these terms. The same goes for the "inner witness of the Holy Spirit" in the context of a Christian life. In any case, this "contextual sensitivity" of the meaning of the biblical text must not be set against its inspiration: in these very diverse uses of the letter of the biblical text, believers hear and read the Word of God in the present tense.

THESIS 6: INTERPRETATION SHOULD NOT BE GIVEN TOO MUCH CREDIT

It is important, as Wittgenstein does, to distinguish carefully between the sign, which can be interpreted, and the meaning, which cannot. Saying to someone who has just arrived for a meeting, "There's coffee on the table," does not need to be interpreted (if at least the visitor knows the use of coffee, which is likely). Ordinary language performs its function correctly, and the visitor immediately understands the sentence. It is the philosophers who introduce difficulties, believing they see ambiguities to be removed to reach timeless meaning where there is only sensitivity to context.

Jesus' words in Matthew 5:3, "Blessed are the poor in spirit, for theirs is the kingdom of heaven," can bless a child without necessarily requiring a few years' study of the Galilean context of Jesus' preaching (or of the *Sitz im Leben*, the cultural and social context in which Matthew's gospel was written). Scholars will undoubtedly be able to enrich our understanding of the verse. The difficulty lies not in interpreting the phrase, as if it were a coded language, but in putting it into practice.

If we insist on talking about interpretation, then it does not mean replacing one symbol with another but identifying the context and life forms that give meaning to words. In the Gospels, the Pharisees never understand Jesus' parables (Luke 18:34; John 10:6): this does not mean that Jesus speaks a coded language, but it is a symptom of their closure to the coming kingdom.

THESIS 7: WE MUST NEITHER REDUCE THE TEXT TO ITS INTERPRETATION, NOR BELIEVE WE CAN REACH A SINGLE, DEFINITIVE MEANING

The appeal to a community of interpretation is neither a reduction of the text to its interpretation, nor a definitive solution to the diversity of readings. On the first point, it seems to me that the suspicion we are reducing the text to its interpretation by readers is linked to an overvaluation of the role of interpretation, which we have just contested: this overvaluation consists in taking the plurality of results of reading practices for a diversity of the text's meaning. On the second point, the objection[58] can be formulated as follows: appealing to a reading community[59] does not account for the divergence of readings of the Bible, unless we make them depend on different practices linked to different communities, but then who will be able to say which reading is the most important? First, dogmatic divergences do not totally determine either Christian practice in general or the practice of Bible reading (e.g., the monastic practice of *lectio divina* in Catholicism has not been contaminated by the "two sources" theory). Second, divergences in Bible reading do not correspond absolutely with confessional divergences (just think of ethical questions, for example). Third, whatever the importance of a canonical reading of the Bible (a reading that reads each text in the context of all the other books that make up the Bible), it does not necessarily lead to the denial of any diversity of theologies within the Scriptures.[60] Finally, it would be astonishing if any principle could tell us, without dogmatism and without being a postulation of principle, which reading of the Bible is the right one. No reading of the Bible has the status of a final reading.

One of the finest refutations of a conception of the Bible as representation is undoubtedly provided by Ezekiel 3:1–4: "He said to me, Son of man, eat what you find, eat this scroll, and go, speak to the house of Israel! I opened my mouth, and he made me eat this scroll. He said to me: Son of man, feed your belly and fill your bowels with this scroll I am giving you! I ate it, and it was as sweet as honey in my mouth. Then he said to me: Son of man, go to the house of Israel and tell them my words!" This is a book that you have to eat before you can understand.

FOR FURTHER READING

Abraham, William J. *Canon and Criterion in Christian Theology from the Fathers to Feminism*. Oxford: Oxford University Press, 1998.

Congar, Yves. *Tradition and Traditions: An Historical and a Theological Essay*. New York: Macmillan, 1967.

58. "Commentary is our drug. Like sleepwalkers, we are protected from the often harsh and imperious radiance of naked presence by the soporific drone of the journalist or theorist." G. Steiner, *Réelles présences. Les arts du sens*. Folio Essais (Paris: Gallimard, 1994), 73.

59. A perusal of a few recent authoritative theological dictionaries, in French, German, or English, quickly reveals that the entry on inspiration has either disappeared altogether or has been briefly dealt with, the essential being developed at best in an entry on Scriptures or the Word of God.

60. For a recent claim to theological interpretation of the Bible, see, in this volume, Anthony Thiselton, "Biblical Hermeneutics and Meaning," sec. 6.9.

Dahan, Gilbert. *L'Exégèse chrétienne de la Bible en Occident médiéval, XIIe-XIVe siècles.* Paris: Cerf, 1999.

Levering, Matthew. *Participatory Biblical Exegesis: A Theology of Biblical Interpretation.* Notre Dame, IN: University of Notre Dame Press, 2008.

Olhausen, William P. "Towards a Relational Hermeneutic: An Investigation in Historical Pragmatics with Special Reference to the Appropriation of Speech Act Theory in the Biblical and Theological Hermeneutics of Anthony Thiselton." PhD diss., University of Liverpool, 2007.

Rahner, Karl, and Joseph Ratzinger. *Revelation and Tradition*. Quaestiones Disputatae 17. New York: Herder and Herder, 1966. (Original edition: *Offenbarung und Überlieferung.* Fribourg: Herder, 1965.)

Steiner, George. *Real Presences: Is There Anything in What We Say?* London: Faber and Faber, 1989.

Theobald, Christoph. *Histoire du Concile Vatican II.* Vol. 5. Paris: Cerf, 2005.

Vanhoozer, Kevin J. *Biblical Authority after Babel. Retrieving the Solas in the Spirit of Mere Protestant Christianity*. Grand Rapids: Brazos, 2016.

CHAPTER 5

The Bible

A Foundational Text for Christian Ethics

Karsten Lehmkühler

INTRODUCTION

How can the Bible be used in Christian ethics? There is no doubt that question is one of the most important questions in theological ethics. For it is precisely the constant reference to the biblical texts, understood as the foundational texts of the Christian faith, and to the tradition that derives from them, that justifies the use of the adjective *Christian* in the formula *Christian ethics*. For Protestant ethics in particular, the problem arises against the backdrop of *sola scriptura*, by Scripture alone, which marks, in the form of the famous "scriptural principle," the approach to *all* doctrinal questions, including morality. This principle stipulates that the books of the Old and New Testament "constitute the only rule and guiding principle according to which all teachings and teachers are to be evaluated and judged."[1]

At the same time, it is a difficult and controversial issue in the field of theological ethics: the most diverse and contradictory positions claim to be based on

1. *Formula of Concord* (1577), in *The Book of Concord: The Confessions of the Evangelical Lutheran Church*, ed. Robert Kolb and Timothy J. Wengert (Minneapolis: Fortress, 2000), 486.

biblical texts, and the hermeneutical question of applying texts that are 2,000 years old (or more) to modern ethical issues remains open.

We are currently witnessing a new interest in these questions, reflected in a large number of publications on the subject. Recent discussion often refers to seminal works from the 1970s and '80s, such as James F. Gustafson's important article, "The Place of Scripture in Christian Ethics: A Methodological Study,"[2] the book of Bruce C. Birch and Larry L. Rasmussen, *Bible and Ethics in the Christian Life*,[3] first published in 1976 and recently reissued in a new version, written by four authors and entitled *Bible and Ethics in the Christian Life: A New Conversation*,[4] as well as the book *What Are They Saying about Scripture and Ethics?* by William Spohn.[5] In 2015, Bruce C. Birch published a relevant bibliography of more than 200 titles.[6] The German-speaking world has also seen lively debates on these issues, as illustrated by the proceedings of conferences and thematic issues of journals.[7]

The current debate includes not only ethicists and systematic theologians but also exegetes of the Old and the New Testament, who comment on the implicit or explicit ethics of the texts in question and, sometimes, also on the possible applicability of these rules and values within Christian ethics today. In this way, exegetes and ethicists enter into a fascinating and promising debate. For example, one discusses the question of whether the canon of biblical texts bears witness to a centre, to one or more central themes and values that would still be able to guide our current ethical reflection. An example of this is the recent work on *Biblical Ethics and Application*, edited by R. Zimmermann and S. Joubert.[8] A good overview of the different possibilities (and limits) of ethical

---

2. James M. Gustafson, "The Place of Scripture in Christian Ethics: A Methodological Study," in *The Use of Scripture in Moral Theology*, ed. Charles E. Curran, A. McCormick, Ramsey (New York: Paulist, 1984), 151–77.

3. Bruce C. Birch and Larry L. Rasmussen, *Bible and Ethics in the Christian Life* (Minneapolis: Augsburg, 1976).

4. Bruce C. Birch, Jacqueline E. Lapsey, Cynthia Moe-Lobeda, and Larry L. Rasmussen, *Bible and Ethics in the Christian Life: A New Conversation* (Minneapolis: Fortress, 2018).

5. William Spohn, *What Are They Saying about Scripture and Ethics*, 2nd ed. (New York: Paulist, 1989).

6. Bruce C. Birch, "Biblical Studies: Ethics," *Oxford Online Bibliographies*, last updated March 10, 2015, https://doi.org/10.1093/OBO/9780195393361-0093.

7. For example: Marco Hofheinz and Frank Mathwig, eds., *Wie kommt die Bibel in die Ethik? Beiträge zu einer Grundfrage theologischer Ethik* (Zürich: Theologischer, 2011); Themenheft, "Theologische Ethik und biblische Exegese," *Zeitschrift für Evangelische Ethik* 55, no. 4 (2011); Marianne Heimbach-Steins, Georg Steins, eds., *Bibelhermeneutik und Christliche Sozialethik* (Stuttgart: Kohlhammer, 2012); Christoph Breitsameter and Stephan Goertz, eds., *Bibel und Moral: Ethische und Exegetische Zugänge*, Jahrbuch für Moraltheologie 2 (Freiburg, Basel, Wien: Herder), 2018.

8. Ruben Zimmermann and Stephan Joubert, eds., *Biblical Ethics and Application: Purview, Validity, and Relevance of Biblical Texts in Ethical Discourse*, WUNT 384 (Tübingen: Mohr Siebeck, 2017).

interpretations of biblical texts can be found in the important article "The Bible and Ethics: Pathways for Dialogue" by Volker Rabens, published online in 2017 and, in a more complete version, in 2021.[9] Concerning interdisciplinary approaches, see also the anthology *Key Approaches to Biblical Ethics. An Interdisciplinary Dialogue*, published in 2021.[10]

In the remainder of this chapter, we shall proceed in four parts. First, with the help of concrete examples, we will address the question of *hermeneutical rules* in relation to the use of the Bible for Christian ethics. How can we avoid, on the one hand, a literalism that does not respect the cultural difference between the time of a biblical text and our own? And how can we prevent, on the other hand, an interpretation that is satisfied with the mere formulation of certain general principles (such as loving one's neighbour) without reflecting on the concrete rules that, according to the biblical text, derive from these principles?

In the other three parts, we will then turn to the *three major moral theories* that are currently discussed, not only in theology but also in moral philosophy, namely *deontological* ethics, *consequentialist* ethics, and *virtue* ethics.[11] Our question will be whether the Bible can nourish and guide each of these ethical approaches. Final considerations will conclude the study.

ARE THERE ANY RULES FOR THE APPROPRIATE USE OF THE BIBLE IN ETHICS?

THE PROBLEM

The authors of *Bible and Ethics in the Christian Life* rightly begin their reflection with a *two-part consensus*, affirming two central theses: "Christian ethics is not synonymous with biblical ethics," and "the Bible is somehow formative and normative for Christian ethics."[12] In fact, it is the systematic use of the Bible that makes ethics *Christian* ethics. Biblical texts have a *normative* value: they contain rules, values and aims that, for Christian ethics, guide and determine moral positions and decisions. They also have *formative* value since

9. Volker Rabens, "The Bible and Ethics: Pathways for Dialogue," *In die Skriflig* 1, no. 3 (2017): a2138. https://doi.org/10.4102/ids.v51i3.2246; Volker Rabens, "Inspiring Ethics: A Hermeneutical Model for the Dialogue between Biblical Texts and Contemporary Ethics," in *Key Approaches to Biblical Ethics: An Interdisciplinary Dialogue*, ed. Volker Rabens, Jacqueline N. Grey, and Mariam Kamell Kovalishyn (Boston: Brill, 2021), 80–126.

10. Rabens, Grey, and Kovalishyn, eds., *Key Approaches to Biblical Ethics.*

11. There are still other moral theories, such as value ethics, but our discussion here is limited to the three major theories mentioned.

12. Birch, Lapsey, Moe-Lobeda, and Rasmussen, *Bible and Ethics in the Christian Life*, 3.

they are the founding texts of the Christian community, texts that are read, meditated, and preached upon in Christian worship as well as in personal piety. In this way, they shape the vision of the world, the habits, and, ultimately, the character of the believer.

At the same time, Christian ethical reflection is not nourished by the Bible alone, and *sola scriptura* cannot mean that nothing outside the biblical texts should come into play in Christian reflection. The biblical texts have given rise to a whole Christian tradition over the centuries, a tradition that interprets and continues the biblical witness. Furthermore, Christian ethics cannot ignore today's context, with its own questions (often unknown in biblical times), its modern scientific knowledge, and its culture that, generally, differs considerably from that of the biblical text.

Moreover, the Bible is not primarily a manual of moral rules. On the contrary, apart from the Old Testament laws found mainly in the books of Exodus and Leviticus (with some repetitions in Deuteronomy), direct moral instructions do not occupy much space. Instead, we find stories and prophecies, poetry and, in the epistolary literature of the New Testament, doctrinal developments. Finally, the biblical texts were written over a period of several centuries, after a long history of oral tradition, and so we find different cultural and social contexts and, sometimes, different moral phenomena within the Bible itself. The question of polygamy, accepted in some Old Testament accounts but excluded in the New Testament, is a well-known example.

Can we establish hermeneutical rules that will enable us to make reasonable and judicious use of biblical texts for modern Christian ethics? Together with Volker Rabens,[13] I would like to distinguish between rules concerning *cultural differences* and rules concerning the existence of a *biblical canon*.

BIBLICAL AND MODERN CULTURES

It is clear that certain biblical texts bear the mark of cultural data that are so profoundly different from our own culture that we must speak of a manifest contradiction.

One of the most frequently cited examples is the discourse on slavery. In both testaments, slavery is an institution that is hardly questioned. Certain Old Testament laws regulate proper behavior towards slaves. While a certain protection of the slave can be observed (which may be surprising in the context of the time when these texts were written), slavery itself is accepted, and the slave may suffer violent acts from his master, as we read in Exodus

13. Cf. Rabens, "The Bible and Ethics," *passim*.

21:20–21:[14] "Anyone who beats their male or female slave with a rod must be punished if the slave dies as a direct result, but they are not to be punished if the slave recovers after a day or two, since the slave is their property."

In the New Testament, slaves are exhorted to "obey your earthly masters with respect and fear" (Eph 6:5). No one today would deduce from this that slavery is an institution willed by God. On the contrary, the Christian subversion of this institution can already be seen in Paul's advice to Philemon that his slave Onesimus may no longer be considered as a slave, "but better than a slave, as a dear brother" (Phlm 16), and above all in the affirmation that in Christ there is "neither slave nor free" (Gal 3:28).[15]

A first rule can be deduced from this: the use of the Bible in the field of ethics must take into account any "cultural conformity and cultural limitation"[16] of the author in question. Certain statements cannot be transferred to the present day as moral instructions. The thorny question is how today's reader will be able to differentiate between culturally limited statements and those that seem to retain their full importance for Christian ethics at all times. From the outset, it can be said that this is one of the most difficult (and disputed) tasks of Christian ethics, which will again require listening, research, and joint reflection within a community. Some help can be found in the reflections on the biblical canon (see the following section).

A text marked by cultural limitations can *nevertheless* have a contemporary significance. There may be an aim, an important intention that is expressed through culturally limited ethical advice. Rabens gives the example of the Pauline exhortation "Greet one another with a holy kiss" (Rom 16:16), an exhortation that is also found in four other New Testament texts (1 Cor 16:20; 2 Cor 13:12; 1 Thess 5:26; 1 Pet 5:14). Admittedly, this is a piece of advice rooted in the prevailing culture, and Christians of all cultures will not be required to opt for this way of greeting each other. However, it is clear that Paul is appropriating a well-known gesture and turning it into an act that will be significant for the life of the Christian community. According to Rabens, the idea behind the apostle's exhortation was probably "to establish a (ritualized) gesture that expresses the belonging to a kinship-like group on a one-to-one level in the form of a warm-hearted greeting."[17] This aim remains as important as ever for the Christian community today, and we could add some stimulating reflections on

14. Quoted by Rabens, "The Bible and Ethics," 2. Biblical texts are quoted according to NIV.

15. Cf. also the condemnation of "slave traders" in 1 Tim 1:10, as well as the obligation to free a "Hebrew servant" after six years in Exod 21:2.

16. Rabens, "The Bible and ethics," 5.

17. Rabens, "The Bible and Ethics," 4.

the warm welcome and living together within Christian parishes (without necessarily repeating the same gesture as the one mentioned by the apostle). As a hermeneutical rule of thumb, we can remember that in some cases, "the justifications are weightier than the rule *qua* rule,"[18] or, in other words, that "that the purpose behind a biblical command carries greater weight than the cultural particulars of its application in the biblical context."[19] In the same vein, M. Beintker emphasizes, with regard to New Testament parenesis,[20] that it is the *approach chosen* that is exemplary for us, not the concrete state of ethical reflection, and he formulates the following rule: "The more specifically a norm is formulated, the more likely it is that it can be relativized. The more universal a normative requirement, the more likely its unlimited validity."[21]

Notably, a biblical author can also turn *against* the culture of his time and formulate ethical demands and values that contradict current opinion. The love of the enemy, demanded by Christ in the Sermon on the Mount, is an example of this. In such cases, a universal significance that goes beyond the historical context of the time is particularly likely.[22]

THE BIBLICAL CANON AND HOW TO READ IT

The biblical canon "functions as a framework of interpretive control" since it presents as a whole "the ongoing activity of God."[23] Certain biblical passages can shed light on others that deal with the same issue, which the Reformers already referred to as a phenomenon of intrabiblical interpretation (*sacra scriptura sui ipsius interpres*), a principle that also relates to ethical reflection.

We can then legitimately ask whether there are *central values* in the canon of biblical writings that play a decisive role in ethical reflection and can therefore help in the discussion of a concrete ethical issue. Such a phenomenon may be called "canonical centrality," and one could speak of "overarching trajectories" that mark the biblical witness in general.[24] We also observe that certain concrete

---

18. Charles H. Cosgrove, *Appealing to Scripture in Moral Debate: Five Hermeneutical Rules* (Grand Rapids: Eerdmans, 2002), 50, quoted in Rabens, "The Bible and Ethics," 5.

19. Rabens, "The Bible and Ethics," 5.

20. The term *parenesis* designates the exhortative parts of New Testament texts; they are found, for example, at the end of Paul's letters.

21. Michael Beintker, "Die Verbindlichkeit biblischer Aussagen für die ethische Entscheidungsfindung der Christen," in *Sexualität – Lebensformen – Liebe*, ed. Wilfried Härle and Reiner Preul, Marburger Jahrbuch VII (Marburg: Elwert, 1995), 130.

22. Such universal importance is likely but not automatically given. Rabens, "The Bible and Ethics," 8, gives the example of certain laws of purity that do not seem to fit in with the prevailing culture of the time but do not lend themselves to universal application.

23. Birch, Lapsey, Moe-Lobeda, and Rasmussen, *Bible and Ethics in the Christian Life*, 84–85.

24. For "overarching trajectories," see Birch, Lapsey, Moe-Lobeda, and Rasmussen, *Bible and Ethics in the Christian Life*, 66. For "canonical centrality," see Rabens, "The Bible and Ethics," 9.

ethical assessments appear in *different* parts of the Bible, particularly in the Old *and* New Testaments; this would be the phenomenon of a "canonical consistency."[25] Consistency is not necessarily central. For example, slavery is accepted in both Testaments, without playing a dominant role. The notion of canonical centrality is therefore more important; and *if centrality and canonical consistency coincide, the ethical assessment in question is particularly important.* We can also add the criterion of *intracanonical progression*: when certain moral practices of the Old Testament, such as polygamy, are abandoned in the New Testament, New Testament ethics will carry more weight for Christian ethics.

It is not surprising that, in this context, the *double commandment of love* is often mentioned as a central biblical theme. According to Jesus, it can be found as a summary of the Old Testament law (cf. Mark 12:28, which combines Deut 6:4–5 and Lev 19:18). This is why it has become a general hermeneutical rule, stipulating that "every ethical determination must ultimately be able to be verified before the double commandment of love."[26] But other values and commandments are also eminent candidates, such as the Golden Rule, justice and mercy, care for the poor, the vulnerable, and the weakest, human liberation (with the central motif of the exodus), or, according to some, "the flourishing of all creation and all humanity."[27]

Considering these central themes is certainly important, and we can imagine cases where the values mentioned can guide concrete ethical choices in our modern societies: the debate on the situation of immigrants is a telling example. However, for other questions of applied ethics, their use seems more problematic. What, for example, is the case with preimplantation genetic diagnosis? Should we argue for the protection of every embryo in the name of the principles of the preservation of human life and the concern for vulnerable life or in favour of the possibility, for the couples concerned, of avoiding a high-risk pregnancy in the name of the principle of mercy? The answer will depend on the respective weight given to the various principles mentioned and on their applicability (always debated within the community) to such concrete cases.

Lutherans also refer to Luther's famous "*Was Christum treibet*" ("What conveys Christ") as one of the key readings. For the Reformer, the purpose of this reading key was to place justification by Christ at the centre of all theology and thus to combat any tendency to make works a condition of salvation.

25. For this terminology, see Rabens, "The Bible and Ethics," 8–9.

26. Beintker, "Die Verbindlichkeit biblischer Aussagen," 134.

27. Birch, Lapsey, Moe-Lobeda, and Rasmussen, *Bible and Ethics in the Christian Life*, 68.

This key prohibits making Christian ethics a path to salvation. Nevertheless, it will be difficult to use the same key to decide on concrete ethical questions.[28]

It therefore seems more promising, when faced with questions of different spheres of *applied ethics* (such as family ethics, economic ethics, bioethics), to look for consistency and canonical centrality not only in the form of *general principles* but also with a view to *certain areas of human life*: Are there, *for this or that sphere of human life*, key orientations that mark the biblical testimonies? Family ethics is a good example here. Even though different historical forms of marriage are present in different texts of the Bible, we can see that marital fidelity, prohibition of adultery and mutual concern between spouses are central and recurring themes.[29] There is no doubt that these are fundamental principles of Christian marriage ethics. Such specific biblical values, which play a central role in biblical testimonies concerning a *certain* sphere of human life, must guide applied ethics in Christian theology.

THE BIBLE AND THE THREE MORAL THEORIES

To make further progress in the reflection on a relevant use of the Bible in ethics, and on rules likely to help us in this matter, we need to take into account the different possible approaches in the field of ethics. Today, there are three major moral theories: the *deontological* approach, the *teleological* (or consequentialist) approach, and the *virtue* ethics approach.

In any human action, three different elements can be distinguished: the *agent*, the *action*, and the *result*. The *deontological* approach focuses on the *action* to be performed, that is, *the duty* (obligations, actions according to universal principles), by asking: What should I do? Such an approach will put forward moral rules and require obedience to these rules and standards. Immanuel Kant's ethics with his "categorical imperative" is the most famous example. The *teleological* approach focuses on the result of an action; we ask: What is the result of my action? Such consequentialist ethics will be marked by the quest for *the good*, understood as *happiness*. Utilitarianism, a variant of this kind of ethics, would stipulate that an action is good if its result is the greatest happiness for the greatest number of people. Finally, *virtue* ethics will focus on the active person and the formation of his or her *character*, asking: What kind of person should I be?

28. Cf. Karsten Lehmkühler, "L'usage de l'Écriture dans l'éthique appliquée: l'exemple du débat à propos de l'homosexualité," in *Usages et mésusages de l'Écriture: Approches interdisciplinaires de la référence scripturaire*, ed. Daniel Frey, Christian Grappe, and Madeleine Wieger (Strasbourg: Presses universitaires de Strasbourg, 2014), 225–43.

29. Cf. Rabens, "The Bible and Ethics," 9.

These three perspectives need to be *distinguished*, but it is not appropriate to *separate* them radically, to the point of making them necessarily opposing approaches. Rather, *together* they shape concrete ethical reflection, even if it is true that they can sometimes lead to different ethical decisions.[30] This is also true for theological ethics: the unilateral emphasis on just one of these three approaches leads to an impoverishment of ethics. In the *ongoing dialogue* between rules, aims, and quest for virtues, the Christian *ethos* takes shape.

Let us take a closer look at the extent to which the Bible could guide each of these approaches to ethics: Are there *biblical deontology*, *biblical teleology*, and *biblical ethics of virtue*? If so, could we formulate rules for their use when faced with a concrete ethical question?

THE COMMANDMENT: THE BIBLE AND THE DEONTOLOGICAL APPROACH

The deontological approach (i.e., the search for norms and commandments that guide our actions) is probably the best-known approach in Christian ethics. Even as children and adolescents, we learn that the Christian faith implies certain rules of conduct that correspond to biblical requirements. In the catechisms of the Reformers, for example, the reader learns about the Ten Commandments as a founding text of Christian ethics, as well as the rules of conduct that follow from them. Other texts in the Bible also give direct commands or exhortations, such as the Sermon on the Mount and the parenetic passages of the New Testament epistles.

The Decalogue is mostly formulated in the form of prohibitions and, in the case of only two commandments, in the form of positive commandments (sanctifying the Sabbath and honouring one's parents). In particular, the prohibitions of the Decalogue have often encouraged Christian ethics to focus on rules and norms. From this point of view, Christian ethics explains, with the help of concrete commandments, what *not* to do. Catechisms always pay attention to this *prohibitive* aspect of the law. The law is a shield that prevents evil, and this inhibition of evil is facilitated by prohibitions: *you shall not kill; you shall not commit adultery*, and so on.

This prohibitive aspect has often been linked to the "first use" (*usus primus*)

30. Cf. the remark in Birch, Lapsey, Moe-Lobeda, and Rasmussen, *Bible and Ethics in the Christian Life*, 190: "But however elegant the theories, we still feel the tug and tensions of all three moral realities – character, consequences, and duty – often without settled resolution. That should show us that no one of these approaches itself captures the whole."

of the law according to Luther,[31] which is the *political* use: the prohibition of evil makes it possible, for society as a whole, to live together. We have to underline the importance of such rules. This is why every human society has such catalogues of deontological rules. However, it would be wrong to limit the prohibitive force of the biblical commandments to the sphere of the common good and politics. This force also acts in the life of every Christian (and if we want to, we can call this force, as in Calvinist theology, a "third use" of the law): the commandment prevents evil in the life of the individual Christian also. We should not, therefore, denigrate the deontological approach within Christian ethics or diminish the importance of the law in the theological sense of the term: these are concrete moral rules that mark out the path that leads to the good.[32]

Nevertheless, it is also important to remember the limits of the moral rules in the Bible, as we set out earlier. First, like any historical text, these rules were formulated in a certain historical context that is no longer ours, and it is important to consider this historical context. This is obvious if we think, for example, of the commandment requiring the sanctification of the Jewish Sabbath. Christian ethics appropriated this commandment but applied it to the Christian Sunday. We should also remember that the last commandment, prohibiting covetousness, mentions another man's wife in a list of his possessions, which could possibly indicate that at the time the text was written, the husband had property rights over his wife.[33] If this interpretation is correct, this is another example of the importance of distinguishing between the essential aim of a moral statement and its concrete formulation and justification.[34]

Second, it is obvious that the biblical commandments cannot give a precise answer for every concrete situation. They are guidelines, but they do not predetermine any future ethical decision. A certain wisdom or prudence is therefore required in applying these rules – and the Greek philosophers already knew that prudence is a very precious gift, without which moral decisions cannot be relevant. What does it mean, for example, to "honour one's parents" in a concrete situation? In this sense, the theologian Karl Barth emphasised that "the Ten Commandments do not contain any direct commands, but only prohibitions

31. For Calvin, this is the second use.

32. From this point of view, it is regrettable that some comments devalue the deontological approach within theology, suggesting that an approach based on virtue ethics is necessarily superior. Cf., e.g., Birch, Lapsey, Moe-Lobeda, and Rasmussen, *Bible and Ethics in the Christian Life*, 138, where the understanding of the formative power of the Bible in terms of its "rules for living perceived as God's rules" is devalued in relation to formation within the community, through its "grand story."

33. Cf. Rabens, "The Bible and Ethics," 5.

34. On the importance of the Torah for Christian ethics, see "Torah et éthique," *Revue des Sciences Religieuses* 82, 2008, no. 3 (thematic issue, ed. Jan Joosten and Karsten Lehmkühler).

or rather delimitations."[35] Therefore, according to Barth, the Decalogue is more like "the indication of a definite sphere," "a framework and programme of the divine action and corresponding human conduct."[36] The faithful orients his actions according to this framework, but the individual decision will depend on a "concrete commandment" that will only be revealed in the given situation.

Let us take the example of lying: Does the commandment "Thou shalt not bear false witness against thy neighbour" forbid lying in any situation? Does it require us to tell the truth even if a person's life is at stake – as Kant stipulated in his ethics? Questions like these give us cause for concern, and the text of the commandment alone does not provide the answer. The law provides the rule, the point of reference: you shall not lie. This rule is important, but it cannot take into account all the possible circumstances of human life.

How can we move forward? The second ethical approach, called the teleological approach, provides some orientations.

THE QUEST FOR THE GOOD: THE BIBLE AND THE TELEOLOGICAL APPROACH

Paul formulates a kind of program of Christian teleological ethics (Rom 12:2): "Do not conform to the pattern of this world, but be transformed by the renewing of your mind. Then you will be able to test and approve what God's will is – his good, pleasing and perfect will."

A teleological ethic focuses on a goal, an aim, a vocation: it seeks *the good*. The question is not so much what is *permitted or forbidden*, but what are the *goals to be pursued*. It is important to note that this perspective is present in biblical texts and in the Christian tradition. The most impressive example of teleological thinking may be found in the mouth of Christ himself. Jesus' disciples are criticised by the Pharisees for plucking ears of corn as they walk through the fields (Mark 2:23–27). As this happened on the Sabbath, the Pharisees considered this action as forbidden work, as "unlawful." In a way, they opt for a deontological view and focus on the (rabbinical) rule in question. In his response, Jesus quotes an event from the Old Testament (v. 25–28): "He answered, 'Have you never read what David did when he and his companions were hungry and in need? In the days of Abiathar the high priest, he entered the house of God and ate the

35. Karl Barth, *Church Dogmatics II,2*, § 38, study ed., vol. 12 (Edinburgh: T&T Clark, 2009), 171, which is *Church Dogmatics II,2* (Edinburgh: T&T Clark, 1957), 684. The study edition is the primary source cited.

36. Barth, *Church Dogmatics II,2*, § 38, 172–73.

consecrated bread, which is lawful only for priests to eat. And he also gave some to his companions.' Then he said to them, 'The Sabbath was made for man, not man for the Sabbath. So the Son of Man is Lord even of the Sabbath.'"

In this text, the issue of lawfulness appears twice, in the criticism of the Pharisees and in the mouth of Jesus, who speaks of the consecrated bread. Jesus refers to an astonishing event in the life of David (1 Sam 21): in a case of necessity, David *transgresses* the cultic law of the people of Israel, a law which is found in the Old Testament (cf. Lev 24:9), and Jesus seems to approve this transgression.

"It is unlawful" is a technical formula in the rabbinic interpretation of the Torah. It enables one to break down a commandment into different decrees and, in this way, leads to a casuistry that interprets the commandment for each particular situation. The biblical commandment forbids work on the Sabbath; the decrees are able to specify which actions represent such work and therefore fall under this prohibition.

The negative form of the commandment (i.e., the form of a prohibition) leads one to think that it would be *by avoiding what is prohibited* that man would fulfil his human vocation and the meaning of his life. Ethical reflection would thus boil down to a strategy for avoiding the forbidden action. However, the prohibition aims at something else: *it protects a good*. The commandment on murder protects life, the commandment on adultery protects marriage, and the commandment on theft protects property. The first commandment above all, by the prohibition of idolatry, protects the possibility of having God as one's God and of living in a relationship of trust with God. In this way, Jesus' response gives rise to a kind of "revolution of thought," a kind of *radical reorientation*: the commandment wants us to discover a good, a possibility and a vocation of human life: "The Sabbath was made for man, not man for the Sabbath." *Human beings are not created to keep the commandments*. They have commandments to *discover the gifts that God offers and to learn living with and through those gifts*. This opens up a new perspective on the Decalogue, one that invites us to discover the goodness of a life with God, the goodness of rest, the goodness of solidarity between generations, the goodness of bodily life, the goodness of marriage, the goodness of a life in truth, and the goodness of satisfaction and gratitude.

The teleological approach therefore encourages in-depth reflection on the *goods* and *positive values* that are protected by biblical texts. This reflection has a long tradition, and we can refer once again to the texts of the Reformation. The interpretation of the Decalogue in the various catechisms of the Reformers is entirely consistent with this *positive reading*. Luther's *Small Catechism* is a good example: each commandment of the Decalogue is explained in a single sentence.

Luther begins by emphasising the prohibition of certain actions and then leads on to a new discovery of what the commandment can produce in the life of the Christian. Let us take again the example of lying, that is, the commandment concerning false witness: "You shall not bear false witness against your neighbor. What does this mean? We should fear and love God, so that we do not lie about, betray, or slander our neighbor, *but excuse him, speak well of him, and put the best construction on everything*."[37] Clearly, a certain *good* is intended here: the good of true and honest relationships, the attempt to protect the honour and dignity of others. Calvin proceeds in the same way, for example, in his explanation of the Decalogue in his *Institutes of the Christian Religion*.[38]

The example of the Reformers is interesting and promising for the orientation of Christian ethics today. Ethical reflection is not primarily about prohibition. It is about the divine gifts given to human beings and about a "successful life" oriented according to these gifts and values.[39] From this point of view, it can be argued – taking our example of lying again – that the commandment "Thou shalt not bear false witness against thy neighbour" is aimed precisely at *protecting others*, in particular (here is the historical context) by avoiding false testimony against them in court. If we make the prohibition against lying absolute, for example, by demanding the truth even in the face of the murderer asking if his victim is in our house, we distort the purpose of this commandment, turning the truth into a "satanic truth."[40]

In the Matthean account of the ears of corn picked on the Sabbath, Jesus quotes Hosea's adage (Matt 12:7; Hos 6:6): "I desire mercy, not sacrifice." The exegete Matthias Konradt sees this as "the guideline for Matthew's interpretation of the Torah" and says: "In the event of conflict, the demand for mercy takes precedence."[41] He then applies this rule to the strict prohibition of divorce, which can be based on Mark 10:1–11. Konradt explains: "From the point of view of mercy as the main criterion of Christian ethics, it is possible to transform Jesus' words on the Sabbath with a view to marriage: marriage was made for man,

---

37. Martin Luther, *The Small Catechism*, 1529, emphasis added. Quoted according to https://els.org/beliefs/luthers-small-catechism/the-ten-commandments/.

38. Cf. John Calvin, *Institutes of the Christian Religion*, ed. John T. McNeill, trans. Ford Lewis Battles (London: SCM, 1961), 2.8.

39. For a consequentialist – and more specifically eudemonist – approach to Christian ethics, see Jean Porter, "Eudaimonism and Christian Ethics: A Scriptural Perspective," *Journal of Religious Ethics* 47 (2019): 23–42.

40. Thus Dietrich Bonhoeffer, in his famous text: "Fragment of an Essay: What Does It Mean to Tell the Truth?" (1943), in *Dietrich Bonhoeffer Works*, vol. 16, *Conspiracy and Imprisonment 1940–1945* (Minneapolis: Fortress, 2010), 601–8.

41. Matthias Konradt, "Neutestamentliche Wissenschaft und Theologische Ethik," *Zeitschrift für Evangelische Ethik* 55, no. 4 (2011): 280.

not man for marriage."[42] He thus argues for the possibility of dissolving a failed marriage and opening up the prospect of a fulfilled life in a new relationship.

Such a teleological interpretation will give rise to debate within the Christian community, as well as between different Christian confessions and denominations. As far as such concrete questions are concerned, we cannot expect a unanimous consensus. However, a consensus is possible on the relevance of the teleological approach in general: following the example of Christ, Christian ethics will seek to find *the good protected by the commandment*, a good that aims to put human beings back on their feet and enable them to live. Faced with a concrete question, the answer has to be sought in common reflection, in renewed listening to the biblical witness, and in the responsibility of each person before God.

BEING FORMED IN THE IMAGE OF CHRIST: THE BIBLE AND VIRTUE ETHICS

Over the last few decades, virtue ethics, long overshadowed by Kantian deontology, has been rediscovered in philosophy and theology, and this is to be welcomed. Virtue ethics focuses on the *character* of the active person. The general idea is as follows: very often, a person's actions and behaviour depend not on a concrete decision but on their habits, way of seeing the world, and character traits. In other words, a person can acquire certain ways of being, dispositions, and abilities: virtues. These virtues become a "second nature" that allows the person to act "naturally" according to their character traits. For example, a truthful and reliable person will no longer ask himself or herself each time whether he or she wants to act according to the virtues of truthfulness and reliability. These virtues have become traits of their character, and the actualisation of these acquired abilities occurs in a quasi-natural way: when the time comes, they will act truthfully and reliably, for example, by keeping a promise, even if it costs them a lot.

Such virtue ethics have been rediscovered in theological ethics. Influenced by the work of Alasdair MacIntyre,[43] Stanley Hauerwas has emphasised the importance of the virtues and character formation for Christian ethics.[44]

42. Konradt, "Neutestamentliche Wissenschaft und Theologische Ethik," 280.

43. Notably Alasdair MacIntyre, *After Virtue. A Study in Moral Theory* (Notre Dame, IN: University of Notre Dame Press, 1981).

44. Cf. Stanley Hauerwas, *Character and the Christian Life: A Study in Theological Ethics* (Notre Dame: University of Notre Dame Press, 1994). Concerning the important role of the Bible for virtue ethics, see also William C. Spohn, "Scripture," in *The Oxford Handbook of Theological Ethics*, ed. G. Meilaender, W. Werpehowski (New York: Oxford University Press, 2005), 93–111.

The link between the Bible and ethics becomes decisive here. For character formation requires two important elements: *texts* that bear witness to a specific story and a *community* in which these texts and this story are read and meditated upon and in which they figure as an authority that guides the whole life of the individual and the community. The central question for the members of a community of faith could be formulated as follows: "What character and conduct is in keeping with who we are *as a people of God?*"[45] From this perspective, one can say that the character of the faithful is formed within the Christian community, a community that reads, meditates on, and discusses the biblical texts. In this context, the *liturgy* of worship also plays an important role.[46]

Hauerwas argues for ethics that is truly and properly *theological*, that is, *linked to the biblical narrative.*[47] This narrative also calls for a form of *fidelity*: the Christian community remains faithful to the narrative on which it is based and therefore, above all, faithful to Christ, to his example, and to the relationship with him that is expressed in the various worship practices. In this way, Hauerwas emphasises the importance of the life of the church and the communal nature of the faith: the Christian community is a living social body, a "*distinctive people.*"

Let us try to be more concrete: What virtues may be encouraged from reading the Bible and will therefore be important for the Christian community? It goes without saying that we could name a large number of character traits that may be forged by the biblical stories. Here we briefly present, by way of example, three virtues that seem fundamental to us.

The message of the Bible, particularly the gospel proclaiming the grace given to us in Christ, encourages the development of a character trait that might be called the *courage of truth.* This virtue relates first and foremost to *truth to ourselves.* The quest for truth to oneself is undoubtedly a human characteristic, including the quest for authenticity. But how do we know who we are? How can we assess the motives and justifications for our actions? First of all, the Bible opens up the possibility of trusting in *divine* knowledge: *another* knows me and declares me righteous (cf. Ps 139; 1 Cor 4:3–5; 1 John 3:19–21).

Moreover, the courage of truth relates to the *connection between truthfulness and forgiveness.* Already on a human level, it is easier to be true in a relationship when we know that the other person is prepared, in that specific relationship,

45. Birch, Lapsey, Moe-Lobeda, and Rasmussen, *Bible and Ethics in the Christian Life*, 17.

46. See Vigen Guroian, "Bible and Ethics: An Ecclesial and Liturgical Interpretation," *The Journal of Religious Ethics* 18 (1990): 129–57.

47. Cf. his reference work: Stanley Hauerwas, *The Peaceable Kingdom: A Primer in Christian Ethics* (Notre Dame: University of Notre Dame Press, 1983).

to *forgive*. Knowing oneself to be accepted often corresponds with knowing oneself to be forgiven. Hannah Arendt spoke impressively of this uniquely human capacity to forgive and, in doing so, to *come to terms with the past*.[48] Forgiveness frees us from the past and breaks the irreversibility of our actions. It also frees us from the fear of facing up to our faults: it becomes easier *to assume our existence*, our responsibility, because we know we are accepted and forgiven. For the Christian faith (particularly for the Protestant tradition), there is an essential link here with the doctrine of *justification by faith alone* (*sola fide*): it is not my works that reveal to me the truth about myself; rather, knowledge of myself depends on a word from outside, a word that no one can give to himself or herself, the word announcing the forgiveness of sins. Therefore, the benevolence of God enables a new openness and truthfulness with regard to oneself.[49]

In the context of the New Testament, this courage of truth is called *parresia*, a term that is often translated as "freedom" or "assurance," but which primarily means freedom of speech, the freedom to speak frankly to God and to others. A believer "may approach God with freedom (*parresia*) and confidence" (Eph 3:12), and Christ's disciples can speak "the word of God boldly (with *parrhesia*)" (Acts 4:31).[50] Truthfulness *coram Deo* ("before God") gives rise to *greater freedom of speech in relationships with others*. Those who know that they are accepted by God will depend less on the evaluations and judgements of others and will be able to develop truthfulness in their relationships.

A second virtue encouraged by the biblical narrative and likely to be embodied in the life of the Christian community is *generosity*. The Bible proclaims the generous gift of God's love. Those who have received this love will be able to show generosity to themselves and to others. We might think here of the parables of the kingdom of God, which praise divine abundance, such as the parable of the mustard seed (Matt 13:31–35), the parable of the prodigal son, which describes the generosity of the father (Luke 15:11–32), or the parable of the unforgiving debtor (Matt 18:21–35), which provides a counterexample. Such generosity could affect the most diverse aspects of human life: generosity in love, generosity in our relationship with money, but also generosity in our way

48. Hannah Arendt, *The Human Condition* (1958), 2nd ed. (Chicago: University of Chicago Press, 1998), 243–47.

49. The apostle Paul speaks of this state of "being known" in 1 Cor 13:12b: "Now I know in part; then I shall know fully, even as I am fully known." Cf. also 1 Cor 8:3: "But whoever loves God is known by God." And Gal 4:9: "But now that you know God – or rather are known by God." See also, against self-judgment, 1 Cor 4:3–4: "I care very little if I am judged by you or by any human court; indeed, I do not even judge myself. My conscience is clear, but that does not make me innocent. It is the Lord who judges me."

50. For the *parresia*, cf. Karsten Lehmkühler, "Les vertus de la vérité," *Revue d'Histoire et de Philosophie Religieuses* 99 (2019): 138–39.

of thinking, a kind of *intellectual hospitality* that welcomes the truth of others like a guest who first asks for my respect.[51]

Finally, the biblical witness encourages us to develop another character trait, that of empathy and *concern for the weak and the most disadvantaged*. In the New Testament, Christ lives his life for others. He is Christ *pro nobis* ("for us"). In particular, he turns towards the despised, the sinners, the sick, the excluded, and those who cannot defend themselves. This attitude has a profound effect on Christian ethics and is destined to become a character trait of the Christian. Dietrich Bonhoeffer spoke of this "being for the other" of Christ, and he affirmed that through *participation* in Christ Christians can become, in turn, a *person for others*.[52]

The virtue of sensitivity and concern for the most vulnerable mark various *spheres* of applied ethics, not only economic and political ethics but also, for example, bioethics, where this virtue leads us never to neglect concern for life in gestation, for the sick or disabled, and for people at the end of life – all situations of particular vulnerability.

The three virtues mentioned – courage of truth, generosity, and concern for the vulnerable – are not specifically Christian. However, within the Christian community, they are rooted in a particular narrative, that of God's history with human beings, a history that culminates in the proclamation of divine grace in Christ. From this centre of the Christian faith, they derive their specific colour and shape and in particular their power to shape the character of the Christian.

CONCLUSION

Christian ethics is marked profoundly by the Bible: by the *norms and obligations* that it transmits, by the understanding of the *good* that is expressed in biblical texts, and by the *character traits* that the Bible elicits through its stories and

51. This virtue of intellectual hospitality plays an important role in the comparative theology of religions. Cf. Klaus von Stosch, *Komparative Theologie als Wegweiser in der Welt der Religionen*, Beiträge zur Komparativen Theologie 6 (Paderborn: Schöningh, 2012), 163–64; the author refers to Catherine Cornille, *The Im-possibility of Interreligious Dialogue* (New York: Crossroad, 2008), 177.

52. Concerning Christ "for me," see Dietrich Bonhoeffer, "Lectures on Christology (Student Notes)," in *Dietrich Bonhoeffer Works*, vol. 12, *Berlin 1932–1933* (Minneapolis: Fortress, 2009), 310–15. The designation of Christ as "the human being for others" is found in his "Outline for a Book," in *Dietrich Bonhoeffer Works*, vol. 8, *Letters and Papers from Prison* (Minneapolis: Fortress, 2010), 501. For Bonhoeffer's idea of participation, see Karsten Lehmkühler, "L'éthique comme participation au Christ: La démarche théologique de Bonhoeffer," in *Dietrich Bonhoeffer: Autonomie, suivance et responsabilité*, ed. Alberto Bondolfi, Denis Müller, and Simone Romagnoli, *Revue d'éthique et de théologie morale*, Hors-série 4 (Paris: Les Éd. du Cerf, 2007), 171–91.

examples of a life with and before God. In this way, the Bible shapes not only our general vision of ethics but also the positions we take and the *concrete* decisions we make (i.e., decisions concerning questions that belong to *applied ethics*).

In these choices, the norms and goods indicated in the Bible act like a *compass* pointing the way. The metaphor of the compass helps us to understand the enduring nature of certain standards and goods named in the Bible. The compass always points north, and the biblical witness points to certain fundamental goods of the Christian community, such as (to take up the Decalogue) intergenerational solidarity, the protection of marriage, and the quest for a life in truth. This orientation towards the key values of the Bible is of paramount importance for the Christian community, and the task of Christian ethics is to give an account of these fundamental orientations.

Every hiker knows that, despite his compass pointing north, he will sometimes have to take a diversion – an unavoidable obstacle will cause him to do so – but he will never forget the direction he has chosen, which leads to the destination. In this way, life can also lead us to take detours, to deviate from the rule. Textbook examples include the "white lie" or self-defence examples where, in a situation of necessity and distress, a commandment or an intended good is not fully assumed. Alongside these classic examples, there are obviously issues that are much more discussed within the Christian community, such as the beginning and end of life, or questions of family and sexual ethics. Whatever we may say about these difficult issues, possible "detours" must not relativize the fundamental duties, goods, and virtues in question, and ethics should not make the case of necessity a new value or rule to follow – just as no one would adjust his compass according to the detours he had to make.

In this way, ethics is the art of discernment (*discretio*) in the face of individual cases. Thomas Aquinas already said, in relation to concrete decisions:

> Practical reason deals with contingent realities, about which human actions are concerned. Therefore, although there is some necessity in the general principles, the more we descend to particular matters, the more we encounter indeterminacy. . . . In matters of action, truth or practical rectitude is not the same for all in its particular applications, but only in its general principles: and where there is the same rectitude in particular actions, it is not equally known to all. . . . And here, the more one descends to particulars the more the indeterminacy grows.[53]

53. Thomas Aquinas, *Summa theologiae*, I-II, q. 94 a. 4, quoted in International Theological Commission, *In Search of Universal Ethic: A New Look at the Natural Law* (Rome, 2009), § 53, https://www.vatican.va/roman_curia/congregations/cfaith/cti_documents/rc_con_cfaith_doc_20090520_legge-naturale_en.html.

The same idea applies to the use of the biblical witness in the face of an individual and concrete ethical decision. This witness indicates the rules, goods, and character traits that mark and inspire Christian existence. The concrete ethical decision is forged by an act of *prudence* (*prudentia*, *phronesis*), by a discernment that weighs up all the elements that mark this unique situation.[54] This prudence itself is a *charism* that develops throughout a life with the Bible, on an individual level as well as in community life. Finally, such an act of prudence, faced with a concrete decision to be taken, always includes a risk, what Bonhoeffer called a *Wagnis*, and the believer, in the end, can only abandon his action, like himself, to God in the confidence that it is God who guides, enlightens, and forgives.[55]

FOR FURTHER READING

Birch, Bruce C., Jacqueline E. Lapsey, Cynthia Moe-Lobeda, and Larry L. Rasmussen. *Bible and Ethics in the Christian Life: A New Conversation*. Fortress: Minneapolis, 2018.

Cosgrove, Charles H. *Appealing to Scripture in Moral Debate: Five Hermeneutical Rules*. Grand Rapids: Eerdmans, 2002.

Lehmkühler Karsten. "L'usage de l'Écriture dans l'éthique appliquée: l'exemple du débat à propos de l'homosexualité." In *Usages et mésusages de l'Écriture: Approches interdisciplinaires de la référence scripturaire*, edited by Frey, Daniel, Grappe, Christian, Wieger, Madeleine, 225–43. Strasbourg: Presses universitaires de Strasbourg, 2014.

Rabens, Volker. "The Bible and Ethics: Pathways for Dialogue." *In die Skriflig* 1, no. 3 (2017): a2138, https://doi.org/10.4102/ids.v51i3.2246.

Rabens, Volker, Jacqueline N. Grey, Mariam Kamell Kovalishyn, eds. *Key Approaches to Biblical Ethics: An Interdisciplinary Dialogue*. Boston: Brill, 2021.

Spohn, William C. "Scripture." In *The Oxford Handbook of Theological Ethics*, edited by G. Meilander and W. Werpehowski, 93–111. New York: Oxford University Press, 2005.

Zimmermann, Ruben, and Stephan Joubert, eds. *Biblical Ethics and Application: Purview, Validity, and Relevance of Biblical Texts in Ethical Discourse*. WUNT 384. Tübingen: Mohr Siebeck, 2017.

---

54. Cf. Renate Kirchhoff, "Ethik in der Bibel – Bibel in der Ethik: über die Verwendung biblischer Texte im ethischen Kontext," *Zeitschrift für Neues Testament* 6, no. 11 (2003): 29, who speaks of a "mature handling [*mündiger Umgang*]" of the biblical text.

55. For the notion of risk, linked to that of freedom and representing one of the elements of a responsible life, see the chapter on "The Structure of Responsible Life," in *Dietrich Bonhoeffer Works*, vol. 6, *Ethics* (Minneapolis: Fortress, 2005), 257–89.

PART 2

The Bible and Its Interpretation

CHAPTER 6

Biblical Hermeneutics and Meaning

Anthony Thiselton

To ask whether a biblical text has meaning or sense and to ask what that sense might be is to engage in the set of explorations known as hermeneutics. Where interpretation denotes the actual process of understanding and expounding texts, hermeneutics asks what we are doing when we interpret texts. It denotes the critical theory on the basis of which we begin to interpret texts, especially biblical texts.

WHAT IS HERMENEUTICS? THREE DIMENSIONS OF THE SUBJECT

The fundamental meaning of *hermeneutics* is *interpretation*, as when Luke writes, "Then beginning with Moses and all the prophets, he (Jesus) interpreted [Gk., *diermēneusen*, or in some manuscripts, *hermēneusen*] to them the things about himself in all the Scriptures" (Luke 24:27).[1] Luke uses as a parallel, "He was opening the Scriptures" (24:32). These verses provide us with a glimpse of what interpretation involves. First, it refers to a specific content, in this case "all the Scriptures." Second, it involves reference to the self: understanding relates to "him" and to "them." Third, meaning and understanding may often transcend a direct and immediate literal reference: How do "all the Scriptures," including

1. Unless otherwise stated, the Bible quotations in this chapter follow the *New Revised Standard Version*.

the Old Testament, speak of Jesus Christ if we cannot transcend the immediate intentions of authors?

To understand the specific content of a biblical text, we need to explore its historical context, its literary genre, the mind of the author, and the circumstances of the utterance. Texts, we shall argue, usually have a determinate and specific meaning. Sometimes a semantic investigation is also necessary. One problem in Christian theology is the danger of generalizing about biblical texts as a whole, as if all biblical texts function in the same way. Part of the purpose of my 1992 book on hermeneutics was to match various hermeneutical models of operation to *various kinds and functions* of biblical texts.[2]

Since hermeneutics comes into play because of the need for interpretation, its second dimension concerns the *interpreter's capacity* for understanding. Many of the biblical writers speak of reading and seeking to understand with blinded eyes or a veiled heart (e.g., Matt 23:16–28; John 12:38–43; 2 Cor 3:14–16). This is why a multitude of specialist scholars in hermeneutics rightly speak of the need for a *preliminary* understanding (German, *Vorverständnis*, often translated *preunderstanding*) before interpretation can begin. It then involves the active interaction or practical engagement between the horizons of an author or text and the horizons which today's reader brings with him.[3]

One of the most widely known examples of the emphasis on preliminary understanding is Rudolf Bultmann's essay, "Is Exegesis without Presuppositions Possible?"[4] He acknowledges that Wilhelm Dilthey (1833–1911) originated the term, drawing it ultimately from Friedrich Schleiermacher (1768–1834), because Dilthey saw that understanding is bound up with the interpreter's life experience. How can we understand a musical or mathematical text, Bultmann asks, unless we have at least a preliminary understanding of music or mathematics? Preunderstanding is integral to all the great hermeneutical writers in the German tradition, including Martin Heidegger, Karl-Otto Apel, and Hans-Georg Gadamer. But it is also recognized by other traditions. We may cite the more linguistic traditions of Paul Ricœur in France and John Searle in America. Searle prefers to speak in linguistic terms of "pre-intentional background."[5]

In the third place, we have spoken of instances where the meaning of a text

2. Anthony C. Thiselton, *New Horizons in Hermeneutics: The Theory and Practice of Transforming Biblical Reading* (London: Harper Collins, 1992).

3. I addressed this in Anthony C. Thiselton, *The Two Horizons: New Testament and Philosophical Description* (Grand Rapids: Eerdmans, 1980).

4. Rudolf Bultmann, "Is Exegesis without Presuppositions Possible?," in *Existence and Faith. Shorter Writings of Rudolf Bultmann* (London: Fontana, 1964), 342–51.

5. John Searle, *Intentionality. An Essay in the Philosophy of Mind* (Cambridge: Cambridge University Press, 1983), 19–20 and 144–59.

transcends the immediate intention of the author. This gave rise in the early church fathers, especially among the Alexandrians, to the notion of allegorical interpretation. Some modern writers have often preferred to use the term *sensus plenior*, or "fuller sense," especially in the context of seeing references to Jesus Christ in the Old Testament. This is still often controversial, but we shall address this issue later. Some, for example Henri de Lubac and Andrew Louth, claim that it constitutes a vital dimension of hermeneutics.[6] Further, hermeneutics raises sociological issues, such as those discussed by Habermas, Apel, Schutz and Luckman, and others.[7]

CAN A TEXT (OR A BIBLICAL TEXT) MEAN WHATEVER WE WANT IT TO MEAN?

Some postmodernist writers maintain that few literary texts have a determinate meaning. Stanley Fish, Richard Rorty, and Paul de Man from America and Roland Barthes, Jacques Derrida, and others from the French tradition have tended in effect to evaporate the stable content of many literary texts. Admittedly, Barthes and Derrida do not claim that the meaning of *all* texts is indefinitely postponed. But in the case of literary texts, their "deconstruction" tends to replace genuine intersubjectivity between authors and readers. They tend to substitute intertextuality between texts. In Derrida's more extreme examples, a text stands under "erasure" and meaning stands under "postponement." This applies not to every utterance in ordinary life but to large tracts of literature.

This subject is complex and cannot be discussed exhaustively here. It owes much in origin to what Ferdinand de Saussure (1857–1913) called "the arbitrary nature of the sign."[8] Saussure writes, "Language is a system of interdependent terms in which the value (*la valeur*) of each term results solely from the simultaneous presence of the others."[9] Meaning is generated by the possibility of alternative choices of words. These may be paradigmatic relations (e.g., opposition between red and green in traffic signals) and syntagmatic relations of adjacent terms from the same field. The concrete act of speech (*la parole*) is

6. Henri de Lubac, *Mediaeval Exegesis*, vol. 1, *The Four Senses of Scripture* (Grand Rapids: Eerdmans, 1998); Andrew Louth, "Return to Allegory," in *Discerning the Mystery* (Oxford: Clarendon, 1983).

7. Jürgen Habermas, *The Theory of Communicative Action*, 2 vol. (Cambridge: Polity, 1987); Karl-Otto Apel, *Understanding and Explanation. A Transcendental-Pragmatic Perspective* (Philadelphia: Westminster, 1981); Alfred Schutz and Thomas Luckman, *The Structures of the Life-World* (London: Heinemann, 1974).

8. Ferdinand de Saussure, *Course in General Linguistics* (London: Owen, 1960), 68.

9. de Saussure, *Course in General Linguistics*, 114.

selected from a potential storehouse of words (*la langue*). There are no pure "givens." In 1931, J. Trier argued, "Only within a field do words convey meaning."[10] In many cases and types of literature, especially in poetry, this approach has advantages.

How, however, does it apply to biblical texts? As Paul Ricœur has pointed out, there are many types of biblical texts, not least differences between prophetic discourse, narrative discourse, prescriptive discourse, wisdom discourse, and hymnic discourse.[11] Admittedly the Psalms and other writings represent poetic discourse, but Ricœur also calls them hymnic discourse. Most are addressed to God and are not wholly indeterminate. Prophetic discourse, he says, "should be taken as the basic referent for a meditation on the idea of revelation. . . . The prophet presents himself as not speaking in his own name, but in the name of another."[12] We cannot separate it, he urges, from its context. In the case of all modes of discourse we find endless variations.

Some narratives, for example, concern specific people, times, and events. Some founding narratives concern Abraham, Moses, David, and the Exodus from Egypt. In the New Testament, the Passion narrative culminating in the crucifixion of Jesus under Pontius Pilate constitutes such a text. No one could emphasize more clearly than Ricœur that biblical narratives are not merely factual report.[13] Their specificity of time and place is essential to many of them. In some, "Confession takes place through narration. . . . God's mark is in history before being in speech. It is only secondarily in speech in as much as this history itself is brought to language in the speech-act of narration."[14]

Kevin Vanhoozer has written a volume largely to attack Derrida's deconstruction as far as biblical literature is concerned.[15] Vanhoozer is passionate about the inapplicability of Derrida's proposals to biblical texts. Under the heading "Undoing Interpretation," he discusses undoing the author, undoing the book, and undoing the reader. He defends the author's intention, attacks indeterminacy, and defends the aims of reading other than for mere enjoyment. He comments, "Derrida's deconstruction of the author is a more or less direct consequence of Nietzsche's announcement of the death of God."[16] He disputes the supposed Kantian legacy (or more accurately, Fichte's legacy) that noth-

10. J. Trier, *Der Deutsche Wortschatz im Sinnbezirk des Verstandes* (Heidelberg: Winter, 1931), 6.
11. Paul Ricœur, *Essays on Biblical Interpretation* (London: SPCK, 1981), 75–90.
12. Ricœur, *Essays on Biblical Interpretation*, 75.
13. Paul Ricœur, *Time and Narrative*, 3 vols. (Chicago: University of Chicago, 1984–88).
14. Ricœur, *Essays on Biblical Interpretation*, 9.
15. Kevin J. Vanhoozer, *Is There a Meaning in This Text?* (Grand Rapids: Zondervan), 199.
16. Vanhoozer, *Is There a Meaning in This Text?*, 48.

ing is "given," and everything is processed by the mind. Some may reply that Vanhoozer overstates his case, but Fichte's and Derrida's effect on biblical interpretation has been severely negative.

This mood of scepticism led to my lecture, published in 2004, *Can the Bible Mean Whatever We Want It to Mean?*[17] In the first part, I traced the change from older questions about the authority of biblical teaching to the subjectivation of what we *take it to mean*, with criticisms that its sixty-six books conveyed only contradictory and ambiguous messages. In the second part, I tried to show that careful and patient exegesis usually resolved alleged "contradictions" into something more profound, often akin to stereoscopic points of view. Among various examples, Robert Alter, a Jewish scholar, has shown how two apparently contradictory accounts of the call of David in 1 Samuel 15–16 describe David's call in one narrative from the point of view of divine call and providence and from a different point of view of "the everyday hurly-burly of human life." The narrator uses stereoscopic lenses.[18] Mikhail Bakhtin has also contributed influentially to the principle of "polyvalent discourse." In the third part, I borrowed Ricœur's term "Doing Away with Idols" to offer a modest critique of much in postmodernism, echoing Richard Bauckham's claim that the Bible is not a "totalizing" system but often a collection of diverse narratives, which hold together a dialectic of coherence and diversity.[19]

Such a countermove is necessary because much literary theory has been influenced first by formalism, then by more radical reader-response theories, and finally by postmodernism, which has often invaded biblical studies without recognition of the distinctive concerns of biblical literature. Admittedly biblical hermeneutics has been enriched by such contributions from literary criticism as A. J. Greimas and Roland Barthes on structuralism and Mikhail Bakhtin on polyphony.[20] But the so-called Yale school in America (e.g., Paul de Man and J. Hillis Miller, following Derrida) tended to focus on exclusively literary texts. Often their contribution to biblical hermeneutics has been marginal.[21]

---

17. Anthony C. Thiselton, *Can the Bible Mean Whatever We Want it to Mean?* (Chester: Chester Academic Press, 2004).

18. Robert Alter, *The Art of Biblical Narrative* (New York: Basic, 1981), 147–53.

19. Richard Bauckham, *Bible and Mission: Christian Witness in a Postmodern World* (Carlisle: Paternoster, 2003).

20. Cf. Gary S. Morson and Caryl Emerson, eds., *Mikhail Bakhtin, Creation of a Prosaics* (Stanford: Stanford University Press, 1990), 13–268.

21. Roger Lundin, Clarence Walhout, and Anthony C. Thiselton, *The Promise of Hermeneutics* (Grand Rapids: Eerdmans, 1999).

THE EARLY CHURCH: ALLEGORICAL, TYPOLOGICAL, AND LITERAL MEANING

The Christian Church inherited various forms of interpretation. Even Judaism was never simply "one thing."[22] Numerically, Hellenistic or Diaspora Judaism eclipsed the "Palestinian" Judaism of the homeland. Further, rabbinic Judaism differed from the Judaism of Qumran (the community that produced the Dead Sea Scrolls). Some Jewish writings represented apocalyptic Judaism. Within rabbinic Judaism the School of Hillel was producing (or would shortly produce) its rules of interpretation.

Rabbi Hillel was born c. 25 BCE in Babylon and formulated seven "rules" (Hebrew, *middoth*) of interpretation. Some of these are mainly logical. For example, the first rule is that the greater includes the lesser. However, the sixth and seventh are genuinely hermeneutical. The sixth concerns finding support for a text from another scripture, and the seventh declares that the meaning depends on its context. Hillel's pupil, Rabbi Ishmael Ben Elisha, expanded these into thirteen rules, and Rabbi Eliezer Ben Jose the Galilean is said to have formulated thirty-two such rules. Rabbi Akiba (AD 50–135) interpreted the Song of Solomon allegorically to denote God's love for Israel. In later years the Mishnah and then the Palestinian and Babylonian Talmuds represented the belief that Scripture applies to every aspect of life. These represented an interpretive supplement to Scripture.

Philo (c. 20 BC–AD 50) notoriously uses allegorical interpretation of Scripture. While he reveres Moses, to whom he was loyal, he also speaks of him as "the great Plato."[23] In expounding the Old Testament, he excludes any "literal meaning" that appears to say anything supposedly unworthy of God or appears to reduce the transcendence of God. For example, Adam cannot be said to "hide" from God (Gen 3:8), for this might seem to reduce God's omniscience. The notion of God's "planting fruit trees" (Gen 2:8–9) would be unacceptable to educated Alexandrian readers and is therefore sheer "silliness." This is an allegory for God's planting virtues in the soul.[24] For Philo, the narrative of the Tower of Babel (Gen 11:1–9) has nothing to do with languages but speaks of divine sovereignty and human folly.[25] Numbers in the Bible seldom denote numerals but denote symbolic qualities.[26]

---

22. Jeremiah Unterman, "Jewish Biblical Interpretation," in this volume.
23. Philo, *On the Life of Moses*, 3.23.
24. Philo, *On Husbandry*, 8–9.
25. Philo, *On the Confusion of Tongues*, 38.
26. Philo, *On Allegorical Interpretation*, 2.1.

Philo turns to Plato's distinction between the physical or earthly and the spiritual or eternal realm as a basis for such interpretation. He wants not only to be loyal to the Old Testament but also to retain the respect of educated Greeks and Romans. We need not look beyond Philo of Alexandria for the use of allegorical interpretation in the early church, especially among the Alexandrian Fathers, Clement, Origen, and Cyril. Henry Chadwick comments, "Of all the non-Christian writers of the first century Philo is the one from whom the historian of emergent Christianity has most to learn."[27] Allegorical interpretation also has an older place of honour among the Greeks. It goes back to Theagenes of Rhegium and Hecataeus in the sixth century BCE and to Metrodorus of Lampsacus in the fifth. Metrodorus understood the tales of deities in Homer to be allegories of parts of the human body or natural forces. Then Zeno (c. 334–262 BCE), founder of the Stoic School, read Hesiod in this way. Even Plato, who held reservations about the overuse of allegorical interpretation, preferring the term *huponoia* ("undermeaning") to allegory, recognized that certain passages in Homer, especially about the conflicts between deities, could not be interpreted literally. The early Stoic philosophers use allegorical interpretation regularly.

It is difficult to say with clarity whether the New Testament writers used allegorical interpretation. Paul the apostle appears to use allegory when he compares Hagar and her son, Ishmael, with Sarah and her son, Isaac, in Galatians 4:21–31, on the basis of Genesis 16:1–16 and 21:1–21. He comments in Greek, *hatina estin allēgoroumena*, which the NRSV translates as "This is an allegory" (v. 24). However, F. F. Bruce comments, "He is not thinking of allegory in the Philonic sense.... He has in mind that form of allegory which is commonly called typology."[28] Otto Michel and Leonhard Goppelt emphatically agree.[29] However, other scholars dissent from this, including notably Andrew Louth.[30] In favour of Bruce's view, Richard Hanson explains that whereas allegory rests on parallels between persons, objects, or ideas, "typology is based on *historical parallels between events.*"[31] Similarly, Ulrich Luz uses the term *typology* when Matthew applies, "Out of Egypt have I called my Son" (Matt 2:15), to his quotation from Hosea 11:1.[32]

---

27. Henry Chadwick, "St. Paul and Philo of Alexandria," *Bulletin of John Rylands Library* 48 (1965), 288, cf. p. 286–307.

28. F. F. Bruce, *The Epistle to the Galatians: A Commentary on the Greek Text* (Grand Rapids: Eerdmans, 1982), 217.

29. Bruce, *The Epistle to the Galatians*, 217.

30. Louth, *Discerning the Mystery*, 138–39.

31. Richard P. C. Hanson, *Allegory and Event: A Study of the Sources and Significance of Origen's Interpretation of Scripture* (London: SCM, 1959), 7 (my italics).

32. Ulrich Luz, *Matthew 1–7: A Commentary* (Minneapolis: Augsburg, 1989), 146–47. Other examples from the New Testament are discussed in Anthony C. Thiselton, *Hermeneutics: An Introduction* (Grand Rapids: Eerdmans, 2009), 76–99.

In the second century, allegorical interpretation can be found in Justin, Irenaeus, and the Gnostic writers. Justin (c. 37–100) understands the narrative of Gen 49:10–11 to be an allegory of Christ.[33] Many Old Testament events, he says, "prefigure" Christ, including Isaiah's prophecy, "A virgin shall conceive."[34] He explicitly uses the term for "types" and "signs" (*sēmeia*) some eighteen times.[35]

Irenaeus (c. 130–c. 200) quotes Isaiah 45:1 to show that "my anointed Cyrus" points to Christ. But Hanson argues that neither Irenaeus nor Justin use allegorical interpretation in the full Alexandrian sense. He regards the parallels between the Old Testament and the cross as typological. Yet in his later work he does use the parable of the Good Samaritan (Luke 10:30–35) more allegorically, seeing the injured man as Adam, the inn as the church, and so on, while the parable of the wedding garment speaks of the Holy Spirit as resting on us (Matt 22:11–13).[36] Many might prefer to leave aside whether we should regard this as allegorical or typological interpretation and simply call it *sensus plenior*, or "fuller sense." We shall return to this subject in section 4.

With the Alexandrian Fathers we enter the world of genuine allegorical interpretation. Clement of Alexandria (c. 150–c. 215) offers a clear example. Hanson observes, "With Clement of Alexandria we reach an author whose allegory is not only Alexandrian but openly and unashamedly Philonic."[37] Because of Clement's partial sympathy with Gnosticism, he delights in finding hidden meanings which he finds everywhere. The tree in the midst of Eden is "divine thought."[38] He prizes a secret tradition in contrast to Irenaeus, who seeks a tradition that is rational and public. However, Clement prepares for his successor, Origen.

Origen (c. 185–c. 254) was known as a creative thinker with a prodigious output. He was apologist, preacher, philosophical theologian, biblical exegete, and textual critic. He was thoroughly familiar with Greek philosophical traditions. Yet at the same time he believed in the importance of apostolic tradition and debated with Gnostic opponents. He believed that Scripture was inspired by the Holy Spirit. Between 238 and 245 he wrote various homilies on the Old Testament and his *Commentary on Ezekiel*. After 245 he wrote eight books of

33. Justin, *Apology*, 1.52.43 and 1.53.1–6.

34. Justin, *Dialogue with Trypho*, 4.1; 68.7.

35. L. W. Bernard, *Justin Martyr: His Life and Thought* (Cambridge: Cambridge University Press, 1967).

36. Irenaeus, *Against Heresies*, 4.30.3–4; cf. Warren S. Kissinger, *The Parables of Jesus. A History of Interpretation* (Metuchen, NJ: Scarecrow, 1979), 1–4.

37. Hanson, *Allegory and Event*, 117.

38. Clement, *Stromata*, 5.11.72.

apologetics, *Against Celsus*. He believed that every word of Scripture had profound meaning.

Every biblical passage, Origen argued, has a literal meaning comparable to a human body, a moral meaning, comparable to the soul, and a spiritual sense comparable to the spirit.[39] At the literal level Scripture may seem to contain contradictions, "but spiritually it is true."[40] Hence, he used allegorical method (as Philo did) as an apologetic tool.[41] Origen declares, "The interpretation is 'spiritual' when one is able to show of what heavenly things the Jews 'according to the flesh' served as an example and a shadow [Gk., *hupodeigma kai skia*]."[42] All Scripture, he said, is coherent and harmonious, "one perfect instrument of God."[43] Karen Jo Torjesen has convincingly argued that Origen's motivation was pastoral as well as apologetic.[44]

The Alexandrian tradition is later represented to some extent by Athanasius (c. 296–373), Didymus the Blind (c. 313–397), and more fully by Cyril of Alexandria (c. 378–344). Athanasius used Scripture especially for apologetic and theological purposes. Didymus followed the biblical interpretation of Origen. Cyril regarded the Old Testament as primarily christological and produced commentaries on Isaiah, the Minor Prophets, and seven New Testament books. He was more restrained than Origen, although he broadly followed his methods.

THE ANTIOCHENE SCHOOL, *SENSUS PLENIOR*, AND LEVELS OF MEANING

In spite of the widespread use of allegorical interpretation, it would be a mistake to regard this method as universal. In particular the tradition called "the Antiochene School" resisted it on the whole. These were chiefly Diodore of Tarsus (c. 330–90), Theodore of Mopsuestia (c. 350–428), John Chrysostom (c. 347–407), and Theodoret of Cyrrhus (c. 393–460).

Diodore is generally regarded as the founder of the Antiochene School. He reacted strongly against Origen's exegesis. He saw Origen's concern as being for

39. Origen, *De principiis*, 4.2.4.

40. Origen, *Commentary on John*, 10:4.

41. Joseph W. Trigg, *Origen. The Bible and Philosophy in the Third-Century Church* (London: SCM, 1983), 82–86.

42. Origen, *De principiis*, 4.2.4.

43. Origen, *Commentary on Matthew*, 2.

44. Karen Jo Torjesen, *Hermeneutical Procedure and Theological Method in Origen's Exegesis* (Berlin: De Gruyter, 1986).

readers rather than for authors, an issue that is still controversial today. He wrote that he preferred "the historical understanding of the text rather than the allegorical."[45] But this is not to say that he or the school were "wooden" literalists, as if they rejected the use of metaphors or typology. They meant that texts were conditioned by their setting in life. Diodore wrote, "We do not forbid the higher interpretation of *theoria* [allegory], for the historical narrative does not exclude it. . . . We must, however, be on our guard against letting *theoria* do away with the historical basis, for the result would be allegory."[46]

Theodore of Mopsuestia studied under Diodore at Antioch. He wrote commentaries on almost all of the books of the Bible, examining their date, authorship, canonicity, and historical background. However, because of his association with Nestorianism, few of his works have survived. Many of his conclusions coincide with modern biblical studies. He did recognize the need for christological exegesis, for example of Psalms 2 and 110.

John Chrysostom also studied under Diodore. His preaching was outstanding and earned him the popular title "golden-tongue" (*chrysostoma*). He produced some six volumes (in English translation) of *Homilies*, which often represent exegetical insights followed by broader pastoral applications.[47] In these commentaries he expounds the content and style of the biblical authors and opposed allegorical interpretation. He expounds both biblical doctrine and practical application to the times. His commentaries are a model of sober, succinct, exegesis, with a ready eye to application. His concern is always "to hear apostolic voices."[48]

Theodoret became bishop of Cyrrhus in Syria, some eighty miles from Antioch, and invited the hostility of Cyril of Alexandria. He wrote many exegetical commentaries but allowed that the Song of Solomon spoke of Christ and the church, allowing sometimes for a "fuller meaning." He allowed for metaphor and for typology, in spite of his opposition to allegory. The debate between allegorical and historical interpretation often overlaps, and it would be an oversimplification simply to equate the former with the Alexandrian School and the latter with the Antiochenes, in spite of its broad truth.

This leads to a discussion of *sensus plenior*. In modern times this "fuller sense" is associated especially with the Roman Catholic New Testament scholar

45. Cited in Dmitri Z. Zaharopoulos, *Theodore of Mopsuestia on the Bible. A Study of Old Testament Exegesis* (New York: Paulist, 1989), 12.

46. Diodore, *Commentary on the Psalms*, preface.

47. John Chrysostom, *Homilies*, in *Nicene and Post-Nicene Fathers*, series 1, vol. 9–14 (Grand Rapids: Eerdmans, reprinted, 1975).

48. John Chrysostom, *Concerning the Statutes*, hom. 1.1.

Raymond Brown (1928–1998). Brown defines this as "that additional, deeper meaning, intended by God but not clearly intended by the human author, which is seen to exist in the words of the biblical text (or group of texts, or even a whole book) when they are studied in the light of further revelation or development in the understanding of revelation."[49] However, Walter Kaiser and Brown himself point out that the term derives from F. André Fernandez in 1927.[50] Although the term was first coined by Catholic writers, it is widely used among Protestant authors today. Brown insists that the *sensus plenior* should be "homogeneous" with the literal sense.[51]

Brown devoted his doctoral dissertation to this subject in 1955. The proponents were mainly Catholic, including Pierre Benoit, Joseph Coppens, and Bruce Vawter. In these early years Brown wrote regularly on *sensus plenior*. He discussed especially such passages as the application to Jesus Christ of passages about King David in the Psalms, and the application of "Emmanuel" in Isaiah to Jesus. But as time passed, he began to address three problems about *sensus plenior*. First, he began to doubt its usefulness. If it required "homogeneity," how could this be measured? Second, responses to the notion seemed to vary, even among Catholic scholars.[52] Third, it seemed to depend on controversial ideas of biblical inspiration.[53] Brown therefore tended to discard the term in favour of speaking of "levels of meaning."

"Levels of meaning" has a respectable ancestry not least through the writings of the learned Catholic philosophical theologian Bernard Lonergan.[54] Paul Ricœur learned from Freud that psychoanalysis may constitute a first level of reading, but there needs to be "the second understanding of hermeneutics."[55]

We have no need to resort to Origen's unbiblical and Greek understanding of a dualism of body and soul or spirit. Lonergan traces these levels of

49. Raymond E. Brown, "The History and Development of the Theory of a Sensus Plenior," *Catholic Biblical Quarterly* 15 (1953): 141–62.

50. Walter C. Kaiser, "Single Meaning, Unified Referents, Accurate and Authoritative Citations of the Old Testament by the New Testament," in *Three Views on the New Testament Use of the Old Testament*, ed. Kenneth Barding, Jonathan Lunde (Grand Rapids: Zondervan, 2007), 47.

51. Raymond Brown, "The *Sensus Plenior* in the Last Ten Years," *Catholic Biblical Quarterly* 25 (1963): 277; cf. 262–85.

52. Joseph Coppens, "Nouvelles réflexions sur les divers sens des Saintes Écritures," *Nouvelle Revue Théologique* 74 (1952) : 3–20; Pierre Benoit, "La plenitude de sens des livres saints," *Revue Biblique* 67 (1960): 161–96.

53. James T. Burtchaell, *Catholic Theories of Inspiration since 1810: A Review and Critique* (Cambridge, Cambridge University Press, 1969); Raymond Brown, "The Problems of the Sensus Plenior," *Ephemerides Theologiae Lovanienses* 43 (1967): 460–69.

54. Bernard J. F. Lonergan, *Method in Theology* (London: Darton, Longman & Todd, 1971), throughout, especially 57–100; and Lonergan, *Insight* (New York: Harper, 1978), especially 13–19 and 319–47.

55. Paul Ricœur, *Freud and Philosophy: An Essay on Interpretation* (New Haven, CT: Yale University Press, 1970), 27. This will be discussed later in this chapter.

meaning from the everyday empirical world to that which transcends it. Music, for example, is more than what can be seen in an oscilloscope. Poetry is more than "literal" discourse. Nevertheless, the "higher" meaning must remain rooted in the historical meaning, as reactions against extreme allegorical interpretation have shown.

FROM THE FIFTH CENTURY TO THE REFORMATION: THE CLARITY OF SCRIPTURE

Augustine of Hippo (354–430) was one of the most influential fathers of the Western church. He was an outstanding theologian and biblical exegete and massively influenced the mediaeval church. His many theological writings include *On Christian Doctrine, On the Holy Trinity, The Enchiridion on Faith, Hope, and Love*, and *City of God*, among others. Most famously he wrote a theological autobiography, *The Confessions*. He also wrote a series of biblical commentaries on Genesis, Matthew, Romans, and Galatians (all in 394), and these reached the high point in his works *On the Psalms* and *On John* in 414–17. Gerald Bonner has commented on the importance of his biblical work.[56]

Robert Marcus has shown the importance of Augustine's exploration of signs, much of which anticipates Saussure in modern times.[57] Alexander Jensen comments, "We convey information by using signs. Signs always point away from themselves at what they signify. Augustine defines the sign as 'a thing which of itself makes some other thing come to mind, besides the impression that it presents to the senses.'"[58] This view of signs may seem to soften the polarity between allegorical interpretation and typology. Augustine did use allegorical interpretation, but he fundamentally believed that biblical language is rooted in its historical situation. Jensen comments further, "The significance of this thought can hardly be overestimated; just as the eternal Word of God became incarnate in Jesus Christ, so our thought becomes incarnate in our spoken word."[59]

Andrew Louth has shown that the significance of allegorical interpretation

56. Gerald Bonner, "Augustine as Biblical Scholar," in *The Cambridge History of the Bible*, ed. P.R. Ackroyd and C. F. Evans (Cambridge: Cambridge University Press, 1975), 541–63. Cf. Emmanuel Durand, "Augustine of Hippo and Thomas Aquinas as Biblical Exegetes: Their Ways of Reading and Interpretations of the Sorrows of Christ" in this volume.

57. Robert Marcus, *Signs and Meanings: World and Text in Ancient Christianity* (Liverpool: Liverpool University Press, 1996).

58. Alexander S. Jensen, *Theological Hermeneutics* (London: SCM, 2007), 40.

59. Jensen, *Theological Hermeneutics*, 46.

lies largely in its attention to Christian *theology* rather than biblical exegesis alone.[60] Augustine was equally skilled in both disciplines. He in effect formulated the four senses or levels of meaning that Scripture generated, but it was left to his successor, Gregory of Rome, to formulate them explicitly. These were (1) the literal or historical sense, which could include figurative or metaphorical language; (2) allegorical interpretation, which may include christological or theological interpretation; (3) moral meaning, which embodied practical application; and (4) anagogical meaning, which embraced the horizon of eschatology.

In the Middle Ages the influence of Augustine cannot be exaggerated on such writers as the Venerable Bede of Jarrow (673–736), Alcuin of York (c. 735–804), Bernard of Clairvaux (1090–1153), Hugh of St Nicholas (1096–1141), Peter Lombard (c. 1100–1161), especially Thomas Aquinas (1225–74) and Nicholas of Lyra (c. 1270–1349). Hugh wrote, "Scripture is understood in terms of history, allegory, and tropology. These points . . . are separate, because it separately kindles in souls the love of God and neighbour."[61] He focused on the historical sense in his notes on the Psalms, Lamentations, and Joel. Hugh greatly influenced Peter Lombard. Peter emphasized the historical or literal meaning more than most mediaeval writers. Some actually criticized him for devaluing a more contemplative aspect.

Thomas Aquinas spoke of the Holy Spirit as the author of the Bible, but he also paid attention to its literary and linguistic diversity. He has sometimes been regarded as the first truly scientific commentator on the Bible, although others accord this credit to John Calvin later. Aquinas continued the tradition of the fourfold sense of Scripture, though he insisted that the four parts should be relevant to Scripture and not forced artificially. The three senses other than the historical, he said, were not to become an argument for Christian doctrine. Thomas produced verse-by-verse commentaries on a variety of biblical books and passages.

Martin Luther (1483–1546) is generally regarded as the founder of the Reformation. This is not to deny that others had urged reform even before the Reformation. One clear example was John Wycliff (1328–84), who urged the abolition of the papacy and transubstantiation, claiming to build on Scripture, Augustine, Ambrose, and Anselm. He delivered a series of lectures at Oxford, *On the Truth of Holy Scripture*. He produced extensive commentaries. But in 1382 the Archbishop of Canterbury prosecuted him for his views, and he retired from Oxford to work as a priest in Lutterworth.

---

60. Louth, *Discerning the Mystery, passim*.

61. Hugh, *On Noah's Ark Moralia*, 1.100.2; or J.-P. Migne, *Patrologia Latina*, Paris, 1844–64, vol. 116, p. 124.

Luther was born at Eisleben in Saxony and gained entry to the University of Erfurt, near Leipzig. He was initially influenced by Nicholas of Lyra. In 1505 at twenty-two years old, he entered the Augustinian Order at Erfurt. From 1505 to 1508 he entered a monastic order, was made deacon, and was ordained as priest. In 1508 he was called to the new University of Wittenberg to teach philosophy. In 1512 he became professor of biblical studies.

James Atkinson and others argue that the dawn of Reformation consciousness emerged as Luther was preparing lectures on the Psalms during April and May 1513.[62] In his early writings from 1517 to 1521, Luther emphasised that faith is the work of God. He wrote, "Faith . . . is more the work of God than ours."[63] In this early period in his lectures on the Psalms, he followed the method of Nicholas of Lyra and Peter Lombard, which at that time included the mediaeval "fourfold sense." The literal sense conveyed the acts of God in history; other senses recorded their appropriation by the community of believers. Throughout, his concern was christological. He observed, "Every word of the Bible peals the name of Christ"; and "The whole of Scripture deals with Christ throughout."[64]

Luther is known popularly for three things: his opposition to indulgencies and Ninety-Five Theses; his opposition to allegorical interpretation; and his emphasis on the perspicuity or clarity of Scripture. The first point is integrally related to his understanding of the sovereign and totally free grace of God, who accepted sinners as they were. The notion that anyone could *pay for* exemptions from punishment or *buy* these seemed to Luther to undermine the heart of the gospel. The second point is only partly true. Luther did declare, "The Christian reader should make it his first task to seek out the literal sense, as they call it. For it alone is the whole substance of faith and Christian theology; it alone holds its ground in trouble or trial."[65] He adds, "It is the historical sense alone which supplies true and sound doctrine."[66] Yet in many cases Luther is willing to use allegorical interpretation, especially in his earlier works. Many argue that his use of allegory is illustrative rather than an appeal directly to Christian doctrine. At all events, his forthright declarations are often qualified by his practice.

In his developed works we come to the third point – namely, to his controversy with Erasmus, which forms the context of his pronouncements about the clarity of Scripture. Luther's assertions about the perspicuity or clarity of

---

62. James Atkinson, *Martin Luther and the Birth of Protestantism* (London: Penguin, 1968), 32–33.

63. Martin Luther, *Commentary on the Epistle to the Hebrews*, in *Luther's Early Theological Works*, ed. James Atkinson, Library of Christian Classics, vol. 16 (London: SCM, 1962), 201.

64. Atkinson, *The Birth of Protestantism*, 101 and 116.

65. Martin Luther, *Luther's Works*, vol. 9 (Philadelphia: Muhlinberg, 1960), 24.

66. Luther, *Luther's Works*, 1:283.

Scripture arise from his debate with Erasmus about the *nature of knowledge*. Luther's approach has often been misunderstood. Until about 1524 Erasmus had helped to forward the Reformation positively by reviving classical, biblical, and patristic studies and also negatively by exposing inadequacies, excesses, and distortions within practices in the church of the time. On the other hand, he did not share Luther's confidence that the foundations of knowledge were clear enough to allow the radical action which Luther urged, and furthermore, he did not fully share Luther's doctrines of sin, grace, and human nature.

The watershed came sometime between 1520 and 1524. Atkinson writes, "As long as Reformation was being *discussed*, Erasmus went along with the idea. As soon as Luther burned the papal bull and the decretals in 1520, and had taken his stand at Worms in 1521, Erasmus began to withdraw."[67] Atkinson comments that Erasmus's very decency and goodness paradoxically constituted an obstacle to his fully appreciating the radical nature of grace and sin which Luther emphasised. The same might be said of his theory of knowledge, where his generosity of judgement could give the opponent sufficient benefit of the doubt to question a theological decision that could result in firm action. Richard Popkin comments, "Erasmus's . . . dislike of rational theological discussions led him to suggest a kind of *sceptical basis* for remaining within the Catholic Church. . . . Human affairs are so obscure and various that nothing can be clearly known."[68]

Against this background Luther asserted the clarity or perspicuity of Scripture in his well-known work *On the Bondage of the Will* (1525). Luther never suggested that clarification through commentaries and careful study was unnecessary. He argued that knowledge was sufficiently clear to allow *action, or the next step*. His many commentaries witness to this fact. Luther commented, "If the laws were equivocal and uncertain, not only would no issues be settled, but no sure standards of conduct would exist."[69] Some kind of yardstick or measure must be clear and determinate; otherwise, how could the Psalmist describe God's Word as a lamp and a light? (Ps 119:105).

Scripture is described as a path, Luther claims, because of its "entire certainty." Christians possess "a sure word of prophecy" (2 Pet 1:19). It is "a shameless blasphemy" to say that the Scriptures are obscure: "Those who deny the perfect clarity and plainness of the scriptures leave us nothing but darkness. . . . I would say in the whole of Scripture that I do not allow any part

---

67. James Atkinson, *The Great Light: Luther and the Reformation* (Grand Rapids: Edmunds, 1968), 80 (his italics).

68. Richard H. Popkin, *The History of Scepticism from Erasmus to Spinoza* (Berkely: University of California Press, 1979), 5; cf. pp. 1–17.

69. Luther, *The Bondage of the Will* (Edinburgh: Clarke, 1957), 125.

of it to be called obscure."[70] Luther concludes, "You see, then, that the entire content of the scriptures has now been brought to light, even though some passages which contain unknown words remain obscure."[71] By contrast, Erasmus asserts, "Human affairs are so obscure and various that nothing can be clearly known."[72] By way of reply Luther responds, "You would readily take up the sceptics' position whenever the inviolate authority of Holy Scripture or the Church's decisions permit."[73]

This entirely puts into perspective what is at issue in Luther's defence of the clarity of Scripture. Clarity, for him, is a *working clarity*; it does not suggest that every obscurity is dissolved. The concept is provisional and practical. It relates to Erasmus's epistemology. For further detail concerning Luther's concept of *claritas scripturae*, we refer to the work of Friedrich Beisser, among others.[74] Luther, however, did in principle oppose the use of allegorical interpretation, even if he admits to using it in early years. Now, he said, "I know that they [allegories] are nothing but rubbish."[75] He appealed to the plain or natural meaning. We may now compare this further with the approach of Calvin.

John Calvin (1509–64) was born in Picardy, northern France, and studied law at Orléans. He was forced to leave France and travelled to Basel, Switzerland. He began to write *The Institutes of Christian Religion* in 1536. He was persuaded to lead the Reformed rejection of the papacy in Geneva. There he wrote commentaries on virtually all the books of the Bible. In his first commentary, on Romans, he acknowledges the exegetical work of Philipp Melanchthon and the influence of Martin Bucer. Whereas Luther was the founder of the Reformation, Calvin belonged to the second generation of Reformers and was its outstanding systematic theologian. He wrote the last edition of *The Institutes* in 1560, four years before his death.

Calvin believed that an interpreter of Scripture should aim at "lucid brevity" and should "unfold the mind of the writer whom he has undertaken to expound."[76] He compared the right interpretation of the Scriptures to the addition of glasses to provide a vision of God.[77] The Bible, he said, was inspired by the Spirit of God. The Gospel of John "fulminates in majesty" and "strikes down

70. Luther, *The Bondage of the Will*, 128–29.

71. Luther, *The Bondage of the Will*, 71.

72. Desiderius Erasmus, *The Praise of Folly* (Chicago: Packard, 1946), 84.

73. Luther, *On the Bondage of the Will*, 66.

74. Friedrich Beisser, *Claritas Scripturae bei Martin Luther* (Göttingen: Vandenhoeck & Ruprecht, 1866); and Gerhard Ebeling, *Luther. An Introduction to His Thought* (London: Collins, 1972), 107–9.

75. Luther, *Luther's Works*, 54:406.

76. John Calvin, *The Epistles of Paul to the Romans and the Thessalonians* (Edinburgh: Oliver & Boyd, 1964), preface.

77. John Calvin, *Institutes of the Christian Religion* (London: James Clarke, 1957), 1:64.

more powerfully than any thunderbolt."[78] His Old Testament commentaries were mostly lectures; the New Testament commentaries were mostly dictated, probably at home. He never spared himself but worked with intense energy. His primary concern was for the honour of God.

Calvin insisted that allegories were "contrary to the humanistic canon of interpretation," and the mind of the author was the "essence" of the interpreter's task.[79] He is even less tolerant than Luther of allegorical interpretation. The goal of the interpreter is to apprehend "the true sense of Scripture which is genuine and simple (*verum sensum scripturae, qui germanus est et simplex*)."[80] The natural sense of Scripture, he said, compared with Demosthenes or Cicero, "will so affect you, so pierce your heart, so work its way into your very marrow, that in comparison of the impression so produced, that of the orator and philosopher almost disappear, making it manifest that there is truth divine."[81] Calvin's detailed attention to language, historical background, the situation of the author, and literary genre is such that he has rightly been called the first of the modern commentators.

In the post-Reformation period a number of Protestant interpreters followed the tradition of Calvin, including Mattias Flacius Illyricus (1520–75) of the University of Wittenberg, where he was appointed professor of Hebrew and lectured on Paul's epistles. He wrote a book under the title *Clavis Scripturae Sacrae* in 1567.

THE ENLIGHTENMENT AND ROMANTICIST HERMENEUTICS OF SCHLEIERMACHER AND DILTHEY

Johann Martin Chladenius (1710–59) was also a professor at Wittenberg and wrote an *Introduction to the Correct Interpretation of Reasonable Discourses and Writings*. He insisted that there should be no difference between fully understanding speech or writing and understanding the person speaking or writing. But he also stressed that interpretation is conditioned by the strength of the interpreter's ability to think. His most important contribution, however, concerned the place he gave to "point of view" (*Sehe-Punkt*). The interpreter's

78. Calvin, *Institutes*, 1.8.11 (1:81).

79. Joseph Haroutunian and Louise Pettibone Smith, general introduction to *Calvin's Commentaries*, ed. Haroutunian and Pettibone Smith (London: SCM, 1958), 28.

80. John Calvin, *The Epistles of Paul to the Galatians, Ephesians, Philippians and Colossians* (Edinburgh: Oliver & Boyd, 1965), 85.

81. Calvin, *Institutes*, 1.1.8 (1:75).

description of an act or event is always conditioned by the viewpoint from which he perceives it.[82]

In Christian hermeneutics a breakthrough occurred in the work and writings of Friedrich D. E. Schleiermacher (1768–1834). David Klemm has called him "the founder of modern hermeneutics" as well as "the father of modern Protestant theology."[83] In 1804 he taught as professor in the University of Halle, before entering the University of Berlin at its foundation in 1810. Concurrently with his work as professor of theology, he regularly preached on Sundays at Trinity Church, Berlin. Karl Barth, who is often critical of Schleiermacher, wrote of him, "It is here [in preaching] that we must seek . . . the centre of his work. Preaching to the congregation to awaken faith was by far the sweetest desire of his life."[84] Schleiermacher himself observed that preaching a good sermon is like "striking up the music" or awaking "the slumbering spark."[85]

Schleiermacher provided a great turning point in hermeneutics, comparable only with Gadamer's second great turning point in the later twentieth century. He defined hermeneutics not as "rules of interpretation" but as "the art of understanding."[86] Because of his concern for creative thought rather than mechanical rules, he is often thought of as a romanticist interpreter. He stressed the "divinatory" (*divinatorisch*) and the "feminine" dimension of hermeneutics. He regarded women as able to bring a more creative aspect to interpretation, while men, he thought, could bring a more comparative, rational, and analytical aspect to the subject. But he stressed that both were essential to the task; one could not do without the other.

Schleiermacher tried to combine an indebtedness to Pietism and an appreciation of the Enlightenment. In his early years he had been at the Moravian theological college. But when he transferred to the University of Halle, he felt that he had entered a world in which there was freedom to breathe. The combination of these two elements led him to describe himself as a "Pietist of a Higher Order." From the influences of the Enlightenment he valued particularly the transcendental philosophy of Immanuel Kant. Schleiermacher's great rival in the University of Berlin was Hegel, who saw theology as addressing intellectual

82. Cf. Kurt Mueller-Vollmer, ed, *The Hermeneutics Reader: Texts of the German Tradition from the Enlightenment to the Present* (Oxford: Blackwell, 1986), 54–71.

83. David E. Klemm, *Hermeneutical Inquiry*, vol. 1, *The Interpretation of Texts* (Atlanta: Scholars, 1986), 55.

84. Karl Barth, *The Theology of Schleiermacher*, Lectures at Göttingen 1923–24 (Grand Rapids: Eerdmans, 1982), xiii.

85. Friedrich Schleiermacher, *On Religion: Speeches to Its Cultured Despisers* (London: Paul, 1893), 119.

86. Friedrich Schleiermacher, *Hermeneutics: The Handwritten Manuscripts*, Eng. (Missoula, MT: Scholars, 1977), 35–79 and 113.

curiosity, while Schleiermacher saw it as a training for professional clergy and for preaching.

In his hermeneutics Schleiermacher paid attention not only to the biblical text's origins and motivation but also to its effects, or to what texts set going. He commented that we must consider "the content of the text and its range of effects."[87] It is often said that for Schleiermacher hermeneutics is "the reverse of composition."[88] He wrote, "The interpreter must try to become the immediate reader of a text in order to understand its allusions, its atmosphere, and its special field of images."[89] Following Friedrich Ast, Schleiermacher produced a sophisticated version of the hermeneutical circle. He observed, "One must already know a man in order to understand what he says, and yet one must first become acquainted with him by what he says."[90] He added, "The understanding of a given statement is always based on something prior, of two sorts – a preliminary knowledge of human beings, a preliminary knowledge of the subject matter."[91]

Schleiermacher's complementary attention to human beings and the subject matter of texts gave rise to his equally important distinction between *grammatical hermeneutics* and *divinatory* understanding (i.e., an understanding of the text *as a whole*). In the first place, our understanding of a biblical book depends on our understanding of its words, phrases, or parts. In the second place, every understanding is based on a provisional and preliminary understanding of what the text is about. We have already discussed this notion of preliminary understanding or preunderstanding in Rudolf Bultmann and others.

Preunderstanding (*Vorverständnis*) became an ongoing theme in the hermeneutics of Dilthey, Heidegger, Bultmann, and Gadamer.[92] Sometimes Schleiermacher alludes to the complementary nature of "comparative" and "divinatory," or psychological, methods of interpretation. He illustrated the so-called feminine and masculine contributions to hermeneutics in his well-known essay *The Celebration of Christmas* or *Christmas Eve*. Men and women gather to discuss the meaning of Christmas. The "masculine" principle is largely that of comparison and analysis, involving a debate on the nature of the incarnation. Meanwhile the women sing hymns to Jesus, whom they know suprarationally.

87. Schleiermacher, *Hermeneutics*, 151.

88. Richard E. Palmer, *Hermeneutics: Interpretation Theory in Schleiermacher, Dilthey, Heidegger, and Gadamer* (Evanston, IL: Northwestern University Press, 1969), 86.

89. Schleiermacher, *Hermeneutics*, 43 and 53.

90. Schleiermacher, *Hermeneutics*, 56.

91. Schleiermacher, *Hermeneutics*, 59.

92. Cf. Anthony C. Thiselton, "Hermeneutical Circle," in *Dictionary for Theological Interpretation of the Bible*, ed. Kevin J. Vanhoozer (London: SPCK, 2005), 281–82.

Schleiermacher comments, "Divinatory knowledge is the feminine strength in knowing people; comparative knowledge, the masculine. Each method refers back to the other."[93] If we follow only the divinatory method, we become "nebulists." If we follow only the comparative, we risk "pedantry."[94]

Wilhelm Dilthey (1833–1911) was effectively Schleiermacher's successor in hermeneutics. He was also his biographer, writing *Life of Schleiermacher*. He became professor at Basel in 1866 and then at Berlin in 1882. He is best known for his attempts to make hermeneutics the basis of the *Geisteswissenschaften*, or the humanities and social sciences. Dilthey's key concept was that of "life" (*Leben*), or lived experience (*Erlebnis*), partly in contrast to Hegel's *Geist* ("mind" or "spirit"). Dilthey wrote, "In the veins of the knowing subject (for example of Descartes, Locke, and Hume) *no real blood flows*."[95] "Life" is the shared flow of human activities and experiences, in both social diversity and individual experience. Life brings a "connectedness" (*Zusammenhang*), which finds expression in a common language and also in human institutions. Part of Dilthey's distinctive contribution to hermeneutics was to include the interpretation not only of texts but also of social institutions and human life.

In common with Heidegger and Gadamer, Dilthey paid attention to the place in history, or historical allergy, of both texts, institutions, and interpreters. The aim of interpretation is for the interpreter to "relive" (*nacherleben*) the experience of the other by stepping out of his or her shoes and exercising "empathy" (*Hineinversetzen*) or transposition. He famously wrote, "Understanding is a rediscovery of the 'I' in the 'You.'"[96] It is a matter of measuring their feelings by our own.

THE EXISTENTIAL HERMENEUTICS OF HEIDEGGER AND BULTMANN

Martin Heidegger (1884–1976) was an eminent philosopher, who immensely influenced existentialist philosophy and existentialist hermeneutics on the European Continent, although he had only indirect influence on biblical hermeneutics and relatively little influence in Britain.

93. Schleiermacher, *Hermeneutics*, 150.

94. Schleiermacher, *Hermeneutics*, 205.

95. Wilhelm Dilthey, *Gesammelte Schriften*, vol. 5, *Die geistliche Welt: Einleitung in das Philosophie des Lebens* (Leipzig: Teubner, 1927), 4.

96. Dilthey, *Gesammelte Schriften*, 7:191; and H. P. Rickman, ed., *Wilhelm Dilthey. Selected Writings* (Cambridge: Cambridge University Press, 1976), 208.

Heidegger's main principle was that "objectification" or "objective description" amounts to depersonalization. "Description," he urged, does not do justice to the particularities of life. In contrast to most British philosophers, he argued that we must go behind the subject-object relation. "Objectivity" is artificial. In conjunction with this, Heidegger insisted on the "historicity," or the historical conditionedness and historical finitude, of every perspective. Not only the text but also the interpreter are historically conditioned. Heidegger begins not with scientific detachment but with a given being-there (*Dasein*). From this standpoint everything is interpreted in terms of pregiven practical concerns. Heidegger expounds this in his monumental book *Being and Time*. A hammer, he says, is not primarily a piece of metal to which a handle is attached but a tool used for hammering. This is quite different from the empirical tradition and the perspective of John Locke.

Heidegger builds on the notion of preunderstanding in hermeneutics. We "project" forwards certain anticipations that will make sense of what we seek to understand. Understanding, as Heidegger's title leads us to expect, is bound up with time and temporality (*Zeitlichkeit*, the ground and possibility of time). He writes, "*Time* needs to be *explicated primordially as the horizon for the understanding of Being, and in terms of temporality as the Being of Dasein.*"[97] Similarly he writes, "*Meaning is the 'upon-which' of a projection in terms of which something becomes intelligible as something. It gets its structure from a fore-having, a fore-sight, and a fore-conception.*"[98]

Between 1935 and 1949, and more clearly in 1953 with the publication of *What Is Metaphysics?* Heidegger's thought took a "turn" that a few interpreters called a "reversal." He further published *On the Way to Language, Discourse on Thinking* (*Gelassenheit*), and other works.[99] Macquarrie carefully compared his earlier and later work and concluded that the "turn" was not a "reversal."[100] Heidegger argued that language and thinking in the Western tradition had fallen out of Being. Fallenness from Being, he believed, is bound up with the disintegration and fragmentation of life, which reflects the cultural tradition of technology and "levelling down." This, he writes, is seen in "the transformation of men into a mass, the hatred and suspicion of everything free and creative."[101]

---

97. Martin Heidegger, *Being and Time* (Oxford: Blackwell, 1962), 39 (his italics).

98. Heidegger, *Being and Time*, 193 (Heidegger's italics).

99. Martin Heidegger, *On the Way to Language* (New York: Harper, 1971); Heidegger, *Discourse on Thinking* (New York: Harper, 1966).

100. John Macquarrie, "Heidegger's Earlier and Later Work Compare," *Anglican Theological Review* 49 (1967): 3–16.

101. Martin Heidegger, *Introduction to Metaphysics* (New Haven, CT: Yale University Press, 1959), 38.

Heidegger's answer is to turn now *to art and poetry*, in contrast to what he calls day-to-day cash-value meanings, which are born after the interests of specialised fields of narrow pragmatic concerns. He writes, "Time has ceased to be anything other than velocity, instantaneousness, and simultaneously, and time as history has vanished from the lives of all peoples."[102] Heidegger's critics dismiss this as mere mysticism. But in terms of hermeneutics, it paves the way for what is called "a new coming to speech" and the related "Language-Event" (*Sprachereignis*) in Gadamer, Fuchs, and Ebeling, whom we shall discuss in the next section.

Meanwhile, we must first consider the influential works of Rudolf Bultmann in theology. He is most widely known for his programme of demythologising the New Testament and his programme of existential interpretation. Bultmann (1884–1976) was one of the foremost New Testament scholars of his time and exercised widespread influence, not least through his former pupils Käsemann, Fuchs, and Bornkamm. As in the case of Heidegger, the key to his programme of demythologisation was his desire to deobjectify the texts of the New Testament. He also built extensively on Wilhelm Dilthey. Like Heidegger, he regarded the New Testament authors as "historically conditioned."[103] Like Schleiermacher and Dilthey, he argued that a presupposition of the interpreter's understanding is "*the interpreter's relationship in his life is the subject which is expressed in the text.*"[104] This is part of the general programme of deobjectification.

In spite of his claims that he was primarily a New Testament scholar, Bultmann was heavily indebted to liberal theology (with Harnack), to neo-Kantian philosophy (with Paul Natorp), and to various philosophical assumptions. Like Heidegger, he held to a radical devaluing of "describing objects." The interest of the New Testament evangelists, he argued, was not to describe objective facts but to confess their faith. The two poles of his thought were *kerygma* and *myth*, which became the working title of many essays on his demythologising project.[105] The *kerygma* ("preaching") stressed that the New Testament was *confessional* literature; *myth* stressed that the primary vehicle of expression was supposedly *mythological.*

Almost every principle of Bultmann's programme has been challenged and discussed. Most recently, Wolfhart Pannenberg has called into question almost

102. Heidegger, *Introduction to Metaphysics*, 38.

103. Rudolf Bultmann, *Essays Philosophical and Theological* (London: SCM, 1955), 236.

104. Bultmann, *Essays*, 241 (Bultmann's italics).

105. Hans-Werner Bartsch, ed., *Kerygma and Myth*, 2nd ed., 2 vols. (London: SPCK, 1962 and 1964); German original: *Kerygma und Mythos. Eine theologisches Gespräch*, 6 vol. (Hamburg: Reich & Heidrich, 1948). A later English edition is Bultmann, *New Testament and Mythology and Other Basic Writings*, ed. Schubert M. Ogden (Philadelphia: Fortress, 1984).

every aspect of Bultmann's approach, not least his debt to Heidegger, his devaluation of assertion, propositions, and rationality.[106]

First, Bultmann's view of myth is radically open to question. He provides three definitions, each of which contradicts the two others. He writes that myth is a way of speaking "of the other world in terms of this world, and of the gods in terms derived from human life."[107] This would cover virtually all analogical language. As G. Miegge points out, "This includes every form of expression which represents the divine by way of analogy, parable, or symbol."[108] In Bultmann's second formulation of myth, he regards myth as explaining the unusual or surprising phenomena in terms of an invasion of supernatural forces. He writes, "The cosmology of the New Testament is essentially mythical in character. The world is viewed as a three-storeyed structure, with the earth in the centre, the heaven above, and the world beneath."[109] This does not concern mythology; it concerns what Bultmann regards as a primitive worldview. The third aspect of myth is to prepare the way for the programme of deobjectification. Bultmann writes, "The real purpose of myth is not to present an objective picture of the world as it is, but to express man's understanding of himself in the world in which he lives. Myth should be interpreted not cosmologically, but anthropologically, or better still, existentially."[110] This borrows the concept of objectification from Heidegger. The British philosopher Donald Hepburn devastatingly argues that these definitions are not merely different, but contradictory.[111]

Bultmann is on even weaker ground when he explains his proposals for the interpretation of myth. Strangely, Bultmann himself writes, "Our radical attempt to demythologize the New Testament is in fact a perfect parallel to St Paul and Luther's doctrine of justification by faith alone."[112] This is because intellectual achievement of any kind is regarded as "works" in the negative sense. Any rational attempt to ground belief in truth is difficult within the horizons of Bultmann's programme. Bultmann writes, "If we follow the objective representations of the New Testament, the cross is indeed understood as a mythical event."[113]

106. Cf. Anthony C. Thiselton, *Understanding Pannenberg, Landmark Theologian of the Twentieth Century* (Eugene, OR: Wipf and Stock, 2018); Wolfhart Pannenberg, *The Idea of God and Human Freedom*, trans. R. A. Wilson (London: SCM, 1973).

107. Rudolf Bultmann, "New Testament and Mythology," in *Kerygma and Myth*, 1:10.

108. G. Miegge, *Gospel and Myth in the Thought of Rudolf Bultmann* (London: Butterworth, 1960), 98–99.

109. Bultmann, "New Testament and Mythology," 10.

110. Bultmann, "New Testament and Mythology," 10.

111. Ronald W. Hepburn, "Demythologising and the Problem of Validity," in *New Essays in Philosophical Theology*, ed. Antony Flew and A. McIntyre (London: SCM, 1955), 227–42.

112. Rudolf Bultmann, "Bultmann Replies to His Critics," in *Kerygma and Myth*, 1:210.

113. Bultmann, *Kerygma and Myth*, 1:33–34.

His most extreme critics call this not news about the cross and the resurrection of Jesus Christ, but news about humankind itself. Pannenberg's critique of his devaluation of history suggests that such a criticism is not entirely wide of the mark.

GADAMER'S ONTOLOGICAL HERMENEUTICS AND THE "NEW HERMENEUTIC"

Hans-Georg Gadamer (1900–2002) was born in Marburg, and his magisterial book *Truth and Method* has become one of the most influential works on hermeneutics at the end of the twentieth century. In his early years he was a friend and admirer of Heidegger with whom he was a colleague at Freiburg in 1923 and studied many of the great philosophers, including especially Plato. He also valued the concept of "wisdom."

In part 1 of *Truth and Method*, he criticized the method of Descartes (1596–1650) and followed instead the historical tradition of Giambattista Vico (1668–1744). He regarded Vico's historical approach as far superior to the narrow rationalism of the Enlightenment. This first part is entitled "The Question of Truth as It Emerges in the Experiences of Art." "Method" is all very well for natural sciences, but not for the *Geisteswissenschaften*. The latter are based on *Bildung*, or culture. Vico, Gadamer says, preserved the communal wisdom of the ancient world. The "common sense" of Thomas Reid is also relevant.

In the second half of part 1, Gadamer turns to the ontology of the work of art. Here his analogy of the theatre, art, or the game is significant. He writes, "All encounters with the language of art is an encounter with an unfinished event and is itself part of this event."[114] This is because "play fulfils its purpose only if the player loses himself in play."[115] Gadamer adds, "The primacy of the play over the consciousness of the player is fundamentally acknowledged."[116] The play or "performance" is not a mechanical replication of some previous game, but players lose themselves in the spontaneity of each game: "Play draws him into its domain."[117] All this applies to the "performance" of understanding and reading. It cannot be rigidly directed by the author. Part of the event occurs in its presentation.[118] The actuality of play, or a festival, or a work of art, cannot

114. Hans-Georg Gadamer, *Truth and Method*, 2nd ed. (London: Sheed & Ward, 1989), 99 (his italics).
115. Gadamer, *Truth and Method*, 102.
116. Gadamer, *Truth and Method*, 104 (Gadamer's italics).
117. Gadamer, *Truth and Method*, 109.
118. Gadamer, *Truth and Method*, 116.

be detached from its presentation. It exists in its presentation or performance. Ontology looks toward a historical and temporal event. We are miles away from Descartes' "consciousness" and his isolated ego.

In part 2 of *Truth and Method*, Gadamer considers truth and understanding in the humanities and social sciences. Here he follows Hegel and Dilthey on historical reason. He observes, "Historical consciousness appropriates what seemed specially reserved to art, religion and philosophy."[119] He endorses Heidegger's view of "historicality," – that is, the historical conditionedness of finite human consciousness. The terms *horizon* and *life-world* now become important. Horizons can move and expand as we move. Further, prejudgements (*Vorurteile*) become more important than human judgements. Gadamer declares, "*It is not so much our judgements as it is our 'prejudices'* [or prejudgments] *that constitute our being.*"[120]

This allows for a rehabilitation of authority. Authority, Gadamer says, "rests on acknowledgement and hence on an act of reason itself which, aware of its limitations, trusts in the better insight of others."[121] Here he is far away from the Enlightenment, which extolled individual judgement. The Enlightenment, he says, was guilty of a prejudice against prejudice!

In the second half of part 2 Gadamer writes that understanding is always something like applying a text to the interpreter's present situation.[122] Here he comes near to the later Wittgenstein, who says, "The application (*Anwendung*) is still a criterion of understanding."[123] Gadamer cites theological and legal hermeneutics. Further, he cites Socrates, Plato, and R. G. Collinwood on the importance of questions. He writes, "The logic of question and answer that Collingwood elaborated puts an end to talk about permanent *problems*."[124] He adds, "Reflection on the hermeneutical experience transforms questions back to questions that arise, and derives their sense from their motivation."[125] In other words, questions arise from a concrete situation, whereas propositions or "problems" may be purely abstract and free-standing.

Part 3 of *Truth and Method* is perhaps less influential than the others and is wholly on language, mainly in the German tradition. He does use the analogy of a conversation, out of which issues may simply "arise." The coming together

119. Gadamer, *Truth and Method*, 229.

120. Hans-Georg Gadamer, *Philosophical Hermeneutics* (Berkeley: University of California, 1976), 9; cf. 3–17.

121. Gadamer, *Truth and Method*, 279.

122. Gadamer, *Truth and Method*, 308.

123. Ludwig Wittgenstein, *Philosophical Investigations* (Oxford: Blackwell, 1955), 146.

124. Gadamer, *Truth and Method*, 375 (his italics).

125. Gadamer, *Truth and Method*, 377.

of two distinct horizons may be more fruitful than a monologue. Gadamer uses the concept of "historically-effected consciousness."[126] Like Saussure, Gadamer sees language as actualizing what was potential. His most positive section is on concept formation.[127] New concepts can generate new insights into truth.

Gadamer's notion of a new coming to speech and "language-event" harmonizes with the "new hermeneutic" of Ernst Fuchs (1903–83) and Gerhard Ebeling (1912–2001). Fuchs believes that the New Testament *kerygma* creates rather than presupposes faith. Both writers insist that the Word of God is meant *to live*. Its living language may come to speech today, they stress, not by changing its vocabulary, but through something more fundamental. Fuchs asks, what do we have to do at our desks so that this Word "strikes home" (*treffen*).[128] The key question for hermeneutics is: How does the Word speak to us *anew*? How does it come-to-speech? ("*Das Zur-Sprache-kommen der Sache selbst?*") This is why some philosophical input is needed; the task is to initiate understanding.

Fuchs and Ebeling believe that the biblical text must first address the interpreter. Fuchs writes, "The text has ourselves as its object." And Ebeling writes, "The text becomes a hermeneutical aid in the understanding of present experience."[129] Fuchs, like Heidegger, Gadamer, and later, Ricœur, makes much of the "world" of the text, not in the historical sense, but in what the text sets going. Fuchs declares, "Language makes . . . Being into an event."[130] The community of faith and the text share a common world. This operates especially in the parables of Jesus. In the parable of the labourers in the vineyard (Matt 20:1–16), for example, "We, too, share the reaction of the first (labourers). The first see that the last receive a whole day's wage, and naturally they hope for a higher rate for themselves."[131] Then comes the shock: grace or generosity eclipses supposed natural justice. Fuchs concludes, "Jesus pledges himself to those who, in face of a cry of 'guilty,' nevertheless found their hope on an act of God's kindness."[132]

In the case of the parables of Jesus, this approach works well. Robert Funk and others adopt and expand this approach in great detail.[133] Funk applies this to the parable of the prodigal son (Luke 15:11–32). In this "the righteous" find themselves in the "world" of the elder brother, while "sinners" share in the

126. Gadamer, *Truth and Method*, 389.
127. Gadamer, *Truth and Method*, 428.
128. Ernst Fuchs, *Studies of the Historical Jesus* (London: SCM, 1964), 8, 411, and 418.
129. Gerhard Ebeling, *Word and Faith* (London: SCM, 1963), 33.
130. Fuchs, *Studies of the Historical Jesus*, 207.
131. Fuchs, *Studies of the Historical Jesus*, 33.
132. Fuchs, *Studies of the Historical Jesus*, 34–37.
133. Robert W. Funk, *Language, Hermeneutic, and Word of God* (New York: Harper, 1966).

"world" of the son who is welcomed. The Word divides the audience into elder and younger sons, or into critical Pharisees and penitent sinners.[134]

This approach can be very useful in the case of metaphorical or poetic language. But Fuchs and Funk are less able to show its value for didactic or prophetic texts, as is the case in most of the epistles. Fuchs notoriously calls the resurrection a "linguistic event," and after some enthusiasm in the 1960s and 1970s, the "new hermeneutic" has declined in influence.

SOME REMAINING QUESTIONS: NARRATIVE HERMENEUTICS AND THEOLOGICAL INTERPRETATION

We have referred briefly to Paul Ricœur (1913–2005), mainly on his appreciation of the variety of biblical texts. But Ricœur is a creative and sophisticated figure, whom we must consider further for his positive influence on hermeneutics. He was a committed Protestant but wrote primarily as a philosopher. He studied philosophy in 1934 at the Sorbonne, Paris, where he came under the influence of Gabriel Marcel. In 1939 he served in the French army but was taken prisoner in 1940. He used this opportunity to study the German philosophers Jaspers, Husserl, and Heidegger. From 1948–1954, he studied in Strasbourg, from whom he received his doctorate in 1950. In 1956 he became professor of philosophy at the Sorbonne.

In these early years Ricœur published *Fallible Man* and *The Symbolism of Evil*.[135] These address problems of human will, finitude, guilt, and symbol. He would later produce his magisterial three-volume *Time and Narrative* and his masterly book *Oneself as Another*.[136] These established him as one of the most seminal and creative thinkers of the late twentieth century. He held a life-long fascination for symbol, metaphor, narrative, and hermeneutics.

One turning point came with his encounter with the work of Freud. When a patient described his dreams, Freud could not take dreams at face value. Another text lay beneath the surface. Displacement, condensation, and "scrambling" could result in "overdetermination." Ricœur understood this to imply the necessity for interpretation and hermeneutic. He observed, "Hermeneutics seems to

134. Fuchs, *Studies of the Historical Jesus*, 16–17.

135. Paul Ricœur, *Fallible Man* (New York: Fordham, 1986); Ricœur, *The Symbolism of Evil* (Boston: Beacon, 1969).

136. Paul Ricœur, *Time and Narrative*, 3 vol. (Chicago: University of Chicago, 1984–88); Ricœur, *Oneself as Another* (Chicago: University of Chicago, 1992).

me to be animated by this double motivation: willingness to suspect, willingness to listen; vow of rigour, vow of obedience."[137] This contrast between suspicion and listening became correlated with the distinction in German hermeneutics between *explanation* (*Erklärung*) and *understanding* (*Verstehen*), explored by Apel and others.

In 1975 Ricœur expounded the multilayered nature of language in his book *The Rule of Metaphor*.[138] This followed his books *The Conflict of Interpretations* (1969) and others. He considers time in dialogue with Heidegger and Greimas. He compares Augustine on extended or stretched-out time with Aristotle on the logic of plot, or in his words, "discordance" in Augustine with "concordance" in Aristotle. He comments, "Emplotment gives shape and organization to what otherwise would be bare extension."[139] This makes understanding (*Verstehen*) possible.

Volume 2 of *Time and Narrative* provides a close-up of narrative with particular reference to fiction. He draws examples from Flaubert and Jane Austen, discussing such standard narrative devices as point of view and Bakhtin's polyphonic voices.[140] He explores Gerard Genette's narrative discourse, including speed, flashbacks, and flash forwards. This technique has been much used in biblical interpretation. For example, the gospel of Mark uses high narrative speed in his first eight chapters, slows to a medium pace in the middle chapters, and then portrays the passion of Christ in slow motion. This is his way of emphasizing that the cross is the centre of the gospel.

Volume 3 of *Time and Narrative* reinforces the aesthetics of temporality and the poetics of narrative identity. He discusses Husserl on "internal time-consciousness."[141] He also considers Heidegger on "making possible," and anticipation.[142] History reveals a creative "refiguration of time."[143]

In *Oneself as Another* Ricœur reconsiders the self and self-identity, looking at Descartes, Locke, Hume, Strawson, and Recanati. This is less directly related to hermeneutics, except that he expands on narrative identity and the nature of the personal. The key theme becomes accountability, which contrary to Hume, constitutes the stable thread of self-identity.

---

137. Ricœur, *Freud and Philosophy*, 27.

138. Paul Ricœur, *The Rule of Metaphor. Multi-Disciplinary Studies of the Creation of Meaning in Language* (London: Routledge, 1977).

139. Ricœur, *Time and Narrative*, 1:33.

140. Ricœur, *Time and Narrative*, 2:93–99.

141. Ricœur, *Time and Narrative*, 3:23–44.

142. Ricœur, *Time and Narrative*, 3:69–70.

143. Ricœur, *Time and Narrative*, 3:104.

Ricœur deserves much more attention, but we must finally discuss *the theological interpretation of Scripture*. This is a recent movement, and it is too early to offer a definitive definition. But it is not difficult to name the scholars who are most closely associated with this approach. Probably the nearest to a definitive account comes from Kevin Vanhoozer's introduction to *Dictionary for Theological Interpretation of the Bible*.[144] Vanhoozer is general editor, but his coeditors are Craig Bartholomew, Daniel Trier, and N. T. Wright, which at once provides the names of four scholars who associate themselves with this project. Six pages of contributors list some 200 further authors, among whom I number myself.

Vanhoozer first declares what the theological interpretation of the Bible is not. It is not an imposition of the theological system or confessional grid onto the biblical text, whether Lutheran, Reformed, Roman Catholic, or Anglican. More positively, it is concerned to bridge the "ugly ditch" in much modern biblical interpretation between exegesis and theology and to avoid the modern fashion for postmodernist approaches in which "anything goes." Vanhoozer writes, "The theological interpretation of the Bible is characterised by a governing interest in God, the word and works of God."[145] Its goal is, he adds, to provide a Christian theological evaluation of the contemporary issues and approaches pertaining to biblical interpretation "with a view to assessing how they enable the church better to hear what God is saying to the church and the world today."[146] Within this agreed framework, Vanhoozer acknowledges that there will coexist a variety of views among its advocates.[147]

Prominent among its well-known advocates are Todd Billings, Joel Green, David Lyle Jeffrey, Edith Humphrey, and Stephen Fowl from America; Francis Watson, John Webster, Jeremy Begbie, N. T. Wright, and Walter Moberly from Britain. In French-speaking Europe, one can mention Benoît Bourgine.[148] All stress the importance of the church as the main reading community of the Bible. It is not written for fellow academics. In part this is a reaction against such scholars as Johann S. Semler (1725–91) in the Enlightenment. He regarded biblical interpretation as a purely historical and literary discipline, from which theology should be excluded. By contrast, Francis Watson writes, "A text is not

144. Kevin Vanhoozer, introduction to *Dictionary for Theological Interpretation of the Bible*, ed. Kevin Vanhoozer (London: SPCK; Grand Rapids: Baker, 2005), 19–25.

145. Vanhoozer, *Dictionary*, 22.

146. Vanhoozer, *Dictionary*, 22.

147. Vanhoozer, *Dictionary*, 23.

148. Benoît Bourgine, *Bible oblige: Essai sur la théologie biblique*, coll. "Cogitatio Fidei" (Paris: Cerf, 2019).

to be regarded primarily as a 'historical source.'"[149] He adds, "The primary reading community within which the biblical text is located is the church."[150] He continues, "If theology is to be Christian, the ecclesial community must be seen as its primary point of reference."[151] He later attacks the supposed neutrality of secular viewpoints. He concludes, "The assumption that faith is incompatible with proper academic standards or with openness to alternative viewpoints is ultimately a mere prejudice."[152]

Biblical Studies must be integrated with theology, as it was in the fruitful days, of J. B. Lightfoot, B. F. Westcott, and Fenton Hort. "Theological interpretation" could bring these fruitful days back, when Lightfoot and Westcott, both professors of divinity at Cambridge University, later became bishops of Durham.

FOR FURTHER READING

Bartholomew, Craig, and Anthony C. Thiselton, eds. *Scripture and Hermeneutics.* 8 vols. Grand Rapids: Zondervan, 2000–2008.

LaCocque, Andre, and Paul Ricœur. *Thinking Biblically: Exegetical and Hermeneutical Studies*. Chicago: University of Chicago Press, 1998.

Mueller-Vollmer, Kurt, ed. *The Hermeneutics Reader.* Oxford: Blackwell, 1965.

Ricœur, Paul. *Essays on Biblical Interpretation*. London: SPCK, 1981.

Thiselton, Anthony C. *Thiselton on Hermeneutics: The Collected Works and New Essays of Anthony Thiselton*. Ashgate Contemporary Thinkers on Religion. Aldershot: Ashgate, 2006; Grand Rapids: Eerdmans, 2006.

Thiselton, Anthony C. *Hermeneutics: An Introduction*. Grand Rapids: Eerdmans, 2009.

Vanhoozer, Kevin, ed. *Dictionary for Theological Interpretation of the Bible.* London: SPCK; Grand Rapids: Baker, 2005.

Watson, Francis. *Text, Church, and World. Biblical Interpretation in Theological Perspective.* Edinburgh: T&T Clark, 1994.

149. Francis Watson, *Text, Church, and World: Biblical Interpretation in Theological Perspective* (Edinburgh: T&T Clark, 1994), 2.

150. Watson, *Text, Church, and World*, 3.

151. Watson, *Text, Church, and World*, 6.

152. Watson, *Text, Church, and World*, 9.

CHAPTER 7

The Bible and History

Craig G. Bartholomew

INTRODUCTION

History telling is far more complex than "what happened in the past," but it is never less than this.[1] "What happened in the past" is too comprehensive to define what we mean by history, but the difference between history and fiction is that history telling refers to actual people and events that existed and took place in the past, and good history *intends* to tell us accurately about such events and people. In this sense history telling is never less than about what actually happened.

All history telling involves selection of data and interpretation in an effort to make sense of the past. As Paul Ricœur[2] and others have pointed out

1. Philosophy of history and of historiography is a complex subject with a vast literature. Cf., for example, David Bebbington, *Patterns in History: A Christian Perspective on Historical Thought* (Vancouver: Regent College Publishing, 1979); Mark Day, *The Philosophy of History* (London: Continuum, 2008); Ernst Breisach, *Historiography: Ancient, Medieval, and Modern*, 2nd ed. (Chicago: University of Chicago Press, 1994); Peter Burke, *History and Historians in the Twentieth Century* (Oxford: Oxford University Press, 2003); Langdon Gilkey, *Reaping the Whirlwind: A Christian Interpretation of History* (New York: Seabury, 1976); Gordon Graham, *The Shape of the Past: A Philosophical Approach to History* (Oxford: Oxford University Press, 1997); Gertrude Himmelfarb, *On Looking Into the Abyss: Untimely Thoughts on Culture and Society* (New York: Vintage, 1994); Keith Jenkins, *Re-Thinking History* (New York: Routledge, 1991); Jenkins, *On What is History? From Carr and Elton to Rorty and White* (New York: Routledge, 1995); Genevieve Lloyd, *Providence Lost* (Cambridge, MA: Harvard University Press, 2008); Paul Ricœur, *Memory, History, Forgetting* (Chicago: University of Chicago Press, 2004); M. C. Smit, *Toward a Christian Conception of History*, ed. and trans. Herbert Donald Morton and Harry Van Dyke (Lanham: UPA, 2006); Michael Stanford, *An Introduction to the Philosophy of History* (Oxford: Blackwell, 1998); Ronald Wells, ed., *History and the Christian Historian* (Grand Rapids: Eerdmans, 1998).

2. Ricœur, *Memory, History, Forgetting.*

historical narrative shares its poetics with fictional narrative so that attention to poetics alone cannot determine whether or not we are dealing with historical narrative. It is the intention of the author that is determinative, whether or not we judge the product to be good or bad history telling. Bruce Halpern observes, "Whether a text is history, then, depends on what its author meant to do."[3]

On all accounts large parts of the Bible are *not* historical narrative. In the Old Testament we have the corpus of wisdom books (Proverbs, Job, Ecclesiastes), collections of the sayings of prophets, and poetic books like the Song of Solomon and the Psalms. In the New Testament, apart from the Gospels and Acts of the Apostles, the rest of it is made up of letters, some of which are expanded into lengthy theological expositions. In the Old Testament historical narrative constitutes Genesis through Esther and Daniel.[4] In the New Testament we have four tellings of the story of Jesus in the Gospels. The Acts of the Apostles functions as the indispensable hinge between the Gospels and the letters by telling the story of the development of the early church and the context in which the letters fit and make sense, since they are written to Christians in the churches established after Pentecost. To be sure, the collections of the prophets' sayings in the Old Testament are invariably anchored in concrete historical situations, and the New Testament letters present themselves as written by particular church leaders to congregations or individuals.

History remains indispensable for the nonhistorical narrative parts of Scripture since they were produced in particular cultural and historical contexts and archaeology, studies of ancient culture, and many other aspects of historical studies can illuminate their meaning. However, when it comes to the topic of the Bible and history, the focus is on the historical narratives in the Old and New Testaments and the extent to which they *intend* to narrate what actually happened.

PRE-"CRITICAL" UNDERSTANDINGS

Prior to the rise of modernity, the historical narratives were treated virtually unanimously as history telling. "Critical" is in quotation marks in the heading because we should not think that early, medieval, and Reformation and Catholic scholars were unaware of many of the challenges involved in biblical interpretation and historicity. Origen, for example, produced the *Hexapla* in the

3. Bruce Halpern, *The First Historians: The Hebrew Bible and History* (San Francisco: Harper and Row, 1988), 8.

4. The genre of Esther and Daniel is contested.

third century AD, a critical edition of the Hebrew Bible in six versions, comparing the Hebrew text with the LXX and other Greek versions. The purpose of this massive compilation is contested, but the task indicates the capacity of the early church fathers to wrestle with the complex issues involved in the Old Testament text and its transmission and accuracy – issues that relate, albeit indirectly, to historicity.

Precritical interpretation is often associated with the quadriga, the fourfold interpretation of the Bible. Often this is related in particular to allegorical interpretation but the latter three senses – the allegorical, the tropological and the anagogical – are always rooted in the literal or historical. What sets precritical interpretation apart from much modern interpretation is that it reads the Bible as Scripture, listening primarily for God's address, and its whole hermeneutic operates within a Judeo-Christian perspective on reality so that divine action is not set in opposition to history but makes perfect sense in terms of God's accompanying history towards its goal.

THE RISE OF BIBLICAL CRITICISM: THE HISTORICAL TURN

With the rise of modernity and its entry into biblical studies, history has become one of the most contested areas of biblical studies. Wilhelm de Wette (1780–1849) is regarded by many as the father of modern biblical criticism, although its origins extend back to figures like Spinoza and many others. De Wette was the first scholar to radically rewrite the history of Israelite religion. Prior to attending university, de Wette was deeply influenced by the philosophy of Kant, and in many ways his scholarship is an attempt to fit biblical studies with a Kantian paradigm. A critical approach to the Old Testament demonstrated, according to de Wette, that it has little to offer in terms of authentic history.[5]

As Thiselton notes,

> De Wette's reconstructed history of Israelite religion and the development of New Testament theologies (plural) steadily became institutionalised as a basis for new theological evaluations. What began as a search for freedom from whatever might inhibit inquiry, namely church dogma or manipulative ecclesial interests, itself became transformed into a new institutional structure.

---

5. On de Wette, see John Rogerson, *W. M. L. de Wette: Founder of Modern Biblical Criticism; An Intellectual Biography*, JSOTSup 26 (Sheffield: Sheffield Academic Press, 1992).

> So monolithic does this structure at times appear to have become that some writers speak, though questionably, of "*the* historical-critical method."[6]

There is much debate about the origins and nature of historical criticism and precisely what is involved in this historical turn.[7] Krentz, as Thiselton observes, describes historical criticism as a unified entity. For Krentz, *historical* and *critical* identify key elements in biblical criticism. *Critical* indicates the investigation of the Bible through the lens of the modern worldview. *Historical* signifies that the Enlightenment historical method was applied to the Bible, especially as it developed in nineteenth century Germany. Krentz asserts,

> It is difficult to overestimate the significance the nineteenth century has for biblical interpretation. It made historical criticism *the* approved method of interpretation. The result was a revolution of viewpoint in evaluating the Bible. The Scriptures were, so to speak, secularized. . . . The Bible was no longer the criterion for the writing of history; rather history had become the criterion for understanding the Bible. . . . The Bible stood before criticism as defendant before judge. The criticism was largely positivist in orientation, immanentist in its explanations, and incapable of appreciating the category of revelation.[8]

Thiselton agrees that a preoccupation with historical method developed but rightly advises us not to lose sight of the varied understandings of history in modern interpretation. Indeed, postmodernism has alerted us to the problem with viewing modernity monolithically. "A plea must be made for the application of hermeneutics to the history of interpretation with no less rigor and sensitivity than is invited by the study of biblical texts."[9] Both Krentz and Thiselton make important points in this regard. The story of the historical turn in biblical studies is not straightforward, and we need to tell that story so as to do justice to the historical particularities.[10]

---

6. Anthony C. Thiselton, "New Testament Interpretation in Historical Perspective," in *Hearing the New Testament: Strategies for Interpretation*, ed. Joel B. Green (Grand Rapids: Eerdmans, 1995), 10–36, 17.

7. See the essays by Bartholomew, Sundberg, Riches, Wolters, Mason, Greene, and Möller, in Craig G. Bartholomew et al., eds., *Renewing Biblical Interpretation*, SAHS 1 (Grand Rapids: Zondervan, 2000).

8. Edgar Krentz, *The Historical-Critical Method* (London: SPCK, 1975), 30.

9. Thiselton, "New Testament Interpretation," 36.

10. New Testament studies are well served by several expositions of the way in which New Testament interpretation has developed. For example, Werner G. Kümmel, *The New Testament. The History of the Interpretation of Its Problems* (London: SCM, 1973); Stephen Neill and Tom Wright, *The Interpretation of the New Testament 1861–1986* (Oxford: Oxford University Press, 1988); John K. Riches, *A Century of New Testament Study* (Harrisburg, PA: Trinity Press International, 1993). Old Testament study is, I think, less

Simultaneously, we do need to identify the patterns that emerge and the inseparable link of biblical criticism with modernity. In recent years Jonathan Israel has done rigorous work on the Enlightenment, and he depicts the Enlightenment "however imperfectly and tentatively, ... as a single highly integrated intellectual and cultural movement, displaying differences in timing, no doubt, but for the most part preoccupied not only with the same intellectual problems but often even the very same books and insights everywhere from Portugal to Russia and from Ireland to Sicily."[11] Israel, rightly in my view, foregrounds the importance of the Radical Enlightenment, which was determined to eliminate or marginalize religion from the great public spheres of life including education and the universities. Krentz is thus right to foreground the secularisation of biblical studies that occurred through the historical turn, and any Christian or theological reflection on biblical criticism must attend to this, albeit never simplistically. History continues to be a heavily contested area in biblical studies, and biblical scholars express diverse views on these issues.[12]

Thus, what we make of the Bible and history will be deeply influenced by what we make of secularisation and modernity. To the credit of the early modern German biblical critics, they would set out in their works their philosophy of religion and then apply it to the Bible, thus enabling one to see the whole picture of how they arrived at their view of the historicity of the Bible. However, under the influence of one of the major modern Old Testament scholars, Julius Wellhausen, a major shift occurred. Wellhausen argued that philosophy never precedes biblical criticism but only follows it. Bearing in mind Wellhausen's influence, with this stance he erased from view the philosophies that had influenced and continue to influence historical analysis of the Bible.

---

well served in this respect. H-J Kraus, *Geschichte der historisch-kritischen Erforschung des Alten Testaments*, 4th ed. (Darmstadt: Neukirchener, 1988), is an important volume, and John Rogerson has done very important work on the history of Old Testament interpretation. There remains scope for some major work on the history of Old Testament interpretation that explores the philosophical and theological dimensions of the story.

11. Jonathan Israel, *A Revolution of the Mind: Radical Enlightenment and the Intellectual Origins of Modern Democracy* (Princeton, NJ: Princeton University Press, 2010), v.

12. For a useful introduction to the debate about faith and history, see Gordon E. Michalson, "Faith and History," in *The Blackwell Encyclopedia of Modern Christian Thought*, ed. A. E. McGrath (Oxford: Blackwell, 1993), 210–14. For an influential view that history is not as central to the Bible as some think, see James Barr, "The Concepts of History and Revelation," in *Old and New in Interpretation: A Study of the Two Testaments*, 2nd ed. (London: SCM, 1982), 65–102. On history and Scripture, see also John Goldingay, *Models for Scripture* (Grand Rapids: Eerdmans, 1994), part 1; and V. Phillips Long, *The Art of Biblical History* (Leicester: Apollos, 1994). N. T. Wright's work is well known for its emphasis on the importance of history for New Testament theology. See chapter 9, "History and Theology," in Neill and Wright, *The Interpretation*, and in particular, N. T. Wright, *The New Testament and the People of God* (Minneapolis: Fortress, 1992).

Wellhausen's type of view continues to be promulgated by scholars such as James Barr and John Barton, for example.

Writing in 2000 James Barr asserts that,

> The typical biblical scholarship of modern times has been rather little touched by philosophy – certainly much less than it has by theology. Going back to the last century, one remembers Vatke and his Hegelianism and it has long been customary to accuse Wellhausen of the same thing though the accusation has long been proved to be an empty one. And after that we do have an influence of philosophy, but mostly on the theological use of the Bible rather than on biblical scholarship in the narrower sense.[13]

Writing in 2007, John Barton asserts that bracketing out "questions of theological truth" is "methodologically essential" for biblical criticism.[14]

Such approaches perpetuate the myth of modernity as neutral, scientific, and objective. In fact, philosophy and views of religion have always influenced biblical criticism in powerful ways. We noted above, for example, the profound influence of Kant on de Wette. One only needs to explore Kant's view of religion and of historical narrative in the Bible to see what implications this would have for someone like de Wette. For Kant religion is all about morality and historical revelation is of no importance for true religion. In his well titled *Religion within the Bounds of Mere Reason*, Kant is clear:

> For the final purpose of even the reading of these holy books, or the investigation of their content, is to make better human beings; whereas their historical element, which contributes nothing to this end, is something in itself quite indifferent, and one can do with it what one wills. – (Historical faith is "dead, being alone,"[15] i.e. of itself, considered as a declaration, contains nothing, nor does it lead to anything that would have a moral value for us.)[16]

His antihistorical approach to the Bible surfaces repeatedly in "The Conflict of the Faculties." Kant asks, "Why should we get entangled in all these

13. James Barr, *History and Ideology in the Old Testament: Biblical Studies at the End of a Millennium* (Oxford: Oxford University Press, 2000), 26–27.

14. John Barton, *The Nature of Biblical Criticism* (Louisville: Westminster John Knox, 2007), 164.

15. The reference is to James 2:17.

16. Immanuel Kant, *Religion within the Boundaries of Mere Reason and Other Writings*, ed. Allen Wood and George di Giovanni, Cambridge Texts in the History of Philosophy (Cambridge: Cambridge University Press, 1998), 119. For similar statements see Kant, "The Conflict of the Faculties," in *Religion and Rational Theology*, trans. and ed. Allen W. Wood (Cambridge: Cambridge University Press, 1996), 242.

learned investigations and disputes because of a historical narrative that should always be left in its proper place (among matters that are indifferent)?"[17] Kant asserts, "For if God should really speak to a human being, the latter could still never *know* that it was God speaking. It is quite impossible for a human being to apprehend the infinite by his senses, distinguish it from sensible beings, and *be acquainted with* it as such."[18]

Kant's influence oriented de Wette towards the Bible and history in a very particular way. However, his critical approach to the Bible left de Wette somewhat bereft, and he found help in Fries's view that religious sentiments are mediated through literature and aesthetics, not historical narrative. The result was the construction of a very different view of the history of Israel to that presented in the Old Testament, a characteristic and tension that is found through much Old Testament biblical criticism. The sort of challenge that modern historical reconstructions of the history of Israel presented to Christian scholars is well captured in Von Rad's statement:

> These two pictures of Israel's history lie before us – that of modern critical scholarship and that which the faith of Israel constructed – and for the present, we must reconcile ourselves to both of them . . . The one is rational and "objective". . . . The other . . . is confessional. . . . The fact that these two views of Israel's history are so divergent is one of the most serious burdens imposed upon Biblical scholarship.[19]

Christians have reacted to this gap in different ways. Some have attempted to close the gap. Others argue that history is not as central to Old Testament theology as is often thought.[20] In this way a minimalist-maximalist distinction among Christian biblical scholars has developed. According to some, God's revelation in Israel and Christ means that the historical accuracy of the biblical narratives is of great importance – such scholars tend to be maximalists. Minimalists, by contrast, seek to ascertain the minimum of historical truth required for the Bible to be taken seriously as Scripture.

The radical Enlightenment sought to marginalise or eliminate religion from the great spheres of public life, including universities, as noted above. Religion could be studied through the lens of the modern worldview(s) but could not inform modern study at a foundational level. When this approach entered into

17. Kant, *Religion and Rational Theology*, 266.
18. Kant, *Religion and Rational Theology*, 283, emphasis original.
19. Gerhard von Rad, *Old Testament Theology*, vol. 1 (Edinburgh: Oliver and Boyd, 1973), 108.
20. Barr, "The Concepts of History and Revelation."

biblical studies, it had major consequence for the historicity of the Bible. The historical narratives in the Bible are awash with the language of divine action, but if such action is ruled out by "scientific" biblical study, then such narratives are reduced to categories like myth, saga, or superstition.

Once again it is vital to note that such approaches *include* very strong views of the nature of religion. Spinoza was hugely influential on the radical Enlightenment and is widely recognized as a key figure in the development of historical criticism, particularly his *Tractatus Theologico-Politicus*. Jonathan Israel points out, "In fact, no one else during the century 1650–1750 remotely rivalled Spinoza's notoriety as the chief challenger of the fundamentals of revealed religion, received ideas, tradition, morality, and what was everywhere regarded, in absolutist and non-absolutist states alike, as divinely constituted political authority."[21] In his *Ethics* Spinoza sets out his view of religion and his metaphysics. His approach to the Bible turns out to be the logical consequence of approaching religion through his pantheistic monism. For Spinoza, "faith in historical narratives, no matter how certain that faith may be, cannot give us any knowledge of God. So it also cannot give us the love of God. For love of God arises from knowledge of him, and knowledge of God must be drawn from common notions certain and known through themselves. So it is far from true that faith in historical narratives is necessary for us to attain our supreme good."[22]

As we noted above, John Barton insists that biblical criticism must bracket out theology; theology may follow biblical criticism but not precede it. However, what Spinoza shows us is that strong views of religion are always already present in biblical criticism so that such bracketing out merely obscures their influence.

In the latter half of the twentieth century, biblical studies' preoccupation with historical method was increasingly challenged. In his 1981 inaugural lecture at Oxford University,[23] Ernest Nicholson wondered whether historical criticism might be a Sisyphean toil, but then dismisses the thought. It simply cannot be that all this historical critical effort is of little value! As time has passed, the challenge has grown stronger, and it has become harder to dismiss that thought so easily.

Some of the above relates in particular to Old Testament studies. A reason

---

21. Jonathan Israel, *Radical Enlightenment: Philosophy and the Making of Modernity 1650–1750* (Oxford: Oxford University Press, 2001), 159.

22. Spinoza, *The Collected Works of Spinoza*, trans. and ed. Edwin Curley, vol. 2 (Princeton, NJ: Princeton University Press, 2016), 129–30.

23. Ernest Nicholson, *Interpreting the Old Testament: A Century of the Oriel Professorship* (Oxford: Clarendon, 1981).

for this is that Old Testament studies has been, and continues to be, far more polarized between minimalists and maximalists than New Testament studies. Whitelam's "death of biblical history"[24] represents a growing scepticism and hardened secularism about Old Testament history, whereas Provan, Long, and Longman's *A Biblical History of Israel* represents a maximalist approach.[25] New Testament studies has never been as polarised as Old Testament studies. Westcott, Hort, and Lightfoot played a major role in developing a moderate, believing New Testament criticism early on,[26] a tradition sustained through the work of scholars such as F. F. Bruce, C. E. B. Cranfield, C. F. D. Moule, I. H. Marshall, and more recently Richard Bauckham[27] and N. T. Wright. There was no such equivalent movement in Old Testament studies early on, which have as a result been far more polarised between radical and conservative approaches to historical issues.[28]

Simultaneously, scholars in New Testament studies such as N. T. Wright and Richard Bauckham have creatively and rigorously revived the notion of history as of fundamental importance for New Testament interpretation. Wright is close to completing his massive series entitled Christian Origins and the Question of God, a rigorous defence of the historicity of the Gospels, Acts, and Paul.[29] Bauckham has similarly done major work on the historicity of the Gospels and of John in particular. According to Wright, "We go back to the past because this is where God acted decisively and uniquely."[30]

---

24. Keith W. Whitelam, *The Invention of Ancient Israel: The Silencing of Palestinian History* (London: Routledge, 1996), 69.

25. Iain Provan, V. Phillips Long, and Tremper Longman III, *A Biblical History of Israel* (Louisville: Westminster John Knox, 2003). Cf. also K. A. Kitchen, *On the Reliability of the Old Testament* (Grand Rapids: Eerdmans, 2003).

26. See Neill and Wright, *The Interpretation*, chap. 3.

27. Cf. Richard Bauckham, *Jesus and the Eyewitnesses: The Gospels as Eyewitness Testimony* (Grand Rapids: Eerdmans, 2006, 2017); *Gospel of Glory: Major Themes in Johannine Theology* (Grand Rapids: Baker Academic, 2015); *The Christian World Around the New Testament* (Tübingen: Mohr Siebeck, 2017); *Jesus: A Very Short Introduction* (Oxford: Oxford University Press, 2011); *The Testimony of the Beloved Disciple: Narrative, History, and Theology in the Gospel of John* (Grand Rapids: Baker Academic, 2007). In the latter work, Bauckham notes that "what most Johannine scholars have failed to take seriously is that the Gospel's theology itself requires a concern for history. . . . We should not expect the history to have been lost behind the interpretation but rather to have been highlighted by the interpretation" (*The Testimony of the Beloved Disciple*, 14). Cf. also Richard Bauckham, ed., *The Book of Acts in Its First Century Setting*, vol. 4, *The Book of Acts in Its Palestinian Setting* (Grand Rapids: Eerdmans, 1995).

28. I am indebted to Brevard Childs for this point.

29. N. T. Wright, *The New Testament and the People of God* (Minneapolis: Fortress, 1992); *Jesus and the Victory of God* (Minneapolis: Fortress, 1996); *The Resurrection of the Son of God* (Minneapolis: Fortress, 2003); *Paul and the Faithfulness of God*, parts 1 and 2 (Minneapolis: Fortress, 2013).

30. N. T. Wright, "A Reformation and Revival Journal Interview with N. T. Wright," in *Reformation and Revival Journal* 11, no. 1 (2002): 117–39, 132.

THE LITERARY TURN AND HISTORICITY

In the last quarter of the twentieth century, the historical emphasis in biblical studies experienced some major challenges. A useful way of visualising this larger context is to think in terms of several *turns*:[31]

- the historical turn
- the literary turn
- the postmodern turn
- a theological turn

As with all models, this one has limitations. It is important to note, for example, that one turn does not erase an earlier one. Nor are the turns uniform in the sense that, for example, only one philosophy of history informs the historical turn, as discussed above. However, the model helpfully alerts us to the dominance of history in biblical interpretation during the twentieth century and to the ways this historical emphasis has had to readjust to other turns. In this way the model enables us to discern the challenges of addressing history and the Bible today.

In the 1970s onwards, biblical studies experienced a literary turn with the rediscovery of the Bible as literature. When they published *The Literary Guide to the Bible* in 1987, Robert Alter and Frank Kermode, the two editors, were able to write that "over the past couple of decades, however, there has been a revival of interest in the literary qualities of these texts, in the virtues by which they continue to live by something other than archaeology."[32] Indeed, Alter was a major figure in this revival. They note that in biblical criticism prior to this turn the literary nature of the Bible received scant attention; biblical criticism "treated the biblical texts as relics, probably distorted in transmission, of a past one needed to recover as exactly as possible."[33]

By the conclusion of the nineteenth century and the beginning of the twentieth, positivism dominated philosophy in Europe. In literary studies this yielded a focus on questions of genesis, context, and authorial intent. What it

---

31. The metaphor of a "turn" has become commonplace in scientific and philosophical literature. See Botha, M. Elaine, "Understanding Our Age: Philosophy at a Turning Point of the 'Turns'? – The Endless Search for the Elusive Universal," *Tydskrif Vir Christelike Wetenskap* 30, no. 2 (1994): 16–31.

32. Robert Alter and Frank Kermode, "General Introduction," in *The Literary Guide to the Bible*, ed. Robert Alter and Frank Kermode (London: Fontana, 1987), 102.

33. Alter and Kermode, *The Literary Guide to the Bible*, 1; cf. p. 3: "It diverted attention from biblical narrative, poetry, and prophecy as *literature*, treating them instead as more or less distorted historical records."

neglected was the *literary text* itself, a neglect paralleled in biblical criticisms' focus on questions of origin and what lies behind the text, and a neglect of the literary shape of the text itself as we have received it. Alter and Kermode note of historical criticism:

> This "scientific" criticism was of great cultural and doctrinal importance; but, as we have said, it diverted attention from biblical narrative, poetry, and prophecy as *literature*, treating them instead as more or less distorted historical records. The characteristic move was to infer the existence of some book that preceded the one we have – the lost documents that were combined to make Genesis as it has come down to us, the lost Aramaic Gospel, the lost "sayings-source" used by Matthew and Luke, and so on. The effect of this practice was curious: one spoke of the existing books primarily as evidence of what must once have been available in an original closer to what actually happened. That was their real value – as substitutes for what had unfortunately been lost.[34]

Alter and Kermode rightly note the connections between the literary turn in biblical studies and developments in literary criticism. New Criticism developed in response to the neglect of the literary text itself, and the literary turn developed in biblical studies to fill a parallel gap. Alter and Kermode rightly identify Erich Auerbach's extraordinary *Mimesis* (1946; Eng. trans. 1953) as a landmark in the literary turn.

Auerbach's work developed out of the tradition of Romance philology, Hegel, and Vico. *Mimesis* is a fascinating work and not least because it is "ideologically unintelligible without the Christian doctrine of Incarnation."[35] In chapter 1 of *Mimesis* Auerbach compares Genesis 22 – the story of Abraham journeying to sacrifice Isaac – with book 19 of Homer's *Odyssey*. From Genesis 22 Auerbach comments in general on the biblical stories. Intriguingly, he notes that

> their religious intent involves an absolute claim to historical truth. The story of Abraham and Isaac is not better established than the story of Odysseus, Penelope, and Euryclea; both are legendary. But the Biblical narrator, the Elohist, had to believe in the objective truth of the story of Abraham's sacrifice – the existence of the sacred ordinances of life rested upon the truth of this and similar stories. He had to believe in it passionately; or else (as many

---

34. Alter and Kermode, *The Literary Guide to the Bible*, 3.

35. Edward W. Said, introduction to *Mimesis: The Representation of Reality in Western Literature*, by Erich Auerbach, 50th anniversary ed., Princeton Classics (Princeton, NJ: Princeton University Press, 2003), xi.

> rationalistic interpreters believed and perhaps still believe) he had to be a conscious liar . . . lying in the interest of a claim to absolute authority.[36]

The Elohist aimed not primarily at realism but at *truth*:

> The Bible's claim to truth is not only far more urgent than Homer's, it is tyrannical – it excludes all other claims. The world of the Scripture stories is not satisfied with claiming to be a historically true reality – it insists that it is the only real world, it is destined for autocracy. . . . Far from seeking, like Homer, merely to make us forget our own reality for a few hours, it seeks to overcome our reality: we are to fit our own life into its world, feel ourselves to be elements in its structure of universal history.[37]

Auerbach argues that the Old Testament presents *universal history*, beginning with creation and concluding with the last days, the fulfilling of the covenant. "As a composition, the Old Testament is incomparably less unified than the Homeric poems, it is more obviously pieced together – but the various components all belong to one concept of universal history and its interpretation."[38]

An intriguing aspect of Auerbach's analysis of the Bible is that its literary nature develops a vision in which the sublime (divine) and the everyday are woven together.[39] In chapter 2 of *Mimesis* Auerbach compares chapter 37 and part of 38 of Peronius's *Fortunata*, the ancient view of the instability of fortune, and part of Tacitus's *Annals*, book 1, with the narrative of Peter's denial of Jesus in the Mark's gospel. In contrast with the ancient literature Peter "is the image of man in the highest and deepest and most tragic sense"[40] and the scene of his denial "fits into no antique genre."[41] Auerbach explores why this narrative arouses in us strong sympathy.

> Because it portrays something which neither the poets nor the historians of antiquity ever set out to portray: the birth of a spiritual movement in the depths of the common people, from within the everyday occurrences of

36. Auerbach, *Mimesis*, 14. This is not to suggest that Auerbach simply sees all Old Testament narratives as historical. There is legendary material present, but "the material of the Old Testament comes closer and closer to history as the narrative proceeds" (19). C. S. Lewis held a similar view.

37. Auerbach, *Mimesis*, 14–15. The reader should note that Lesslie Newbigin makes comparable points.

38. Auerbach, *Mimesis*, 17.

39. Cf. Auerbach, *Mimesis*, 22–23.

40. Auerbach, *Mimesis*, 41.

41. Auerbach, *Mimesis*, 45.

> contemporary life, which thus assumes an importance it could never have assumed in antique literature. What we witness is the awakening of "a new heart and a new spirit." All this applies not only to Peter's denial but also to every other occurrence which is related in the New Testament.... Peter and the other characters in the New Testament are caught in a universal movement of the depths which at first remains almost entirely below the surface and only very gradually... emerges into the foreground of history.... What we see here is a world which on the one hand is entirely real, average, identifiable as to place, time and circumstances, but which on the other hand is shaken in its very foundations, is transforming and renewing itself before our eyes. For the New Testament authors who are their contemporaries, these occurrences on the plane of everyday life assume the importance of world-revolutionary events, as later on they will for everyone.[42]

In terms of the Bible and history, Auerbach's work alerts us first to the value of historical, *comparative study* but of a certain sort.[43] Auerbach focuses on the world represented by the text; such a focus makes Auerbach's work fresh and powerful and foregrounds the issue of history. Second, Auerbach's work demonstrates the need for developing a *literary sensibility* when it comes to the Bible. Indeed, the most creative work on the Bible as literature has largely emerged from Jewish scholars whose specialty is not biblical studies but literature. Third, it is clear from Auerbach's work that in the Bible the literary, the historical, and the theological are intertwined.

The literary turn in biblical studies can be tracked from a growing awareness of the limitations of historical criticism through Brevard Child's Canon Criticism[44] and New Criticism (including Muilenberg's rhetorical criticism) to the narratology of Alter, Berlin, and Sternberg[45] with parallel developments in New Testament studies. In 1981 Alter wrote that "over the last few years, there has been growing interest in literary approaches among the younger generation of biblical scholars... but, while useful explications of particular texts have

42. Auerbach, *Mimesis*, 43.

43. Cf. C. S. Lewis, *Undeceptions: Essays on Theology and Ethics* (London: Bles, 1971), 126, for his critique of seeing the Gospels as legends. He notes that "now, as a literary historian, I am perfectly convinced that whatever else the Gospels are, they are not legends.... Apart from bits of the Platonic dialogues, there are no conversations that I know of in ancient literature like the Fourth Gospel. There is nothing, even in modern literature, until about a hundred years ago when the realistic novel came into existence."

44. John Barton, *Reading the Old Testament: Method in Biblical Study*, 2nd ed. (London: Darton, Longman & Todd, 1996), notes the similarities between New Criticism and Childs's canonical approach, but Childs insists his is a theological hermeneutic.

45. David M. Gunn, "New Directions in the Study of Biblical Hebrew Narrative," *JSOT* 39 (1987): 65–68.

begun to appear, there have been as yet no major works of criticism, and certainly no satisfying overview of the poetics of the Hebrew Bible."[46] Alter's *The Art of Biblical Narrative* and his other such works are seminal, but Sternberg's *The Poetics of Biblical Narrative* is the major work on Old Testament narrative. Gunn observed, "Sternberg's recent book on poetics moves such a narratology into a whole new dimension of discrimination and sophistication and will be fundamental to the emerging generation of narrative critics."[47]

The literary turn has major implications for historical criticism. For example, what was thought to be a doublet, and thereby signalling a source, is now considered an example of careful, artistic repetition. Of course, it was always possible to see the literary turn as another method and to get on with analysing the Bible as literature while ignoring historical issues. Some have practiced literary analysis of the Bible without concerning themselves with historical issues. N. T. Wright identifies this as a particular danger amidst postmodernism: "While history and theology work at their stormy relationship, there is always a danger, particularly in postmodernism, that literary study will get on by itself, without impinging on, or being affected by, either of the others."[48] But clearly the historical turn is not unaffected by the literary turn. Sternberg, Wright, Thiselton,[49] and others rightly argue for a careful integration of the historical and literary dimensions of the Bible, as well as the ideological or theological.

What needs to be noted is that the best literary work on the Bible has foregrounded the issue of history and the Bible's unique insights in this respect. Sternberg, for example, is critical of tendencies to categorise Hebrew Bible / Old Testament narratives as fiction. Fiction and history can only be distinguished in terms of overall purpose. When the Hebrew Bible / Old Testament narratives are assessed in this way, "the product is neither historicized fiction nor fictionalised history, but historiography pure and uncompromising."[50] For Sternberg, everything points this way: the obsession with memory of the past and its relevance for the present among the Israelites and Israel's uniqueness in this regard in the ANE – such factors confirm that the historical narratives of the Hebrew Bible / Old Testament make a strong historical truth claim. "Were the narrative written or read as fiction, then God would turn from the lord of history into

46. Robert Alter, *The Art of Biblical Narrative* (New York: Basic, 1981), 15.

47. Gunn, "New Directions," 68.

48. This is a real danger in our postmodern context, as Wright, *The New Testament*, 13, points out.

49. Anthony C. Thiselton, "On Models and Methods. A Conversation with Robert Morgan," in *The Bible in Three Dimensions*, ed. D. J. A. Clines et al., JSOTSup 87 (Sheffield: JSOT, 1990), 337–56.

50. Meir Sternberg, *The Poetics of Biblical Narrative: Ideological Literature and the Drama of Reading* (Bloomington: Indiana University Press, 1985), 35.

a creature of the imagination, with the most disastrous results."[51] Sternberg's approach is by no means uncontested. But it demonstrates well how the literary turn complicates historical criticism.

THE POSTMODERN TURN AND HISTORICITY

Before the literary turn could be fully appropriated in biblical studies and its implications for the Bible and history properly assessed, the postmodern turn was upon us with its wild pluralism and smorgasbord of methods. Postmodernism developed in literary studies – while structuralism was still in vogue Derrida famously gave his lecture on poststructuralism – and then extended into a critique of Western culture as a whole, mauling many of the central pillars of postenlightenment thought. Christopher Norris argues that "literary theory, through its colonizing drive into other disciplines, bids fair to reverse that entire movement of progressive or enlightened critique which has sought to establish adequate protocols for the discrimination of truth from falsehood, of factual from fictive or historical from mythic modes of utterance."[52] Postmodernism questioned central assumptions of modernity, including its views of history, and inevitably such questioning threatened the dominance of the quintessentially modern biblical criticism. With its pluralism, its view of texts as indeterminate, its suspicion of getting behind texts, much postmodernism has rendered the historical critical enterprise untenable. If, as Munslow says, "the past is not discovered or found," and "it is created and represented by the historian as a text, which in turn is consumed by the reader,"[53] then where does this leave the enterprise of historical criticism or any strong sense of the historical narratives in the Bible as history telling?

On the one hand the depth provided by the postmodern challenge must be noted. As long as what Toulmin and others refer to as the standard narrative of modernity of scientific, rational progress was assumed, biblical criticism did not need to pay much attention to defending its philosophical presuppositions. However, postmodernism questioned such neutrality and alerted us to the fact that particular epistemologies and philosophies of history undergird biblical criticism, and these cannot simply be assumed.

51. Sternberg, *Poetics*, 32.

52. Christopher Norris, *Truth and the Ethics of Criticism* (Manchester: Manchester University Press, 1994), 114.

53. Alun Munslow, *Deconstructing History* (New York: Routledge, 1997), 178.

Postmodernism spread like wildfire, and it is through postmodern philosophies of history that both biblical criticism *and* maximalist views of the Bible and history are challenged. Munslow, in his *Deconstructing History*, identifies three major options in historiography: reconstructionism, constructionism, and deconstructionism. Reconstructionism argues that the more rigorously we practice history, the closer we get to what happened. Constructionism invokes general laws of history, Marxism being the most well-known example. Munslow groups postmodern approaches under the label of deconstructionism, including authors like Hayden White and Keith Jenkins. Postmodern approaches stress that historiography always involves literary production with all its attendant complexities.

At the heart of postmodern debates about history is the extent to which historiography can represent the past accurately through narrative. Proponents invoke the interpretative and hermeneutical element in historiography, and many draw extremely radical conclusions from these characteristics.[54] Munslow, for example, proposes that "history is best viewed epistemologically as a form of literature producing knowledge as much by its aesthetic or narrative structure as by any other criteria."[55] "All such narratives make over events and explain why they happened, but are overlaid by the assumptions held by the historian about the forces influencing the nature of causality."[56]

Although postmodernism did open the door for a reengagement with religion, at its extreme it virtually erased the distinction between fiction and history and introduced questions about the possibility of history telling the truth about the past. Furthermore, although postmodernism challenged many of the tenets of modernity, it remained deeply committed to human autonomy. One way to think of postmodernists is as sitting on the Enlightenment branch of a tree and sawing it off at the same time. Postmodernism was always more deconstructive than constructive, and the result is that in biblical studies historical criticism tends to remain as the default position as postmodernism looses its attractions.

A THEOLOGICAL TURN?

In his inaugural lecture at Oxford University, John Barton attends to the crisis in Old Testament interpretation and notes the call for a *religious* hermeneutic.[57]

---

54. For a taste of the radicality of this, see F. W. Burnett, "Historiography," in *Handbook of Postmodern Biblical Interpretation*, ed. A. K. M. Adam (St. Louis: Chalice, 2000).

55. Munslow, *Deconstructing History*, 5.

56. Munslow, *Deconstructing History*, 10.

57. John Barton, *The Future of Old Testament Study* (Clarendon: Oxford, 1993).

Barton is wary of this call and advocates for a recovery of Enlightenment values at the heart of Old Testament studies. Barton rightly recognizes that many have argued for the recovery of a theological hermeneutic in biblical studies.

Karl Barth, Childs's canonical hermeneutic, and Yale's postliberal theology are important ingredients in this development. This theological turn has two major approaches. One is that of simply getting on with reading the Bible for doctrine and the church. This tends to allow a limited approach for historical criticism, as with Childs, but makes the focus theological interpretation. The other is somewhat different. It argues that we need a theology of history (and literature, etc.) to inform biblical interpretation. Neill and Wright express this as follows:

> Similarly, there has, alas, been little progress in the areas of a theology of history, or of New Testament ecclesiology. It is an exciting idea, as was mooted in the first edition of this work, that "An understanding of history which is incompatible with a Christian doctrine of revelation is bound to land the New Testament scholar in grave perplexities; a true theological understanding of history would not of itself solve any New Testament problems, but it would, so to speak, hold the ring within which a solution can be found." But where are the scholars sufficiently familiar with actual history-writing, sufficiently at home in philosophy and the history of ideas, and sufficiently committed to the study of the New Testament, to undertake the task?[58]

Wright himself has gone on to make a major contribution in this area with his magisterial, multivolume series, Christian Origins and the Question of God. Kevin Vanhoozer comparably argues, "The *best general hermeneutics is a Trinitarian hermeneutics*. Yes, the Bible should be interpreted 'like any other book'; but *every* book should be interpreted with norms that we derive and establish from Trinitarian theology."[59] This second approach has yielded major work on the New Testament and history, as evidenced in Wright's work.

A THREEFOLD CORD

There has been a growing recognition that three dimensions of the Bible need to be taken into account in biblical interpretation – namely, the historical,

58. Neill and Wright, *The Interpretation*, 366.

59. Kevin Vanhoozer, *Is There a Meaning in This Text? The Bible, The Reader, and the Morality of Literary Knowledge* (Grand Rapids: Zondervan, 1998), 456.

the literary, and the theological, or kerygmatic. This is an important insight in many ways. First, it reminds us that the Bible is not a history book. Its goal is to tell us about God's involvement in his world, and it does this through his immersion in the life of an ANE nation (Israel) and in the Christ event (the New Testament). History is, of course, a vital part of this. As Goldingay says of the Old Testament, "It remains true that the major overt emphasis of much of the OT is that Yahweh has acted, acts and will act in Israel's history for her salvation. The importance of this emphasis should not be lost in the course of emphasising complementary features of OT faith."[60]

Second, it alerts us to the fact that the history telling of the historical narratives is from a committed, religious perspective. For secular scholars this perspective often rules it out as seriously historical. However, much depends upon the view of the religious perspective informing the history telling of the Bible. The Jewish scholar Will Herberg argues that "the uniqueness – the 'scandal' – of biblical faith is revealed in its radically historical character."[61] He insists that we cannot eliminate the historicity of the Bible without destroying faith itself.

Herberg identifies three major ways humans have sought to understand history. First, there is what I call the pagan approach, which equates reality with nature, a type of immanence philosophy. Second, there is the Greek approach, which focuses not on nature but on the timelessly eternal beyond nature. Third, there is the biblical view, which breaks with both of the first two – both nature and time are real but contingent, dependent upon God. This, for Herberg, allows history to come into proper focus for the first time. "It is in and through history that God calls to man; it is in and through history, human action in history, that man responds; and it is in and through history that God judges."[62] The Bible presents us with a great drama of existence in a threefold pattern: our present woes result from *falling* away from *the original good creation*, and the fallen creation is destined for *restoration* in the kingdom of God. All human history is contained within this drama. Its range is universal, but its centre is particular: exodus-Sinai for Judaism and the Christ event for Christians. Herberg discerns a double inwardness to the biblical view of history: it interprets events through the lens of faith, "acts and events that, from another standpoint, might well be interpreted

60. John Goldingay, *Approaches to Old Testament Interpretation* (Leicester: InterVarsity Press, 1981), 69. See Craig G. Bartholomew, *The Old Testament and God*, Old Testament Origins and the Question of God (Grand Rapids: Baker Academic, 2022), especially chap. 4.

61. Will Herberg, *Faith Enacted as History: Essays in Biblical Theology*, ed. Bernhard W. Anderson. (Philadelphia: Westminster, 1976), 32.

62. Herberg, *Faith Enacted as History*, 35.

in an altogether different way."[63] Second, it is inward in that the biblical view can only become redemptive for me personally if I indwell it as my history.

This backs us into the very common view expressed, for example, by Bruce Halpern, who sets believing reading against historical reading: "Worshippers do not read the Bible with an intrinsic interest in human events. . . . Confessional reading levels historical differences."[64] Herberg's approach, and here I think too of the work of philosophers like Alvin Plantinga and Nicholas Wolterstorff, suggests precisely the opposite: that biblical faith increases one's interest in the historicity of the Bible and orients one towards history in a particular way so that one can take the historical aspect of the Bible with full seriousness.

HISTORICAL CONTEXT REVISITED

Since biblical criticism emerged and came to dominate biblical studies, a great deal of historical information about the cultures in which the Bible came into existence has emerged. An intriguing case is now being made that traditional biblical criticism, especially in relation to the Old Testament, does not fit with recent discoveries. In an important work, Joshua Berman describes a conference in Jerusalem in 2013 titled "Convergence and Divergence in Pentateuchal Theory: Bridging the Cultures of Israel, North America and Europe." This conference was the culmination of a yearlong research group made up of eight of the most prominent scholars in Pentateuchal criticism. The result demonstrated crisis and gridlock. Berman writes of a new movement in historical critical analysis of the Pentateuch:

> The root of the problem, heretofore, according to this movement, is that scholars have rooted their compositional theories for the growth of the biblical text entirely in their own intuition of what constitutes literary unity. For those of us working in this new movement, the time has come to root compositional theory in the so-called empirical findings of the writings of the ancient near East. We must canvas and analyze documented examples of compositional growth and editing across a wide field of ancient near eastern texts, both within ancient Israel and outside it.[65]

63. Herberg, *Faith Enacted as History*, 40.

64. Halpern, *First Historians*, 4.

65. Joshua A. Berman, *Inconsistency in the Torah: Ancient Literary Convention and the Limits of Source Criticism* (Oxford: Oxford University Press, 2017), 2–3.

Thus, Berman and others are making that case that we need to take the criterion of similarity far more seriously in our assessment of how Old Testament documents came into existence.

THE GOD QUESTION

Herberg's work alerts us to a fundamental issue when it comes to the Bible and history: one's view of the God depicted in the Bible. The Bible is awash with historical narratives about divine action in history, but in so much modern biblical interpretation, the one issue excluded is one's view of God. Affirm the biblical view of God as creator and redeemer, the God who sustains, governs, and acts in history, and then one is far more positively oriented towards the Bible and history.[66] This does not solve all the many historical issues that emerge in biblical studies, but as Wright and Neill note, it creates a ring within which solutions may be found.

FOR FURTHER READING

Auerbach, Erich. *Mimesis: The Representation of Reality in Western Literature.* Princeton Classics. Princeton, NJ: Princeton University Press, 1953.

Barr, James. *History and Ideology in the Old Testament: Biblical Studies at the End of a Millennium*. Oxford: Oxford University Press, 2000.

Bartholomew, Craig G. *God Who Acts in History: The Significance of Sinai*. Grand Rapids: Eerdmans, 2020.

———. *The Old Testament and God: Old Testament Origins and the Question of God.* Grand Rapids: Baker Academic, 2022.

Herberg, Will. *Faith Enacted as History: Essays in Biblical Theology*. Edited by Bernhard W. Anderson. Philadelphia: Westminster, 1976.

Israel, Jonathan. *Radical Enlightenment: Philosophy and the Making of Modernity 1650–1750*. Oxford: Oxford University Press, 2001.

Krentz, Edgar. *The Historical-critical Method*. London: SPCK, 1975.

Kümmel, Werner G. *The New Testament. The History of the Interpretation of Its Problems*. London: SCM, 1973.

---

66. Cf. Craig G. Bartholomew, *God Who Acts in History: The Significance of Sinai* (Grand Rapids: Eerdmans, 2020); "Old Testament Origins and the Question of God," *Bulletin for Biblical Research* 27, no. 2 (2017): 169–84.

Michalson, Gordon E. "Faith and History." In *The Blackwell Encyclopedia of Modern Christian Thought*, edited by A. E. McGrath, 210–14. Oxford: Blackwell, 1993.

Neill, Stephen, and Tom Wright. *The Interpretation of the New Testament 1861–1986*. Oxford: Oxford University Press, 1988.

Provan, Iain, V. Phillips Long, and Tremper Longman III. *A Biblical History of Israel*. Louisville: Westminster John Knox, 2003.

Sternberg, Meir. *The Poetics of Biblical Narrative. Ideological Literature and the Drama of Reading*. Bloomington: Indiana University Press, 1985.

Wright, N. T. *The New Testament and the People of God*. Minneapolis: Fortress, 1992.

CHAPTER 8

Jewish Biblical Interpretation

Jeremiah Unterman

The Jewish Bible is what Christians refer to as the Old Testament. It is also known as the Hebrew Bible or, in Hebrew terminology, the Tanakh[1] or Miqra ("Scriptures"). The history of the Jewish interpretation of its Bible is the history of the Jewish religious civilization, affecting the development of law, liturgy, ritual, literature, music, art, philosophy, mysticism, institutions – indeed, all of Jewish life. From earliest times, every age and every literate segment of the Jewish people has interpreted their Bible in accord with their own historical, religious, and social situations and outlooks, as well as their own needs and purposes.[2] For example, in the land of Israel, Jewish exegesis was invariably influenced by the conquests by Persia, Hellenists, Rome, Christians, and Muslims.[3] Additionally, their interpretations were very frequently, even normally, influenced by previous interpretations. Such interpretation is ongoing.

This chapter will attempt to present a very brief overview of the various periods in the history of Jewish Bible interpretation, along with a few of its main

1. An acronym for: T = *Torah* (i.e., the Pentateuch or the Five Books of Moses: Genesis, Exodus, Leviticus, Numbers, and Deuteronomy); N = *Neviim* (Prophets: Former Prophets – Joshua, Judges, 1 and 2 Samuel, 1 and 2 Kings – and Latter Prophets – Isaiah, Jeremiah, Ezekiel, Hosea, Joel, Amos, Obadiah, Jonah, Micah, Nahum, Habakkuk, Zephaniah, Haggai, Zechariah, Malachi); Kh = *Ketuvim* (Writings: Psalms, Proverbs, Job, The Song of Songs, Ruth, Lamentations, Ecclesiastes, Esther, Daniel, Ezra, Nehemiah, 1 & 2 Chronicles).

2. As did the Jewish first followers of Jesus, and whose interpretations comprise some of the New Testament. As other chapters examine Christian Bible interpretation, that and the New Testament will not be discussed here.

3. As Jewish exegesis in the diaspora was influenced by Christian persecution and Muslim subjugation. On the other hand, those times of humane Muslim and Christian rule had happier influences.

goals and achievements. The primary focus will be on actual interpretation, as opposed to, for example, simple allusions. That overview will be supplemented by a small number of detailed examples.

Jewish biblical interpretation is an exceptionally large field of study – an activity that has been taking place for the better part of three millennia in many countries, under many influences, and by many groups and individuals. As such, it is impossible to truly do justice to it in a brief essay. Let the reader imagine going on a wine-tasting trip to an area filled with dozens of wineries, each with dozens of wines of different types. Herein, we will sample only a few wines from a few varieties at a few wineries.

INNERBIBLICAL

Biblical authors often quoted, clarified, expanded, revised, and generally utilized previous biblical texts.[4] These reference types occur across the board, that is, within the Torah itself, other biblical books citing the Torah, and other biblical books citing each other. Also, an individual book may reuse another text in the same book. Sometimes the source is mentioned explicitly, but most times it is not – so only one who is familiar with the source texts will be able to recognize the allusion. The kinds of referencing that takes place are done by original authors, compilers/editors, and copyists.[5]

A classic example of a formative interpretation by compilers is the fact that the Torah is immediately followed by the Former Prophets and the Latter Prophets. Such an arrangement creates a chronological consistency: the Torah encapsulates the period from creation through the end of the desert wanderings; the book of Joshua fulfills God's promise of the people's conquest and settlement of Canaan; Judges through Kings tells the story of that settlement in chronological order until the Babylonian destruction and exile in 586 BCE (viewed as a fulfillment of the curses for disobedience in Leviticus 26 and Deuteronomy 28). Most of the Latter Prophets belong to the period covered by 2 Kings, the last of which (most of Ezekiel, Isaiah 34–35 and 40–66, Haggai, Zechariah, and Malachi), on face value, historically go through and beyond the exile and into the return to Zion under Persia by approximately another century. The Latter Prophets follow the Torah and Former Prophets both because the literary

4. The classic study of inner-biblical interpretation is M. Fishbane, *Biblical Interpretation in Ancient Israel* (Oxford: Oxford University Press, 1988).

5. This is not the place to discuss the development of the text of the Jewish Bible. For a comprehensive treatment, see E. Tov, *Textual Criticism of the Hebrew Bible*, 4th ed. (Minneapolis: Fortress, 2022).

prophets explicitly explain why the kingdoms of Israel and Judah were destroyed for disobedience to the divine covenant and laws of the Torah *and* to assure the people that God's promises of redemption for them will also be fulfilled.[6] In other words, the structure created by the compilers follows the prophecies in the prophetic books, which themselves are often commentaries – on the laws of the Torah as the stipulations of covenant, on the Torah's blessings and curses, and on the Torah's emphasis on the Israelites as having a special relationship with God that will never be sundered (as in Gen 12:2–3, 14–16; Exod 4:22–23; 19:5–6; Lev 25:55; 26:40–45; Deut 1:31; 4:5–8, 19–20, 29–39; 8:5; 14:1; 30:1–10; 32:9–12, etc.). The Jewish Bible, then, primarily interprets the relationship of the Israelites (in their land, but also in exile) to their God through their obedience or disobedience to his[7] will as revealed in the Torah.

That major theme includes a type of interpretation that is common until this very day – that the source text is referring to a specific historical event at the time of or in the knowledge base of the interpreter. For example, the Assyrian exile of the inhabitants of the Northern Kingdom of Israel is explained in 2 Kings 17:23 by these words: "In the end the Lord removed Israel from His presence, as He had warned them through all His servants the prophets. So the Israelites were deported from their land to Assyria, until this day."[8] No prophet is named here, but Amos and Hosea come to mind as an appropriate fit, even though both predicted exile without mentioning Assyria as the destination (Amos 9:9; Hos 9:17).

A well-known example of revision, which includes both expansion and substitution,[9] appears in the Ten Commandments in Deuteronomy 5, as opposed to the original text in Exodus 20. Both texts are virtually identical until the Sabbath pericope, where, instead of Exodus 20:8, "*Remember* (Heb. *zachor*) the Sabbath day to sanctify it," Deuteronomy 5:12 has, "*Observe* (Heb. *shamor*) the Sabbath day to sanctify it, *as the Lord your God commanded you*." Deuteronomy here not only replaces the first word, but at the end of the verse appends a statement alluding to an earlier text (if not Exod 20:8, then perhaps Exod 31:14, which contains the word *observe* in connection with sanctifying

6. On the other hand, in Christian Bibles, the Latter Prophets are placed immediately before the New Testament in order to show how the divine promise of salvation is fulfilled in the advent of Jesus.

7. On the masculine gender used in Hebrew in reference to God, see J. Unterman, *Justice for All: How the Jewish Bible Revolutionized Ethics* (Lincoln, NB: Jewish Publication Society; University of Nebraska, 2017), xxii–xxiii.

8. All translations of biblical verses are based upon the *JPS Hebrew-English Tanakh*, 2nd ed. (Philadelphia: Jewish Publication Society, 1999) – with occasional changes as deemed necessary by the author.

9. This type of revision occurs in both legal and nonlegal texts.

the Sabbath). Further, while the *raison d'être* for the Sabbath is articulated in Exodus as God's resting on the seventh day of Creation (verse 11 there), the reason given in Deuteronomy is the exodus from Egypt (v. 15).[10]

An important type of biblical legal interpretation, which was to have a major effect on the development of Judaism, is what came to be known as *midrash halakhah*, an explication in which specific behaviors related to individual laws were written down after the laws themselves first appeared in the Torah. So, for example, the Sabbath law in the Ten Commandments only states the prohibition of "work" on the Sabbath (Exod 20:10; Deut 5:14) but does not delineate what that work entails. Jeremiah 17:19–27 is a prophecy that specifically states that that prohibition requires the cessation of "carrying burdens" on the Sabbath day (vv. 22 and 24) – ostensibly, for the purposes of commerce (see Amos 8:5; Neh 10:32; 13:15–17).[11] For later rabbinic authorities, the evidence of such innerbiblical interpretations attested to the existence of the "Oral Law," a verbal tradition that was transmitted along with the "Written Law" (the divine commandments in the Torah) during the Sinai revelation and beyond. Thus, *Mishnah Shabbat* 7:2 listed thirty-nine categories of labor prohibited on the Sabbath.

It is noteworthy that the many different types of interpretation that appear in the Bible itself reappear throughout subsequent ages of interpretation.

FROM THE HELLENISTIC UNTIL THE BEGINNING OF THE TANNAITIC PERIOD

The Jewish texts relating to the Bible in this section were written from the Hellenistic period[12] until the beginning of the Tannaitic period[13] but were not

10. Other, more minor, additions appear further in the Sabbath commandment, in the commandment to honour one's parents, and the commandment against coveting.

11. Other Sabbath prohibitions appear in the Torah: cooking (Exod 16:32), plowing and harvesting (Exod 34:21), lighting fire (Exod 35:23), and wood gathering (Num 15:32–36).

12. It is possible that the latest compilation to become a part of the Jewish Bible was the last six chapters of Daniel – apparently written during the time of the persecutions of Antiochus IV and the beginnings of the Maccabean Revolt (early 160s BCE). In other words, extrabiblical interpretation was taking place before the Bible was completed.

13. The Tannaim were the first Jewish religious authorities termed *rabbis*. Their teachings are contained in the Mishnah, the edited compilation of their statements on the oral law/tradition, which comprise the first part of the Talmud, completed by 220 CE (and in quotations in the Gemara, the commentary on the Mishnah completed by the Amoraim several centuries later [see below], and early midrashic texts), and they flourished from approx. the first century BCE through the early third century CE, although some of these preserved teachings may be older. Among the early texts preserved in rabbinic circles were the Aramaic translations of biblical books.

preserved by rabbinic Judaism. These texts are frequently referred to as intertestamental literature, apocrypha, and pseudepigrapha. They also include such diverse texts as the Septuagint (the earliest extant Greek translation of the Hebrew Scriptures), the Samaritan Pentateuch (the Samaritans saw themselves as a Jewish sect but were not accepted by most Jewish authorities as such), the Judean Desert Scrolls (also called the Dead Sea Scrolls),[14] and the writings of Philo and Josephus.

In the above-mentioned literature are texts that "rework" the Bible – that is, rewrite biblical texts and stories, sometimes to solve interpretive problems, and sometimes to advance legal or theological objectives. These readings of the Bible set forth interpretations that affected future understandings in the ensuing millennia.[15] Such texts include the *Genesis Apocryphon* and *Reworked Pentateuch* from the Judean Desert Scrolls, as well as the book of *Jubilees*.[16]

A new type of interpretation is found in the philosophic writings of Philo of Alexandria and the histories of Flavius Josephus: to interpret the Bible in such a way to authenticate and justify Judaism to non-Jews who belonged to a rival and dominant culture. Philo (20 BCE–50 CE) was actually writing for Jews also and was interpreting the Septuagint translation since that was written in the language of the competing culture, Greek.[17]

THE CLASSICAL RABBINIC PERIOD

The classical rabbinic period lasted from the first through the sixth century CE.[18] The rabbinic interpretive tradition developed predominantly in the lands of Israel and Babylonia (the latter eventually became more influential). The great written achievements of this tradition – the Talmud (the Tannaitic Mishnah and its commentary, the Amoraic Gemara[19]) and the midrashic col-

---

14. For a detailed study of the relationship of the Septuagint, Aramaic translations, the Samaritan Pentateuch, and the Judean Desert Scrolls to the Hebrew Bible, see Tov, *Textual Criticism*, and his other works, such as *The Text-Critical Use of the Septuagint in Biblical Research*, 3rd ed. (Winona Lake, IN: Eisenbrauns, 2015). It is a truism that all translations are interpretations.

15. See J. Kugel, *The Bible As It Was* (Cambridge, MA: Harvard University Press, 1997); *Traditions of the Bible* (Cambridge, MA: Harvard University Press, 1999).

16. See examples in H. Najman, "Early Nonrabbinic Interpretation," in *The Jewish Study Bible*, ed. A. Berlin and M. Z. Brettler (Oxford: Oxford University Press, 2004), 1836–38.

17. See examples in Najman, "Early Nonrabbinic Interpretation," in *The Jewish Study Bible*, 1840–44.

18. Much of this section, unless otherwise indicated, is taken from "Classical Rabbinic Interpretation," by Yaakov Elman, of blessed memory, in *The Jewish Study Bible*, 1844–63.

19. The Amoraim, the rabbinic sages whose words appear in the Gemara, lived from the third to the sixth centuries. They produced two Talmuds: that of the Land of Israel (until 370) and that of Babylon

lections – encapsulated the methodological approaches and arguments of their authors (including minority opinions), as well as the development of law, ritual, morality, and Jewish thought. Both content and method have had an enormous impact on subsequent Jewish interpretation onwards through modern times.

The ancient rabbis (and their successors) viewed the Tanakh as sacred literature, imbued with the divine spirit. As such, the texts – already the product of a bygone age – were embodied with timeless wisdom and knowledge that needed to be explained to contemporaries. If this was true of the Tanakh as a whole, it was even of greater importance when it came to the Torah – perceived not only as authored by God (Moses was only the transmitter) but also as the repository of God's commandments to the Jewish people. The Torah, more than any other text, represented God's will. The words of the Torah had omnisignificance. Every letter was meaningful in a spiritual, ethical, or legal sense, for the commandments were the foundation of all Jewish law – civil, criminal, and ritual.

Yet the ancient rabbis never developed a uniform, systematic way to treat every word of every text. Ultimately, only what was significant to an individual sage, or group, was addressed, and much of that was due to contemporary needs. One goal was to more exactly define legal duties. To accomplish that precise goal, as well as to explain how nonlegal texts in the Hebrew Bible related to the contemporary Jew, uniform methods had to be developed. The rabbis put forward lists of various logical types of biblical interpretation – the best-known and shortest of which was the list of seven types attributed to the first century BCE sage Hillel: "deduction from a minor case to a major case," "drawing an analogy between texts based on a word in common," "applying a principle derived from one verse," "applying a principle derived from two verses," "modification of a general principle derived from a particular principle," (the reverse) "principles derived from similar passages," and "deduction from context."[20]

Even though the ancient rabbis devoted themselves to understanding the relevance of the Tanakh in their own day *because* of its divine inspiration, they recognized that their legal decisions by majority might be challenged as lacking scriptural authority in ritual matters. The following story about the arguments among the rabbis concerning the legal status of "the oven of Akhnai" is therefore included in the Babylonian Talmud, *Bava Metzia* 59b:

(completed in the sixth century). The little understood Savoraim, who lived and worked in the sixth century, may have been the last editors/compilers of the Talmud. It is thought that the anonymous statements in the Talmud are attributable to them.

20. Elman, in *The Jewish Study Bible*, 1847–48. Two other lists are the thirteen rules of Rabbi Ishmael and the thirty-two rules of Rabbi Eliezer ben Yossi Haglili.

> It has been taught: On that day R. Eliezer brought forward every imaginable argument, but they did not accept them. [Finally, in frustration,] he said: If the law follows my opinion, let this carob-tree prove it! Thereupon the carob-tree was torn a hundred cubits out of its place – others affirm, four hundred cubits. No proof can be brought from a carob-tree, they retorted. Again he said to them: If the law agrees with my opinion, let the stream of water prove it! Thereupon the stream of water flowed backwards. No proof can be brought from a stream of water, they rejoined. Again he urged: If the law agrees with my opinion, let the walls of the schoolhouse prove it! Thereupon the walls inclined to fall. But R. Joshua rebuked them, saying: When scholars are engaged in a legal dispute, what have you to interfere? Hence [the walls] did not fall, out of deference to R. Joshua, nor did they resume standing, in deference to R. Eliezer; and they still stand inclined. Finally he said to them: If the law follows my opinion, let it be proved from Heaven! Thereupon a heavenly echo cried out: Why do you dispute with R. Eliezer, seeing that in all matters the law agrees with his opinion? But R. Joshua arose and exclaimed: "It is not in Heaven!" (Deut 30:12)
>
> What did he mean by that? Said R. Jeremiah: Since the Torah has already been given at Mount Sinai, we pay no attention to a heavenly echo, because You have long since written in the Torah at Mount Sinai: "After the majority must one incline" (Ex 23:2).[21]
>
> R. Nathan met Elijah [the Prophet] and asked him, What did the Holy One, Blessed be He, do at that time [in response to this statement]? He laughed [with joy], he replied, saying, My sons have defeated Me, My sons have defeated Me.[22]

Thus, Rabbi Joshua's reinterpretation of Deuteronomy 30:12 (the plain meaning of which was to state that the divine commandments are humanly achievable), applying it to rabbinic majority authority and its use of reason, is affirmed by God.

At the same time, however, that is not the end of the story. The rabbis not only proceeded to excommunicate Rabbi Eliezer but burnt everything he had previously ruled to be pure. On that day, a third of the olive, wheat, and barley crops in the world were destroyed – apparently by God. The obvious message is that rabbinic power has limits, and if the rabbinic authorities, whose responsibility is to effect justice, treat a person unfairly, tragedy will ensue.

---

21. The end of the verse in Hebrew is ambiguous, which allowed the ancient rabbis to find here a source for their oral tradition that a judicial majority was decisive in legal questions.

22. Elman, in *The Jewish Study Bible*, 1862.

Along with the actual explication of laws, the most important literary creation of this period was midrash and midrashic collections. By this time, *midrash* – from the Hebrew root *d-r-sh*, "to seek" or "to inquire" – came to refer to rabbinic study and interpretation of the Bible. However, in a technical sense, midrash became particularly akin to the nonlegal material of the Talmud known as *aggadata* (such as the story cited above). These comprise stories, interpretations, and homilies. Collections of homiletical *midrashim* (the plural of *midrash*; a homiletical midrash is called a *midrash aggada*), which were originally oral traditions (some dating back to the Tannaim), were beginning to be transcribed in the early Amoraic period.[23] One such collection is the *Midrash Rabbah* ("the great midrash"), which is actually ten collections, one for each of the five books of the Torah and one for each of the "five scrolls" (Song of Songs, Ruth, Lamentations, Ecclesiastes, Esther).[24]

Homiletical midrashic interpretations have a creative openness of the imagination that would hardly be suitable for legal exegesis. For example, on Genesis 25:22, which relates of Rebekah's twins (Jacob and Esau) that "the children struggled in her womb," Genesis Rabbah has the following interpretations:[25]

> R. Yochanan said: This one *ran* to kill the other, and the other one *ran* to kill the first one [a play on the word "struggled" which, in Hebrew, contains the root for 'run'] . . .
>
> R. Shimon ben Lakish said: This one permitted [what was forbidden] by command to the other, and the other one permitted [what was forbidden] by command to the first [meaning that each one's laws and practices were in conflict with the other. This interpretation may be based on an aural similarity in Hebrew between the word "struggled" and "permitted by command"]. . . .
>
> "The children struggled in her womb" means that they tried to run out of her womb. When Rebekah passed by a pagan temple, Esau would kick her to let him leave; this is what is written, "The wicked are defiant from the womb" (Psalm 58:4). And when Rebekah passed by a synagogue and a study-hall (*beit midrash*), Jacob would kick her to let him out; this is what is written, "Before I created you in the womb, I knew you" (Jeremiah 1:5). [By a different

23. D. Stern, "Midrash and Midrashic Interpretation," in *The Jewish Study Bible*, 1863. Collections of legal exegesis – midrash halakhah – were also transcribed during this period, such as: the Mekhilta of Rabbi Ishmael and the Mekhilta of Rabbi Simon bar Yochai (both on the legal sections of Exodus); Sifra on Leviticus; Sifre on Numbers; Sifrei on Deuteronomy.

24. In the liturgy, each of the Five Scrolls is read on a different holy day – in order: Passover, Feast of Weeks, the 9th of Av, Feast of Tabernacles, Purim.

25. Quoted from Stern, "Midrash and Midrashic Interpretation," 1869–70, with some minor adjustments for the sake of space.

vocalization, the phrase "I knew you" – one word in Hebrew – could mean "I caused you to know."]

The last interpretation, by an anonymous rabbi, is based on the fact that early biblical texts were written entirely in consonants. Therefore, by vocalizing words with different vowels (which were written in at a later period), one had the ability to draw new meanings from a text. The pun found in the first interpretation (plus a possible aural similarity at the basis of the second) and the technique of the third are illustrative of the freedom of midrashic interpretation.[26] Words and phrases could now be taken out of context, and associations between disparate verses and topics became completely dependent upon the imagination of the interpreter. Such midrashic comments are quintessentially eisegesis.

The multiplicity and idiosyncrasy of creative midrashic interpretations has continued throughout Jewish history and is still found commonly today in rabbinic sermons.

THE MEDIEVAL PERIOD

Christian commentaries on biblical books were already being produced as early as the third century.[27] However, it wasn't until the ascent of Islam, combined with qur'anic exegesis, and its assertion of religious supremacy that individual Jews in the Muslim orbit began writing commentaries on biblical books. These commentaries were also influenced by the rationalism of Islamic philosophy and particularly by Islamic attention to philology and linguistics. Imitating Arabic study, Jews began writing Hebrew grammars and dictionaries that invariably referenced biblical verses. The new Jewish commentators recognized that the specific rules of the Hebrew language must now be used in elucidating the text.

The Karaites, a break-away Jewish movement that rebelled against rabbinic midrashic exegesis, were actually the first Jews to write such commentaries, in the ninth century. They, in turn, were opposed by the preeminent rabbinic commentator (and philosopher) of that time, Saadia Gaon (882–942), who was the head of the foremost talmudic academy of his day. In his introduction to his commentary on the Torah, he stated the necessity of comprehending the text according to the *peshat* – the simple, plain, literal meaning of the words – with four exceptions:

---

26. Stern, "Midrash and Midrashic Interpretation," 1870.

27. Most of this section is taken from the excellent article by B. D. Walfish, "Medieval Jewish Interpretation," in *The Jewish Study Bible*, 1876–1900.

> (1) If experience and sense perception contradict the plain meaning (e.g., that Eve was the mother of all living things [Gen 2:20]); (2) if reason contradicts the plain sense (e.g., Deut 4:24, that "the Lord your God is a consuming fire," which must be interpreted metaphorically); (3) when verses contradict each other (e.g., Mal 3:10, "thus put me to the test," which must be interpreted so as not to contradict Deut 6:16, "do not test the Lord, your God," which takes precedence); (4) when a verse contradicts established tradition (e.g., in the prohibition against seething a kid in its mother's milk [Exod 23:19; 34:26; Deut 14:21]). In the last case, an oral tradition (the complete separation of meat and milk products) was transmitted by the people, who saw how the prophets behaved in this matter. . . . Exegetical freedom has to be limited by the dictates of tradition, which sometimes led to interpretations far from the plain sense.[28]

Although interpretation according to the plain or contextual meaning of words and phrases becomes a conscious goal at this time, the concept of *peshat* originates in the classical rabbinic period in maxims such as, "the text does not leave its *peshat*" (Babylonian Talmud, Shabbat 63a; that is, it cannot be interpreted without attention to its plain meaning) and "the Torah speaks in the language of humans" (e.g., B. T. Berachot 31b; Zevachim 108b; Sifre Numbers 112). The latter statement will now imply that one must be knowledgeable of biblical Hebrew – lexicography, grammar, syntax – to understand fully the basic nuances and allusions in the text.

The systematic biblical commentaries of the Karaites and the Geonim[29] continued to develop. They attained even greater sophistication with the transfer of the intellectual center of Jewry from Babylonia (modern day Iraq) to Muslim Spain in the tenth century. In that century and the next, Hebrew grammatical treatises were composed under the influence of Islamic rhetoric and poetry. One such author, the eleventh century grammarian Jonah ibn Janah, was the first scholar to recognize that Isaiah 40–66 was written by a different prophet than Isaiah ben Amoz (a section termed by modern scholars Deutero-Isaiah or Second Isaiah).

At the same time that Jewish exegesis in Muslim Spain was reaching its zenith, a different school of *peshat* interpretation emerged independently in Northern France. The leader of that school was unquestionably Rashi (an acronym for Rabbi Shlomo son of Yitzchak, 1040–1105). Not only did he write commentaries on almost the entire Tanakh, but he also wrote them on the

28. Walfish, "Medieval Jewish Interpretation," in *The Jewish Study Bible*, 1878.

29. The period from the 589 to 1038 is known as the Geonic period. The Geonim were the leaders of the Babylonian academies, and they also began the first systematic legal studies of the Talmud.

majority of the Talmud. His commentaries – models of clarity and relevant detail – became so popular that it became inconceivable to study either the Jewish Bible or the Talmud without them. Indeed, every printing of the Hebrew Bible or the Talmud with rabbinic commentaries always included Rashi in primacy of place. Further, more than 300 "supercommentaries" – commentaries on *his* commentaries – have been composed! A classic example of Rashi's commentary concerns the first words of Genesis. While moderns are used to the translation, "In the beginning, God created the heavens and the earth," Rashi states, "And if you have come to explain the text according to its *peshat,* this is its interpretation . . . , 'At the beginning of God's creating the heavens . . .' in similarity to 'When God began to speak to Hosea'" (Hosea 1:2). Rashi, here, recognizes that the first word in Hebrew is *beraisheet,* a construct form. Therefore, he understands that it means "In the beginning *of,*" that is, "At the beginning of God's creating," or "When God began to create." He finds a parallel in Hosea where a different Hebrew word, a synonym of "beginning," also appears in the construct state, and brings it here. Therefore, he also understands that the second word, *bara,* usually translated as a past (perfect) tense, "created," is actually the infinitive absolute, i.e., "(to) create" or "creating."

In his exegesis of Genesis 3:8, Rashi states as his goal to comment on "the contextual meaning (*peshuto*) of Scripture," while only adding rabbinic midrashic material that relates to the contextual meaning. Rashi did have some knowledge of tenth century Spanish Jewish grammarians, but his work was almost entirely original. Furthermore, he reworked some of his commentaries over the course of his lifetime and was constantly searching for new insights into the *peshat* of the text. His grandson Rashbam (Rabbi Shmuel ben Meir, ca. 1080–1160) writes in his own (famous) commentary on the Torah (at Gen 37:2) that, during an argument he was having with his grandfather on interpretation, Rashi "admitted to me that, if he had more time, he would have to write other commentaries based upon new insights into the *peshatot* (*peshat* meanings) which occur every day." An example of Rashbam's interpretation is on Genesis 11:4, the Tower of Babel, when the builders say, "let us build a city, and a tower with its top in the sky . . . else we shall be scattered all over the world." Rashbam states, "According to the *peshat,* what was the sin of the generation of dispersion? . . . The Holy One Blessed be He had commanded them 'Be fruitful and increase, and fill the earth,' and they chose for themselves a place to settle there and said 'else we shall be scattered.'"[30] In other words, as opposed to many moderns who view the Tower as an attempt to attack Heaven, Rashbam understands

30. My translation of the Hebrew from https://www.sefaria.org.il/Rashbam_on_Genesis.11.4?lang=he.

that the purpose of a tower as part of a city is defensive in nature, and therein lies the people's sin – their disobedience to God's command in 9:1.

Rashbam's commentaries, and those of Joseph Kara (1050–1125), Eliezer of Beaugancy (mid-twelfth cent.), and Joseph Bekhor Shor (1130–1200) all followed Rashi in focusing on the contextual meaning of the text but (with the exception of Bekhor Shor) shifted away from midrashic material in their exegesis. Their works can still be mined today for exceptional insights into the *peshat* of the text. For example, Rashbam was the first to recognize the literary technique of foreshadowing – presenting information in anticipation of later need for it. However, after the end of the twelfth century, Rashi's combination of the plain, contextual meaning along with midrashic material became the most accepted and influential commentary approach throughout the rest of the Middle Ages and into the modern period. The vast majority of rabbinic scholars were unwilling to abandon midrash. Nonetheless, the *peshat* approach would have a significant effect on Jewish biblical interpretation in modernity.

Two more Spanish medieval *peshat* exegetes must be mentioned – Rabbi Abraham ibn Ezra (1089–1164) and Rabbi David Kimchi (ca. 1160–1235). Ibn Ezra left Spain in 1140 and traveled to Rome, France, and eventually England, where he died. His many commentaries were based on grammar, lexicography, and reason. He believed that the text could have only one meaning which would be revealed by the rules of grammar, syntax, and rhetoric. He emulated Saadia in his insistence that the rabbinic "oral tradition" must be followed in terms of legal interpretation, that is, that a *peshat* interpretation that contravened Jewish law could not happen. In that, he differed from Rashbam, Bekhor Shor, and others of the Northern French school. One of his unique aspects is his indication of later additions to the text, although he does this indirectly. For example, regarding Deuteronomy 1:1, "on the other side of the Jordan," Ibn Ezra states, "If you understand the secret of the [last twelve verses of Deuteronomy], and 'as Moses wrote' (Deut 31:9), 'and the Canaanites were then in the land' (Gen 12:6), 'on the mountain of the Lord will be seen' (Gen 22:14), 'and here is his bedstead, an iron bedstead' (Deut 3:11), you will recognize the truth."[31] Assumedly, the "truth" is that these verses and phrases were written later than Moses' time but were included in the Torah as if they were Moses' words.

A greater claim to fame, though, is Ibn Ezra's lasting contribution in the transmission of the best of Spanish-Jewish exegesis to the Jews of Christian Europe. By the late Middle Ages, he had become an iconic personality for nearly all the intellectual schools. Later still, Spinoza would cite him as the first biblical

31. My translation of the Hebrew from http://mg.alhatorah.org/Full/Devarim/1.1#e0n6.

critic. He was also esteemed by the Christian Hebraists of the early modern period (who both quoted him and translated his works).

In somewhat similar fashion, the Spanish *peshat* tradition was transported to Provence by the scholarly Kimchi family. Their foremost exegete (whose father and brother both wrote biblical commentaries) was Radak (acronym for Rabbi David Kimchi, 1160–1235), who wrote commentaries on the Torah, the Prophets, Psalms, Proverbs, Job, and Chronicles. These commentaries, together with his important grammatical works, exemplified the best of Spanish textual understanding. Unlike some of his older counterparts in Northern France, Radak integrated midrashic tendencies, including moral and spiritual sensibilities, into his *peshat* interpretations. Additionally, his acute historical sense, for example, enabled him to explain aural and written variations in textual readings[32] as due to the upheaval caused by the Babylonian exile (sixth cent. BCE) – when books went missing and traditions were lost. Radak's commentaries and grammars became standards – frequently copied and printed throughout the succeeding centuries.

A new era in exegesis was introduced by Ramban (acronym of Rabbi Moshe ben Nachman, also known as Nachmanides, 1194–1271), as he was the first interpreter to write under the influence of both Spanish and North French traditions. Living in Gerona in Christian Spain, he was heir to Spanish exegesis, but was also an admirer of Rashi and his school. He also was fully knowledgeable of and utilized the vast, variegated rabbinic literature. While refining the approaches of Rashi and Ibn Ezra, he also expanded exegesis judiciously to include theology, philosophy, mysticism, history, ethics, and psychological insights. His commentaries, which were intended to be popular, were systematic to a higher degree than his predecessors, as he concerned himself with issues of structure and thematic unity – for example, when he explains the order of verses in Exodus 21–23, groups of laws that are written in no obvious logical order. Scholars have detected some fourteen hierarchical categories in his commentary on the Torah (such as birth order, preferential order, order of significance, and order of severity). He also introduced kabbalistic (Jewish mystical) insights in his commentaries, which stimulated and legitimized mystical understanding of the Torah in his audience.

Commentaries with a philosophical emphasis also appeared at this time. For example, Ralbag (acronym for Rabbi Levi ben Gershon, also known as

32. The Masoretic Text (MT) is the traditional rabbinic text of the Jewish Bible edited and copied by a group called the Masoretes (from Hebrew *masorah*, meaning "tradition") between the seventh and the tenth centuries. In their notations, the Masoretes indicated that certain words are vocalized differently than what is written or are even replaced vocally by other words.

Gersonides, 1288–1344), perhaps the most creative and important Jewish thinker of the later Middle Ages, followed the teachings of Maimonides.[33] He was the first interpreter to provide lists of philosophical and moral lessons on given passages in his commentaries, perhaps under the influence of Christian exegesis.

At the end of the Middle Ages, the method of problematization (whereby questions about problems in the text are posed and then solutions are given) was used consistently by Isaac Arama (1420–94) in his homiletic commentaries, which combined homiletics with philosophical and psychological insights, on the Torah and the Five Scrolls. His student, the greatest interpreter of the fifteenth century Don Isaac Abravanel, wrote extensive commentaries on the Torah and the Prophets (and Daniel) using this method. While he stressed *peshat*, he also made frequent, careful use of selective midrashic interpretations. He rejected the rationalist philosophy of his day in favor of an emphasis on traditional rabbinic faith. Since he himself held high positions in government (serving monarchs in Portugal, Spain, and Italy), his exegesis of Samuel and Kings – as an expert on monarchy, political theory, and medieval history – are particularly important. Nor did Abravanel hesitate to include contemporary Renaissance thought.

THE POST-MEDIEVAL PERIOD

Exegesis in the sixteenth and seventeenth centuries continued the disparate approaches of the Middle Ages. Although Baruch (Benedict) Spinoza (1634–77) became famous in more recent modernity for raising questions about biblical authenticity, reliability, and authorship, he was really out to undermine rabbinic traditional understandings and biblical authority. Due to the fact that his ground-breaking *Theologico-Political Treatise* (1670) was composed in Latin, Spinoza had no effect on seventeenth through eighteenth century Jewish interpretation.[34]

The key development in the eighteenth century to have an impact on exegesis was the rise of the *Haskalah* ("the Jewish Enlightenment"),[35] which wished

33. Ralbag was a physician, as were a number of other medieval Jewish exegetes. He was also an extraordinary mathematician and astronomer, the first to have correctly estimated the distance from the earth to the stars.

34. E. Breuer, "Post-Medieval Jewish Interpretation," in *The Jewish Study Bible*, 1901. Much of this section is summarized from this article.

35. The Haskalah sought to encourage Jewish integration into European society due to a new tendency for tolerance to Jews in some locales, resulting from a decrease in Christian political power over secular society.

to transmit to Jewish society some of the achievements of German culture while advancing the Jewish study of the Bible. An important German translation and Hebrew commentary was spearheaded by the well-known Jewish philosopher Moses Mendelssohn (1729–86). As a thoroughly Jewish approach based upon the best of medieval scholarship, the commentary added new literary and linguistic insights.

As a consequence of the continuation of the Haskalah, in the nineteenth century contemporary German intellectual discourse and academic methods influenced the Jewish study of Jewish literature and history, emphasizing textual and linguistic analysis – called the *Wissenschaft des Judentums*.[36] The founders of this academic study of Judaism included Leopold Zunz (1794–1886) and Abraham Geiger (1810–74, also a founder of the Reform movement), both of whom wrote significant critical works on biblical topics. Another member of this academic movement was Shmuel David Luzatto (1800–1865), scion of an Italian scholarly family, who wrote a brilliant, detailed commentary on the Torah (and Isaiah).

The antitraditional approach of some of this group was challenged by Orthodox traditionalists, who were nonetheless aware of developments in the world around them. Of the foremost of these were Malbim (acronym of Rabbi Meir Leibush ben Yechiel Michel, 1809–79), whose systematic commentaries used the problematization style; Rabbi Shimshon Raphael Hirsch (intellectual founder of modern Orthodox Judaism, 1808–88), whose commentary on the Torah explicates its ethical and spiritual worldview; Rabbi David Zvi Hoffmann (1843–1921, younger colleague of Hirsch who was familiar with contemporary non-Jewish biblical scholarship), whose discerning and perceptive commentaries on Genesis, Leviticus, and Deuteronomy exhibit a broader scholarly range than any other Jewish exegesis of his age.

At the end of the nineteenth century, Solomon Mandelkern (1846–1902, an Orthodox rabbi and poet who studied at the Universities of St. Petersburg and Jena, receiving a PhD in law at the latter) produced a tool which would prove invaluable for research into the Hebrew Bible into the computer age: a concordance in Hebrew of every word in the Tanakh.[37]

---

36. Simultaneously, the new Reform movement arose in Germany – an attempt by Jews who wished to assimilate into European culture without losing their Jewish identity. At the same time, these Jews attempted to restructure Judaism to make it more acceptable in European society, a goal which also led to the elimination of much of rabbinic traditional ideology and practice.

37. H. Rosenthal, P. Wiernik, "Mandelkern, Salomon B. Simchah," in *Jewish Encyclopedia*, ed. I. Singer et al. (New York: Fund & Wagnalls, 1906), http://www.jewishencyclopedia.com/articles/10351-mandelkern-solomon-b-simhah-dob; and S. D. Sperling, "Modern Jewish Interpretation," in *The Jewish Study Bible*, 1911.

THE LATE MODERN PERIOD

As mentioned above, in nineteenth century Europe, some Jews began to study their Bible no longer within a traditional rabbinic milieu but with cognizance of non-Jewish approaches, tools, and thought (as opposed to drawing from both rabbinic tradition and contemporary approaches used in the host society). Further, in reaction to the rise of Reform Judaism, not only did modern Orthodoxy consolidate itself, but a new perspective began to form, one which would ultimately become the Conservative movement (that is, to "conserve" Judaism). That movement, which began to amalgamate at the end of the nineteenth century, also had roots in *Wissenschaft des Judentums*. While it was more traditional than the Reformers, it was firmly convinced that, alongside divine inspiration, human involvement in the historical development of Jewish texts and practices was critical (as opposed to the primary emphasis that the Orthodox put upon divinely given Torah and law).[38] In addition to the establishment of the Conservative movement, another important element laid the foundation for new Jewish approaches to biblical interpretation in the twentieth century – Zionism.

In the late nineteenth century, the advent of Zionism – the national[39] Jewish movement to establish an autonomous Jewish state in its ancestral home of the Land of Israel – was influenced by several factors: the age-old love of the Jews for their ancient homeland, the rise of nationalism in Europe, the European Enlightenment and resulting democracy, socialism, and ongoing – and new forms of – anti-Semitism (such as pogroms – state-sponsored attacks on Jewish communities). One of the achievements[40] of Zionism was the establishment of institutions such as the Hebrew University of Jerusalem – a university which

38. Reform, early on, had defined its major principle as "personal autonomy." No longer were the commandments seen to be obligatory (although ethics was always advocated), but rather traditional Jewish practice came to be viewed as a "guideline" to be voluntarily accepted or rejected as the individual's choice. Thus, interpretation by traditional rabbis (no matter how progressive in their own social and intellectual contexts) could now be minimized. Conservatives, however, would take standard rabbinic approaches very seriously as these would be essential in understanding how Jewish thought and religion developed.

39. Many people fail to understand that Judaism is not just a religion. Rather, it is the only surviving ancient civilization carried on by a nation characterized by its own religion. Thus, for example, conversion to Judaism also means becoming a member of the Jewish nation/people. Zionism, then, originates in the ancient history of the Jews in their land and the biblical prophetic promises of a return to that land.

40. Let those who think otherwise examine the facts: (1) since the second millennium BCE, Jews and their ancestors have resided in the Land of Israel (which only became designated as Palestine by the Romans in the second century CE); (2) those Jews who came to live in Israel from the end of the nineteenth century through the 1930s did so peacefully with the express permission of the Ottoman and, later, the British authorities. Until the Arab war against the Jewish community, every single place in which Jews lived in the Land of Israel was legally bought and paid for.

did not suffer or expel Jews, but permitted them to develop their own biblical studies organically, without the external pressure of second-class citizenship in a host environment of disapproving Christians. Furthermore, institutions such as Hebrew University were open to all streams of Jews – Orthodox, Conservative, Reform, and secular, male and female, none of whom were required to accept any particular academic theory.

The upshot of all of the above elements was a new outpouring of Jewish exegesis of the Tanakh. The modern academic study of philology, linguistics, literature, and history, combined with ancient Near Eastern archaeological textual discoveries and ancient languages (such as Egyptian, Akkadian, Hittite, and Ugaritic), by Jews who also know traditional Jewish biblical interpretation have resulted in (1) studies focused on the historical development of biblical religion, (2) studies integrating the finds of archaeology and exegesis, and (3) a reinvigoration of the *peshat* approach within literary analysis.

STUDIES FOCUSED ON THE HISTORICAL DEVELOPMENT OF BIBLICAL RELIGION

The most important Jewish composition in the twentieth century on the historical development of biblical religion was Yehezkel Kaufmann's epic *Toldot HaEmunah HaYisraelit* ("The History of Israelite Faith").[41] Although Kaufmann agreed in the main with source criticism, Kaufmann argued that (1) the Priestly source was earlier even than the monarchy, that (2) supernatural monotheism did not naturally evolve from polytheism, but that it was an original creation of Israelite religious thought, and (3) that the prophets extrapolated from the ethics of the Torah in positing the primacy of morality over ritual. Although a number of Kaufmann's positions have not been generally accepted, his views on biblical ethics have not been refuted,[42] and he had a profound impact on the study of biblical ideas in modern Jewish scholarship, particularly among the non-Orthodox.

---

41. In eight volumes, published in Hebrew in Israel, 1937–56; English: Y. Kaufmann, *The Religion of Israel*, trans. and abridged by M. Greenberg (Chicago: University Chicago Press, 1960). In the nineteenth century, Julius Wellhausen's version of the Documentary Hypothesis stated that the Torah was actually composed of four sources (all of which were written much later than the time of Moses), and that the Priestly source was written after the preexilic ethical messages of the prophets. Thereby, Wellhausen, who was a Protestant German anti-Semite, claimed that Judaism, which he saw as a post-Babylonia exile phenomenon, was ethically inferior for it emphasized "legalism" – a minutiae of laws centred on ritual.

42. On the primacy of morality over ritual, see recently, Unterman, *Justice for All*, 85–108. Although Kaufmann's very early dating of P has not been accepted, meticulous studies in comparative linguistics and philology date the Priestly source as preexilic. Most academics also think that ethical monotheism evolved out of polytheism, but no one has convincingly showed how or why it happened only among the ancient Israelites.

The most significant work that combines Jewish and modern academic scholarship to elucidate the ideology behind Israelite ritual (such as the priestly concept of repentance) has been the studies of Jacob Milgrom. His three-volume Leviticus commentary is a masterpiece.[43]

A major work on prophetic ethics was Abraham Joshua Heschel's *The Prophets.*[44] To this day, it is the best analysis of the prophetic personality, particularly in his depiction of how the prophets understood anthropopathy – the ascription of human emotions to God. Just as biblical descriptions of God's "hand" or "arm" (anthropomorphisms) were comprehended as metaphoric, so, too, were mentions of divine emotions such as "love" or "anger." The prophets discerned that the difference between divine and human emotions was that God's emotions were always justifiable. Unlike humans, who often became incensed or enamored concerning matters of no account, the portrayal of God's emotions was always morally based.

In 1937, Joseph H. Hertz (1872–1946), chief rabbi of the United Kingdom, published his commentary on the Torah,[45] which became the standard interpretation used along with the synagogue liturgy throughout the English speaking world until the 1980s. Hertz not only used traditional Jewish exegesis but also referred to Christian academic scholars and included essays on perceived conflicts between academic and traditional Jewish understandings.

STUDIES INTEGRATING THE FINDS OF ARCHAEOLOGY AND EXEGESIS

Two very different modern Israeli commentary series have focused on archaeology and the Tanakh: the secular academic *Olam HaTanakh* ("The World of the Bible") and the Orthodox *Da'at Mikra* ("The Knowledge of Scriptures"), which combines some academic exegesis with traditional rabbinic

---

43. J. Milgrom, *Leviticus 1–16, Leviticus 17–22, Leviticus 23–27,* Anchor Bible (New York: Doubleday, 1991, 2000, 2001).

44. A. J. Heschel, *The Prophets* (Philadelphia: Jewish Publication Society, 1962). Heschel was a professor at the Jewish Theological Seminary in New York who lived the ethics that he studied. He was an activist in the 1960s civil rights movement (marching with Martin Luther King in Alabama).

45. J. H. Hertz, *The Pentateuch and Haftorahs* (London: Soncino, 1937). W. G. Plaut, *The Torah: A Modern Commentary* (New York: Union of American Hebrew Congregations, 1981), replaced Hertz in the Reform movement. It included homiletics and essays on the Torah and the ancient Near East by W. W. Hallo. Afterward the Jewish Publication Society published a Conservative academic approach to the Torah, including many footnotes and excursuses: N. Sarna, *Genesis* (Philadelphia: Jewish Publication Society, 2001); N. Sarna, *Exodus* (Philadelphia: Jewish Publication Society, 2003); B. Levine, *Leviticus* (Philadelphia: Jewish Publication Society, 2003); J. Milgrom, *Numbers* (Philadelphia: Jewish Publication Society, 2003); J. H. Tigay, *Deuteronomy* (Philadelphia: Jewish Publication Society, 2003). That series is continuing with other biblical commentaries.

interpretation.[46] As archaeological research in Israel and the ancient Near East is ongoing and constantly undergoing reevaluation, exegesis that relies on archaeology is always in danger of quickly becoming outdated.

THE REINVIGORATION OF THE *PESHAT* APPROACH WITHIN LITERARY ANALYSIS

The first significant Jewish biblical exegete to apply modern methods of literary analysis was Umberto Cassuto in his works on Genesis.[47] However, the person who truly introduced modern literary methodology (through the "New Criticism") to Tanakh study in Israel was Meir Weiss (1908–98) in his trailblazing work *HaMikra Kidmuto*.[48] Weiss was a Hungarian rabbi and academic scholar who survived the Holocaust with his family. A professor of Tanakh at the Hebrew University of Jerusalem, his approach has had tremendous influence over generations of students both in Israel and abroad.[49] Briefly, Weiss describes his method thusly:

> [It is a] methodological imperative to pay close attention to the text, to every word, to the word-order and syntax, to synonyms and metaphors, to unusual syntactical phenomena, to the structure of every sentence and to the structure of the work as a whole. All this must not be done from a statistical perspective, by classifying and counting, not by enquiring into separate elements as such but by examining the function of each linguistic and structural element within the whole work, by answering the question of how all the individual parts are welded to make up the formal unity of the whole . . . interpretation does not mean the explanation of every detail in the work by itself but rather

---

46. *Olam HaTanakh*, ed. Menachem Haran (Tel-Aviv: Revivim, 1982–94); *Da'at Mikra*, ed. Yehuda Kiel (Jerusalem: Mosad HaRav Kook, 1971–2003). A new series has recently gone into publication: The Koren Tanakh of the Land of Israel, edited by D. Arnovitz (editor in chief) and J. Unterman (academic editor) (Jerusalem: Koren, 2020–), with volumes on *Exodus* (2020), *Samuel* (2021), *Leviticus* (2023), *Numbers* (2023), and *Genesis* (2024). This series in English, by an Orthodox publisher in Jerusalem, is not a commentary *per se* but focuses on presenting each book of the Tanakh within its own ancient Near Eastern historical, geographical, social, literary, and religious context – as best as new archaeological finds can be immediately integrated.

47. U. Cassuto, *From Adam to Noah* (Jerusalem: Magnes, 1961); *From Noah to Abraham* (Jerusalem: Magnes, 1964).

48. M. Weiss, *HaMikra Kidmuto* (Jerusalem: Bialik, 1962); *The Bible From Within*, trans. A. Cooper (Jerusalem: Magnes, 1984).

49. His work influenced Nechama Leibowitz, Moshe Greenberg, Jacob Milgrom, Uriel Simon, Adele Berlin, Sara Japhet, Yair Zakovitch, and others – and preceded biblical Hebrew literary publications of such scholars as James Kugel and Robert Alter. Weiss called his approach "total-interpretation." Moshe Greenberg followed in his footsteps but added a historical component; see M. Greenberg, "The Vision of Jerusalem in Ezekiel 8–11: A Holistic Interpretation," in *The Divine Helmsman*, ed. J. L. Crenshaw, S. Sandmel (New York: KTAV, 1980), 143–64.

> the explanation of every detail in the light of the whole creation and the explanation of the whole creation on the basis of all its details.[50]

The "new critical" approach dovetailed to a certain extent with Jewish exegesis because of its similarity to the *peshat* tradition in such aspects as "close reading." Recently, Weiss's literary approach has become the dominant influence (not always recognized) in modern Orthodox study of the Jewish Bible – through the Herzog College in the Jerusalem environs. A brief example of Weiss's method is his analysis of Amos' response, "I am not a prophet nor am I the son of a prophet" (Amos 7:14), to Amaziah's implication that Amos is a prophet for hire. Why the mention of both "prophet" and "son of a prophet"? Many moderns think that Amos is saying that he is neither a prophet nor the member of a prophetic band. However, Weiss points out that the latter is known in the Bible in the plural as "sons of the prophets," not the singular of "son of a prophet." Rather, Weiss points to the decisive linguistic parallel in Psalm 116:16, "I am Your servant, the son of Your handmaid," as an indication of the superlative in biblical Hebrew, that is, "I am completely Your servant." Thus, Amos is really saying, "I am in no way the professional prophet you think I am." Weiss, then, shows sensitivity to the grammar and syntax of the verse within the greater context of the Tanakh.

The most significant series of academic biblical commentaries being produced in modern Israel is *Mikra LeYisrael*.[51] Written for the interested layperson, it eschews academic jargon and footnotes. Nonetheless, all the commentaries are written by Jewish academics.

The greatest influence on the popular study of the Bible in Israel were the worksheets with questions on the weekly Torah portion that Nechama Leibowitz (1905–97) mailed out to all who were interested, starting in 1942 (Leibowitz received a PhD at the University of Marburg in 1925 and immigrated to the land of Israel in 1930, eventually becoming a professor at Tel-Aviv University). People all over Israel would send these sheets back to her, and she would mark every one and return them, often with comments. An expert on medieval rabbinic commentary and knowledgeable of the New Criticism (she and Meir Weiss would occasionally coauthor material on biblical pedagogy), she was adept at explaining to her students the textual logic at the basis of sophisticated rabbinic interpretation. It is estimated that she had 40,000 correspondents! In the 1950s

---

50. Weiss, *The Bible from Within*, 26–27.

51. In Hebrew by Am Oved Publishers (Tel-Aviv) and Magnes (Jerusalem). The current editor is S. Ahituv. Some of the commentaries, those written by American-trained scholars, have appeared in English in a different edition.

and 1960s, her studies were gathered together and published.[52] At her request, on her tombstone is written below her name only one word, *morah* – "teacher."

CONCLUSIONS

Throughout the history of the Jewish religious civilization, the Tanakh has been understood as its formative document, even its constitution. Furthermore, for thousands of years – until the secularism of modernity – every word has been considered at least divinely inspired, if not actually spoken by God. As such, Jews of all times and places have seen the biblical text as omnisignificant – the key to comprehending God's relationship to the Jews as both a people and individuals and how Jews must guide their thoughts, emotions, and behavior.

The Jews were always aware of their requirement to know and act according to God's will as written in the Tanakh – particularly, the Torah. Thus, the regular public reading of the Torah (already attested by Hecataeus of Abdera in the fourth century BCE,[53] and which over two thousand years ago became a weekly event), accompanied by the universal public education of Jewish boys (B. T. Bava Bathra 21a), assured the Torah's dissemination. Already in antiquity, a selection from the Prophets became attached to the weekly Torah reading for the purpose of hermeneutics. However, as mentioned above, Jewish exegesis had already taken place *within* the biblical text.

These testaments point to the reality that the Jewish people en masse had an intimacy with their Bible that was not duplicated in the ancient world – and perhaps not among other peoples at all until the advent of the printing press. From time immemorial, the Jews focused on their Bible with laser-like concentration, studying texts repeatedly – as in Joshua 1:8, "You shall recite it day and night" (see also Ps 1:2) – to mine every possible meaning and lesson for daily living. Jewish interpretation, then, did not arise out of an intellectual pursuit but out of an existential need. Therefore, any new idea or method that could further illuminate the text was integrated into Jewish exegesis.

Perhaps, that is the most important contribution of Jewish interpretation of the Bible. When one takes the Bible seriously – every book, every chapter, every verse, every word – in the search for the meaning of the text for one's life, that

52. Originally published in Hebrew; for English, see N. Leibowitz, *New Studies in the Weekly Parashah: Genesis, Exodus, Leviticus, Numbers, Deuteronomy*, 7 vols., trans. A. Newman (Jerusalem: World Zionist Organization, 1972–80).

53. M. Stern, *Greek and Latin Authors on Jews and Judaism*, vol. 1 (Jerusalem: Israel Academy of Sciences and Humanities, 1974).

becomes a model for how to study. The accumulation of countless generations of such study, always incorporating the new while maintaining respect for the old, itself creates a civilization that can withstand any tragedies or other obstacles, even the challenge of secularism.[54]

Whatever future methods or trends in biblical interpretation take hold among the Jews, Jewish tradition – in its manifold variegations – must play a role in order for such interpretations to be called Jewish. In the words of famous Israeli intellectual and educator Ernst Simon (1900–88), "The Jew is like a man in a rowboat; in order to go forward, he must look backward."

FOR FURTHER READING

Arnovitz, D. A., ed. *The Koren Tanakh of the Land of Israel: Exodus, Samuel, Leviticus, Numbers, Genesis.* J. Unterman, academic ed. Jerusalem: Koren, 2020–24.

Berlin, A., and M. Z. Brettler, ed. *The Jewish Study Bible.* Oxford: Oxford University Press, 2004.

Fishbane, M. *Biblical Interpretation in Ancient Israel.* Oxford: Oxford University Press, 1988.

Hertz, J. H. *The Pentateuch and Haftorahs.* London: Soncino, 1937.

Heschel, A. J. *The Prophets.* Philadelphia: Jewish Publication Society, 1962.

Kaufmann, Y. *The Religion of Israel.* Translated and abridged by M. Greenberg. Chicago: University Chicago Press, 1960.

Kugel, J. *The Bible as It Was.* Cambridge, MA: Harvard University Press, 1997.

Kugel, J. *Traditions of the Bible.* Cambridge, MA: Harvard University Press, 1999.

Leibowitz, N. *New Studies in the Weekly Parashah: Genesis, Exodus, Leviticus, Numbers, Deuteronomy.* 7 vols. Translated by A. Newman. Jerusalem: World Zionist Organization, 1972–80.

Levine, B. *Leviticus.* Philadelphia: Jewish Publication Society, 2003.

Milgrom, J. *Leviticus 1–16*; *Leviticus 17–22*; *Leviticus 23–27.* Anchor Bible. New York: Doubleday, 1991, 2000, 2001.

Milgrom, J. *Numbers.* Philadelphia: Jewish Publication Society, 2003.

Plaut, W. G. *The Torah: A Modern Commentary.* New York: Union of American Hebrew Congregations, 1981.

54. In the last few years, the popular study of the Bible has been reinvigorated in Israel among secular Jews through a project called "929" (the number of chapters in the Jewish Bible), precisely because the Bible is so fundamental to the Jewish people. This project makes it possible to go online (or to public lectures) to access a great many new biblical interpretations, as well as for individuals to contribute their own understandings.

Saebo, M., ed. *Hebrew Bible/Old Testament: The History of Its Interpretation*. 2 vols. Göttingen: Vanderhoeck & Ruprecht, 1996, 2008.

Sarna, N. *Genesis*. Philadelphia: Jewish Publication Society, 2001.

Sarna, N. *Exodus*. Philadelphia: Jewish Publication Society, 2003.

Tigay, J. H. *Deuteronomy*. Philadelphia: Jewish Publication Society, 2003.

Tov, E. *Textual Criticism of the Hebrew Bible*. 3rd ed. Minneapolis: Fortress, 2011.

Unterman, J. *Justice for All. How the Jewish Bible Revolutionized Ethics*. Lincoln, NB: Jewish Publication Society and University of Nebraska Press, 2017.

Weiss, M. *The Bible from Within*. Translated by A. Cooper. Jerusalem: Magnes, 1984.

CHAPTER 9

Augustine of Hippo and Thomas Aquinas as Biblical Exegetes

Their Ways of Reading and Interpretations of the Sorrows of Christ

Emmanuel Durand[1]

It would be wrong to think that Augustine and Thomas Aquinas had access to the Bible that we can hold in our hands today. At the time of his conversion, recounted in book 8 of *Confessions*, Augustine only possessed a collection of the letters of Saint Paul. For the bishop of Hippo, the Bible was first of all a list of works in circulation whose canonicity needed to be verified because they were not bound together in a single approved volume. Several centuries later, Thomas Aquinas did not travel through the European Universities and schools *(studia)* with a Bible that belonged to him. His biblical commentaries show that he used the Bibles made available to him in the Dominican priories where he stayed during this or that period of time.[2] To understand the biblical exegesis of these two grand masters, it is necessary to look at their own ways of approaching Scripture and its proper use, at the resources and textual tools available to them in their own times, and at the methods of reading that they favoured. After having

1. This chapter was translated by David McIlroy. We use the Douai-Rheims translation of the Bible, as it is the closest to the Latin texts available to both Augustine and Aquinas.

2. I owe this information to Gilles de Grandpré, OP (†), editor of Aquinas's *Commentary on the Letter to the Romans.*

outlined these essential features, we offer a case study comparing Augustine's and Thomas's exegesis of Jesus' words: "My soul is sorrowful even unto death" (Matt 26:38; par. Mark 14:34).

AUGUSTINE AS EXEGETE: HIS PRINCIPLES AND METHOD OF READING

THE READING OF SCRIPTURE: AN INVITATION TO TRAVEL AND AN APPRENTICESHIP IN HUMILITY

For Augustine, the Bible is the mysterious map of a long journey whose outcome is nonetheless already known: the full enjoyment of the love of the triune God.[3] To love God as the ultimate end and to love one's neighbour as a partner and as a signpost towards God, that is for the bishop of Hippo the perspective that leads to a good use of Scripture. The interpretation of the map is sometimes laborious and sometimes pleasant. It is possible to forget the purpose of the journey on the way, to be captivated by the subtleties of the map, to be seized by the excitement of deciphering it, or to be distracted by the strangeness of the landscape.[4] To make good use of the Scriptures, one must first understand the goal that controls all intermediate exploration and then cultivate the faith, hope, and love that connect the traveller to the ultimate end of the journey. Understanding the Scriptures is essentially a matter of reaching the exact thought of the biblical authors and growing in love for God and neighbour.[5]

The Scriptures require the attentive and persevering reader to learn humility. They are a divine pedagogy and a salutary remedy against pride. For Augustine, sin numbs the soul, trapping it in material concerns, and rendering it deaf to the call of the Word. The Scriptures and the gospel, however, offer believers the possibility of reconnecting with the intimate teaching of the creative Word.[6] God's words are expressed in human words, just as the Word of God made human flesh his own. In both manners, God has embraced the ways of descent to call out to his disorientated creatures on their own level and in their own language. With foolish condescension, Wisdom boldly adapts to human

---

3. Augustine of Hippo, *De doctrina christiana*, 1.4.4–5, 5; on the status of Scripture for Augustine, see Isabelle Bochet, *"Le firmament de l'Écriture": L'herméneutique augustinienne* (Paris: Institut d'Études Augustiniennes, 2004), 33–53.

4. *De doctrina christiana*, 1.34.38.

5. *De doctrina christiana*, 1.36.40.

6. *De Genesi ad literam*, 1.5.10; *Confessionum*, 11:7.9–8.10; 8.10–9.11.

weakness.[7] The abasement of the flesh and the simplicity of the Scriptures demand that sinners and readers are prepared to accept a certain humbling of their (vain or proud) minds. This treatment is suited to the disease that prevents the soul from understanding the Scriptures.

In the opening pages of his treatise *De Trinitate*, Augustine points out the difficulty of the theological enterprise, the common errors of method, and the virtue of debate in the matter. He denounces the quibbling of those who argue rationally without starting from the foundation of faith. Augustine identifies three common errors in rational discourse about God.[8] They consist in either a mistaken transposition from creation to God or the elevation of human reason above creation in order to speculate about God. The three erroneous approaches can be summarised as follows:

- transposing onto God what has been observed of bodily realities by the senses
- transposing onto God what belongs to the nature of the human mind and its affects
- elevating human reason above creation, without being able to identify or to grasp the nature of God

In Augustine's view, the third error is the most deceptive, for it produces seductive statements without any real referent. To prevent believers from going astray in this way, Scripture nurtures and regulates the possibilities for the elevation of human reason. The elevation of the human spirit towards God presupposes a prior abasement, of which the ways of speaking in Scripture are an applied grammar. For Augustine, therefore, the third approach is simply to be discarded, whilst the first two (which seek to draw inferences about God from creation) are useful if they have been tamed:

> Consequently, in order that the human mind may be cleansed from errors of this kind, Sacred Scripture, adapting itself to little ones (*parvulis congruens*), has employed words from every class of objects in order that our intellect, as though strengthened by them, might rise as it were gradually to divine and sublime things. For when it spoke of God, it made use even of words taken

7. *De doctrina christiana*, 1.11.11; *De Genesi contra Manichaeos*, 2.5.6; *Contra Adimantum*, 13.2; *Enarrationes in Ps.* 103, serm. 4.1. Condescension (*katabasis* in Greek, *condescensio* in Latin) does not carry here a pejorative connotation, unlike its usual contemporary usage. The word signifies simply that God "descends" in some manner in order to address his people or in order to raise up human beings.

8. *De Trinitate*, 1.1.

> from material objects. . . . For, it is from created realities that the divine Scripture is wont to prepare enticements, as it were, for children (*infantilia oblectamenta*). Its purpose is to arouse the affections of the weak, so that by means of them, as though they were steps, they may mount to higher things and abandon the lower things, step by step, as much as they are able.[9]

Augustine does not reject the use of reason, but it must be guided, instructed, and healed by the Scriptures because these speak in a language suitable for human weakness. The intellectual limitations of the human condition are coupled with a form of illness: a darkening of the mind due to sin. Not only does God radically exceed the human capacity for understanding, but our rational faculties must also be healed. Readers of the Bible are thus led to ascend to God by degrees, but not to let their reason work on its own. The bodily and spiritual similes used in the Bible to talk about God, such as the shadow of wings, jealousy, and repentance, are like educational toys, which are developed to lead children gradually to understand truths that are deeper than the heuristic devices. Such approximations are apt to persuade those who are ready to learn and to humble the proud. Practising theology is a gradual learning process, an ongoing conversion, and a long-term spiritual exercise.

KEYS TO OVERCOMING OBSCURITIES AND AMBIGUITIES IN THE TEXT

The written words and the propositions contained in the Bible have been formed by letters so that they can be read with our eyes. These signs are the extension of the words that are spoken to be heard by our ears. Both the written and the spoken words are signs of the thoughts which gave rise to them.[10] For Augustine, the challenge of interpretation is to reach the thoughts of the biblical authors and, beyond that, to discover what God wanted to reveal. But the interplay of signs and the diversity of languages inevitably lead to obscurities and ambiguities. Moreover, to make the message more attractive, to overcome boredom, and to tame the pride of the readers, the Bible uses figures, metaphors, parables, and allegories, the exact meaning of which is not always easy to determine.[11] To deal with the difficulties of reading and interpretation, the bishop of Hippo gives several rules of hermeneutics.

Augustine adopts the following presupposition: what is obscurely stated in

9. *De Trinitate* 12, trans. Stephen McKenna (Washington, DC: Catholic University of America, 1963), translation adjusted.

10. *De doctrina christiana*, 2.1.1–4, 5.

11. *De doctrina christiana, II*, 5, 6–6, 8.

one passage of Scripture is clearly expressed elsewhere. It is therefore appropriate to seek to resolve obscurities in one text by recourse to other, more obvious passages.[12] The legitimate space for such intertextuality is delimited by the canon of Scripture. This varied somewhat from church to church. Augustine therefore provides a list that takes into account the authority of the apostolic sees and leaves out writings not accepted as canonical by certain churches.[13]

A lack of understanding of the text is due either to the reader not understanding the signs or to finding them ambiguous. The signs are either proper or figurative. To understand a proper term whose meaning is unknown to the reader, it is necessary to have recourse to knowledge of the original language, to compare translations and to favour the most literal ones, to choose the most reliable ancient versions.[14] To decipher a figurative term whose meaning is unknown, one must have recourse not only to linguistic resources but also to knowledge of the things themselves – for example, the properties of animals, plants, trees, and stones used as figures in the biblical texts. For instance, it is inevitable that a Latin reader will not immediately know the potential meanings of hyssop. Occasionally, the interpreter must call upon the science of numbers (whose possible combinations deliver meaning, in the wake of Plato), musical notions, astronomy, indications from secular history, dialectics, logic and philosophy. In short, he must make good use of the "spoils of the Egyptians" (cf. Exod 12:36), all the ancillary knowledge from secular culture that nevertheless helps the reader to understand the words and things spoken of in Scripture.[15]

If ignorance of the signs can be partially overcome, what about their ambiguities? With regard to ambiguous signs, Augustine sets out his hermeneutical framework: once possible solutions have been explored in terms of punctuation, pronunciation, or intonation, one must "consult the rule of faith, which one has derived from clearer passages of Scripture, or from the authority of the Church."[16] When neither faith nor context can overcome an ambiguity, the interpretation is left to the reader.[17] Overall, Augustine remains convinced that the vast

12. *De doctrina christiana*, *II*, 6, 8; 9, 14.

13. *De doctrina christiana*, *II*, 8, 12–13.

14. *De doctrina christiana*, *II*, 11, 16–15, 22.

15. *De doctrina christiana*, 2.16.24–42, 63.

16. *De doctrina christiana*, 3.2.2. Bibliothèque Augustinienne, 11/2. (Paris: Institut d'Études Augustiniennes, 197), 237. Augustine chooses the following example: "In the beginning was the Word and the Word was with God and God was" (*in principio erat Verbum et Verbum erat apud Deum et Deus erat*) taken from John 1:1 but wrongly transcribed: the last proposition has been truncated, which means that it no longer says "the Word was God" (*Deus erat Verbum*). All of the words used can be understood in their proper sense, but the significance of the passage as a whole is ambiguous, as a result of the doubtful, or rather heretical, transcription which avoids affirming the divinity of the Word.

17. *De doctrina christiana*, 3.2.5.

majority of ambiguities can be overcome. As for ambiguous figurative signs, they sometimes require the integration of another hermeneutical key associated with the truth of faith: honesty of morals.[18] Questionable or cruel actions imputed to God or the saints in the Scriptures (e.g., the polygamy of the patriarchs or the cruelty of the anathemas) are to be interpreted in a spiritual sense rather than endorsing lust or wickedness.

Augustine incorporated a Platonic scheme into his conception of the human spirit, according to which the soul's dependence on the material[19] is a consequence of the fall.[20] Interpreting material signs such as words and letters is not an innate function of the human intellect in search of God. The exercise must overcome many obstacles: obscurity, ambiguity, confusion, pride, and so on. This prism distinguishes Augustine from the Christian authors of the Aristotelian tradition, for whom the mediation of the material is the most natural and reliable mode of operation of the human intelligence. Thomas Aquinas is one of the most prominent representatives of this tradition.

THOMAS AQUINAS AS BIBLICAL EXEGETE: HIS PRINCIPLES AND METHOD OF WORKING

Unlike Augustine, Thomas Aquinas did not set out his method of reading the Bible in a specific large-scale treatise. Nevertheless, Aquinas provides valuable insights into his methods in his handling of *sacra doctrina* – specifically, the use of similitudes and the four senses of Scripture.[21] After a brief synthesis of Aquinas's theoretical reflections on the function of Scripture, it is appropriate to consider the new tools of textual criticism and new techniques of reading developed in his time.

THE ROLE OF THE SCRIPTURES, THE VALUE OF THE MATERIAL, AND THE PRIMACY OF THE LITERAL SENSE

For Thomas Aquinas, the Scriptures transmit the revealed principles of sacred doctrine, that is, the complete teaching of the faith. These revealed

18. *De doctrina christiana*, 3.10.14.

19. Translator's note. The original French word used is *sensible*, which could be translated into English as "sensible" in the sense of that which is capable of being perceived by the senses. As this usage is somewhat uncommon I have translated unless otherwise stated, as "material."

20. *De Genesi contra Manichaeos*, 2.4.5; Isabelle Bochet, *"Le firmament de l'Écriture,"* 37.

21. Thomas Aquinas, *In I Sent.*, prologue, a .5; *Quodlibet* 7, q. 6; *Sum. theol.* I, q. 1, a. 9–10; *In Gal.*, 4.24, ed. Marietti, n.°253–254. See Gilbert Dahan, *L'Exégèse chrétienne de la Bible en Occident médiéval, XIIe–XIVe siècles* (Paris: Cerf, 1999); Id., *Lire la Bible au moyen âge. Essais d'herméneutique médiévale* (Geneva: Droz, 2009).

truths are received in two mutually responsive ways: *revelation* on the part of the transmitter and *prayer* on the part of the receiver. In the Scriptures, these two aspects of reception can be seen in the prophetic revelations and the prayers of the psalms.[22]

Since it is natural for the human intelligence to progress from sensations in its operations of knowledge,[23] Aquinas gives full value to the confirmations and sensible expressions that corroborate the truths of faith: miracles, signs and signifiers (e.g., metaphors), symbolic statements, and parables. Based on the principles of revelation that it transmits, Scripture has three main functions: to refute errors, to teach morals, and to contemplate the truth. Scripture proceeds in various ways along the axes of refutation and contemplation.[24]

In addition to the literal sense of the biblical texts, also called the "historical" sense, Thomas identifies three registers of the spiritual sense, also called the "mystical" sense:

- the moral sense is capable of guiding human action on the basis of an accomplished reality, often an action or a gesture of Christ himself;
- the allegorical sense proceeds in particular by referring a reality featuring in the Old Testament to a reality or a person from the New Testament; and
- the anagogical sense announces by anticipation certain realities or modalities of future glory, such as the heavenly Jerusalem.

This classification of the four meanings of Scripture was already well established in the twelfth and thirteenth centuries.[25] Because of the progression of the stages of fulfilment within the Bible, Thomas believes that one should not seek to interpret every text according to the four senses.[26] In some cases, explaining in the literal sense is sufficient.

In ordinary human writing, words refer to realities through the mediation of words and thoughts. The principal author of the Scriptures (in the sense of

22. Thomas Aquinas, *In I Sent.*, prologue, a .5, resp. For an innovative and contemporary discussion on the subject of prophecy and prayer as the epistemological foundations for a confessional exegesis, see Adrian Schenker, "De la validité de l'exégèse croyante de la Bible," *Revue des sciences philosophiques et théologiques* 97 (2013) 449–57.

23. *Sum. theol.* I, q. 1, a. 9, resp.

24. *In I Sent.*, prologue, a .5, resp.

25. The classification presented by Thomas differs from the one Augustine had proposed: history, aetiology, analogy, allegory. According to Thomas, the first three proposed by Augustine form part of the literal sense, whilst Augustine's category of allegory encompassed the three different spiritual senses Thomas distinguished. See Augustine of Hippo, *De utilitate credendi*, 3.5–8; Thomas Aquinas, *Sum. theol.* I, q. 1, a. 10, ad 2.

26. Thomas Aquinas, *Quodlibet* 7, q. 6, a. 2, ad 5.

founder and organiser), the Holy Spirit, is the author not only of the words but also of the realities signified. It is therefore a unique feature of the Scriptures that the realities themselves (narrated or announced) are arranged in such a way that they can also signify other realities.[27] Thus, the ram offered as a sacrifice in place of Isaac is both an animal and a figure of Christ. The exit from Egypt is read both as a historical event and as a figure of the passion of Christ. The Egyptians are the figure par excellence of enemies or pagans. The anointing of the king applies first to David and then to Christ, and so on.

The literal sense of the Scriptures is that according to which words signify realities, while the spiritual sense is that according to which one reality (e.g., a person, an action, a quality, a place, a time, a number) is the figure of another.[28] Not only the main author, the Holy Spirit, but also the instrumental author, the biblical writer, are able to aim at several meanings under the same statement, with a reference from the literal meaning to a spiritual meaning.[29]

The spiritual meaning is always based on the literal meaning and develops from it. Such a requirement delegitimises imaginary "spiritual" derivations without an assured textual foundation.[30] According to Aquinas, the literal meaning can include both the literal and the figurative. The metaphors and parables used by the prophets and by Christ are figures of speech and imaginary similes, not realities, and therefore fall within the literal meaning of Scripture.[31] Following Augustine, Thomas believes that only the literal meaning of biblical texts is suitable as an argument to refute errors, since it is not exposed to confusion of referents and false deductions.[32]

NEW TOOLS AND TECHNIQUES OF EXEGESIS

In *De doctrina christiana*, Augustine was concerned to overcome the obscurities and ambiguities of the words used in the biblical text. One resource was to seek out the most reliable text and then to discern the variations in meaning offered by punctuation, pronunciation, or intonation. In the twelfth and

---

27. *Quodlibet* 7, q. 6, a. 1, resp.; *In Gal.* 4.24, ed. Marietti, n.°254.

28. These distinctions were conventional at the time when Thomas used them; see Hugh of Saint-Victor, *De sacramentis*, prologue, 5, PL 176, 185 cited by Dahan, *L'exégèse chrétienne de la Bible en Occident médiéval*, 300. Dahan demonstrates convincingly that the spiritual sense is based not only on the reference from one reality to another but also on the reference from one word to another; see Dahan, *L'exégèse chrétienne de la Bible en Occident médiéval*, 302–25.

29. *Quodlibet* 7, q. 6, a. 1, ad 5.

30. *Quodlibet* 7, q. 6, a. 1, ad 1; *Sum. theol.* I, q. 1, a. 10, resp.

31. *Quodlibet* 7, q. 6, a. 2, ad 1; *Sum. theol.* I, q. 1, a. 10, ad 3; *In Gal.* 4.24, n.°254.

32. *In I Sent.*, prologue, a. 5, resp. [in fine]; *Quodlibet* 7, q. 6, a. 1, ad 4; *Sum. theol.* I, q. 1, a. 10, ad 1 referring to Augustine.

thirteenth centuries, textual criticism and biblical study acquired new tools. An eminent specialist in medieval exegesis, Gilbert Dahan (on whom I am largely dependent in this section), presents and illustrates them in several of his works. In the twelfth century, preachers and commentators had "lexicons of biblical terms, dictionaries of translations of proper names from the Bible, dictionaries specialising in the spiritual meanings of biblical realities (bestiaries, lapidaries, herbariums, treatises on numerology)."[33] In the thirteenth century, to support the missions of preaching and university teaching, the Order of Preachers, to which Thomas belonged, participated in the creation of new tools:

- biblical concordances, the first of which was attempted in Paris between 1230 and 1240, under the direction of Hugh of Saint-Cher; and
- collections of "distinctions," explaining the spiritual meanings of biblical words or more complex expressions.[34]

As the demand for books increased, in the context of the nascent universities and Dominican study centres, a new technique for producing copies of works was to entrust the various sections of a single work to different copyists. This increased the efficiency of reproduction but required great vigilance on the part of publishers or booksellers. The general chapters of the Dominicans requested that the Bibles in use in the order's priories be corrected and punctuated according to the work of critical editing carried out by the friars in Paris. Under the direction of Hugh of Saint-Cher, a first "correctory" was composed from 1230 to 1235. Several others followed. These corrected the texts in circulation and indicated with precision the variants or errors, referring the reader of the Bible to the oldest versions (Latin, Hebrew, and Greek), as well as to the Fathers and the authorised commentators.[35]

Let us move on to the exegesis itself. Among the methods of reading and interpreting the Bible in the thirteenth century, Thomas Aquinas especially developed the hermeneutical resources of the prologue, the division of the text (*divisio textus*), the "notes," and the "question."

- The prologue is the introductory lesson to a biblical commentary (or to another type of commentary). Based on a well-chosen Bible verse, the

---

33. Gilbert Dahan, *Dominique et ses frères lecteurs de la Bible au XIIIe siècle*. Cahiers Évangile, Supplément 177 (Paris: Cerf, 2016), 17. I am heavily dependent on the work of this author in this section.

34. See Dahan, *Dominique et ses frères lecteurs de la Bible au XIIIe siècle*, 17–22.

35. See Dahan, *Dominique et ses frères lecteurs de la Bible au XIIIe siècle*, 37–43.

prologue offers the reader a perspective on the intention, the author, the mode(s) of expression, or the usefulness of the book being commented on.[36] Prologues are sometimes structured using the four Aristotelian causes.

- The *divisio textus* is not a formalization of the text's plan, which can be extracted from the writing being commented on, but a creative subdivision that is the key to the interpretation developed by the exegete himself.[37] The exegete then refers to it constantly in the course of his commentary, for the *divisio textus* is the roadmap of exegetical analysis.
- The "notes" resemble the "distinctions" already mentioned in the collections, but they are included in the biblical commentary and provide conceptual or doctrinal clarifications on the possible meanings of a term or expression.
- The "question" is the treatment of an apparent contradiction, doubt (*dubium*) or theological debate, which marks a brief pause within the commentary. The development is often signalled by a (*sed*) *contra* and leads to a resolution by the commenting teacher. In Thomas Aquinas's works, the questions most often raise doctrinal points.

The working tools and methods of exegesis employed by Aquinas favour a distinction (without exclusion) between literal exegesis and spiritual interpretations of biblical texts, often indicated by "in the mystical sense" (*mystice*). The exegesis practised by Thomas is primarily literal and doctrinal because he considers that the affirmations of faith are part of the literal meaning of the biblical texts. Hence the fundamental coherence between the biblical commentaries and the systematic works of Aquinas, which is verified on several points of doctrine.[38] Some of the biblical commentaries were taught in sync with the writing of this or that part of the *Summa Theologiae*, for which the biblical texts Thomas commented on (notably the gospel of John and the epistle to the Romans) were particularly decisive.[39] It should be borne in mind, however, that in the Middle Ages the theological act par excellence remains the commentary on Scripture, not the theological synthesis or the disputed question.

---

36. See, e.g., the prologue of the *Super Isaiam* or that of the *Super Psalmos* of Thomas Aquinas.

37. See Dahan, *L'exégèse chrétienne de la Bible en Occident médiéval*, 273.

38. For example, this has been illustrated by Gilles Emery, "Biblical Exegesis and the Speculative Doctrine of the Trinity in St. Thomas Aquinas's Commentary on St. John," in *Trinity in Aquinas* (Ypsilanti, MI: Sapientia, 2003), 271–319.

39. For the dates of these works, see Jean-Pierre Torrell, *Initiation à saint Thomas d'Aquin: Sa personne et son œuvre* (Paris: Cerf, 2002).

CASE STUDY: "MY SOUL IS SORROWFUL UNTO DEATH"

THE EXEGESIS OF MATTHEW 26:38 IN AUGUSTINE

Let us consider the main texts in which Augustine examines Christ's words in Gethsemane: "My soul is sorrowful even unto death." The major occurrences are in the eightieth of the *Eighty-Three Questions*, the *Discourses on the Psalms* and a section of book 14 of *The City of God*. The exegesis of the bishop of Hippo has a clear doctrinal purpose.

In the fourth century, the Apollinarians (heretics named after Apollinaris of Laodicea) denied that the Word had assumed a "whole man" (*totus homo*), soul and body. Based on John 1:14, they dismissed both the spirit (*mens*) and the soul (*anima*) of Christ, believing that the Word was united solely with the flesh and took the place of the soul. Augustine's refutation proceeds in stages.[40] First, he offers an exegesis – rooted in the Alexandrian Fathers – of John 1:14: "The Word was made flesh." The assumption of humanity by the Word extends to the "visible flesh." In the unity which the incarnation achieves, the two extremes are the Word and the flesh: the highest and the lowest. The Johannine formulation thus reveals "the excess of God's humility," playing on the contrast between the two extremes. The soul remains implicit, as is often the case in Scripture, when one part (the flesh) refers to the whole human.[41]

Augustine's counterattack draws on a range of Scriptures. The Lord's human "affections" or "passions," often attested to in the Gospels, require a soul. Augustine, however, takes account of a hermeneutical objection: in theory, the Lord's words, such as "My soul is sorrowful even unto death," could be figurative language, as Christ often spoke in parables. But the narratives (*narrations*) of the Evangelists leave no ambiguity as to the truth of what happens to the body: being born, being seized, being scourged, being crucified, being killed, being buried in the tomb. It is impossible to hear these narrative elements as fictional or figurative. The same narrative realism must apply to the mentions of the affections that presuppose the soul: "As these [facts] prove that [Christ] had a body, so do they show that he had a soul, those affections which there can be only in a soul [and] which, with this, we read in the narratives of the same Evangelists: Jesus was astonished (Mt. 8:10), and angry (Jn. 11:15), and grieved (Mk. 3:5), and rejoiced (Jn. 11:15), and so on and so forth."[42] The same reasoning also applies to

40. Augustine of Hippo, *Quaestio* 80 *Adversus Apollinaristas*, in *De Diversis Quaest. LXXXIII*, Bibliothèque Augustinienne 10 (Paris: DDB, 1952), §1, 354–57.

41. *Quaestio* 80, §2, 356–59.

42. *Quaestio* 80, §3, 360–61 (translation adjusted).

the joint functions (*officia*) of body and soul, such as being hungry, sleeping, sitting down tired after a walk, and so on. These narrated facts attest that the Lord was endowed with a humanity like our own, soul and body. Augustine later explains that Christ was not subjected to the affections of his soul as a matter of necessity, but that he assumed them by a divine will applied in time (*voluntas dispensationis*).

The *Discourses on the Psalms* were delivered at various times but most often in a liturgical setting. Gathered and ordered to cover the whole psalter, they offer a striking testimony to Augustine's pastoral exegesis in the act of preaching. Complaints are frequent in the psalms. The bishop of Hippo shares with his predecessors the conviction that the voice of Christ is constantly heard in these songs.

To understand how the afflicted Christ expresses himself on behalf of the martyrs and the "weak," we must place ourselves in the context of the choral singing of the psalms, as it is practised in the Christian assembly or community gathered by the bishop of Hippo. In the liturgical setting, the choir (*chorus*) responds to the voice of the first cantor, who is comparable to the head (*caput*) of the body formed by the members of the community.[43] The cantor and the choir speak to each other, personifying Christ and the church, who respond to each other. In the singing of the psalms, certain words spoken by Christ the Head – especially those characteristics of sinners and martyrs – are said in the name of the suffering members of his body, while other words sung by the choir of the faithful belong to Christ the Head – especially those which testify to innocence and glory. The swapping of words between Christ and the faithful is made possible by the close solidarity between the head and the members. They can speak for each other because they ultimately share the same Passover, even if the head (the Christ of glory) is ahead of the members (the faithful pilgrims). This is clearly the case at the ascension, where, as in a birth, the head precedes the rest of the body.[44] The Augustinian theology of the "total Christ" (*totus Christus*), head and body, is intuited by the choral singing of the Psalms.

The swapping of voices, scripted by the alternation of choral singing, reveals for Augustine a deeper truth: Christ has assumed our condition in his weakness in order to share with us certain properties of his. In the face of the paradoxes of faith, centred on the contrasts of the divine condition (*forma Dei*) and the

---

43. See *Enarr. in Ps.* 87.3, Corpus Christianorum Series Latina [subsequently abridged as CCSL], 39 (Turnhout: Brépols, 1956), 1210.

44. See *Enarr. in Ps.* 122:1, CCSL 40, 1814; *in Ps.* 142:3, 2061; Emmanuel Durand, "La variété des langues dans le *Christus totus*, selon saint Augustin," *Ephemerides Theologicae Lovanienses* 86 (2010) 1–25, here 2–8.

human condition (*forma servi*), we must recognise that as "Christ speaks, I speak." This rule applies especially to the human "weaknesses" of Christ, as reported in the gospel: "Jesus was displeased, Jesus was tired, Jesus slept, he was hungry, he was thirsty, he prayed."[45] The "admirable exchange" between the conditions is not fictitious, since it is incarnation and passion on the side of Christ, life and salvation on the side of the beneficiaries.

The measure of any particular "assumption" of the weaknesses of the slave condition is the fundamental realism of the incarnation. As he really took on flesh, he really assumed the weaknesses that go with it: passions, affections, weaknesses, and so on. When he speaks on our behalf, Christ is not playing a game. He is not just a model. He bears and lives in his own way – without sin – what he has received from us by taking on our condition.

Accepting the realism of the incarnation means making allowances for the "infirmities" of the flesh. Recognising the truth of Christ's fear and sadness in Gethsemane, Augustine refutes the Stoic teaching – known through Cicero and Virgil – that exempts the wise man from sadness. For the bishop of Hippo, this is tantamount to exalting the "hardness" of the heart, which often stems from pride (*superbia*).

> If I have no fear, I may not fear through hardness of heart; for many fear nothing through excessive pride. Let your charity be attentive; one thing is the health of the body, another thing the insensibility of the body, another thing the immortality of the body. Perfect health is immortality, and that which we enjoy in this life is also called [health] in a certain way. When he is not sick, anyone is called healthy; and the physician who examines him declares him healthy; as soon as anyone begins to be sick, health itself is impaired; and when he is cured, he is restored to health. Observe and examine these three different states of the body: health, insensibility and immortality. Health is free from disease; nevertheless, [the body] would suffer if it were struck or injured. Insensibility does not suffer; [the insensitive body] has lost the sense of pain and is all the more insensitive the worse it is. As for immortality, it does not suffer; all corruption has been overcome; the corruptible has been clothed with incorruptibility, and the mortal with immortality. There is no suffering in an immortal body, and there is also no suffering in a body that has become insensible. Let not the insensible man think himself immortal; the health of him who suffers is nearer to immortality than the insensibility of him who feels nothing. You meet a haughty, proud and insolent man who has

45. See *Enarr. in Ps.* 85:1, CCSL 39, 1176–77.

> persuaded himself that he fears nothing; do you think he is stronger than he who said: "Fight outside, fear inside" [2 Cor 7:5]? Do you think he is stronger than our Head, our Lord God, who said, "My soul is sorrowful unto death" [Matt 26:38]? No, this one is not stronger: let not his insensibility charm you; he has not put on immortality, he is stripped of all feeling.[46]

To feel no fear would be a sign not of excellence but of a defect of sensitivity, an insensitivity of the soul comparable to the stupor of the body. The body can experience three states: health, insensitivity (*stupor*), and immortality. The last two remove suffering, but the insensitive man should not believe that he has attained immortality, for "the health of one who suffers is closer to immortality than the insensibility of one who feels nothing." Immortality – declared by the Christian faith in the resurrection of the body – does not imply a suspension of human affections but an elevation and integration of noble passions by a clearly oriented and fully stabilised will. The field is open for a full integration of human "infirmities" into the coherence of the incarnation: Christ's emotions are as true as his body and flesh.

In book 14 of *The City of God*, Augustine sets out the logic of life "according to the flesh," which governs the city of Cain, in contrast to the logic of life "according to the spirit," which prevails in the city of Abel. The two cities are not exclusive domains in terms of locatable spaces. Pilgrims in the city of God walk the streets of the worldly city here and are in constant contact with its citizens. Do the pitfalls of the world lead to a wholesale condemnation of the passions? Not at all. Augustine is mainly concerned with the morality of the passions, whether they are coupled with a right or a wrong will. He also pays attention to the health and balance of our emotional responses, allowing for human limitations and frailty in our earthly condition. He is in direct opposition to the rigorism and inhumanity of the Stoics, for whom the wise man should not feel any disturbance of the soul.[47] Augustine argues that there is such a thing as good sorrow. He takes as an example the sorrow that the apostle Paul praised in the Corinthians, namely, the sorrow of repentance.[48]

Apatheia (absence of the passions) is not favoured by Augustine. He is realistic and benevolent. He recognises that even the right affections are partly beyond our control in our earthly condition. However, this is not the case with Christ, who voluntarily experiences certain passions, notably fear and sadness, in the very design (*dispensatio*) of his incarnation. Sadness and fear are very real

46. *Enarr. in Ps.* 55:6, CCSL 39, 681.
47. See Cicero, *Tusculanes*, 4.4.8–26, 57.
48. See 2 Cor 7:8–11; *De civitate Dei*, 14.8.

in Christ: as the Son took on our flesh, so he took on our passions.[49] The truth of the incarnation, involving soul and body, is the basis for the truth of Christ's affections. To have no passion would be the sign not of excellence but of infirmity: an insensitivity (*impassibilitas*) of the soul, comparable to the stupor of the body. "What is rigid is not therefore right, and insensibility is not health."[50]

In his works, Augustine interprets Christ's words in Gethsemane from a doctrinal and pastoral perspective. He seeks above all to show the truth of the incarnation through the affections. He does this in response to various currents of his time, notably the Apollinarian heresy and Stoicism. In the background is also the classic argument against the Arians, who denied Christ's divinity: the weaknesses that seem to contradict his divine condition, he actually assumed for us, in order to deliver us from those weaknesses.[51] In Augustine, this line of exegesis is linked to the Pauline theology of head and body (cf. Eph 1:22–23; 3:13–16), already translated by Tyconius into a rule of scriptural hermeneutics.[52] The sorrow of Jesus is thus part of a theological argument within the doctrinal and literary context of antiquity.

THOMAS AQUINAS'S EXEGESIS OF MATTHEW 26:38

In his collation of patristic explanations of Matthew 26:38, Thomas incorporates the specific contributions of Augustine (question 80 and *The City of God* 14). He also incorporates the diverse positions of Hilary, Jerome and John Damascene on the motives for Christ's sorrow.[53] In the whole of Aquinas's work, the exegesis of "My soul is sorrowful even unto death" unfolds in two main strands: the refutation of christological heresies and the overcoming of the Stoic sage.

Like his predecessors, Thomas uses Christ's sorrow to show that the Word in the flesh had a human soul, the home of his passions. This doctrinal argument comes into play especially in the commentary on Matthew 26, where Thomas treats Jesus' sorrow according to three questions: What? Why? How? The first

49. *De civitate Dei*, 14.9.3.

50. *De civitate Dei*, 14.9.6.

51. See Ambrose of Milan, *Expositio Evangelii secundum Lucam*, 22, 42, book IV, n. 61, CCSL 14, 363; Hilary of Poitiers, *De Trinitate*, 10.35–39; Athanasius of Alexandria, *Contra arianos*, 1.46–48; Gregory Nazianzus, *Orationes*, 30.5–6.

52. See Augustine of Hippo, *De doc. christ.* 3.31.46, BA 11/2, 297; Tyconius, *The Book of Rules*. Sources chrétiennes, 488 (Paris: Cerf, 2004). Tyconius was a Christian author in fourth-century Africa. His first rule of biblical hermeneutics is that the words of the Head (the Lord) or the body (the church) are sometimes understood as coming from the same person. Augustine uses this key reading, especially when commenting on the Psalms, to justify the fact that the (glorious) Head sometimes speaks for the (suffering) members and vice versa.

53. See *Catena Aurea*, Matt. 16:36–38, lectio 10.

question leads to three clarifications. First, Christ was not saddened according to his divinity. Second, against Apollinaris and the Arians, Christ had a human soul and was therefore capable of feeling sadness. Finally, against Manichaean dualism, Christ truly suffered.[54] Elsewhere, Thomas uses Jesus' sorrow, attested in word and deed, to distinguish between Christ's human and divine nature.[55]

Thomas also seeks to legitimise Jesus' sorrow in the eyes of the Stoic sage. In his approach, his desire to reconcile philosophy and exegesis is discernible. When commenting on Job 3:1, "After this Job opened his mouth . . . ," Thomas qualifies Job's and Christ's sadness by contrasting the Stoic and Aristotelian views:

> On the subject of the passions of the soul, the opinion of the ancients was twofold: the Stoics said that sadness is not found in the wise man, while the Peripatetics held that the wise man grieves but behaves moderately, according to reason, in his sorrows.
>
> This opinion is consistent with the truth. For reason can take nothing away from the condition of nature. Now it is natural to human nature to take pleasure in what is good for it and to rejoice in it, and to suffer from what is harmful and to be sad about it. Reason therefore cannot remove this [condition], but moderates it in such a way that reason is not diverted from its rectitude by sadness.
>
> This view also agrees with Scripture, which places sadness in Christ, in whom is all virtue and fullness of wisdom.[56]

Thomas goes on to explain that the delay of seven days after which Job opened his mouth shows that he did not speak under the influence of passion. Although he opens his mouth to curse the day of his birth, Job is in line with the model of the reflective peripatetic, to which Thomas also links Christ and Paul: "It is customary among the wise to express, from reason [*ex ratione*], the movements of passion they feel, and so spoke Christ: 'My soul is sorrowful even unto death,' as well as the Apostle in Romans VII: 'the good I want I do not do,

54. Thomas Aquinas, *Super Mat.* 16, lectio 5, ed. Marietti, n. 2221–24; see *Super Io.* 1.14, lectio 7, n. 167; *Compendium theologiae*, I, 204; *In Symbolum Apostolorum*, art. 3; *Sum. theol. III*, q. 5, a. 3.

55. See *Summa contra gentiles*, *IV*, 27, n. 3.

56. *Super Iob* 3.1, lectio 1. For a more complete theological refutation of the stoic position, in line with Aristotle's *Nicomachean Ethics* 2.6.7, see *Sum. theol.* I-II, q. 59, a. 3 which considers the following question: "Is sorrow compatible with moral virtue?" Albert the Great, Thomas Aquinas's teacher, responded to his pupil with his own commentary *Super Iob* in which he was more favourable to the ideal of the stoic sage than Aquinas; see Ruth Meyer, "A Passionate Dispute over Divine Providence: Albert the Great's Commentary on the Book of Job," in *A Companion to Job in the Middle Ages*, ed. Franklin Harkins and Aaron Canty, Brill's Companions to the Christian Tradition 73 (Leiden: Brill, 2016), 201–24.

and the evil I hate I do' [v. 15]."[57] Here the interpretation falls within the framework of Aristotelianism, which humanises the figure of the wise man without exempting him from sadness. Philosophical reason and Scripture work together in the explanation. About a decade later, Thomas commentes on Psalm 54, where the psalmist says in verse 3: "I was contrite [*contristatus sum*]." Thomas then raises the biblical figure of the righteous man as a counterpoint (*sed contra*). He resolves the problem in the following way through a "question" typical of his exegesis:

> *Sed contra*: "Whatsoever shall befall the just man. it shall not make him sad." (Prov 12:21). It ought to be said that a just person is not grieved by the sadness of the age that threatens [him with] death, but by the sadness of repentance, which is in relation to God. Or it ought to be said that there is one kind of sadness which is an emotion; and this imitates sufferance in a corporeal fashion; but this does not befall a wise man. The other sadness, that is spoken of as a "propassion," which is a sudden movement or change, is something else; and this sadness was in Christ.[58]

Let us clarify the first answer. The sorrow of penitence does not fit Christ directly, as far as he is concerned. Elsewhere, Thomas specifies that Christ voluntarily assumed a sorrow for others, analogous in its aim to that of penance, in consideration of the sin of certain men, and with a view to the redemption of the human race.[59]

Let us return to the second answer. According to Jerome, "propassion" designates the first beginning of a passion, without it developing to the point of escaping the control of reason. This answers the question of *how* regarding Christ's sorrow in the commentary on Matthew 26:37–38.[60] The syntax of verse 37 lends itself particularly to the interpretation of sadness as the beginning of a passion, since the Evangelist himself writes: "He began to grow sorrowful [*coepit constristari*]." Following Jerome, Thomas notes this explicitly when he

57. Meyer, "A Passionate Dispute over Divine Providence," in *A Companion to Job in the Middle Ages*, 201–24.

58. Thomas Aquinas, *Super Psalmos* 54.3, ed. Uccelli, *ad locum*; see also *Super Rom*. 12.2, lectio 1, ed. Marietti, n. 738, where the sorrow of Christ is justified by the natural human aversion to bodily deficiencies.

59. See *In III Sent*., 15.2.2.1, ad 3; *Sum. theol*. III, q. 15, a. 6, resp. et ad 4; *Super Rom*. 9.2, n. 738.

60. See *Super Mat*. 26:37–38, n. 2226; *Catena Aurea*, Matt. 26:36–38, lectio 10; Jerome, *Super Mat*. 26:37, SC 259, 253; 5.28.119. On the context for the use of this notion, see Donna Trembinsky, "[Pro]passio Doloris: Early Dominican Conceptions of Christ's Physical Pain," *The Journal of Ecclesiastical History* 59 (2008) 630–56.

deals with Christ's sorrow in the *Summa Theologiae*.[61] Understood in terms of propassion, Christ's sorrow does not contradict either the model of the wise man (in its peripatetic version) or the biblical figure of the just.

In addition to fine-tuning the compatibility of sorrow and wisdom in Christ, Thomas Aquinas clarifies the purpose of the sadness of Gethsemane by assembling and weighing a vast patristic dossier. Thomas shows, in the patristic record he compiled, how Hilary of Poitiers, Jerome, and Augustine each considered, in their own way, that Christ was deeply saddened for others. Drawing on a fine distinction between the natural movement of the will and the deliberate will taken from John Damascene, Aquinas held that Christ was naturally saddened by his own death, to which his natural will was repugnant, while also being deliberately saddened for those who would be affected by his death: Judas, his disciples, the Jews, and Jerusalem, among others.[62] The integration of the Greek tradition summarized by John Damascene's *The Orthodox Faith*, a seventh-century synthesis translated into Latin in the twelfth century, allowed Aquinas to clarify and deepen the exegesis of Christ's sorrow.

CONCLUSION

The exegeses of Augustine and Thomas Aquinas do not differ radically from each other in the doctrinal themes they deal with. The bishop of Hippo comments on the Bible most often with a pastoral aim, while Aquinas develops his exegesis primarily in an academic manner. Writing several centuries after Augustine, Thomas has access to a wider collection of patristic writings and engaged with a new interlocutor: the philosophy of Aristotle. In engaging with Aristotle, Thomas proceeds in line with the principles laid down by Augustine in *De doctrina christiana*, concerning the use of related disciplines in biblical interpretation. Thomas gives permanent value to the material because he believes that the forms received from the senses are a natural mediation of the human intellect. Thomas emphasizes the primacy of the literal sense, which

---

61. See *Sum. theol.* III, q. 15, a. 6, ad 1. In his commentary on the fourth Gospel, Thomas readily interprets Christ's recurring "trouble" as a sadness about death; see Richard Schenk, "'And Jesus Wept': Notes towards a Theology of Mourning," in *Reading John with St. Thomas Aquinas: Theological Exegesis and Speculative Theology*, ed. Michael Dauphinais & Matthew Levering (Washington, DC: Catholic University of America Press, 2005), 212–37.

62. See Thomas Aquinas, *Catena Aurea*, Matt. 26:36–38, lectio 10; *Super Mat.* 26:37–38, n. 2225; *Sup. Io.* 12.27, n. 1653; *Super Rom.* 9.2, n. 738; *Super Psalmos* 29.12; John Damascene, *De fide orthodoxa*, 59 [3.15]; 62 [3.18]; 67 [3.23], ed. E. M. Buytaert (New York: Franciscan Institute, St. Bonaventure, 1955), 239–40, 253–54, and 265–66.

Augustine had already emphasized. However, the academic framework and the tools of medieval exegesis, notably the division of the text and the question, call for a new type of reader, the student of Scripture.

Some fundamental questions remain for us. Augustine adopts the presupposition that things that are obscure in one part of Scripture are clearly stated elsewhere in Scripture. Thomas Aquinas follows him on this point.[63] Is this not too simple? There seems to be a great risk of systematically reducing the unknown or the enigmatic to the known. Such a process is natural in the search for an explanation, but it should be handled cautiously, in order not to reduce the depth of meaning intrinsic to some exegetical complexities and difficulties. For example, if metaphors referring to God's wrath are systematically understood as primarily meaning judgement, it is very likely that other meanings of divine wrath are obscured.[64]

The Scriptures must be interpreted together with the Rule of Faith, of which the symbols or creed are stabilized versions. Augustine uses this method in a particularly fruitful way in *De Trinitate*, when he refutes Arian interpretations of Scripture.[65] But some of the exegetical choices to be made are not explicitly covered by the Rule of Faith. It is then appropriate to extend the hermeneutical framework to the tradition of the church. However, how can we distinguish between the tradition and traditions? How can we possibly criticize traditions that are confused with the tradition of divine revelation? For example, slavery was accepted and practiced for centuries in Christian circles. In his time, Paul attempts to evangelize people on both sides of the hostile divides between Jew and Gentile, man and woman, free and slave, but this did not transform social conventions in any significant way.[66] In the context of the colonization of the Americas, it was not until the preaching of Antonio de Montesinos in Santo Domingo in 1511 that consciences were challenged on the subject of enslaving the native population. For the Scriptures to be better interpreted, the Rule of Faith is not enough. The Scriptures must be read with the Spirit who inspired them. Only through conversion can certain scales fall from the eyes of the readers. For this reason, the prophets and saints are the most innovative and faithful interpreters.[67]

The reception of the sorrow of Jesus continues at various times. Imprisoned

63. Thomas Aquinas, *Quodlibet* 7.6, ad 3; *Sum. theol.* I, q. 1, a. 9, ad 2.

64. See Emmanuel Durand, *Les Émotions de Dieu, indices d'engagement* (Paris: Cerf, 2019), 165–211.

65. Augustine of Hippo, *De Trinitate*, 1.7.

66. See Michel Gourgues, *Ni homme ni femme: L'attitude du premier christianisme à l'égard de la femme. Évolutions et regressions* (Paris: Cerf, 2013).

67. See Thomas Aquinas, *Sup. Io.* 18.23, n. 2321; Augustine of Hippo, *Tract. in Io.* 63.4.

in the Tower of London, under the threat of a terrible punishment for the crime of high treason, the humanist Thomas More wrote his *De Tristitia Christi* (1534–35). Unfinished, the work is a meditation on the passion narratives, through which More accompanies his future readers in the quest for a prudent and theological way of living through trials. Much emphasis is placed on the management of fear and imagination in preparation for unwanted martyrdom. More argues that martyrs who courageously and faithfully endure the troubles of fear are (*de facto*) more like Christ than martyrs who eagerly expose themselves to death, for in order to sustain the fearful, Jesus willingly assumed the most acute fear.[68] Thomas More's exegesis draws on the suggestions of the fathers, the resources of humanism, and his own experience of trial. Such a reading is the result of a lifelong process of spiritual growth.[69]

FOR FURTHER READING

Bochet, Isabelle. *"Le firmament de l'Écriture": L'herméneutique augustinienne*. Paris: Institut d'Études Augustiniennes, 2004.

Dahan, Gilbert. *L'exégèse chrétienne de la Bible en Occident médiéval. XIIe–XIVe siècle*. Paris: Cerf, 1999.

Dauphinais, Michael, and Levering, Matthew, eds. *Reading John with St. Thomas Aquinas: Theological Exegesis and Speculative Theology*. Washington, DC: Catholic University of America Press, 2005.

Durand, Emmanuel. *Les Émotions de Dieu, indices d'engagement*. Paris: Cerf, 2019.

Durand, Emmanuel. *Divine Speech in Human Words: Thomistic Engagements with Scripture*. Washington, DC: Catholic University of America Press, 2022.

Loiseau, Stéphane. *De l'écoute à la parole: La lecture biblique dans la doctrine sacrée selon Thomas d'Aquin*. Paris: Cerf, 2017.

Meyer, Ruth. "A Passionate Dispute over Divine Providence: Albert the Great's Commentary on the Book of Job." In *A Companion to Job in the Middle Ages*, edited by Franklin Harkins and Aaron Canty, Brill's Companions to the Christian Tradition 73, 201–24. Leiden: Brill, 2016.

---

68. See Thomas More, *De Tristitia Christi*, 1565, Complete Works of St. Thomas More, 14/1. ed. C. H. Miller (New Haven, CT: Yale University Press, 1976), specifically 39–109, 237–57; Travis Curtright, "From Thomas More's Workshop: *De Tristitia Christi* and the *Catena Aurea*," *Logos* 18 (2015): 100–126.

69. See Jeffrey L. Morrow, "Thomas More on the Sadness of Christ: From Mystagogy to Martyrdom," *Heythrop Journal* 58 (2017): 365–73. For further developments, see Emmanuel Durand, "La tristesse de Jésus à Gethsémani selon une théologie des figures, avec Augustin d'Hippone, Thomas d'Aquin et Thomas More," in *Une théologie à l'école de saint Thomas d'Aquin*, Festschrift Gilles Emery, ed. Nicole Awais (Paris: Cerf, 2022), 491–509.

Roszak, Piotr, and Vijgen, Jörgen, eds. *Reading Sacred Scripture with Thomas Aquinas: Hermeneutical Tools, Theological Questions and New Perspectives.* Turnhout: Brepols, 2015.

———. *Towards a Biblical Thomism: Thomas Aquinas and the Renewal of Biblical Theology.* Pamplona: EUNSA–Ediciones Universidad de Navarra, 2018.

Trembinsky, Donna. "[Pro]passio Doloris: Early Dominican Conceptions of Christ's Physical Pain." *The Journal of Ecclesiastical History* 59 (2008): 630–56.

Valkenberg, W. G. B. M. *Words of the Living God: Place and Function of Holy Scripture in the Theology of St. Thomas Aquinas.* Thomas Instituut Utrecht 6. Leuven: Peeters, 2000.

CHAPTER 10

The Historical-Critical Method in Biblical Studies

Its History, Potential, and Limitations

Armin D. Baum

The expression *historical-critical method* is ambiguous. Not just one but (at least) two different methods of analyzing a given text are called "historical-critical." Therefore, I will first look at this somewhat confusing terminology.

Most influential books on New Testament methodology usually give much more room for exegetical than for historical method. For this reason, I will describe both the exegetical and the historical method. In due course, I will not only highlight their strengths but also point out their limitations.

Regarding both methods, the question arises about what difference it makes whether exegetes or historians interpret biblical texts as Christian believers. This pneumatic or spiritual dimension of biblical studies is often omitted in textbooks on New Testament method. I will deal with it in relation both to exegetical and to historical interpretation of the New Testament.

Finally, I will look at the relationship between the historical-critical method and *a priori* criticism of the miraculous. What is the main difference between a dogmatic or absolute and an open-minded approach to the supernatural elements in the biblical texts?[1]

1. As a German scholar, I write this text from a German perspective, but I will also include some

As a New Testament scholar, I discuss various aspects of the "historical-critical method" significant for New Testament studies but am quite confident that my observations and explanations also apply to Old Testament studies.

TERMINOLOGY

The English word *method* derives from the Greek word *methodos*, which generally means "following after, pursuit" and can refer specifically to "pursuit of knowledge, scientific inquiry, investigation, method of inquiry."[2] The Latin word *methodus* also refers to "a mode of proceeding."[3] Accordingly, our modern word *method* means "procedure" and refers to a systematic procedure for obtaining knowledge.

Different objects require different methods. This also applies to biblical studies. Biblical scholars use an exegetical method and a historical method.

EXEGESIS AND THE EXEGETICAL METHOD

The English word *exegesis* derives from the Greek word *exēgēsis*: "the explanation and interpretation of a text which is not easily comprehensible."[4] The *exēgētēs* is an "expounder, interpreter,"[5] among other things of law and poetry. In Latin, the word *interpretatio* means "explanation, interpretation." The *interpres* or *interpretor* is "one who explains or expounds," "interpreter," or "expositor."[6] The exegetical method is thus a systematic procedure to explain the meaning of a text.

Already in pre-Christian times, Greek exegetes applied different methodological tools. They defined the meanings of words, analyzed syntactical structures, explained historical backgrounds, formulated paraphrases, and determined the scope of their texts. In addition, already in ancient times the principle of explaining Homer from Homer (Porphyrius) or explaining Hippocrates from

important English titles. However, due to the limited space in this chapter, I will focus on the classical and most influential contributions to my topic. Cf. my article, "Die historisch-kritische Methode in der Bibelwissenschaft: Ihre Geschichte, ihre Leistungsfähigkeit und ihre Grenzen," *Biblisch erneuerte Theologie* 3 (2019): 53–87. I would like to thank Martin Webber for his help with the English version of this article and for many helpful suggestions.

2. H. G. Liddell, R. Scott and H. S. Jones, *A Greek-English Lexicon* (Oxford: Clarendon, 1985), *s. v.*; cf. J. Ritter, "Methode," in *Historisches Wörterbuch der Philosophie*, ed. J. Ritter, K. Grunder, and G. Gabriel (Basel: Schwabe, 1971–2007), 5:1304–5.

3. *Oxford Latin Dictionary* (Oxford: Clarendon, 1968), *s. v.*

4. H. Schreckenberg, "Exegese I (heidnisch, Griechen u[nd] Römer)," in *Reallexikon für Antike und Christentum* (Stuttgart: Hiersemann, 1950–), 6:1174.

5. Liddell, Scott, and Jones, *A Greek-English Lexicon*, s. v.; *Oxford Latin Dictionary*, s. v.

6. *Oxford Latin Dictionary*, s. v.

Hippocrates (Galen) was applied by comparing parallel passages from the analyzed authors.[7]

In addition to the question of what a text means, some exegetes (like Xenophanes) also dealt with questions of truth and authenticity. They examined whether a text came from the author whose name it carried and whether the content of a text was historically accurate.[8]

The first exegetical commentaries were written in the famous library of Alexandria in the Hellenistic period. These ancient commentaries were called "exegesis" or "exegetics." Both Galen and Origen used this terminology.[9]

Our current expressions exegesis *and* exegetical method *originate from these ancient, partly pre-Christian roots. Likewise, the different steps of our exegetical method do not differ fundamentally from those already applied in pagan and Christian antiquity.* I discuss the exegetical method used today, especially in biblical studies, in more detail below.

HISTORY AND THE HISTORICAL METHOD

The English word *history* derives from the Greek word *historia*, which designated "(a learning by) inquiry," "the knowledge so obtained, information" and "an account of one's inquiries, a narrative, history."[10] The Latin word *historia* also meant "investigation, inquiry, research" as well as "a written account of past events, a history."[11]

Since the end of the fourteenth century, the terms *ars historica* and *methodus historica* have been used to describe the work of the historian.[12] Already in antiquity, historians were obliged to report only what really had happened. They worked with oral and written sources, had to check their authenticity to distinguish between primary and secondary sources, and had rules for dealing with conflicting testimonies and for rendering historical speeches. They omitted questionable information or, if they reproduced it, informed their readers that they considered it doubtful or untrustworthy.[13] Early Christian authors also used a historical method and worked with historical criteria. This is clear

---

7. Schreckenberg, "Exegese I," 6:1175–77, 1182, 1186.

8. Schreckenberg, "Exegese I," 6:1178–82.

9. L. Fladerer and D. Börner-Klein, "Kommentar," *Reallexikon für Antike und Christentum*, 21:276–77, 282–283.

10. Liddell, Scott, and Jones, *A Greek-English Lexicon*, *s. v.*

11. *Oxford Latin Dictionary*, s. v.

12. J. Rüsen and W. Schulze, "Methode, historische," in *Historisches Wörterbuch der Philosophie*, 5:1345–46.

13. See J. Marincola, *Authority and Tradition in Ancient Historiography* (Cambridge: Cambridge University Press, 1997), 62–127 on ancient source criticism, and 280–86 on ancient handling of contradictory sources.

not only from the prologue of the gospel of Luke (Luke 1:1–4)[14] but also from ancient discussions about the authenticity of the words of Jesus.[15]

Thus, *our present terms* history *and* historical method *also have ancient roots, and the rules of our historical method developed from rules already being applied in pre-Christian and Christian antiquity.* Below I will return to the role of the historical method in modern biblical studies.

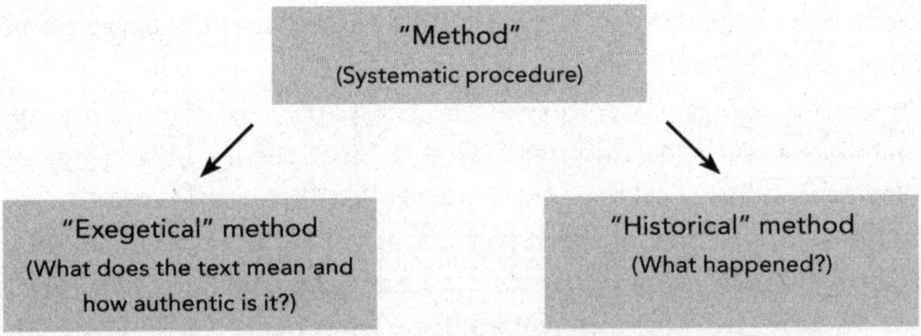

Figure 1: The Exegetical and the Historical Method

CRITICISM AND THE CRITICAL METHOD

Another technical term to consider in a description of the historical-critical method is the adjective *critical* or the related noun *criticism*. The adjective *critical* is often combined with the adjective *historical* in the compound adjective *historical-critical*.

The English word *criticism* comes from the Greek word *kritikē*, meaning the "evaluation" of written works. Since Hellenistic times (from about 300 BC), the Greeks called a literary scholar not only a "philologist" or a "grammarian" but also a "critic" (*kritikos*).[16] This terminology was adopted in the Middle Ages, when interpreters of poetic or other texts were called not only "grammarians" but also "critics (*critici*)." The philological art of correcting, explaining, and commenting on texts was called *ars critica*.[17]

Since the sixteenth century, the expression *ars critica* has also been used to designate the interpretation of the biblical writings.[18] In the seventeenth century, the French exegete Richard Simon used the word *critique* to describe the scholarly method that he applied to the biblical writings and understood himself in

14. See A. D. Baum, *Einleitung in das Neue Testament. Evangelien und Apostelgeschichte* (Gießen: Brunnen, 2017), 274–97.

15. See A. D. Baum, "Die Diskussion der Authentizität von Herrenworten in altkirchlicher Zeit: Ein Beitrag zur Geschichte der Leben-Jesu-Forschung," *Theologische Beiträge* 30 (1999): 303–17.

16. C. von Bormann, "Kritik," in *Historisches Wörterbuch der Philosophie*, 4:1251–52.

17. G. Tonelli and C. von Bormann, "Kritik," in *Historisches Wörterbuch der Philosophie*, 4:1263–64.

18. Tonelli and von Bormann, "Kritik," 4:1264.

this respect as a biblical critic,[19] that is, a biblical scholar.[20] In this sense, biblical criticism is the scholarly interpretation of the Bible. This use of the expression *biblical criticism* is still very common.[21]

Parallel to this particular use, multiple meanings of the word *criticism* melted together into one general sense: "exercise of reason."[22] Immanuel Kant used the word in this general sense when he called his major philosophical works *Critique of Pure Reason* (*Kritik der reinen Vernunft*, 1781), *Critique of Practical Reason* (*Kritik der praktischen Vernunft*, 1788), and *Critique of Judgment* (*Kritik der Urteilskraft*, 1790).[23]

Since the eighteenth century at the latest, the adjective *critical* appears in combination with the adjective *historical*. Since then, scholarly treatises on philological and historical topics have been called "historical-critical" investigations. Thus, in 1747 the Lutheran pastor Gottfried Ephraim Müller published a *Historical-Critical Introduction* to the knowledge and use of the old Latin writers. In 1818, the Lutheran church historian Johann Karl Ludwig Gieseler (1792–1854) published his *Historical-Critical Essay* on the origin of the written Gospels, in which he answered the synoptic question with the tradition hypothesis. This terminology is still widespread.

Thus, for centuries, the words *critique* and *criticism* have meant more or less the same thing as the word *method*. Therefore, the expression *philological criticism* often means nothing other than application of a philological or exegetical method. For this reason, the expression *historical criticism* often means the same thing as *historical method. In this context, the historical-critical method is the historian's scholarly method, the roots of which go back to pre-Christian times.*[24]

In the nineteenth century, however, some theologians began to add a layer of meaning to the word *criticism*, using it to describe certain philosophical assumptions (see section 4 below) that should guide biblical studies. *Critical* came to mean a kind of exegesis that in principle no longer recognized the philosophical possibility of miracles. From this point of view, *biblical criticism*, in the

19. M. Reiser, *Bibelkritik und Auslegung der Heiligen Schrift: Beiträge zur Geschichte der biblischen Exegese und Hermeneutik*, WUNT 217 (Tübingen: Mohr Siebeck, 2007), 204–9.

20. Reiser, *Bibelkritik und Auslegung der Heiligen Schrift*, 220–22.

21. See for instance J. Barr, "Biblical Criticism," in *History and Ideology in the Old Testament: Biblical Studies at the End of a Millennium* (Oxford: Oxford University Press, 2000), 32–58; F. F. Bruce, *Understanding Biblical Criticism*, ed. D. Capes (Nashville: Kingsley, 2017).

22. Tonelli and von Bormann, "Kritik," 4:1266.

23. See H. Holzhey, "Kritik," in *Historisches Wörterbuch der Philosophie*, 4:1268–72.

24. Cf. R. Riesner, "Sollen wir das Neue Testament unhistorisch-unkritisch auslegen?," in *Gotteswort im Menschenwort? Zum Verstehen und Auslegen der Bibel*, ed. S. Grosse and J. Walldorf, Porta-Studien 30 (Marburg: SMD, 1999), 29–31.

traditional sense of the expression that considered the raising of Jesus from the dead to be a historical event in space and time, was regarded as "precritical."

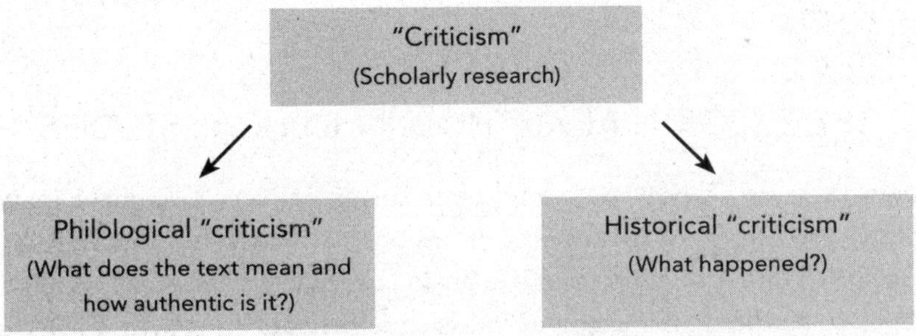

Figure 2: Philological and Historical Criticism

Since this philosophical criticism concerned historical statements of the Bible, the adjective *critical* was combined with the adjective *historical*. This new approach was called "historical-critical research" and the related method the "historical-critical method."[25] *Until today, the historical-critical method in this sense presupposes an a priori denial of the supernatural claims of the biblical texts.* This variant of biblical criticism will also be analyzed below.

The expression *historical-critical method* thus has two different meanings that need to be distinguished. On the one hand, *critical* simply means "scholarly," and *historical-critical* means "historical-scholarly." It does not presuppose any *a priori* decision about the possibility of supernatural actions of God and is in this respect open-minded. On the other hand, *critical* can have the ideological sense "miracle-critical," and in these cases *historical-critical* means "historical and miracle-critical" and in principle excludes supernatural acts of God.

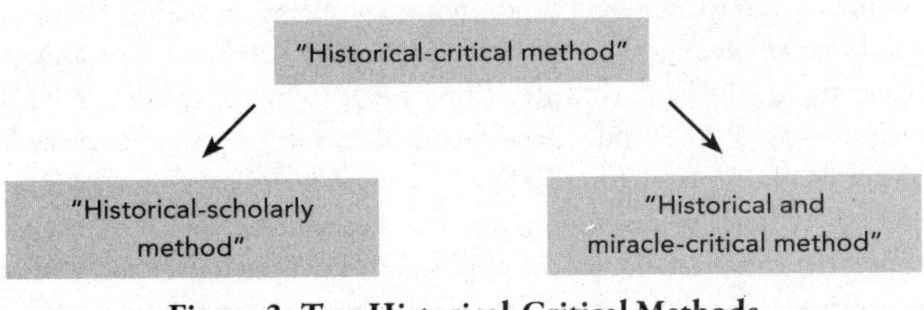

Figure 3: Two Historical-Critical Methods

The fact that the term *historical-critical method* has these two different meanings is often overlooked outside the scientific community (and even in

25. Reiser, *Bibelkritik und Auslegung der Heiligen Schrift*, 34–38.

scholarly discussions, it is not always considered). In any case, the question of whether someone advocates *the* historical-critical method cannot be answered with a simple yes or no.

THE EXEGETICAL METHOD IN BIBLICAL STUDIES

Modern exegesis analyzes not only the meaning of New Testament texts but also their prehistory. In this respect, it has both a synchronic and a diachronic dimension. Which of these two dimensions receives more room varies from textbook to textbook. For example, Udo Schnelle treats the synchronic meaning of the New Testament texts only briefly, while he discusses the diachronic prehistory of the texts extensively.[26] Wilhelm Egger and Peter Wick, on the other hand, deal at length with synchronic but much less with diachronic exegesis.[27]

SYNCHRONIC TEXTUAL ANALYSIS

Synchronic exegesis of New Testament texts concentrates on four aspects, supplemented by other aspects as necessary: form, language, literary, and historical contexts.

First, the form of a text is analyzed. Where does it begin and end, and how can it be distinguished from its surrounding literary context? What is its structure? Which generic characteristics does it manifest? Is it, for example, a will or a parable? How does the narrative work?

Second, the exegete analyzes the language of the text. With the help of dictionaries, he subjects it to lexical and semantic analyses. With the help of grammars, he examines its syntax and identifies figures of style.

Third, the interpreter looks at the literary context of the text. What precedes, what follows? What does the context of a passage contribute to its meaning?

Fourth, the historical context of the text is to be considered. What light can encyclopedia entries (and other scholarly literature) shed on the background and meaning of the text? Different analyses of the historical context can lead in different directions. Sociohistorical analysis, for example, looks at the explanatory potential of contemporary social phenomena. Religious-historical analysis examines similarities and differences with phenomena in contemporary religion.

---

26. U. Schnelle, *Einführung in die neutestamentliche Exegese* (Göttingen: Vandenhoeck, 2014), 57–67 (text delimitation, context, syntax, etc.) and 68–139, as well as 162–77 (literary, form, tradition, and redaction criticism).

27. W. Egger and P. Wick, *Methodenlehre zum Neuen Testament* (Freiburg: Herder, 2011), 80–219 (text delimitation, context, syntax, etc.) and 222–68 (literary, tradition, and reaction criticism).

Each text requires an individual application of the different methodological tools, and in each of the four areas, further differentiations are possible.

DIACHRONIC TEXTUAL ANALYSIS

In diachronic textual analysis, the exegete examines the oral or written prehistory of the text.

Terminology for the different methods used in diachronic analysis is not uniform. Generally, though, analysis of the oral prehistory of a text is called "tradition criticism," study of the written prehistory of a text is usually referred to as "source criticism," and "redaction criticism" asks how an author has edited his oral or written sources and to what extent he has shaped the final form of his text.

Diachronic textual analysis can in principle be applied to every text. It is not, however, of equal importance for all biblical books. Some diachronic questions have gained such importance that fixed names have been established for them. For instance, analysis of the history of the Synoptic Gospels is called the synoptic question. The search for the prehistory of the gospel of John is called the Johannine question.

In the Synoptic Gospels, tradition criticism asks how pericopes changed during their oral transmission. Have the orally transmitted words and stories of Jesus, for example, grown like snowballs or melted down?

Source criticism asks whether the Evangelists have used written sources, and if so, which ones? Did Mark use the gospel of Matthew, or Matthew the gospel of Mark – or perhaps a proto- or deutero-Mark (that is, an earlier version of or a later revision of the canonical gospel)? Did Luke know and use the gospel of Matthew, or did Matthew and Luke use a second written source besides the gospel of Mark, known as Q?

In contrast to tradition and source criticism, redaction criticism focuses on the processing of oral and written sources by the Evangelists. How did they select, link, and supplement their source material? What theological motives could have guided them?

DANGERS AND LIMITATIONS OF THE EXEGETICAL METHOD

Some theologically uneducated Bible readers disregard a methodological interpretation of the Bible and rely mainly on intuition. Occasionally, they even declare unmethodical Bible reading to be the only true and spiritual approach. To escape the danger of subjectivism, however, an exegetical method is indispensable. No student of theology or preacher can do without an exegetical method that leads him to verifiable results and protects him from an uncritical appropriation of the biblical texts.

Overinterpretation of Details

Nevertheless, every Bible interpreter must remain aware of a danger inherent in the application of an exegetical method. The danger of overinterpretation lurks behind every single word, every biblical sentence, and every theological statement. Colleagues from neighboring disciplines sometimes see these dangers more clearly than do experts in biblical studies themselves.

The classical philologist Olof Gigon (1912–98) emphatically warned New Testament scholars against an uncritical application of literary criticism. Because this method has a

> tendency to hypertrophy. *It is possible to analyze any text in such a way that it dissolves into a conglomerate of heterogeneous fragments.* The philologist is in danger of acquiring a *mal'occhio*, so to speak, and of discovering everywhere only incongruities, leaps of thought and breaks in style . . .
>
> The mistake is, of course, that the interpreter tacitly starts with the image of a perfectly coherent text that is perfect in form and content, as if such a thing could be found in historical reality at all – apart from perhaps the mathematical-logical language of formulas, which, however, has nothing to do with a language in the historical sense.
>
> It's all about recognizing the limitations of this method and getting clarity about the kind of texts to which it can be applied and to what degree. It is just as absurd to abandon it completely as it is inadequate to apply it to every text until it becomes a formless heap of sand.[28]

The Small Size of the New Testament

The systematic theologian Helmut Thielicke (1908–86) observed among his colleagues in biblical studies that they did not always pursue their discipline with the necessary sobriety and restraint: "In every generation – may I say it maliciously and with exaggeration – the New Testament scholars confuse us with new ideas. . . . [This] is certainly due not least to the fact that the New Testament is a quantitatively very small book."[29]

Of course, despite its small size, the New Testament is of unique importance for Christian theology. However, *if the object of investigation is of small size, the danger of overstraining methodological tools is particularly great.* It therefore makes sense that New Testament scholars do not limit themselves to the exegesis of New Testament texts but regularly include the many neighboring

28. O. Gigon, *Erwägungen eines Altphilologen zum Neuen Testament* (Basel: FETA, 1972), 2 (my trans.).

29. H. Thielicke, *Auf dem Weg zur Kanzel: Sendschreiben an junge Theologen und ihre älteren Freunde* (Stuttgart: Quell, 1983), 51 (my trans.).

disciplines of New Testament studies. Such an approach facilitates the finding of new results.

The danger of overinterpretation must, of course, be avoided not only in the application of tools of diachronic exegesis such as source criticism but also in the application of synchronic tools such as determination of word meanings (word-study fallacies) and interpretation of syntactic structures (grammatical fallacies).[30]

Nevertheless, even the most prudent application of exegetical methods cannot guarantee one thing: a consensus about the meaning of a particular text. Such a consensus remains a meaningful goal that we can and must strive for, yet this goal will always only be partially achieved. No exegete, however ambitious and methodically versed, can ever overcome this fundamental limitation.

PLACE AND PURPOSE OF A PNEUMATIC APPROACH

For Christian exegetes, interpretation of biblical texts has another dimension in addition to the purely exegetical one. For them, the New Testament is not merely a collection of interesting ancient texts. It is at the same time the written source of their faith in which they have a deep existential interest. The believing exegete must be aware of this double interest in the biblical text and reflect on the relationship between the scholarly and the spiritual approach.

The Pneumatic Approach as a Complement

Representatives of pneumatic exegesis have particularly emphasized this. They observe that the New Testament scholar Adolf Schlatter (1852–1938) "practiced pneumatic exegesis in a revolutionary new way" and did so "with an eye enlightened by the Holy Spirit." In his writings, they find a "historical-critical-pneumatic interpretation" or "exegesis."[31] Despite his pneumatic approach, however, Schlatter was firmly convinced that it was "a weighty methodological mistake when a work, whether historical or dogmatic, makes the claim to possess a special method in which its theological character consists, and this because it is valid for application only in the religious realm. This is sure to raise such profound suspicion that the work, whatever its merit otherwise, will go unheeded."[32] Thus, the pneumatic approach did not change Schlatter's exegetical method, but added an additional dimension to it.

---

30. For examples see D. A. Carson, *Exegetical Fallacies* (Grand Rapids: Baker, 1996).

31. H. Frey, *Die Krise der Theologie: Historische Kritik und pneumatische Auslegung im Licht der Krise* (Wuppertal: Brockhaus, 1972), 44–46 (my trans.).

32. Quoted according to R. W. Yarborough, "Adolf Schlatter's 'The Significance of Method for Theological Work': Translation and Commentary," *SBJT* 1 (1997): 65.

Proponents of pneumatic exegesis have also regarded the German-Baltic systematic theologian Karl Girgensohn (1875–1925) as a forerunner. He criticized the "distance of the observing researcher from his research object" as a basic prerequisite of historical-critical exegesis. In his opinion, the exegete had to listen to the voice of the living God in the Scriptures, "for which the historical-critical analysis of Scripture simply lacks the organ." Such a spiritual interpretation was only accessible to born-again Christians. For Girgensohn too, however, the historical-critical and the pneumatic method of interpretation were two approaches that should not corrupt but complement each other. *The scholarly approach protects the interpreter from subjectivism, while the pneumatic approach protects him from irreverence towards the Scriptures.*[33]

Pauline Pneumatology

This kind of exegesis, which takes the work of the Holy Spirit into account, corresponds to the pneumatology of the Pauline letters. The apostle Paul, on the one hand, strongly advocates that Christians make use of the gift of reason given to them by God and warns his readers against a disdain for rational thinking: "Do not be children in your thinking; rather, be infants in evil, but in thinking be adults" (1 Cor 14:20 NRSV). Paul challenges his Christian addressees to integrate their rationality as an indispensable element into their spirituality: "I will pray with the spirit, but I will pray with the mind also" (1 Cor 14:15 NRSV).

On the other hand, Paul also emphasizes that people can recognize God as Father only through the Holy Spirit (Gal 4:6; Rom 8:15). Jesus can be recognized as Lord only through the Holy Spirit (1 Cor 12:3). Christian joy is brought about only through the Holy Spirit (Rom 14:17; 1 Thess 1:6). Sinful acts can be abandoned only through the Holy Spirit (Rom 8:13). Christian fellowship develops only through the Holy Spirit (2 Cor 13:13). Such experiences are only accessible to Christians who have received the Holy Spirit. However, *nowhere in the New Testament is there any hint that such pneumatic experiences should restrict the use of reason. Sensible judgment and spiritual experience belong together and complement each other.*

At this point, the German-Baltic Old Testament scholar Hellmut Frey (1901–82) chose a different path by using pneumatic exegesis, at least partly, as an alternative to scholarly exegesis. Frey was convinced that at times pneumatic exegesis would have to produce results that were not methodologically justified but rather imposed themselves through a congenial listening to the text. In textual criticism, in the delimitation of pericopes, in the determination of word

33. Frey, *Die Krise der Theologie*, 62–63, 65–66.

meanings, in the analysis of sentence structures, in the translation of the biblical text, the pneumatic exegete has to make exegetical decisions that lead in a different direction than text-critical rules or dictionaries.[34] This radical form of pneumatic exegesis has rightly been accused of subjectivism and has found only few followers.

THE HISTORICAL METHOD IN BIBLICAL STUDIES

In contrast to the exegetical method, which mainly seeks to explain the meaning of a text, the historical method judges to what extent available sources are reliable and to what extent the events they describe are historical.[35]

Common textbooks of historical-critical exegesis often treat the historical method only marginally or not at all. Egger and Wick deal with it on scarcely ten pages,[36] while it is completely missing from Schnelle's book.[37] In New Testament studies, explanations of the historical method are most likely to be found in textbooks on the life of Jesus. *Students of the Bible can obtain the most comprehensive information on the historical method from textbooks on secular and church history.*[38]

Since the nineteenth century, the principles of historical research have been delineated as follows: heuristics (the collection and classification of sources), criticism (the distinction between historical and doubtful data), interpretation (the connecting of historical data), and historiography (the writing of history books).[39]

After the historian has compiled the available source material as completely as possible, he or she subjects it to a double critique: external and internal source criticism. External criticism deals with the historical quality of the sources, while internal criticism deals with the historicity of related events.

EXTERNAL SOURCE CRITICISM

External source criticism decides whether and to what extent a source is admissible as a historical testimony. To justify this decision, the historian

34. Frey, *Die Krise der Theologie*, 71–72.

35. E. Bernheim, *Lehrbuch der historischen Methode und der Geschichtsphilosophie* (Leipzig: Duncker und Humblot, 1908), 324.

36. Egger and Wick, *Methodenlehre zum Neuen Testament*, 195–203.

37. See Schnelle, *Einführung in die neutestamentliche Exegese*, 7–10, 57–58.

38. For instance, L. Gottschalk, *Understanding History: A Primer of Historical Method* (New York: Knopf, 1950); or M. C. Howell and W. Prevenier, *From Reliable Sources: An Introduction to Historical Methods* (Ithaca, NY: Cornell University Press, 2001).

39. Rüsen and Schulze, "Methode, historische," 5:1350–52.

asks several key questions, including the following: When and where did the source originate? Who wrote it? Is it authentic? On what other sources does it depend?[40]

The date of origin of a source is important because the value of its testimony depends on how chronologically close it is to the event described. The place of origin of a source is important because the value of its testimony may also depend on how geographically close it is to the event. Identification of the author of a source is important because it allows conclusions regarding the quality of the source. Determining the authenticity of a source (and the identification of interpolations) is important because forgeries or errors cannot serve as historical evidence. Interdependence among available sources is important because the value of their testimonies depends on which of them most directly reflects the historical event. The historian must examine "whether the reporting person himself has seen or heard what he communicates, or whether he retells what he heard from others; in the former case his report is regarded as the original source, in the latter as a derived source."[41]

In New Testament studies, these questions of external source criticism are dealt with in books on New Testament introduction, which cover general and special introduction to the New Testament. *Special introduction deals with the origins of the twenty-seven individual New Testament writings and poses the same questions to them as the historian does in external source criticism*: When, where and by whom were the texts written? Are they authentic? To what extent are they interdependent?[42]

Answers to these introductory questions form the basis for the use of the Gospels in life-of-Jesus research. Therefore, introductory questions to the Gospels are also treated in books on the life of Jesus.[43] Introductions to the New Testament deal not only with the Gospels but also with the question of which of the thirteen New Testament (and several apocryphal) epistles of Paul can be regarded as literarily genuine and what historical value the New Testament book of Acts (and the Apocryphal Acts) have for the work and the theology of the apostle Paul. Only based on these answers to the introductory questions can the life of the apostle and his theology be reconstructed.[44]

40. Bernheim, *Lehrbuch der historischen Methode*, 330–464.

41. Bernheim, *Lehrbuch der historischen Methode*, 413 (my trans.).

42. For the current state of research, see Baum, *Einleitung in das Neue Testament*.

43. G. Theissen and A. Merz, *The Historical Jesus: A Comprehensive Guide*, trans. J. Bowden (Minneapolis: Fortress, 1998).

44. See, for example, F. F. Bruce, *Paul: Apostle of the Heart Set Free* (Grand Rapids: Eerdmans, 1977).

INTERNAL SOURCE CRITICISM

Internal source criticism asks whether events mentioned in the sources really happened.[45] New Testament scholars ask, for example, to what extent the transmitted words of Jesus or the apostles are historically authentic, what happened to the apostle Paul in his final years, and whether the bodily resurrection of Jesus was a historical event.

In a first step, internal source criticism examines, based on the results of the external source criticism, the reliability of individual testimonies of the sources. In a second step, the historian asks whether the testimonies confirm or cast doubt on each other. A comparison of the available testimonies can – roughly speaking – lead to three different results: a word of Jesus can be attested several times, only once, or in several different versions.

The Criterion of Multiple Attestation

One of the most fundamental questions of inner criticism is whether a Jesus *logion* is attested only once or more than once. This question is based on psychological experience: "As in ordinary life, in the field of historical tradition we consider ourselves completely convinced of the truth of a testimony when two or more independent witnesses report the same thing."[46] If a *logion* appears in two or more literarily independent sources, this speaks for its authenticity.

In this context, the historian also examines whether a testimony fits with otherwise known facts. In this case, a single direct testimony can be confirmed by indirect evidence. This kind of agreement establishes the inner probability of a fact.[47]

If a Jesus *logion* is attested only once, multiple attestation is missing. Whether this leads to a negative historical judgment depends on the historical value ascribed to the one historical source. This judgment consists of two factors. First, it is important to determine whether the author intended to and was able to reproduce Jesus' words correctly. Second, it is decisive whether the source in question has proven to be historically reliable in places where it can be tested. *A single attestation as such does not give the historian the right to reject such a testimony.*[48]

The most difficult task for the historian is to evaluate sources that contradict each other. Special care is required in such cases. "Before asserting that there

---

45. Bernheim, *Lehrbuch der historischen Methode*, 464.
46. Bernheim, *Lehrbuch der historischen Methode*, 525 (my trans.).
47. Bernheim, *Lehrbuch der historischen Methode*, 533.
48. Bernheim, *Lehrbuch der historischen Methode*, 536.

are mutually exclusive contradictions, we must have carefully examined whether we are dealing with only apparent contradictions. Once we have done this, we have no choice but to look at the degree of reliability of each of the conflicting testimonies and to prefer the more reliable one. If two equally reliable testimonies contradict each other, we have no choice but to leave our judgement in suspense."[49]

The Criterion of Dissimilarity

Generally speaking, the criterion of dissimilarity, which played a major role in life-of-Jesus research, can no longer be found in current textbooks on the historical method. The classical version of the criterion was developed by Rudolf Bultmann's pupil Ernst Käsemann (1906–98): "In only one case do we have more or less safe ground under our feet; when there are not grounds either for deriving a tradition from Judaism or for ascribing it to primitive Christianity."[50] Whatever judgement the researcher makes about the authenticity of Jesus *logia* not covered by the criterion of dissimilarity again depends on his overall judgement about the historical value of his sources. Even Käsemann himself referred to the extremely limited efficiency of the criterion of dissimilarity: "But in so doing we must realize beforehand that we shall not, from this angle of vision, gain any clear view of the connecting link between Jesus, his Palestinian environment and his later community. The frontiers here lie wide open to the most diverse hypotheses."[51]

A main objection against the criterion of dissimilarity is that it prevents Jesus from being historically rooted either in Judaism or in the history of Christianity and thus makes him appear ahistorical.[52] This point has received more attention in the so-called "third quest" for the historical Jesus. Gerd Theissen and Dagmar Winter advocate replacing the criterion of dissimilarity with a plausibility criterion. They want to accept as genuine words of Jesus that are unique but at the same time plausibly fit into the Jewish context and can be interpreted as the historical origin of early Christianity.[53] *With such a plausibility criterion, the methodology of New Testament Jesus research returns to the methodology of profane historical research, which also asks whether an attested event fits into its historical context.*

---

49. Bernheim, *Lehrbuch der historischen Methode*, 542 (my trans.).

50. E. Käsemann, "The Problem of the Historical Jesus," in *Essays on New Testament Themes*, trans. W. J. Montague (London: SCM, 1964), 37.

51. Käsemann, "The Problem of the Historical Jesus," 37.

52. G. Theissen and D. Winter, *The Quest for the Plausible Jesus: The Question of Criteria*, trans. M. Eugene Boring (Louisville: Westminster John Knox, 2002), 135–36, 168–69.

53. Theissen and Winter, *The Quest for the Plausible Jesus*, xv–xvi, 188.

DANGERS AND LIMITATIONS OF THE HISTORICAL METHOD

As in the case of the exegetical method, application of the historical method can lead to aberrations that historians must avoid: methodological suspiciousness, historical hypercriticism, and the historian's overestimation of his capabilities. In this respect also, Bible scholars can learn from the neighboring disciplines. The French historian Henri-Irénée Marrou (1904–77) identified the dangers of historical criticism particularly clearly and vividly.

Methodological Suspiciousness

First, Marrou identified the danger of "methodical distrust":

> [The historian] should not confront the witnesses of the past with an attitude that is surly, fussy, or peevish, like some unpleasant policeman for whom anyone summoned to court is suspect, *a priori*, and regarded as guilty until there is proof to the contrary. Any such exaggeration of the critical spirit, far from being a qualification, would be a radical vice for the historian. It would make him practically incapable of recognizing the real significance, import or value of the documents that he is studying. Such an attitude is as dangerous in the study of history as is the fear of being duped in daily life.[54]

A suspicious and arrogant attitude gives rise to "the history produced by critics who could only deny, diminish or destroy."[55]

A good historian's primary fear is not being deceived but not understanding correctly. His suspicion must be directed first at his own cognitive faculty: "It is no easy matter to understand a document. . . . How many times has it happened that a critic thought he had discovered some oversight or error only to learn that further research proves, to his shame, that he was unable to understand."[56]

Historical Hypercriticism

Closely connected with the danger of arrogant suspicion is the danger of hypercriticism, for a suspicious attitude results in a supercritical handling of historical sources. Marrou illustrated this danger of historical hypercriticism by reminding his readers of Jean Hardouin (1646–1729), who believed that most of the writings of ancient authors were in fact the work of medieval monks, and of Richard Whately (1787–1863), who argued in one of his treatises that Napoleon had never lived.

---

54. H.-I. Marrou, *The Meaning of History*, trans. R. J. Olsen (Baltimore: Helicon, 1966), 103–4.
55. Marrou, *The Meaning of History*, 106–7.
56. Marrou, *The Meaning of History*, 107–8.

The hypercritic succumbs to the danger of demanding "more and more from his documents before deciding to believe them. He will examine them with an eye that becomes more and more suspicious, and that is the end of the possibility of drawing any conclusions."[57]

> But what can we answer to someone who believes that these motives of credibility are insufficient? . . . No one can be forced to have faith. From this (and every generation of historians experiences it) comes the impassioned character, the sharpness, the infinity of discussions engendered by such hypercritical hypotheses: It is impossible to agree, to force anyone to share your conviction.

As an antidote, Marrou recommended willingness to believe the sources until proven otherwise. *"Our consent is asked for taking things simply at their best – testimonies that nothing prevents our believing, and that good reasons encourage us to accept."*[58]

The Historian's Overestimation of His Capabilities

A third danger in application of the historical method is the historian's overestimation of his own capabilities. This danger is particularly acute when historical testimonies of the sources have been called into question because of hypercritical zeal. The Italian historian Arnaldo Momigliano (1908–87), an expert in the history of Greek, Roman, and Jewish antiquity, stressed in 1980 at an annual meeting of the American Society for Biblical Literature: "We have to learn to live with a disproportion between the intelligent questions we can ask and the plausible answers we can give. . . . The most dangerous type of researcher in any historical field is the man who, because he is intelligent enough to ask a good question, believes that he is good enough to give a satisfactory answer."[59] *An overestimation of the historian's own abilities easily leads to a tendency to pile up hypotheses that have hardly any basis in the historical sources.*

Even those, however, who in their historical work on the Bible carefully avoid the dangers that accompany application of the historical method will not be able to achieve one thing: a broad consensus among professional and nonprofessional readers of the Bible. Not only in exegeses but also in historical research does agreement on a majority of issues remain a desirable but unattainable ideal.

---

57. Marrou, *The Meaning of History*, 151.

58. Marrou, *The Meaning of History*, 149.

59. A. Momigliano, "Biblical Studies and Classical Studies: Simple Reflections upon Historical Method," in *On Pagans, Jews, and Christians* (Middletown, CT: Wesleyan University Press, 1987), 5.

PLACE AND PURPOSE OF A PNEUMATIC APPROACH

Just as in the case of the exegetical method, the historical method also raises the question of the extent to which the Christian historian is dependent on the work of the Holy Spirit. As the systematic theologian Karl Heim (1874–1958) has shown, this is primarily the case regarding relative and absolute historical certainty. Gotthold Ephraim Lessing (1729–81) articulated the classic formulation of this problem.

Relative Certainty of the Historian

Lessing claimed that only those who had experienced miracles themselves and seen them with their own eyes could believe in them. That is why the first Christians could believe that Jesus did miracles and why they could invoke the miracles of Jesus to justify their belief that Jesus was the Son of God.[60]

Christians in later centuries, however, found themselves in a different situation. They did not experience the miracles of Jesus themselves but only learned about them through historical reports or sources. However, historical reports only allow indirect access and are therefore too weak to prove the historicity of Jesus' miracles. At best, a miracle report could support the probability of a miracle, but *historical probability judgements are not strong enough to correct the theological and moral judgements of reason.*[61]

For this reason, Lessing argued that one cannot base Christian faith on historical sources about supernatural acts of God in history but exclusively on the more reliable judgements of reason: "When will they stop hanging nothing less than the whole of eternity on a spider's thread."[62]

Pneumatic Certainty of the Believer

Heim responded to Lessing's objection in a section on historical criticism. With reference to Bernheim's textbook on historical method, Heim acknowledged that the evaluation of historical sources never produces absolute certainty. Therefore, the historian can only make probability judgments about the words and deeds of Jesus of Nazareth. The scholarly results of historical research always contain a remainder of uncertainty.

Therefore, Heim regarded the question posed by Lessing as justified: "How can we, in view of the uncertainty of even the best attested historical fact,

60. G. E. Lessing, "On the Proof of the Spirit and on Power," in *Lessing's Theological Writings: Selections in Translation*, ed. H. Chadwick (Stanford: Stanford University Press, 1956), 51–52.

61. Lessing, "On the Proof of the Spirit and on Power," 52–56.

62. G. E. Lessing, "Eine Duplik," in *Theologiekritische Schriften III: Philosophische Schriften*, Gotthold Ephraims Werke 8 (Darmstadt: WBG, 1996), 41.

become so certain of a historical fact that we can build our faith in God on it?"[63] Given the relativity of all historical knowledge, how can Christians know for certain that Jesus of Nazareth is the unique Son of God whom God raised from the dead?

Heim's answer was that the *fides humana*, which comes from historical research, must be accompanied by the *fides divina*, which is created by the inner testimony of the Holy Spirit.[64] *For the Christian historian, Jesus Christ is not only a person of the past and thus an object of historical research but at the same time a present person whom he or she encounters through faith.*[65] Through this present experience, the Christian historian grasps the reality of Christ "with immediate certainty."[66] Heim called this immediate certainty also "pneumatic certainty."[67]

Lucan Pneumatology

Heim's answer to Lessing's question corresponds to a dual emphasis already perceptible in the Acts of the Apostles. On the one hand, the resurrected Jesus commissions his first disciples to be his (historical) "witnesses" (Acts 1:8; cf. Luke 24:46–48). The contents of their testimony are the events they witnessed, from the baptism to the ascension of Jesus (Acts 1:21–22). According to this commission, Peter reports historically on the miracles of Jesus, his crucifixion, and his resurrection (Acts 2:22–24). In another sermon, Peter describes himself and his fellow apostles as historical "witnesses" of the passion and resurrection of Jesus (Acts 3:13–15). Such historical reports about the life and the fate of Jesus of Nazareth also form part of the later missionary speeches in the Acts of the Apostles (Acts 5:30–31; 10:36–41; 13:28–31, etc.).

The importance of historical evidence for the Christian faith is also expressed in the prologue of the gospel of Luke (Luke 1:1–4),[68] in the second epilogue of the gospel of John (John 21:24–25), in the epistles of Paul (1 Cor 15:3–8), in the epistles of John (1 John 1:1–3), in the epistles of Peter (1 Peter 5:1; 2 Peter 1:16–18), and in the epistle to the Hebrews (Heb 2:3).

On the other hand, the New Testament writings at no point give the impression that historical statements are strong enough to produce Christian faith. Rather, the book of Acts reports that the risen Jesus announced an imminent baptism with the Holy Spirit (Acts 1:4–5). This announcement was fulfilled on

63. K. Heim, *Leitfaden der Dogmatik: Erster Teil* (Halle: Niemeyer, [3]1923), 47–48 (my trans.).
64. Heim, *Leitfaden der Dogmatik: Erster Teil*, 59.
65. Heim, *Leitfaden der Dogmatik: Erster Teil*, 47.
66. Heim, *Leitfaden der Dogmatik: Erster Teil*, 55 (my trans.).
67. Heim, *Leitfaden der Dogmatik: Erster Teil*, 57 (my trans.).
68. See Baum, *Einleitung in das Neue Testament*, 274–97.

Pentecost (Acts 2:4, 17, 33). Since this primordial Christian experience, every person who becomes a Christian receives the Holy Spirit. Luke tells in detail how the Holy Spirit falls on the centurion Cornelius and the members of his house and how they are baptized by Peter (Acts 2:44–48; cf. 11:15; 15:8). Historical reports about Jesus of Nazareth and the work of the Holy Spirit are most closely linked in a statement by the apostles before the Jerusalem Sanhedrin: "We are witnesses to these things, and so is the Holy Spirit whom God has given to those who obey him" (Acts 5:32 NRSV).

The fact that Christian faith cannot develop and exist without the Spirit of God is also underlined by the gospel of John (John 15:26), the epistles of Paul (Rom 8:16; 2 Cor 1:22; 5:5; Gal 3:3:5 *etc.*), the epistles of John (1 John 4:3; 5:6–12), and the epistle to the Hebrews (Heb 6:4).

From a New Testament perspective, then, the problem of Christian certainty of faith as formulated by Lessing cannot be solved merely with the means available to the historian. *Only the historian who believes in the risen Christ can obtain sufficient certainty of faith.* Such a pneumatic relationship to the risen Christ seems to have remained alien to Lessing and those who followed his lead.

PHILOSOPHICAL MIRACLE CRITICISM AS A HISTORICAL CRITERION

In Christian theology until well into modern times, it was more or less unanimously assumed that the New Testament texts were historically correct in those places where they reported miraculous healings of Jesus or his resurrection from the dead. Openness to recognize even miracles as historical events resulted from the Jewish-Christian concept of God as already formulated in the first sentences of the Bible (Gen 1:1–2:3) and runs through the Old and New Testaments (Exod 20:11; Neh 9:6; Ps 146:5–6; Is 40:26, etc.). Why should the God who once created heaven and earth and the laws of nature that are ruling them not be able to interrupt them on special occasions by supernatural intervention?[69]

During the nineteenth century, a radical change took place in German theology leading to the formation of two camps: one camp of philosophically open-minded biblical scholars who consider the raising of Jesus from the dead to be historically possible, and another camp of biblical scholars who in principle

69. R. M. Grant, *Miracle and Natural Law in Graeco-Roman and Early Christian Thought* (Amsterdam: North Holland, 1952), 127–52.

exclude the possibility of a resurrection from the dead (without necessarily denying the theological significance of the resurrection).

David Friedrich Strauss (1808–74) was one of the most important fathers of the miracle-critical camp. In his history of historical Jesus research, Albert Schweitzer noted that Strauss divided the history of New Testament research into two periods, "that before Strauss and that after Strauss." For with the advent of Strauss, the question of miracle "found a solution, viz., that these events have no rightful place in the history."[70]

In today's New Testament scholarship, justification for this second position is primarily based on an essay by Ernst Troeltsch (1865–1923) on the difference between a dogmatic and a historical method in theology.[71]

ERNST TROELTSCH'S DEFINITION OF HISTORICAL CRITICISM

In 1898, Ernst Troeltsch published an essay entitled "On Historical and Dogmatic Method in Theology," which some exegetes consider to be the fundamental explanation of the historical-critical method. In it, Troeltsch described a "dogmatic" method by which his opponents justified their Christian faith. He also described his own alternative method, which he called the "historical [-critical]" method.

The Dogmatic Method

Troeltsch called the "dogmatic method" the "old," "absolute," or "apodictically certain" method or approach.[72] He did not describe it as systematically as the historical method with its three main characteristics (criticism, analogy, and correlation). His explanations show, however, that he also attributed three main characteristics to the dogmatic method, in direct contrast to the three main characteristics of the historical method. They can be described as authority, supernaturalism, and separation.

First, according to Troeltsch, the dogmatic method is characterized by the fact that it takes certain statements for granted and regards them as absolute, unchangeable norms.[73] Because of their absolute authority, these dogmatic statements were free from all uncertainty and could not be shaken by anything.[74]

---

70. A. Schweizer, *The Quest of the Historical Jesus*, trans. W. Montgomery (London: Black, 1911), 10.

71. For a comprehensive overview of historical-critical theology, see U. Wilckens, *Historische Kritik der historisch-kritischen Exegese*, vol. 3 of *Theologie des Neuen Testaments* (Göttingen: Vandenhoeck, 2017), 44–353.

72. E. Troeltsch, "Historical and Dogmatic Method in Theology," in *The Historical Jesus Quest: Landmarks in the Search for the Jesus of History*, ed. G. W. Dawes (Louisville: Westminster John Knox, 2000), 29–53.

73. Troeltsch, "Historical and Dogmatic Method in Theology," 35.

74. Troeltsch, "Historical and Dogmatic Method in Theology," 40.

Second, the dogmatic method is based on supernaturalism. Dogmatic statements are justified by supernatural acts of God. *God is capable of extraordinary activities that go beyond the ordinary laws of nature. "Everything depends on this concept of God."*[75]

Third, the dogmatic method makes a strict separation between the ordinary history of normal life and a "history of salvation" or "history of a higher order."[76] For the dogmatic method, ordinary history is "devoid of miracles and subject to the normal working of historical criticism," while the history of salvation is "permeated by miracles and accessible to study only through methods based on inner experience and the humble subjection of reason."[77] This history of salvation with its miracles is "knowable and provable only for the believer."[78]

The "Historical [-Critical]" Method

Troeltsch called his own, alternative method, both in the title of his essay and elsewhere, the "historical method" and synonymously the "critical and relativistic," the "history-of-religion," and the "historical-critical" method. He formulated three main characteristics of his historical method, namely criticism, analogy, and correlation, in direct contrast to the tenets of the dogmatic method.

First, for Troeltsch the "critical" approach of the historical method takes the place of the absolute authority of the dogmatic method. Those who engage in historical criticism must accept that "in the realm of history there are only judgments of probability."[79] Troeltsch used the word *criticism* here in the sense it has in external and internal source criticism of historical research.

Second, the "analogy" of the historical method replaces the miracles of the dogmatic method. For Troeltsch, without analogy there would be no historical criticism or historical research. "Analogous occurrences that we observe both without and within ourselves furnish us with the key to historical criticism."[80] With his principle of analogy, Troeltsch took up the principle of multiple attestation in the historical method: Only events that agree with "normal, customary, or at least frequently attested happenings and conditions as we have experienced them" can be recognized as historically probable.[81]

At this point, however, Troeltsch went one step further by speaking of an "omnipotence of analogy," from which "the similarity (in principle) of all

75. Troeltsch, "Historical and Dogmatic Method in Theology," 43.
76. Troeltsch, "Historical and Dogmatic Method in Theology," 50.
77. Troeltsch, "Historical and Dogmatic Method in Theology," 42.
78. Troeltsch, "Historical and Dogmatic Method in Theology," 41.
79. Troeltsch, "Historical and Dogmatic Method in Theology," 32.
80. Troeltsch, "Historical and Dogmatic Method in Theology," 32.
81. Troeltsch, "Historical and Dogmatic Method in Theology," 32.

historical events" results.[82] He thereby excluded supernatural acts of God *a priori. For Troeltsch, the omnipotence of analogy resulted from his conception of God. He interpreted history (following Hegel) as "a disclosure of the divine reason."*[83] For him, God was "involved in every vital movement only as the purposive will that produces the motion of the total system."[84] Based on this philosophical image of God, Troeltsch considered supernatural actions of God to be impossible in principle.

Third, in Troeltsch's historical method the "correlation" or interaction between all historical events replaces the dogmatic separation between ordinary history and the history of salvation. For Troeltsch, there was no history of a higher order that that existed beyond reason and historical research:

The "Dogmatic" Method:	The "Historical (-Critical)" Method:
1. Authority (absolute judgements) 2. Supernaturalism (miracles possible) 3. Separation (salvation vs. ordinary history)	1. Criticism (only probability judgements) 2. Analogy (miracles impossible) 3. Correlation (only ordinary history)

The "Dogmatic" and the "Historical" Method according to Ernst Troeltsch

Troeltsch was convinced that the historical-critical method, which he advocated, as soon as it was applied to biblical studies acted "as a leaven, transforming everything and ultimately exploding the very form of earlier theological methods."[85] In other words, "give the historical method an inch and it will take a mile. From a strictly orthodox standpoint, therefore, it seems to bear a certain similarity to the devil."[86]

OBJECTIONS TO PHILOSOPHICAL MIRACLE CRITICISM

Relative Certainty of the Historian

Troeltsch was justified in objecting to the dogmatic method (as he defined it) that absolute and unquestionable statements about historical events are impossible. It is one of the generally accepted tenets of historical research that the historian can only make probability judgements and differentiate between

82. Troeltsch, "Historical and Dogmatic Method in Theology," 33.
83. Troeltsch, "Historical and Dogmatic Method in Theology," 47.
84. Troeltsch, "Historical and Dogmatic Method in Theology," 43.
85. Troeltsch, "Historical and Dogmatic Method in Theology," 31.
86. Troeltsch, "Historical and Dogmatic Method in Theology," 35.

different degrees of probability. Lessing rightly insisted on this point, and Karl Heim rightly acknowledged this insight for his historical work with New Testament sources. A theology that wants to dispense with this "critical" insight about the limitations of the historical or historical-critical method would abandon its scholarly character. All historical judgments are probability judgements.

Renunciation of a History of a Higher Order

Further, Troeltsch was justified in objecting to the dogmatic method that no historical events are removed from the historical method and only visible to believers. A division of history into ordinary history and a history of salvation corresponds neither to the secular nor the biblical understanding of history. In the Old and New Testament historical books, the supernatural acts of God are accessible not only to believers but also to unbelievers and sceptics. There is no extra purview for a salvation history distinct from ordinary history. Everywhere the same scholarly rules and methods apply.

Unfoundedness of *A Priori* Miracle Criticism

The situation is different with the philosophical criticism of miracles, which Strauss successfully promoted and which Troeltsch associated with his second keyword, that is, analogy.[87]

When Gerhard Maier published his polemic *The End of the Historical-Critical Method* (in 1974), its main thrust was not directed against methodologically sound historical criticism but against the *a priori* criticism of the miraculous by Strauss, Troeltsch, and their followers.[88] Maier rejected "the compelling principle of analogy." He regarded it as an unjustified dogmatic claim that "set limitations to the divinity of God" in historical research. According to Maier, *the (Christian) historian "must ensure an openness to the methodological principle which will not hastily and insolently curtail divine revelation at any place."* Rather he should develop "a 'wide-angle' methodological attitude which must not prematurely exclude certain possibilities."[89] Many scholars regard this criticism of Troeltsch's historical method as indispensable. (However, Maier did not find many followers for his suggestion to speak of a "historical-biblical method.")

To my knowledge, the "dogmatic" method criticized by Troeltsch does not have many adherents in recent scholarship. The real alternative to the

---

87. For a recent overview of the most important philosophical, theological, and scientific objections to the possibility of miracles (including the ones used by Strauss and Troeltsch), see G. H. Twelftree, *Jesus the Miracle Worker* (Downers Grove, IL: InterVarsity, 1999), 38–53, 241–53.

88. G. Maier, *The End of the Historical-Critical Method* (St. Lewis: Concordia, 1977), 11–16.

89. Maier, *The End of the Historical-Critical Method*, 50–52.

"historical" method represented by Troeltsch is another "historical" method.[90] Representatives of both historical methods agree that even the biblical scholar can only make historical probability statements and that no area of history may be removed from historical research. The essential difference between them is that the historical method defended by Troeltsch starts from an absolute philosophical prejudice, while the historical method advocated by Schlatter, Heim, and others refrains from absolute presuppositions not only in historical but also in ideological terms.

A Closed Historical Method	An Open Historical Method
1. Criticism (only probability judgments) 2. Analogy (miracles impossible) 3. Correlation (only ordinary history)	1. Criticism (only probability judgments) 2. Openness (miracles possible) 3. Correlation (only ordinary history)

A Closed and an Open Historical Method

CONCLUSION

In modern biblical studies, both the exegetical and the historical method are called the *historical-critical* method. The roots of this language go back to antiquity. Since the nineteenth century, the adjective *critical* has also been used in the sense of *a priori* miracle criticism. Since that time, *historical-critical* has also come to mean "historical and miracle-critical."

The exegetical method consists of synchronic and diachronic textual analyses. Exegetes of the limited number of biblical texts must be especially aware of the danger of overinterpretation. However, even if the exegetical method is applied carefully, it cannot offer existential access to the biblical texts. This can only be achieved by pneumatic experience, which of course must never restrict the exegetical method but must complement it.

The historical method consists primarily of external and internal source criticism. The historian must beware of methodical suspicion and the hypercritical evaluation of his sources that results from it. However, as Lessing rightly claimed, even if the historical method is applied perfectly, it cannot produce absolute certainty, only probability judgments. Nevertheless, for Christians, the inner testimony of the Holy Spirit, which presupposes the strong historical

90. Cf. Wilckens, *Historische Kritik der historisch-kritischen Exegese*, 354–84.

evidence of the New Testament sources, reaches beyond the limited possibilities of historical research.

The criterion of philosophical miracle criticism was introduced into biblical scholarship in the nineteenth century and promoted successfully by (David Friedrich Strauss and) Ernst Troeltsch. Critics of this philosophical kind of miracle criticism consider the application of such absolute theological preconditions inappropriate and prefer a methodical openness that encompasses their conception of God.

FOR FURTHER READING

Bruce, F. F. *Understanding Biblical Criticism*. Edited by D. Capes. Nashville: Kingsley, 2017.

Grant, R. M. *Miracle and Natural Law in Graeco-Roman and Early Christian Thought*. Amsterdam: North Holland, 1952.

Lessing, G. E. "On the Proof of the Spirit and on Power." In *Lessing's Theological Writings: Selections in Translation*, edited by H. Chadwick, 51–56. Stanford: Stanford University Press, 1956.

Lucian. *How to Write History*. In Loeb Classical Library 430, translated by K. Kilburn, 1–74. Cambridge: Harvard University Press, 1959.

Maier, G. *The End of the Historical-Critical Method*. Translated by E. W. Leverenz and R. F. Norden. St. Louis: Concordia Publishing House, 1977.

Marincola, J. *Authority and Tradition in Ancient Historiography*. Cambridge: Cambridge University Press, 1997.

Marrou, H.-I. *The Meaning of History*. Translated by Robert J. Olsen. Baltimore: Helicon, 1966.

Momigliano, A. "Biblical Studies and Classical Studies: Simple Reflections upon Historical Method." In *On Pagans, Jews, and Christians*, 3–10. Middletown: Wesleyan University Press, 1987.

Reiser, M. *Bibelkritik und Auslegung der Heiligen Schrift: Beiträge zur Geschichte der biblischen Exegese und Hermeneutik*. WUNT 217. Tübingen: Mohr Siebeck, 2007.

Theissen, G., and A. Merz. *The Historical Jesus: A Comprehensive Guide*. Translated by J. Bowden. Minneapolis: Fortress, 1998.

Troeltsch, E. "Historical and Dogmatic Method in Theology." In *The Historical Jesus Quest: Landmarks in the Search for the Jesus of History*, edited by G. W. Dawes, 29–53 Louisville: Westminster John Knox, 2000.

Yarborough, R. W. "Adolf Schlatter's 'The Significance of Method for Theological Work': Translation and Commentary." *SBJT* 1 (1997): 64–76.

PART 3

The Bible in the Contemporary World

CHAPTER 11

The Bible and Modern Literature

Karen Swallow Prior

Modern literature was birthed by the Bible. Not the Bible as it has existed for thousands of years in a variety of ancient forms, but rather the Bible that, half a millennium ago, took the form of a mass-produced, bound, and printed book. Because of its widespread availability and because of the mass literacy encouraged by that availability, this iteration of Scripture – technologically, culturally, and literarily – helped create the modern subject: a self-defining, authentic self,[1] one whose sense of particular experience and consciousness arises, in part, through the interpretive practices of individual reading. This modern subject is the subject – the theme – of modern literature.

It was, of course, for doctrinal and ecclesial reasons that the Protestant Reformers sought the ability of the masses to be able to read the Bible for themselves, in their own language, unmediated by church authorities. But the coincidence of these church reforms with the emerging technology of the printing press (which was, of course, more than mere coincidence) cultivated an experiential, experimental way of knowing, the very one that brought about the scientific revolution and the Enlightenment as well – in other words, modernity.

All of these developments to some degree shifted authority from the objective and external world toward the inner world of self-consciousness, experience, and agency. Furthermore, this newly accessible ability to read the Bible (or any text) conferred validity upon the authority of that reading self. The validation,

1. Charles Taylor, *Hegel* (Cambridge: Cambridge University Press, 1975), 6; Charles Taylor, *Ethics of Authenticity* (Cambridge, MA: Harvard University Press, 1991), 25–29.

first, of the subjective authority of the self grew over time into the privileging of inner, self-generated authority over external, objective authority. As reading and interpretation became increasingly individual, private acts, so, too, the authority of the inner life increasingly shaped the mode of being of subjects within the modern world. Thus, paradoxically, access by the masses to the words believed by the majority of people in the Western world to be the ultimate source of external, objective authority, increased the very subjectivity that would come to define the secular age. Or as Roland Barthes famously declared: "The birth of the reader must be requited by the death of the Author."[2]

Secular, in this sense, is more than merely the opposite of sacred. Secularity as a cultural condition is older and broader than modernity itself, as Charles Taylor shows in *A Secular Age*. Taylor defines this broader sense of secularity as the shift away from a condition "in which it was virtually impossible not to believe in God, to one in which faith, even for the staunchest believer, is one human possibility among others." This turn was a gradual process which began well before the Enlightenment with which the onset of modernity is usually marked.[3] According to Taylor's account, the secular age emerged, in large part, out of an emphasis on civility that began during the late Renaissance.

Civility, Taylor argues, was a self-interested way for the elites to solidify order for all of society. Civility entailed the reordering of both public and private life through ordered government and "rational moral self-control," along with the cultivation of education, manners, taste-promoted civility, and consequently, the discipline required to achieve all these.[4] Thus, while civility was the project of those in power, it brought with it the side effect of improving and elevating those in the lower classes too. Moreover, civility and discipline were not only ways by which one might improve oneself but ways by which society itself could improve through the collective efforts of the regulated self. As discipline grew into a social obligation, the idea of progress took hold. No longer need one's station or lot in life passively be accepted as the immutable will of God. But rather, through discipline, one might work to improve one's manners, one's morals, one's way of life, and one's life. The "rise of the disciplinary society,"[5] as Taylor describes this development, contributed to secularity in demonstrating what individuals and societies could achieve through the power of human effort, will, and desire. In short, civility cultivated a nonreligious form of

---

2. Roland Barthes, "The Death of the Author," in *The Rustle of Language* (New York: Farrar, Straus and Giroux, 1986), 55.

3. Charles Taylor, *A Secular Age* (Cambridge, MA: Belknap, 2007), 1–3.

4. Charles Taylor, *A Secular Age* (Cambridge, MA: Belknap, 2007), 101.

5. Charles Taylor, *A Secular Age* (Cambridge, MA: Belknap, 2007), 90–145.

humanism.[6] Thus, the modern individual was born: a subjective, increasingly autonomous self, an interpretive being, one actively receiving, reading, and producing texts – both the text of Scripture and endless other texts.

THE MODERN SUBJECT AS A READING SELF

Civility, discipline, social and political reform – these are all outward expressions. But a reading self cultivates the inward state that constitutes modernity's characteristic "turn to the subject" (as the modern age is most succinctly defined). Reading for oneself is inherently an internal, conscious, subjective experience and, as such, is foundational to the seismic epistemological and phenomenological changes that brought about modernity. The ethos of all the epistemologies and belief systems that can be associated with the modernity – the scientific method, empiricism, rationalism, deism (and later agnosticism and atheism) – is derived from, more than anything else perhaps, *reading*. The modern self is a reading self, an interpretive being created by a hermeneutical way of experiencing not only texts but the world too – as a subject.

But if the reading self is a modern subject, then there are parallel implications for the author. Indeed, modern subjectivity was accompanied by the rise of the author, not only as a copyrightable entity and public figure but as a concept that became part of the modern social imaginary. In the same essay quoted above, "The Death of the Author," Barthes explains, "The *author* is a modern character, no doubt produced by our society as it emerged from the Middle Ages, inflected by English empiricism, French rationalism, and the personal faith of the Reformation, thereby discovering the prestige of the individual."[7] Thus, if, as Francois Lyotard famously declared, the "postmodern condition" is defined by "incredulity toward metanarratives,"[8] then the author is, as Barthes says, no longer credible either: the author is dead.

With no author, of course, there can be no unified meaning: "We know that a text consists not of a line of words, releasing a single 'theological' meaning (the 'message' of the Author-God)." Instead, Barthes explains, are a multiplicity of unoriginal, competing meanings that emerge from the surrounding culture.[9] In place of the author, there is only, Barthes says (making this observation on the

6. Charles Taylor, *A Secular Age* (Cambridge, MA: Belknap, 2007), 87–88.

7. Barthes, "The Death of the Author," 49.

8. Francois Lyotard, *The Postmodern Condition: A Report on Knowledge*, trans. Geoff Bennington and Brian Massumi (Minneapolis: University Minnesota Press, 1984), xxiv.

9. Barthes, "The Death of the Author," 52–53.

cusp of the poststructuralist, deconstructive hermeneutical turn that occurred near the end of the twentieth century), a "scriptor." A scriptor is a kind of writer who "no longer contains passions, moods, sentiments, impressions" but simply repeats words drawn from a dictionary. As a result, "life merely imitates the book."[10]

The subjectivity of such a life, one rooted in the interpretive self, is naturally at odds with the earlier reception of the Bible via some external, objective authority (whether the church in a formal way or, less formally, oral tradition, art, and popular culture) by whom the writing is interpreted and applied. This precritical approach to reading the Bible (and other texts) gave way in the modern period to the critical method. Some accounts of the relationship between the Bible and modern literature portray the latter as arising out of an increasingly skeptical or even hostile view of the Bible, Christianity, and religion more generally. These histories emphasize the rivalry between the religious and secular worldviews that grew throughout the eighteenth and nineteenth centuries (which, of course, continues today) and correlates with the hermeneutical shift in Bible-reading to the hermeneutical approach reflected in reading and writing modern literature.

NOVEL HERMENEUTICS: FROM *THE PILGRIM'S PROGRESS* TO *ROBINSON CRUSOE*

Such an analysis is exemplified by Hans Frei's rendering in his seminal work *Eclipse of Biblical Narrative*. According to Frei, before the shift to modern critical methods that took place in the eighteenth century, the hermeneutical approach to the Bible in the West was "realistic," by which he means "at once literal and historical."[11] In other words, according to Frei, biblical narratives were understood to be literally, factually, and historically true – or "realistic." *Literal* in this sense does not preclude the use of allegory, metaphor, and other forms of figurative language by the biblical writers. To the contrary, to understand the Bible "literally" in this sense includes allegorical and anagogical readings of Scripture. All of these kinds of readings were possible with the underlying assumption that the biblical writers were using language in an intentional way. From a word's meaning, (meaning based on but not limited to its literal meaning), the writer's intended meaning could be reliably understood and interpreted. Precritical interpretations of Biblical narratives read the stories as

10. Barthes, "The Death of the Author," 53.

11. Hans W. Frei, *The Eclipse of Biblical Narrative: A Study in Eighteenth and Nineteenth Century Hermeneutics* (New Haven, CT: Yale University Press, 1974), 1.

literally and historically true, Frei says, because the "words and sentences meant what they said," and thereby "accurately described real events and real truths."[12] Thus, the meanings of the words were hermeneutically united with both historical fact and truth. Because the unit of meaning was sealed; the Bible could be seen as "self-interpreting."[13]

It is the opening of this seal that constitutes modern critical or higher interpretation. Frei explains,

> As the realistic narrative reading of the biblical stories broke down, literal or verbal and historical meaning were severed and literal and figural interpretation, hitherto naturally affiliated procedures, also came apart. Figural reading had been literalism extended to the whole story or the unitary canon containing it. But now figural sense came to be something opposite of literal sense.[14]

So while Augustine, for example, could read a passage allegorically *because* he also read (and accepted the truth of) the words "literally," (allowing for two levels of meaning), the modern severing of literal and figural interpretation (the result, in part, of an Enlightenment-based hermeneutics that narrowed truth into mere facts) forces a choice between the two kinds of meanings. A precritical interpretation of Song of Songs, for example, would understand the text to be about both a relationship between a man and a woman and an allegory of Christ and the church, whereas modern interpretations often pit literal and figural readings against one another: the book is either symbolic or literal, depending on which reading is better supported by verifiable "facts."

The shift, particularly as it is reflected in literature, was remarkably quick. The change can be seen occurring over merely four decades when considering the extraordinary difference between John Bunyan's allegorical narrative *The Pilgrim's Progress* (1678) and Daniel Defoe's realistic narrative *Robinson Crusoe* (1719).

Significantly, both Bunyan and Defoe were Puritans. Both were imprisoned for expressing their religious beliefs – Bunyan (jailed for twelve years) for preaching without a license, and Defoe (imprisoned for six months, as well as being put in the pillory three times) for writing satirically (and, apparently, seditiously) against the state church. Both produced literary works that contributed monumentally to literary history. Separated by just a few decades, however, Bunyan and Defoe's works reflect an epoch's difference in their respective narratives.

---

12. Frei, *The Eclipse of Biblical Narrative*, 1.
13. Frei, *The Eclipse of Biblical Narrative*, 18.
14. Frei, *The Eclipse of Biblical Narrative*, 6–7.

Allegory, such as that exemplified by *The Pilgrim's Progress*, invites premodern, precritical, literary readings. Indeed, this is exactly the kind of reading Bunyan aimed to elicit from his audience – even going so far as to convince readers skeptical of the artfulness of allegory with a lengthy prefatory poem written to assuage such fears. It's important to note that reading biblical narratives in a literal way includes reading them symbolically or allegorically. Allegory depends, in one sense, on literalism in that it assumes, more or less, that one-to-one relationship between sign and signified that Frei describes as hermeneutically united. Toward the end of his apology for allegory, Bunyan explains,

> This book is writ in such a Dialect
> As may the minds of listless men affect:
> It seems a Novelty, and yet contains
> Nothing but sound and honest Gospel-strains.[15]

Despite using "feigned words," the poem asserts, its purpose is to "make truth to spangle and its rays to shine." With this defense, Bunyan clearly aimed to thwart the common criticism of his fellow Puritans that fiction was unwholesome and unworthy because it is not truth but a lie.

Defoe, on the other hand, was a Puritan of eighteenth-century (and modern) sensibilities. He fully embraced the possibilities of fictional narrative. Drawing from his background as a journalist, Defoe created in *Robinson Crusoe* a prototype for the novel. Whereas Bunyan's allegory is filled with allegorical characters (Christian, Evangelist, Obstinate, Pliable, and Faithful, to name a few) and places (from the City of Destruction to the Celestial City to the many places in between, such as Doubting Castle and the Delectable Mountains) of obvious (and insightful) symbolic meaning, *Robinson Crusoe* is filled with journalistic details: names of cities, dates, and an inventory of items retrieved from the wrecked ship ("pens, ink, and paper, several parcels in the captain's, mate's, gunner's and carpenter's keeping; three or four compasses, some mathematical instruments, dials, perspectives, charts, and books of navigation"[16]).

Both works give a central place to the Bible. But the differences in the way the Bible is read, interpreted, and applied illuminate the difference between a precritical and a modern critical hermeneutical approach.

The narrative of *The Pilgrim's Progress* begins with the Bible (in two senses, actually: the appearance of the Bible in the fictional story accompanied

15. John Bunyan, *The Pilgrim's Progress* (Oxford: Oxford University Press, 2003), 8.
16. Daniel Defoe, *Robinson Crusoe* (New York City: Penguin, 2003), 52.

by Bunyan's glosses, which cross-reference passages from the real Bible for the benefit of the real-life reader):

> As I walked through the wilderness of this world, I lighted on a certain place where was a Den, and I laid me down in that place to sleep: and, as I slept, I dreamed a dream. I dreamed, and behold, I saw a man clothed with rags, standing in a certain place, with his face from his own house, a book in his hand, and a great burden upon his back. [Isa. 64:6; Luke 14:33; Ps. 38:4; Hab. 2:2; Acts 16:30, 31] I looked, and saw him open the book, and read therein; and, as he read, he wept, and trembled; and, not being able longer to contain, he brake out with a lamentable cry, saying, "What shall I do?" [Acts 2:37][17]

A couple of paragraphs later, the dreamer/narrator continues:

> Now, I saw, upon a time, when he was walking in the fields, that he was, as he was wont, reading in his book, and greatly distressed in his mind; and, as he read, he burst out, as he had done before, crying, "What shall I do to be saved?"
>
> I saw also that he looked this way and that way, as if he would run; yet he stood still, because, as I perceived, he could not tell which way to go. I looked then, and saw a man named Evangelist coming to him and asked, Wherefore dost thou cry? [Job 33:23]
>
> He answered, Sir, I perceive by the book in my hand, that I am condemned to die, and after that to come to judgement [Heb. 9:27]; and I find that I am not willing to do the first [Job 16:21], nor able to do the second. [Ezek. 22:14]
>
> Then said Evangelist, Why not willing to die, since this life is attended with so many evils? The man answered, Because I fear that this burden is upon my back will sink me lower than the grave, and I shall fall into Tophet. [Isa. 30:33] And, Sir, if I be not fit to go to prison, I am not fit, I am sure, to go to judgement, and from thence to execution; and the thoughts of these things make me cry.
>
> Then said Evangelist, If this be thy condition, why standest thou still? He answered, Because I know not whither to go. Then he gave him a parchment roll, and there was written within, Flee from the wrath to come. [Matt. 3.7]
>
> The man therefore read it, and looking upon Evangelist very carefully, said, Whither must I fly? Then said Evangelist, pointing with his finger over a very wide field, Do you see yonder wicket-gate? [Matt. 7:13,14] The man said, No. Then said the other, Do you see yonder shining light? [Ps. 119:105; 2 Pet. 1:19] He said, I think I do. Then said Evangelist, Keep that light in your eye,

17. Bunyan, *The Pilgrim's Progress*, 10.

> and go up directly thereto: so shalt thou see the gate; at which, when thou knockest, it shall be told thee what thou shalt do.
>
> So I saw in my dream that the man began to run.[18]

Thus begins Christian's pilgrimage from the City of Destruction to the Celestial City: the plain reading of the Bible leads to a journey from this world to the heavenly one, both literally and symbolically in the world of the story.

In the case of Crusoe, however, the dramatic scene of his Bible-reading does not lead as directly or immediately to the theologically and hermeneutically correct response as it does for Christian in *The Pilgrim's Progress*. Rather, the narrative presents Crusoe as a subjective agent, one who reads, interprets, questions, and wrestles with the text before finally seeking direction from God (and a little assist from his rum and tobacco):

> I took up the Bible and began to read; but my head was too much disturb'd with the tobacco to bear reading, at least at that time; only, having opened the book casually, the first words that occurr'd to me were these, "Call on Me in the day of trouble, and I will deliver thee, and thou shalt glorify Me."
>
> The words were very apt to my case, and made some impression upon my thoughts at the time of reading them, tho' not so much as they did afterwards; for, as for being *deliver'd*, the word had no sound, as I may say, to me; the thing was so remote, so impossible in my apprehension of things, that I began to say, as the children of Israel did when they were promised flesh to eat, *Can God spread a table in the wilderness?* so I began to say, "Can God Himself deliver me from this place?" And as it was not for many years that any hopes appear'd, this prevail'd very often upon my thoughts; but, however, the words made a great impression upon me, and I mused upon them very often. It grew now late, and the tobacco had, as I said, doz'd my head so much that I inclin'd to sleep; so I left my lamp burning in the cave, lest I should want anything in the night, and went to bed. But before I lay down, I did what I never had done in all my life – I kneel'd down, and pray'd to God to fulfil the promise to me, that if I call'd upon Him in the day of trouble, He would deliver me. After my broken and imperfect prayer was over, I drank the rum in which I had steep'd the tobacco, which was so strong and rank of the tobacco that I could scarcely get it down; immediately upon this I went to bed. . . .
>
> . . . When I awak'd I found myself exceedingly refresh'd, and my spirits lively and cheerful; when I got up I was stronger than I was the day before, and

18. Bunyan, *The Pilgrim's Progress*, 11–13.

> my stomach better, for I was hungry; and, in short, I had no fit the next day, but continued much alter'd for the better.[19]

Crusoe continues to read the Bible over the next several days. In so doing, he is for the first time in his life struck by his need for repentance. He dwells for a while on the word *deliverance*, pondering the way it has taken on a new meaning:

> Now I began to construe the words mentioned above, "Call on Me, and I will deliver thee," in a different sense from what I had ever done before; for then I had no notion of anything being call'd *deliverance*, but my being deliver'd from the captivity I was in; for tho' I was indeed at large in the place, yet the island was certainly a prison to me, and that in the worse sense in the world. But now I learn'd to take it in another sense: now I look'd back upon my past life with such horror, and my sins appear'd so dreadful, that my soul sought nothing of God but deliverance from the load of guilt that bore down all my comfort. As for my solitary life, it was nothing. I did not so much as pray to be deliver'd from it or think of it; it was all of no consideration in comparison to this. And I add this part here, to hint to whoever shall read it, that whenever they come to a true sense of things, they will find deliverance from sin a much greater blessing than deliverance from affliction.[20]

Whereas Christian's understanding of the Bible in *The Pilgrim's Progress* is based on Evangelist's literal application and requires no interpretation from Christian (simply obedience or disobedience), Crusoe's reading of Scripture is a subjective, personal, hermeneutical experience that occurs over time and with struggle. His realization of a spiritual meaning of the word *deliverance* in addition to the physical meaning he already understood is anagogical rather than allegorical. While in allegory, the literal or concrete is used to represent a symbolic or abstract idea of any nature, an *anagoge* points specifically to a spiritual reality; an anagogical reading follows an upward ascent from the visible, physical realm to an invisible, spiritual truth. Crusoe's interpretation of *deliverance* is this kind of spiritual reading.

With *Robinson Crusoe*, Defoe employs the allegory of Bunyan but recasts it by using the language, form, and narrative subjectivity that comes to define the novel. Thus, Defoe opened up a new kind of interpretive space that helped make way for the reader as a modern subject.

---

19. Defoe, *Robinson Crusoe*, 75–76.
20. Defoe, *Robinson Crusoe*, 78.

THE NOVEL AS INTERPRETIVE SPACE

While there is some debate over whether Defoe's fictional works are truly novels or the novel as a genre emerged more formally a few years later with Samuel Richardson (as will be addressed below), there is no dispute that Defoe brought to his narratives the realism that would come to characterize the novel in its emphasis on the particularities of persons, places, and objects. Likewise, the novel's unified narrative around the personal growth and life journey of the main character – a marked development in comparison to early forms of literature – directly reflects the influence of the spiritual autobiographies that were ubiquitous among Puritans, including both Bunyan and Defoe.

The novel is the literary form that reflects and expresses all of these developments. It is written in the prose of everyday language, taking the form of a long narrative, and centered on the particular experiences of an individual, usually and most notably, an ordinary person of modest or no means. In an insightful 2011 essay at the *New York Times*, contemporary novelist Marilynne Robinson observes a significant connection between the modern realism "invented" by both the novel and the Bible:

> The great assumption of literary realism is that ordinary lives are invested with a kind of significance that justifies, or requires, its endless iterations of the commonplace, including, of course, crimes and passions and defeats, however minor these might seem in the world's eyes. This assumption is by no means inevitable. Most cultures have written about demigods and kings and heroes. Whatever the deeper reasons for the realist fascination with the ordinary, it is generous even when it is cruel, simply in the fact of looking as directly as it can at people as they are and insisting that insensitivity or banality matters. The Old Testament prophets did this, too.[21]

This similarity between the novel and the Bible notwithstanding, in both form and content, the early novel contrasted sharply with earlier genres such as heroic epics, tragic dramas, and courtly romances, namely, as noted earlier and observed by Robinson, in the particularity of the detail in the novel and in the ordinariness of the lives it tended to depict. Both constitute and cultivate the subjectivity and agency of the modern self. And from this modern self came

21. Marilynne Robinson, "The Book of Books: What Literature Owes the Bible," *New York Times*, December 23, 2011, https://www.nytimes.com/2011/12/25/books/review/the-book-of-books-what-literature-owes-the-bible.html.

other forms of modern literature, always defined by or against the notions of the self wrought by the ability of the self to read and interpret texts for oneself.

It is not coincidental that such a dramatic shift in narrative form – from allegory to novel – occurred at the same time that a shift in biblical hermeneutics – away from received reading to self-generated reading – was also taking place. As the novel form developed, increasingly reflecting and cultivating modern subjectivity, the place of the Bible in fictional narrative evolved too. Within the space of decades, one can see a kind of reversal take place in narrative works, from reading the biblical text and taking direction for one's life from it to interpreting one's life in light of the biblical text. Significantly, this is not necessarily a relationship of opposition or erasure. To the contrary, it may be that modern literature provides a participatory path to engaging with and understanding not only the words of the Bible but its spirit too.

As Kevin Seidel argues in *Rethinking the Secular Origins of the Novel: The Bible in English Fiction 1678–1767*, the rise of realistic fiction and the novel in the eighteenth century did not turn the Bible and secular narratives into rival texts. Rather, the Bible and modern narratives began to be read differently as widespread literacy began to write the modern subject. Eighteenth century fiction, Seidel argues, shows not a decline in the authority of the Bible, but rather, "a secular imagination not yet hardened in opposition to religion, a religious imagination not yet turned in resentment against secularism, and each side more than tangled with the other."[22] Thus, "the relationship between religious and secular ways of thinking" may not be "necessarily mutually exclusive nor mutually reinforcing, but sometimes mutually fulfilling."[23]

PAMELA: THE INTERPRETED SELF

The work that many literary critics consider to be the first novel, Samuel Richardson's 1740 *Pamela; Or, Virtue Rewarded*, reflects all of these shifts. Presented as a series of letters and journal entries written by a poor servant girl who is relentlessly and even violently pursued by her rakish master, *Pamela* presents itself as being written by its main character. Moreover, the outcome of the plot turns on her writings being read by her antagonist, which makes him repentant. *Pamela*, the novel, is in many ways about interpretation. Pamela, the character – her embodied self and her self as represented in the letters and journal entries

22. Kevin Seidel, *Rethinking the Secular Origins of the Novel: The Bible in English Fiction 1678–1767* (Cambridge: Cambridge University Press, 2021), 26.

23. Seidel, *Rethinking the Secular Origins of the Novel*, 259.

she writes – is the central "text." Additionally, the novel is explicitly Christian, intended, as Richardson states on the title page of the work, to inculcate Christian virtue and morality in its readers, particularly youthful ones. Biblical allusions and quotations appear throughout the narrative but are made use of by the characters much more casually or even tendentiously than we see in Bunyan or Defoe.

Rather than being directly guided or instructed by reading the Bible, as illustrated by both Christian in *The Pilgrim's Progress* and Crusoe in *Robinson Crusoe*, Pamela tends to read herself into biblical texts, recalling familiar passages and interpreting her own situation in light of them. For example, at a critical point in the story – when Pamela has been granted enough agency and freedom to leave her imprisonment but finds herself suddenly doubting her decision and wondering if she should return to her captor – she likens herself to the Israelites, described in Numbers 11:5 as "murmuring" because they "long after the onions and garlick of Egypt, when they had suffered there such heavy bondage."[24] Later, as she is preparing to be married to the wealthy master whom she has won over through her steadfast virtue, she sees herself as being like Mary, exclaiming, "I have seen God's salvation! . . . If any body ever had reason, I have to say, with the blessed virgin, My soul doth magnify the Lord; for he hath regarded the low estate of his handmaiden – and exalted one of low degree"[25] (cf. Luke 1:46ff). Even the wicked servant Mrs. Jewkes, who serves as Pamela's jailer on behalf of their employer, interprets Pamela's life as one that reenacts Biblical narratives, telling Pamela she is "as innocent as a dove, yet . . . as cunning as a serpent"[26] (cf. Matt 10:16). At one point, upon discovering Pamela missing during a failed escape attempt, Mrs. Jewkes fears Pamela has been "carried away, as St. Peter was out of prison, by some angel"[27] (cf. Acts 12:6–10).

Again, over the course of modern literary history, particularly the history of the novel, the interpretive space between the biblical text and its reader widens. Earlier in this history, as with *Robinson Crusoe* and *Pamela*, there seems to be a lack of narrative awareness of this space, on the parts of author, narrator, and character. We might call this posture one of naïve interpretation, one marked by an absent or minimal awareness of the activity of interpreting to which the modern self is subject. The history of modernity is, in significant part, the history of this growing awareness which comes to be self-consciousness as the self grows in awareness of interpreting not only written texts but the self itself as well.

---

24. Samuel Richardson, *The Novels of Samuel Richardson, Esq. Viz. Pamela, Clarissa Harlowe, and Sir Charles Grandison: In Three Volumes; To which is Prefixed, a Memoir of the Life of the Author* (London: Hurst Robinson, 1824), 118.

25. Richardson, *The Novels of Samuel Richardson*, 147.

26. Richardson, *The Novels of Samuel Richardson*, 183.

27. Richardson, *The Novels of Samuel Richardson*, 237.

A SHOCKING READING OF THE BIBLE: *JANE EYRE*

Such self-awareness is arguably the essential characteristic of Charlotte Brontë's 1847 novel *Jane Eyre*, indeed, in some ways the very theme of the work. An early scene finds young Jane – an orphan being raised in the home of a cruel aunt before being sent to live in an even crueler charity school – is being interviewed by Rev. Brocklehurst (whose character embodies a hypocritical evangelical clergyman) before he accepts her into the school:

> "Do you read your Bible?"
>
> "Sometimes."
>
> "With pleasure? Are you fond of it?"
>
> "I like Revelations, and the book of Daniel, and Genesis and Samuel, and a little bit of Exodus, and some parts of Kings and Chronicles, and Job and Jonah."
>
> "And the Psalms? I hope you like them?"
>
> "No, sir."
>
> "No? oh, shocking![28]

The character, Jane, of course, is unaware that her taste in Scripture is "shocking," but the narrator, now an adult looking back at her life (not to mention the author), understands this well. Jane's character as a child as portrayed in this scene develops into a heroine who will go on to "shock" readers by her strength of character and by maintaining a true and genuine Christian faith in the face of severe trials and temptations and in the context of a culture defined by nominal Christianity.

In many ways, *Jane Eyre* is a retelling of the spiritual journey of Christian in *The Pilgrim's Progress*. This more modern narrative is not told in the form of allegory, however, but rather with the particularities of a specific soul named Jane, who lives in a world very like the one of the authors, who finds her way home here in this world. Indeed, the narrator, Jane, refers to Bunyan's allegory explicitly at the end of the novel in comparing Jane's cousin St. John Rivers, a severe Calvinist and Jane's rejected suitor who has become a missionary in India, to Bunyan's Greatheart, "who guards his pilgrim convoy from the onslaught of Apollyon." Concluding the story with St. John's story, Jane conveys St. John as a reader of the Bible less like Jane or Crusoe and more like Bunyan's Christian:

28. Charlotte Bronte, *Jane Eyre* (Nashville: B&H, 2021), 74.

> His is the exaction of the apostle, who speaks but for Christ, when he says – "Whosoever will come after me, let him deny himself, and take up his cross and follow me."[29] His is the ambition of the high master-spirit, which aims to fill a place in the first rank of those who are redeemed from the earth – who stand without fault before the throne of God, who share the last mighty victories of the Lamb, who are called, and chosen, and faithful.
>
> . . . The last letter I received from him drew from my eyes human tears, and yet filled my heart with divine joy: he anticipated his sure reward, his incorruptible crown.[30] I know that a stranger's hand will write to me next, to say that the good and faithful servant has been called at length into the joy of his Lord.[31] And why weep for this? No fear of death will darken St. John's last hour: his mind will be unclouded, his heart will be undaunted, his hope will be sure, his faith steadfast. His own words are a pledge of this – "My Master," he says, "has forewarned me. Daily He announces more distinctly, – 'Surely I come quickly!' and hourly I more eagerly respond, – 'Amen; even so come, Lord Jesus!'"[32]

It is notable that a novel accused of ushering in "the most alarming revolution of modern times"[33] would in fact give the last words to so earnest St. John, who, unlike young Jane, wrestled not at all with the text. Indeed, Jane's final professed belief in the reward and life to come described in Scripture reveals that she too believes the promises in the text to be true.

MOBY-DICK AS A SOCRATIC DIALOGUE WITH THE BIBLE

While Charlotte Brontë wrote a novel that exemplified genuine – if, therefore, shocking – Christian faith, a few years later across the ocean in America, Herman Melville wrote a work drawing even more heavily, and explicitly, on the Bible – not to embody Christianity, but to question it. The biblical references in *Moby-Dick* flow effortlessly, from the famous opening line, "Call me Ishmael," to the epilogue's invocation of the book of Job to the starring character of Ahab (an allusion to the wicked king of Israel) in between. Melville clearly had read the Scriptures. Indeed, more than 600 biblical references have been documented

---

29. Jane is quoting Jesus as recorded in Matt 16:24; Mark 8:34; and Luke 14:27.
30. 1 Cor 9:25.
31. Matt 25:23.
32. Bronte, *Jane Eyre,* 735–36; St. John is quoting Rev 22:20.
33. Margaret Oliphant, "Modern Novelists Great and Small," *Blackwood's* 77 (1855): 557.

within the twelve volumes that comprise Melville's prose writing.[34] Melville's biblical knowledge derives from his Calvinist upbringing, but he employs that knowledge to undermine the faith in which he was raised. The self-awareness of his goal and its accomplishment is evidenced in his remark to his good friend Nathaniel Hawthorne, "I have written a wicked book and feel as spotless as a lamb."[35] Indeed, in *Moby-Dick* Melville has been said to have "wittily spoofed the idea that the Bible should be taken for literal truth instead of for wonderful oral story-telling and mythologies."[36]

Nevertheless, Melville perhaps was his own foil. *Moby-Dick* can be and is often read as a biblical allegory. The work nearly demands it. However, unlike the clear and straightforward symbols of Bunyan, those in this novel are often ambiguous, most especially so the symbol of the whale itself. The whale can be seen as symbolizing God or evil, ambition or madness, redemption or destruction, or all of these and many more. The text cannot easily make a case for a single, unified interpretation.

Indeed, the text explicitly models resistance to such interpretive practices in one of its most famous chapters, "The Whiteness of the Whale." This chapter examines and extols the powerful and ambiguous symbolic meanings of the color white. Whiteness symbolizes beauty, innocence, justice, holiness, panic, terror, the craven soul, and much more. Ishmael says,

> What the white whale was to Ahab, has been hinted; what, at times, he was to me, as yet remains unsaid.
>
> Aside from those more obvious considerations touching Moby Dick, which could not but occasionally awaken in any man's soul some alarm, there was another thought, or rather vague, nameless horror concerning him, which at times by its intensity completely overpowered all the rest; and yet so mystical and well nigh ineffable was it, that I almost despair of putting it in a comprehensible form. It was the whiteness of the whale that above all things appalled me. . . .
>
> But not yet have we solved the incantation of this whiteness, and learned why it appeals with such power to the soul; and more strange and far more portentous – why, as we have seen, it is at once the most meaning symbol of

34. Christopher Sanford, "Obsessed by Good, Evil, and 'Moby Dick'," *America: The Jesuit Review*, October 4, 2019, https://www.americamagazine.org/arts-culture/2019/10/04/herman-melville-obsessed-good-evil-and-moby-dick.

35. Herman Melville to Nathaniel Hawthorne, Pittsfield (November) Monday afternoon, 1851, in "The Hawthornes in Lenox," in *The Century Illustrated Monthly Magazine*, vol. 49 (New York: Century, 1894): 90.

36. Gail Coffler, "Melville's Allusions to Religion," *Leviathan* 8, no. 1 (March 2006): 111.

> spiritual things, nay, the very veil of the Christian's Deity; and yet should be as it is, the intensifying agent in things the most appalling to mankind.[37]

In the essay by Marilynn Robinson quoted above, she includes *Moby-Dick* among the many works of modern literature that owe a debt to the Bible. Of these Robinson explains,

> These texts are not allegories, because in each case the writer has posed a problem within a universe of thought that is fully open to his questioning once its terms are granted. Here the use of biblical allusion is not symbolism or metaphor, which are both rhetorical techniques for enriching a narrative whose primary interest does not rest with the larger resonances of the Bible. In fact these great texts resemble Socratic dialogues in that each venture presupposes that meaning can indeed be addressed within the constraints of the form and in its language, while the meaning to be discovered through this argument cannot be presupposed.[38]

Though the presence of a narrator (of whatever mode) can obscure this fact, novels are – like all literature is, in fact – inherently dialogical. And dialogue, by its nature, both embodies and demands interpretation.

T. S. ELIOT'S DIFFERENT VOICES

Drama and often even poetry place this dialogical nature closer to the surface than most novels do. Perhaps no poem does this more self-consciously and self-referentially than T. S. Eliot's masterpiece *The Waste Land* (1922). Notably, Eliot's working title for the poem was *He Do the Police in Different Voices*, a phrase found in Charles Dickens's *Our Mutual Friend*, which has been described as Dickens's "most 'modern' novel" (alongside the *The Waste Land* being described as the "quintessential 'modern' poem").[39]

Expressive of the moral, spiritual, and existential aftermath of World War I, *The Waste Land* is generally considered the crown jewel of modernism in literature. Written five years before he joined the Church of England, Eliot alludes in the poem to biblical passages and imagery as freely as he does to ancient myth,

37. Herman Melville, *Moby-Dick* (Hertfordshire: Wordsworth Classics, 2002), 156–63.

38. Robinson, "The Book of Books."

39. Keith Hale, "Doing the Police in Different Voices: The Search for Identity in Dust Heaps and Waste Lands," *Dickens Studies Annual* 29 (2000): 303–21.

medieval Romances, and multiple languages. A dizzying array of voices, vignettes, and perspectives, the poem defies, deliberately and defiantly, easy interpretation. The 433 footnotes he included with the 434 lines of poetry make this intention for obscurity even clearer. There is a world of difference between Bunyan's glosses and Eliot's however. Bunyan is determined to direct his reader to the exact biblical texts as a means of justifying his literary art. Eliot, on the other hand, knows that his erudition (biblical and otherwise) outpaces even his peers among his readers. He points his readers as readily to the biblical texts as he does to Ovid, Dante, Shakespeare, Baudelaire, and *The Upanishads*. For the pre-Christian Eliot, authority matters, but the Bible is just another text whose authority is allusive rather than direct.

PIRANDELLO: DESPERATELY SEEKING AN AUTHOR

But the death of the author was looming, as made clear by Luigi Pirandello's 1921 absurdist drama, *Six Characters in Search of an Author* (first produced in America in 1922).[40] In the world of this play, not only is there no God, but there is not even an author. Set in a theatre where a cast for a play within the play is assembled (in a brilliant metatheatrical move, it's a play by none other than Pirandello), the closest approximation to an author is the Manager (who functions like a director, as that role is termed in other translations). It is the Manager who delivers the first line of the play, one that echoes the opening of the Bible: "I can't see. Let's have a little light, please!"[41]

Along with the Manager, there is also the "book," an interesting word to use for the script that is referred to throughout the play – always called the "book" and always appearing with the square quotes around it. For without an author, how can there be a book?

The rehearsal of the play written in the "book" is underway when the play opens. It is soon interrupted, however, by the titular figures, the six characters (all of a family and given only names that correspond to their roles). The characters spend the rest of the play telling bits of their tragic story as a broken family marred by infidelity, near incest, and death in hopes of having the Manager agree to have their story acted out. For in order to make all the parts cohere, in order to find the meaning in their story – and in their suffering – they need not only a manager or director, but an Author. Instead, lacking any coherence

40. There are numerous versions (and translations) of this play, as Pirandello made a series of revisions to the text in the years following the first production. The edition used here is a translation by Edward Storer originally published by E. P. Dutton in 1922.

41. Luigi Pirandello, *Six Characters in Search of an Author* (Mineola, NY: Dover Thrift, 1998), 1.

or conclusion or meaning, the manager can only complain, upon seeing their worst pain acted out – in what is the last line of the play (and another echo of Genesis), "I've lost a whole day over these people, a whole day!"[42] The manager, having "lost" a day, not only alludes to the Genesis account of the days of creation but also anticipates the fall in expressing the loss that accompanies creation. The world of this drama is the fallen one.

Specifically, the play demonstrates the existential condition: if existence precedes essence (the basic postulate of existential philosophy), then the meaning of one's existence must be made by and for oneself. The burden of such freedom (and responsibility) is so heavy that the desire is natural to seek a manager, director, or Author who can provide this meaning. Thus, the essence of the existential condition is a hermeneutical dilemma too: with no Author, there can be no interpretation, let alone a story.

HE'S SURE TO COME TOMORROW: STILL WAITING FOR GODOT

Waiting for Godot fulfills in some ways what Pirandello prophesied. A play by Samuel Beckett first performed in 1953 and part of a dramatic movement called Theatre of the Absurd, *Waiting for Godot* is indeed quite absurd. As one of its two main characters says, "Nothing happens, nobody comes, nobody goes, it's awful!"[43] The main one who never comes (despite promising that "surely tomorrow" he will) is the mysterious figure of Godot. The work is haunted by the Bible. "One of the thieves was saved," Vladimir suddenly blurts as he and Estragon pass the time while waiting. "Suppose we repented," he further muses.

> **Vladimir:** Did you ever read the Bible?
> **Estragon:** The Bible . . . (He reflects.) I must have taken a look at it.
> **Vladimir:** Do you remember the Gospels?
> **Estragon:** I remember the maps of the Holy Land. Coloured they were. Very pretty. The Dead Sea was pale blue. The very look of it made me thirsty. That's where we'll go, I used to say, that's where we'll go for our honeymoon. We'll swim. We'll be happy.
> **Vladimir:** You should have been a poet.[44]

---

42. Pirandello, *Six Characters in Search*, 52.
43. Samuel Beckett, *Waiting for Godot: A Tragicomedy* (London: French, 1957), 28.
44. Beckett, *Waiting for Godot*, 3.

Little changes between the first and second acts of the play. Near the end of the second act, Christ is invoked again:

> **Vladimir:** Your boots, what are you doing with your boots?
> **Estragon:** (turning to look at the boots). I'm leaving them there. (Pause.) Another will come, just as . . . as . . . as me, but with smaller feet, and they'll make him happy.
> **Vladimir:** But you can't go barefoot!
> **Estragon:** Christ did.
> **Vladimir:** Christ! What has Christ got to do with it. You're not going to compare yourself to Christ!
> **Estragon:** All my life I've compared myself to him.
> **Vladimir:** But where he lived it was warm, it was dry!
> **Estragon:** Yes. And they crucified quick. Silence.
> **Vladimir:** We've nothing more to do here.
> **Estragon:** Nor anywhere else.
> **Vladimir:** Ah Gogo, don't go on like that. Tomorrow everything will be better.
> **Estragon:** How do you make that out?
> **Vladimir:** Did you not hear what the child said?
> **Estragon:** No.
> **Vladimir:** He said that Godot was sure to come tomorrow. (Pause.) What do you say to that?
> **Estragon:** Then all we have to do is to wait on here.[45]

The play closes a few lines later with neither character moving.

As surreal as the play is, it nevertheless echoes the allegory of *The Pilgrim's Progress*, taking place in the stark setting described only in the text as: "A country road. A tree. Evening." To be sure, sometimes a road in a literary work is just a road. But more often than not it is the site of a spiritual journey. (See, for example, Cormac McCarthy's 2006 novel, *The Road*. Even the presence of marauding cannibals cannot diminish the allegorical nature of this postapocalyptic novel about no less than the meaning of life and the afterlife.[46])

This quality reflects what Robinson observes in her already-cited *New York Times* essay:

---

45. Beckett, *Waiting for Godot*, 37.
46. Cormac McCarthy, *The Road* (New York: Knopf, 2006).

> Literatures are self-referential by nature, and even when references to Scripture in contemporary fiction and poetry are no more than ornamental or rhetorical – indeed, even when they are unintentional – they are still a natural consequence of the persistence of a powerful literary tradition. Biblical allusions can suggest a degree of seriousness or significance their context in a modern fiction does not always support. This is no cause for alarm. Every fiction is a leap in the dark, and a failed grasp at seriousness is to be respected for what it attempts. In any case, these references demonstrate that in the culture there is a well of special meaning to be drawn upon that can make an obscure death a martyrdom and a gesture of forgiveness an act of grace. Whatever the state of belief of a writer or reader, such resonances have meaning that is more than ornamental, since they acknowledge complexity of experience of a kind that is the substance of fiction.[47]

A CHILDREN'S BIBLE FOR EVERYONE

A contemporary work that demonstrates this utter indebtedness to the Bible is Lydia Millet's 2020 novel, *A Children's Bible*. Reminiscent in a way of the retelling of biblical myth by John Steinbeck's 1952 novel, *East of Eden*, *A Children's Bible* also retells many of the dramatic narratives of the Bible within a modern-day setting. Both works, like the Bible, explore the effects of one generation on another. Both novels tell stories that are propelled by moral failures, but in the dystopian *A Children's Bible*, human errors are compounded by a climate disaster.

Narrated by a child named Eve (called Evie), the main plot echoes events straight out of the biblical narrative: the expulsion from paradise, the gathering of animals before a flood, a ride in a boat, the issuing of certain rules or commandments from on high. In this tale, rather than a providential presence (as in *The Pilgrim's Progress* and *Robinson Crusoe*), or a constructed self (as in *Pamela* and *Jane Eyre*), or countless competing authorities (as in *The Waste Land*), or an absent God (as in *Six Characters in Search of an Author* and *Waiting for Godot*), the authority figures (the children's parents) are simply self-absorbed and negligent.

The novel offers a warning – not only about impending environmental disaster from an author with expertise in environmental science but also about the failure of parents and authorities to read the times and to exercise their rightful

47. Robinson, "The Book of Books."

authority well. It is up to the children – there are twelve (a number of obvious symbolic significance) who journey together toward safety – to recover the truth that has been lost by the previous generation.

"Once we lived in a summer country," the story begins. "Where the water met the sky."[48] Where "deer ambled onto the sweeping lawn. Their grace was deceptive, though: they carried ticks, and ticks carried disease."[49] Here, in the beginning, in just a few lines, we have the Eden, the firmament, the animals, the fall, and the death implied by sickness. That death comes for the deer a few lines later and, by the end of the novel, for Evie's brother Jack, who had clung throughout the narrative to a book given to him that was strangely unfamiliar to and disdained by all the other children: *A Child's Bible: Stories from the Old and New Testaments*.

As he is dying at the end of the story, Jack asks Evie,

> "What happens at the end?"
>
> "The end of what, Jack?"
>
> "You know. The story."

The children's Bible Jack has been reading does not include the final book, the end: Revelation. But Evie tells him that maybe the end will be "like art" or poetry that "still comes from what they used to call God." And Jack repeats, "What they used to call God."[50]

Despite whatever incredulity toward metanarratives may exist on the surface, modern literature – indeed modern life – from *The Pilgrim's Progress* to *A Children's Bible* – reveals an unending desire to read and interpret life and one's self within the framework of the greatest story ever read. In building on and evoking a rich tradition rooted in biblical narratives, images, and language and by demanding critical rather than naïve readings, modern literature cultivates another kind of "people of the book," who turn to the text as a kind of authority. In its own way, modern literature has given us the Bible again.

FOR FURTHER READING

Beckett, Samuel. *Waiting For Godot*. London: French, 1957.

Bronte, Charlotte. *Jane Eyre*. Nashville: B&H, 2021.

48. Lydia Millet, *A Children's Bible* (New York: Norton, 2020), 1.
49. Millet, *A Children's Bible*, 1–2.
50. Millet, *A Children's Bible*, 222–24.

Bunyan, John. *The Pilgrim's Progress*. Oxford: Oxford University Press, 2003.

Defoe, Daniel. *Robinson Crusoe*. Oxford: Oxford University Press, 2007.

Eliot, T. S. *The Waste Land*. London: Penguin Classics, 2003.

Frei, Hans. *The Eclipse of Biblical Narrative: A Study in Eighteenth and Nineteenth Century Hermeneutics*. New Haven, CT: Yale University Press, 1980.

Hall, Donald E. *Subjectivity: The New Critical Idiom*. New York: Routledge, 2004.

McCarthy, Cormac. *The Road*. New York: Vintage, 2006.

McKeon, Michael. *The Origins of the English Novel:1600–1740*. Baltimore: Johns Hopkins University Press, 1987.

Melville, Herman. *Moby-Dick*. Hertfordshire: Wordsworth Classics, 2002.

Millet, Lydia. *A Children's Bible*. New York: Norton, 2021.

Pirandello, Luigi. *Six Characters in Search of an Author*. Mineola, NY: Dover Thrift, 1998.

Prior, Karen Swallow. Introduction to *Jane Eyre*. By Charlotte Bronte. Nashville: B&H, 2021.

Rasula, Jed. *What the Thunder Said: How The Waste Land Made Poetry Modern*. Princeton, NJ: Princeton University Press, 2022.

Seidel, Kevin. *Rethinking the Secular Origins of the Novel: The Bible in English Fiction 1678–1767*. Cambridge: Cambridge University Press, 2021.

Watt, Ian. *The Rise of the Novel: Studies in Defoe, Richardson and Fielding*. Berkeley: University of California Press, 1974.

CHAPTER 12

The Bible and New Reading Habits in the Western World

Philippe de Pol

This will kill that.

—*Victor Hugo*[1]

INTRODUCTION

Long before the advent of the digital world, the demise of the paper book had been predicted.[2] In the nineteenth century, the threat came from the development of newspapers, in the twentieth century it was the television screen followed by the computer, and finally in the twenty-first century came the ebook reader. However, the ominous signs have vanished, and books have remained! Each of these new media has in fact bolstered the use of reading but minimized the practice of writing. (We are writing less and less; typing, while looking at a screen, has become the norm.)[3] Comparative studies between reading from a

1. The title of chapter 2, book 5 of the 2nd ed. of the novel by Victor Hugo, *Notre Dame de Paris, 1482*, 1831.

2. Pascal Durand, "'Quant au Livre.' Prophéties et pouvoirs," in *Éditions et Pouvoirs*, ed. Jacques Michon (Sainte Foy, Québec: Presses de l'Université Laval, 1995), 285–304.

3. M. Melot, "Le dernier livre," *Livraisons de l'histoire de l'architecture* 20 (2010): 116; Cf. Bélisle, ed., *Lire dans un monde numérique* (Paris: Presse de l'ENSSIB, 2011), 21, 41.

screen as opposed to from a hardcopy[4] make us realize that what is written on this subject becomes obsolete as soon as it is published![5] In a technological society undergoing continual change thanks to planned obsolescence, carrying out a study focused on the digital world will inevitably be labelled utopian! (Note to the reader: this is even more so now that this chapter is being translated almost four years after its publication in French.) We will differentiate between what is really new from what is simply a revamping of what is already in place, first by outlining the evolution of the use of writing, reading, and of the media, and then by assessing the innovations brought about by our media saturated society against the yardstick of the particular status of the Bible.

SPEAKING AND READING

"What is written in the Law? . . . How do you read it?" (Luke 10:26). A twofold interrogation that calls into question both writing and reading. Jesus raises the issue with the lawyer – *nomikos*, the one who does the reading (*nemein*) – regarding the law (*nomos*). The law was passed on by a twofold tradition: teaching was transmitted in writing and orally.[6] A text can generate several readings according to the various schools of Judaism. Between Jesus and the lawyer, interpretative cooperation is possible because they belong to the same reading community.[7] "'You have answered correctly,' Jesus replied. 'Do this and you will live'" (Luke 10:28).

This dialogue, from the gospel of Luke, was transmitted in Greek, the *lingua franca* inherited from the empire of Alexander the Great, spoken in the big cities of the Roman Empire such as Jerusalem, whereas the oral exchange between our two protagonists was probably in the Aramaic language, the ancient *lingua franca* spoken by the Jews since their return from the Babylonian captivity, asserting their independence in remote regions such as "the Galilee

4. A. Dillon, "Reading from Paper Versus Screens: A Critical Review of the Empirical Literature," *Ergonomics* 35, no. 10 (1992): 1297–1326; L. Singer and P. Alexander, "Reading on Paper and Digitally: What the Past Decades of Empirical Research Reveal," *Review of Educational Research* 87, no. 6 (2017): 1007–41.

5. F. Waquet, *Parler comme un livre. L'oralité et le savoir (XVIe–XXe siècle)* (Paris: Albin Michel, 2003), 366.

6. B. Gerhardsson, *Memory and Manuscript. Oral Tradition and Written Transmission in Rabbinic Judaism and Early Christianity*, and *Tradition and Transmission in Early Christianity* (Grand Rapids: Eerdmans, 1998), 21.

7. Umberto Eco, *Lector in fabula. Le rôle du lecteur* (Paris: Grasset, 1985), 29 (translated from the Italian [1979] by Myriem Bouzaher).

of Jesus."[8] An intrinsic gap is thus growing for the spread of the message proclaimed by Jesus, passed on by tradition, and translated to be communicated outside its frame of reference. Since this conversation, the space between what is written and the way to read the message has widened. Nowadays nearly six billion readers can have access to this story in their own language – that is 1,430 potential ways of reading in 2019.[9]

The oral tradition taught by Jesus and then put in writing results from the necessity of translation for non-Jewish peoples.[10] The Greek verb translated by "read" in Luke 10:26 is the Attica region verb *anagignôskein* (from *gignôskein*, "knowing").[11] This type of reading requires recognition. A written piece remains meaningless until its reader brings it back to oral comprehension. In the book of Acts, the Ethiopian court official is reading the scroll of the prophet Isaiah. The evangelist Philip asks him: "Do you understand [*ginōskeis*] what you are reading [*anaginōskeis*]?" He answers: "How can I . . . unless someone explains it to me?" (Acts 8:30–31). What is written requires an oral interpretation to give meaning to the text. What is at stake is reducing the gap that separates what is oral from what is written so that it can once again become audible. For Roland Barthes, the transcription of a recorded word is like preparing a dead body for embalming.[12] Likewise, for Régis Debray, "writing scales down for the sake of storage and abridges for conservation. When we wish to preserve a corpse, the water must be removed. Drying out the feeling (by significant abstraction) reduces it to the intellect and therefore enables it to be stored, conserved and moved around."[13] Reading makes the dried out ink more fluid, allowing the oral word to be set free. The reverse side of writing is described by the linguist Claude Hagège as following: "The invention of writing has contributed to obscuring the living word. . . . [Written traces] remain dead and inadequate graphic projections of the accompanying gestures, and of expressive semiotics like facial expression."[14] Writing places itself between two moments of orality, but by writing it down a range of various possible readings open up which can extend indefinitely within the digital sphere.

8. H. C. Kee, ed., *The Bible in the Twenty-First Century* (New York: American Bible Society, 1993), 112; H-J. Martin, *Histoire et pouvoirs de l'écrit* (Paris: Librairie académique Perrin, 1988), 51.

9. Annual Report of the United Bible Societies 2018.

10. C. H. Roberts and T. C. Skeat, *The Birth of the Codex* (Oxford: Oxford University Press, 1983), 59.

11. J. Svendra, "La Grèce archaïque et classique. L'invention de la lecture silencieuse," in *Histoire de la lecture dans le monde occidental*, ed. G. Cavallo and R. Chartier (Paris: Seuil, 1997), 53.

12. R. Barthes, "De la parole à l'écriture," in *Le grain de la voix. Entretiens 1962–1980* (Paris: Seuil, 1981), 9.

13. Régis Debray, *Introduction à la médiologie* (Paris: Presses Universitaires de France, 2000), 76.

14. Cl. Hagège, *L'homme de paroles. Contribution linguistique aux sciences humaines* (Paris: Fayard, 1985), 109.

FROM VOCAL TO SCRIBAL

"In the beginning was the Word" (John 1:1). Such is the reading that the author of the gospel of John takes from the story of the beginning. The Word of the beginning made itself heard as a creative principle, producing what it enunciated. Its action was transcribed to be transmitted. In one of his lectures at the Sorbonne, Father Marcel Jousse, using the image of the shadow as the double of the human being, said: "Shadows spontaneously invented writing. As soon as the sun rises, as soon as a fire is lit, here comes the invention of writing."[15] Writing takes its place as the shadow of the spoken word. Behind this we are conscious of Plato's shadows projected onto a backdrop, which led Socrates to say in the form of a dialogue – and not that of a treatise – that writing is a "simulacrum" of discourse.[16] As for Jacques Derrida, he thinks that "writing is at the same time more exterior to the spoken word, not being its 'image' or its 'symbol,' and more interior to the spoken word being already a form of writing in itself."[17] He considers writing as the "custodian of the spoken word."[18] The written trail which proceeds from the spoken word will gradually become detached. The medievalist Paul Zumthor underlines that "theoretically, writing was conceived, according to the ancient grammatical tradition, as a secondary system of signs reflecting the primary one which the voice manipulates. But in fact, through use, repetition and self-reflection, a writing code has been built up, moving in its turn towards taking on the status of a primary system."[19] The writing will then write its own story in the cradle of history that was Mesopotamia – literally "between two rivers" (The Tigris and the Euphrates) – this place between two flows of orality.

THE EVOLUTION OF WRITING

Occasional instruments used by the first men became tools with a certain repository of know-how that has enabled transmission. Retroactively, tools have favoured their own evolution by being perfected to better fit the predispositions of our brains. This also caused the reduction of cuneiform writing to the Greek

15. M. Jousse, *L'anthropologie du geste* (Paris: Galimard, 1974), 105.

16. Waquet, *Parler comme un livre*, 16; W. J. Ong, *Orality and Literacy: The Technologizing of the Word* (New York: Routledge, 1982), 79.

17. Jacques Derrida, *De la grammatologie* (Paris: Éditions de Minuit, 1967), 65.

18. Derrida, *De la grammatologie*, 326.

19. P. Zumthor, *La lettre et la voix. De la "litterature" médiévale* (Paris: Seuil, 1987), 123.

alphabet, which has turned out to be the simplest transcription system, best adapted to our neural capacities.[20] "Alphabetical writing is the most inaudible since it doesn't immediately correspond to any particular language. Although it is distinct from the voice, it remains the most faithful to it and represents it the best."[21] The shape of the letters depends on configurations already printed in the mind long before the invention of writing.[22] The function of our neurons enabling facial recognition (distinguishing a friend from an enemy) and securing shelter (spotting secure, danger-free places) has been recycled in order to focus on the recognition of distinctive elements of writing.[23] Acquiring the ability to read has thus developed at the expense of primitive skills enabling one to "read" traces of things scored in nature.[24] By using eyesight, reading redirects the neural zones used for seeing so that the words are not treated like images but like items of a lexicon made of meanings and sounds. The surrealist René Magritte in his painting "The Treachery of Images" has made good use of this ambivalence.[25] Writing and reading modify the way the brain functions, moving from the observations of signs to reading, making a distinction between image and writing.

Writing also undergoes the influence of its medium. For Mesopotamia specialist Jean-Jacques Glassner, the invention of cuneiform was intrinsically dependent on the clay tablets largely available in the region where this form of writing emerged. "Writing and its medium, the clay tablet, were invented simultaneously. . . . The invention of the graphic sign required the associated invention of the tablet; they are so congruent and indissociable, that one cannot be conceived without the other."[26] This link between the medium and writing will endure in spite of the technical evolutions which bring about changes in our ways of thinking.[27] Thus, the cuneiform syllabary has made it possible to identify around fifteen languages belonging to a different linguistic group from the Sumerians through a period of three millennia,[28] while another type

20. S. Dehane, *Reading in the Brain: The New Science of How We Read* (New York: Penguin, 2009), 303.

21. Derrida, *De la grammatologie*, 405.

22. Dehane, *Reading in the Brain*, 139; T. Baccino and V. Drai-Zerbib, *La lecture numérique* (Grenoble: Presse universitaire de Grenoble, 2015), 7.

23. Baccino and Drai-Zerbib, *La lecture numérique*, 32.

24. Dehane, *Reading in the Brain*, 213.

25. A. K. M. Adam, "Interpreting the Bible at the Horizon of Virtual New Worlds," in *The Bible in Ancient and Modern Media*, ed. H. E. Hearon and Ph. Ruge-Jones. (Eugene, OR: Cascade, 2009), 169.

26. J.-J. Glassner, *Écrire à Sumer: L'invention du cunéiforme* (Paris: Seuil, 2000), 156.

27. E. Soucher, "L'écrit d'écran, pratiques d'écriture & informatique," *Communication et langages* 107 (1996):105–9, 106.

28. L. Bonfante, John Chadwick, B. F. Cook, W. V. Davies, J. Healey, J. T. Hooker, and C. B. F. Walker, *La naissance des écritures. Du cunéiforme à l'alphabet* (Paris: Seuil, 1994), 71.

of writing more adapted to the consonantal semito-hamitic languages developed on another medium, papyrus, gave birth to a consonantal alphabet called Abjad, devoid of vowels.[29] This reliance of the writing system on its medium led Marshall McLuhan, an expert on "literature" born at the pivotal period of the invention of writing to coin his phrase: "The medium is the message." The message undergoes the influence of the medium that is used and, conversely, because "signs produce meanings and . . . a text is invested with an unprecedented meaning and status which alter the medium which is presenting the text to be read."[30] The medium is an integral part of the message. It alters its content just as reading has changed our way of thinking. The Bible is a perfect illustration of this process.

CODEX

Among the media that has contributed to the evolution of writing, there is one that has played a key role for Christianity: the codex. With the change of medium to printing, this connection will be reinforced during the Reformation, through the distribution of pamphlets by door-to-door salesmen, who foreshadow our social networks.[31] The paginated book, just like the codex, will emerge as Christianity's identity marker. It will eventually become a major part of its organisation.[32]

The Romans used wooden tablets – hence the name codex – covered with malleable wax. In his own inimitable style, Regis Debray wonders: "What was a codex really used for in the Roman world? It was a wretched thingummy, a notepad, a notebook for making the first draft of a text or doing the household accounts."[33] It was by gathering together several tablets, papyri, and then parchments that led to the birth of the codex.[34] As the specialist in the history of books, Henri-Jean Martin, emphasises: "The arrival of the codex, that is a book which is no longer written on scrolls but on lamina bound together and

29. Bonfante et al., *La naissance des écritures*, 264.

30. G. Cavallo and R. Chartier, eds., *Histoire de la lecture dans le monde occidental* (Paris: Seuil, 1997), 8.

31. R. J. Deibert, *Parchment, Printing, and Hypermedia: Communication in World Order Transformation* (New York: Columbia University Press, 1997), 71; J.-F. Gilmont, *La Réforme et le livre. L'Europe de l'imprimé (1517–v.1570)* (Paris: Cerf, 1990), 84; "Réformes protestantes et lecture," in *Histoire de la lecture dans le monde occidental*, 251.

32. Ch. Vanderdorpe, *Du papyrus à l'hypertexte. Essai sur les mutations du texte et de la lecture* (Paris: La Découverte, 1999), 22.

33. Régis Debray, *Cours de médiologie Générale* (Paris: Gallimard, 1991), 131.

34. Roberts and Skeat, *The Birth of the Codex*, 12.

written on both sides, represents surely the most important revolution the book has gone through during our era."[35] It will accompany and support that other revolution, namely Christianity. From its beginning, Christianity adopted the codex in spite of the popularity of the *volumen*,[36] although this was the medium usually adopted for venerable or sacred texts.[37] There is no consensus on the various explanations for such a preference.[38] The historian of early Christianity Larry Hurtado aptly concludes his overview of the so-called advantages with this observation: "If the codex was so obvious a superior book form for reading/use of texts, why did most users of literary texts in the second and the third centuries so firmly prefer book rolls?"[39] Neither the material that was supposed to be cheaper nor the arrangement that was more practical for travelling, nor the easier handling of the paginated format, nor even the possibility of writing on both sides of the material made the codex the medium of Christian identity.[40] Instead, it was the editorial decision of the Bible authors addressing their texts to communities of readers/listeners of every social status, among whom were slaves used to making notes on cheap material. The codex turned out to be the medium perfectly adapted to the transmission of the Christian message that revolutionized the ancient world, just as the invention of printing contributed to the upheaval of the Renaissance world.

PAUL, TANNER AND MANUFACTURER

One of the first missionaries convinced of the need to spread the gospel was the apostle Paul. His letter-writing activity was concurrent with his itinerant ministry. When he was physically absent, his collaborators replaced him by delivering letters that they transmitted in the spirit of the apostle (1 Cor 5:3; Col 2:5). These epistles addressed to local communities were also sent on to other communities. Some epistles acquired the status of circular letters, going to and from Colossae and Laodicea for instance (Col 4:16). All of these letters were gathered

35. Martin, *Histoire et pouvoirs de l'écrit*, 70.

36. *Volumen* is the Latin term for the roll, whose Greek equivalent is *biblos*, based on the town of Byblos, an important Phoenician port town known for commerce in papyrus. (H. Y. Gamble, *Books and Readers in the Early Church. A History of Early Christian Texts* [New Haven, CT: Yale University Press, 1995], 44).

37. Gamble, *Books and Readers in the Early Church*, 49; Larry W. Hurtado, *The Earliest Christian Artifacts: Manuscripts and Christian Origins* (Grand Rapids: Eerdmans, 2006), 49; Roberts and Skeat, *The Birth of the Codex*, 53.

38. Hurtado, *The Earliest Christian Artifacts*, 53–65; Roberts and Skeat, *The Birth of the Codex*, 45.

39. Hurtado, *The Earliest Christian Artifacts*, 65.

40. Gamble, *Books and Readers in the Early Church*, 55.

in a codex[41] mentioned in 2 Peter 3:15–16.[42] Commenting on this passage, the New Testament teacher Samuel Bénétreau writes, "Paul's letters are considered by verse 16 as a collection, a corpus to which an overall authority of Scripture is recognized. They soon became part of the common good even though they targeted specific local communities with their own specific issues, at first."[43] Just as the printing sector benefited from the experience of goldsmiths with the font of movable type, the codex benefited from the handcraft of tent makers as experts in the art of sowing together tanned skins.[44] Paul was one of them; he had left at Carpus's home in Troas some *membrana* (2 Tim 4:13),[45] a Latin word translated as parchments, and these could be codices made by Paul for the circulation of his letters.

The compilation of the various epistles of Paul gave each of them a shared authority regardless of size or content.[46] All of these letters acquired an authority which would not be linked to the local church but to Paul's ministry. Gathered in the same codex, they take on the status of catholicity, addressed to the universal church[47] and form the Pauline corpus.[48] It is the gathering of scattered texts in a codex that will give a new meaning and a recognized authority to the whole, the intrinsic value being more than the sum of its parts.[49]

GOSPEL TRUTH

The form of the codex made it possible to add to the Pauline corpus some texts from various authors. At the end of the second century, two or even several gospels were gathered in the same codex.[50] The format of the codex enabled all four gospels to be retained whereas the attempt to harmonize them into four parts

41. Gamble, *Books and Readers in the Early Church*, 60. J. S. Siker, *Liquid Scripture. The Bible in a Digital World* (Minneapolis: Fortress, 2017), 27.
42. Hurtado, *The Earliest Christian Artifacts*, 80.
43. Samuel Bénétreau, *La deuxième épître de Pierre* (Édifac: Vaux-sur-Seine, 1994), 218.
44. G. Frost, "Adoption of the Codex Book: Parable of a New Reading Mode," in *The Book and Paper Group* 17 (1998): 67–74.
45. Roberts and Skeat, *The Birth of the Codex*, 20.
46. Hurtado, *The Earliest Christian Artifacts*, 39.
47. Gary Frost, "Adoption of the Codex Book: Parable of a New Reading Mode," in *The Book and Paper Group Annual* 17 (1998): 67–74, American Institute of Conservation.
48. Gamble, *Books and Readers in the Early Church*, 63.
49. Siker, *Liquid Scripture*, 29.
50. Hurtado, *The Earliest Christian Artifacts*, 37. Manuscripts P64 and P67 (Matthew) and P4 (Luke) come from the same codex. The Bodmer manuscript contains the Gospels of Luke and John. The Chester Beatty codex contains, in this order: Matthew, John, Luke, and Mark, as does the Codex of Bèze, the Latin versions (*Codex Palatinus*, Vercellensis, *Veronensis*) and the gothic version of the *Argenteus* codex.

had produced the *Diatessaron* of Tatian,[51] which actually did not gain a foothold when confronted with the authority of each gospel. The separated books (*ta biblia*), which carried an authoritative weight, slowly came together the Book (*to biblion*) thanks to the codex. The paleographer Malcom Parkes wrote that "the reader 'eventually considered the various texts comprised in the same book as a single whole' and used them as such, which had a great impact on intellectual practices."[52]

This principle inherent to the codex seems to be related to Jesus' address to the experts in the law in Luke 11:51: "From the blood of Abel to the blood of Zechariah, who was killed between the altar and the sanctuary. Yes, I tell you, this generation will be held responsible for it all." Among the possible identifications of the Zechariah concerned, the one from 2 Chronicles 24:20–22 would lend credibility to the existence of a Hebrew corpus. The two characters would be used as "literary" landmarks: Abel for the first text (Genesis) and Zechariah for the last text (Chronicles).[53] The expert in British literature Alan Jacobs sees here both an anticipation of the development of the codex and an appeal for this technique or the way of thinking it fosters.[54]

This possibility of compilation gave some communities the opportunity to add some texts such as *The Shepherd of Hermas* or *The Epistle of Barnabas* after the Gospels and Paul's letters. The church would thus be required to define a rule, a canon, of authoritative texts commonly agreed upon. By the end of the second century, the Muratorian fragment attests nearly all the biblical texts such as they have been retained and transmitted by the church.[55]

When Christianity became the religion of the empire, the codex became the norm.[56] Régis Debray emphasises that two things happened concurrently: the "victory of the codex over the scroll in the fourth century"[57] and the victory of "Christianity over paganism," and compares that to the "evangelical Reform, which followed step by step the development of the printing-press in Europe."[58]

51. L. Vaganay, *Initiation à la critique textuelle du Nouveau Testament*, 2nd ed. revised by Ch-B. Amphoux (Paris: Cerf, 1986), 56. *Diatessaron* means "through four." This work from the end of the second century harmonised the four Gospels into one.

52. M. Parkes, "Lire, écrire, interpréter le texte: Pratiques monastiques dans le haut Moyen-Âge," in *Histoire de la lecture dans le monde occidental*, 104.

53. F. Bovon, *Commentaire de Luc 9,51–14,35*, *Commentaire du Nouveau Testament IIIb* (Genève: Labor et Fides, 1996), 213.

54. Alan Jacobs, "Christianity and the Future of the Book," *TheNewAtlantis.com*, Fall 2011, https://www.thenewatlantis.com/publications/christianity-and-the-future-of-the-book.

55. J.-D. Kaestli, "Histoire du canon du Nouveau Testament," in *Introduction au Nouveau Testament: Son histoire, son écriture, sa théologie*, ed. D. Marguerat. (Genève: Labor et Fides, 2001), 451.

56. Hurtado, *The Earliest Christian Artifacts*, 47; Roberts and Skeat, *The Birth of the Codex*, 67.

57. Debray, *Cours de médiologie Générale*, 35.

58. Debray, *Cours de médiologie Générale*, 60.

Christianity cannot be separated from the book to such an extent that after the fall of the Roman empire, it was the church that saved and maintained the art of writing right through the Middle Ages until the emergence of universities in the thirteenth century, which resulted in the secularisation of writing.

WHEN THE BIBLE BECOMES SACRED

Reading consists not in identifying the owners of a text thanks to their seal[59] nor in noticing, while passing by, the inscriptions found on Roman monuments, mere images of the glory of the empire.[60] Reading is the fruit of a learning process enabling one to recognize the sense and the sound of what is being transmitted. One of the unfortunate consequences of the development of reading has been the sacralization of the text. To read the Bible, it is not necessary to learn the original languages; it is quite possible to read them in translation. The plurality of the biblical languages reminds us that there can be no sacred language for the Christian, nor is there a sacred text.[61] As the doctor of the church Bernard de Clairvaux said: "The Christian faith is not a religion of the book but of the Word, not of the written and silent word but of the Incarnate living word."[62] The dogmatics professor Louis Panier made the same claim: "Depository [*sic*] of the spoken word that they are expressing and have in their safe-keeping, the Scriptures, the Book, are not per se sacred. They mediate and *resurrect*, for those who can read, the relation to the spoken word."[63]

If the Word was, at the beginning, breathed out, writing slowly fossilized it by setting it in stone. The invention of the alphabet by the Greeks enabled a complete transcription of what was audible.[64] This relation to orality was so strong that the written word was not distinguishable, drowned as it was in the stream of the *scriptio continua* that very closely transcribed the verbal flow.[65] The scribe did not copy what he had before his eyes, but he reproduced what

---

59. Hiéroglyphic writing has a special status, close to that of pictograms; it provides something to see but being unchangeable it wasn't able to reflect the evolution of the Egyptian language (Bonfante et al., *La naissance des écritures*, 141).

60. In the same way that Hellenistic libraries were not public reading places but visible signs of the grandeur of the Greek empire (Cavallo and Chartier, eds., *Histoire de la lecture dans le monde occidental*, 17).

61. Gamble, *Books and Readers in the Early Church*, 231.

62. Quoted in point 108 of the *Catéchisme de l'Église catholique* (Paris: Mame/Plon, 1992), 36.

63. Louis, Panier, "De la sacralisation à la lecture, published in Spanish translation," *Los límites del texto sagrado*, Tópicos del Seminario 22 (Julio-Diciembre 2009): 53–74.

64. Bonfante et al., *La naissance des écritures*, 260.

65. A. Manguel, *Une histoire de la lecture* (Paris, Actes Sud, 1998), (translated from English by Christine Le Bœuf), 81.

he was hearing. Separating the words gave them visibility, which consequently integrated the meaning into the word itself, in the same way that ancient science considered that combustible materials were impregnated with burning substance.[66] The appearance of the printing press increased the dynamics of this process by standardizing the transcription of the vocabulary of the new emerging national languages[67] in support of the *sola scriptura* of the Reformation. In the sixteenth century, the profession of printer was largely characterised by its confessional dimension, with its share of martyrs of the faith.[68] This sacralization still exists today, since librarians and teachers maintain an almost religious relationship with books, any destruction of a publication is seen as sacrilege and the books removed from the shelves end up in hell.[69] Regarding the specificity of the Bible, this process had an influence on the way the message was transmitted. Too many translations have been governed by a sort of *lex talionis* whereby a word of the original language must correspond to word of the target language.[70] Like the *communicatio idiomatum*, the quality of the "sacred" nature of the Word of God has been applied to the printed Scriptures, thus becoming the "Holy" Bible on which people swear an oath, or use like the *Sortes Vergilianae* by choosing verses at random.[71] Translations such as the King James in English or the Louis Segond in French have been given a status nearly equivalent to the original text, to the extent of generating a sort of sacred newspeak, a religious jargon, losing sight of the fact that any translation, even the most literal, is *de facto* an interpretation.[72]

WHEN THE READER BECOMES SACRED

Another change accompanied this phenomenon of the sacralization of the text. It concerns the readers and their ability to interpret the text.[73] The Scriptures are regarded as the Word of God addressed to a community of

66. Adam, "Interpreting the Bible at the Horizon of Virtual New Worlds," 162.

67. Ong, *Orality and Literacy*, 119.

68. Gilmont, *La Réforme et le livre*, 1990, 40, 103.

69. Waquet, *Parler comme un livre*, 55. Hell is the place where books that can't be consulted in libraries are stored.

70. "Instead of benefiting from the work of theoreticians and practitioners of translation, academic biblical scholarship tends to show a persistent inclination toward a fantasy of a perfect one-word-to-one -word equivalence." Adam, "Interpreting the Bible at the Horizon of Virtual New Worlds," 161.

71. Gamble, *Books and Readers in the Early Church*, 237; Manguel, *Une histoire de la lecture*, 300.

72. Kee, ed., *The Bible in the Twenty-First Century*, 51.

73. "The reading revolution came before the book revolution" (Cavallo and Chartier, eds., *Histoire de la lecture dans le monde occidental*, 33).

listeners,[74] who may not necessarily be readers.[75] Our conception of readership is ethnocentric, particularly if we relate it to a culture in which oral tradition has remained significant notwithstanding the use of writing. It is a heritage of the eighteenth-century "fury of reading" on a broad range of subjects, which has favoured secular writings at the expense of religious writings, and which has generated literature and its concepts of plagiarism and of authorship.[76] In a society where illiteracy was not seen as a deficiency,[77] any text was "interpreted" by the person who could read, just as a comedian embodies a role based on the script.[78] For the paleographer Guglielmo Cavallo, the reading of the Greek text was "a *hypokrisis*, that is a vocal and gestural 'interpretation' in the best interests of the literary genre and the author's intentions,"[79] and the reading of Roman poetry was like performing a "musical score."[80] The persons who were reading a biblical text could interpret it because they were its author or because they had been present when the text was dictated; they could therefore re-interpret it *in persona*. The apostle Paul, for example, took great care to convey his letters through the channel of disciples who would then speak in his name.[81]

Most of the interpretation was thus the responsibility of the speaker; however, it allowed the audience to interact and thus to take part in the "transduction"[82] of the text.[83] Sharing this cooperative responsibility has progressively become the listener's responsibility as he took on the status of reader, by interpreting orally what he had before his eyes. With the development of silent

74. "The early Christian community was more a group of listeners than a group of readers; a reading public is more individualistic, scattered, not occupying the same physical space as a listening public who have to meet together frequently to receive and retain an ephemeral message" (Debray, *Cours de médiologie générale*,150).

75. Svendra, "La Grèce archaïque et classique. L'invention de la lecture silencieuse," in *Histoire de la lecture dans le monde occidental*, 55; Pieter J. J. Botha, *Orality and Literacy in Early Christianity* (Eugene, OR: Cascade, 2012), 178.

76. P. Zumthor, *Introduction à la poésie orale* (Paris: Seuil, 1983), 254; Ong, *Orality and Literacy*, 135; Botha, *Orality and Literacy in Early Christianity*, 117.

77. "Orality is presented as an indicator of a *deficiency* whereas reading is seen as something complete. From this position the temptation is to slip from fact to value, from the observation of absence (writing) to a vision of oral culture as a *deprived* cultur." M. Diagne, *Critique de la raison orale. Les pratiques discursives en Afrique noire* (Paris: Karthala, 2005), 15.

78. Botha and Rhoades, *Orality and Literacy in Early Christianity*, 204. Concerning oral medieval culture, Paul Zumthor writes: "The voice brings me to a knowledge of the discourse that the poetry is offering, by representing it (in the theatrical sense)" (Zumthor, *La lettre et la voix*, 186).

79. Cavallo and Chartier, eds., *Histoire de la lecture dans le monde occidental*, 19.

80. Cavallo and Chartier, eds., *Histoire de la lecture dans le monde occidental*, 89.

81. Botha, *Orality and Literacy in Early Christianity*, 207, 243; David Rhoads, "Competing Gospels," in *The Bible in Ancient and Modern Media*, 87.

82. Yves Citton uses this word "transduction" to emphasize the idea of translation produced by interpretative activity. *L'avenir des humanités. Économie de la connaissance ou cultures de l'interprétation?* [Paris: La Découverte, 2010], 91).

83. Manguel, *Une histoire de la lecture*, 358.

reading in the twelfth century, only sight could interpret what was being read. To facilitate this silent work, the words were detached from each other as early as the seventh century; in the thirteenth century the invention of glasses came as a great help and in the fifteenth century, the printing industry with its mechanised layout made visible and thus readable what the author "meant" to say.[84] This hermeneutic principle had been initiated by the copyists of manuscripts in which "the introduction of punctuation signs had enabled them to convey the hermeneutic analysis onto the page so that it could be perceived by the reader as being a part of the process of reading."[85] This change became in turn one of the characteristics of digital reading as Christian Vandendorpe points out: "The text by passing from the realm of the ear to the realm of sight, has changed the way it communicates. It has become an abstract and impersonal entity, which can be detached from its author and from its historical roots, offered for individual consumption and for deconstruction in all its forms."[86] The shift of the interpretative authority is done at the expense of the context which the codex had helped to structure and of the paratext[87] developed by the printing industry. The change of medium means that "a 'same' text is no longer the same when the medium on which it is written changes and thus the ways it is read and the meaning given to it by new readers."[88]

READING AS AN INTERPRETATION

This delegation of interpretation has been carried out with the complicity of authors. For Paul Zumthor, as early as the Middle-Ages, "the act of listening . . . by which the work (probably after a long process) takes shape socially cannot avoid being written in advance into the text, planned in fact, by placing signs of intention, and this partly defines where the discourse finds its place in the person who pronounces it."[89] The intention written into the text requires textual cooperation from the reader, which leads Umberto Eco to write that the text is "a lazy machine which makes the reader do almost all the work,"[90] a task

84. Vanderdorpe, *Du papyrus à l'hypertexte*, 40.

85. Parkes, "Lire, écrire, interpréter le texte," 122.

86. Vanderdorpe, *Du papyrus à l'hypertexte*, 171.

87. "The paratext is made up of factors introduced by printing such as division into chapters, page numbers, typographic items and lay-out . . .".

88. R. Chartier, "Qu'est-ce qu'un livre? Métaphores anciennes, concepts des lumières et réalités numériques," *Le français aujourd'hui* 178(2012/3):11–26, 21.

89. Zumthor, *La lettre et la voix*, 20.

90. Eco, *Lector in fabula*, 251.

which was previously the responsibility of the speaker. The auditory and visual performance that the speaker gave in public has gradually been interiorized by readers who are left to their own devices.[91] For Roland Barthes the emergence of the reader implied the death of the author, this being the title of an article where he pointed out: "We now know that a text is not made up of a line of words, leading to a single meaning, a sort of theological meaning (that is, a message sent by the Author-God), but of a multi-dimensional space, where varied writings intermingle and challenge one another, none of them being the original one: the text is a fabric of quotations originating from thousands of cultural homes."[92] If the performance of a single speaker before an assembly was unique, the multiplication of individual readers makes the text ambiguous. Interpretation is done from out of the reader's intimate world. The person who ends up being in the situation of an art critic vilified by Jacques Ellul about whom he says sarcastically, "Without the critic, the work is fruitless because the critic eventually becomes a role model for the reader: so the work must be studied not in terms of the person who created it but in terms of the person who reads it. It is the reader who writes the work."[93] It seems then that modern readers create for themselves the meaning of texts that they have not written. In fact, the four meanings of the Scriptures, which were the rules for reading laid down by the church fathers, are insignificant compared with the readings that proliferate today.[94] This is called into question by the biblical scholar Moisés Silva: "When Ricœur (with the agreement of many others) tells us that a written text 'escapes the finite horizon lived by its author,' so that 'what the text means now matters more than what the author meant when he wrote it' (1976, p. 30), one wonders whether we are returning to the allegorical method that modern scholarship had fought so hard to vanquish."[95]

This approach to reading is reflected in modern media as studied by the psychiatrist Serge Tisseron; he notes that "a part of the critical attitude that was traditionally directed towards the author must shift towards the spectator. The question of 'knowing what the author meant' must be replaced by a questioning of the effects of images for each of us. This means in fact that if an image surprises and upsets us, it is important to grasp this clue not as a starting point of a questioning about the author but as the source of a questioning of oneself."[96]

91. Zumthor, *Introduction à la poésie orale*, 238.

92. Roland Barthes, "La mort de l'auteur," *Mantéia* 5 (1968): 65.

93. Jacques Ellul, *L'empire du non-sens* (Paris: PUF, 1980), 265.

94. See G. Aichile, et al., *The Postmodern Bible* (New Haven, CT: Yale University Press, 1995).

95. R. Hodgson and P. A. Soukup, eds., *From one Medium to another: Basis Issues for Communicating the Scriptures in New Media* (Kansas City: Sheed & Ward; American Bible Society, 1997), 48.

96. S. Tisseron, *Comment l'esprit vient aux objets* (Paris: Aubier, 1999), 115.

If the text has the same effect on the reader that the image has on the spectator, it means that the text has gone back to being an image. The listener, who had turned into a reader, has turned back into a spectator, admiring himself in the text. The professor of religion Melvin Peter wrote: "Femininity analysis and African-American analysis are not approaches at all, but are . . . examples of particular audiences using the Bible to meet their own perceived needs."[97] In the century of post-truth,[98] every interpretation claims to have value per se, with no regard for the truth, the only norm being individual sincerity, which is scarcely compatible with a recognition of the normative authority of Scripture.

THE CHURCH AS A COMMUNITY OF INTERPRETATION

The interpretation of the Bible is not the monopoly of an individual; it belongs to the community of believers. The church has transmitted through the centuries the texts that have nourished its faith. The performance of the speaker has been shouldered by the church, the community of interpretation. During the Reformation, when this transmission was being called into question, the pastor became the interpreter, giving back its voice to the Word in a context of silent reading, symptomatic of widespread insularity.[99] Reading the Bible and understanding it outside its transmission by the community of believers is like believing that a library can vouchsafe memory apart from the community of readers. This leads Regis Debray to write, "Exalting 'places of memory' above and independently of communities of people who remember would be to make the building a fetish by dissociating, so to speak, the dweller from the dwelling, or the body from the soul."[100] This is the risk of bibliolatry, which consecrates Scripture in disregard of the reader-listener community. The value of a text is prior to the reader; it has been handed down by generations who have borne this heritage from the past through to today. This heritage which is described as follows by the expert in literature Yves Citton:

> [Literary] interpretation is the very act of tradition, i.e. what hands down and brings back [*tradere*] the heritage to the present time. This act tends to be reactionary when it aims at diverting us from the present time to draw our

97. Kee, ed., *The Bible in the Twenty-First Century*, 147.
98. S. Dieguez, *Total Bullshit! Au cœur de la post-vérité* (Paris: PUF, 2018).
99. Gilmont, *La Réforme et le livre* (Paris: Cerf, 1990), 24.
100. Debray, *Introduction à la médiologie*, 9.

> attention to past customs. It becomes a possible source of enrichment and of emancipation as soon as it uses references to the past in order to bring out new attributes of the present – that is to say as soon as it makes the past text say something other than what had been heard so far.[101]

The current difficulty is due to the fact that the role of the reading community is no longer attuned to our information society. In lieu of the global village born from the globalization of communication systems, we are witnessing the emergence of a new tower of Babel amidst a flood of information.[102] The digital society suffers from "infobesity." [103] The role of interpreters was to digest these pieces of information rather than to store them to change them into knowledge, becoming therefore transmissible, just like the first tools of human beings. Knowing where to find a piece of information and how to have access to it is not the same as acquiring knowledge. Dominique Wolton, research director at the Centre national de la recherche scientifique (CNRS), echoes Christlike thoughts when he wonders, "What is the point of having access to all sorts of information if we do not have the keys to understand them?"[104] In the same tone of voice, Ben Witherington III, New Testament professor, writes, "Information – whether from the pulpit, in the classroom, on the e-mail or in print – without transformation availeth nothing."[105] Information without transformation just destroys interpretation.

The value of a piece of information is directly indexed to current affairs. The newspaper has the same value as a baguette; both are stale in a few days. The true challenge of biblical reading is that of interpretation – that is, making "a concerted effort leading to *reconfigure the existing frameworks*, testing their vitality and attempting to lead to the *production of something new*."[106] But for this, it is necessary to have (empty) space and (free) time,[107] two things that are not valued by our information society. The gospel cannot be presented in the same way as a journalistic press release to inform people; rather, it is transmitted from one generation to the next to transform, even to convert, the person to whom the message is addressed. Quite rightly, Yves Citton writes, "Information

---

101. Citton, *L'avenir des humanités*, 89.

102. D. Wolton, *Informer n'est pas communiquer* (Paris: CNRS éditions, 2009), 126.

103. Wolton, *Informer n'est pas communiquer*, 57.

104. Wolton, *Informer n'est pas communiquer*, 118.

105. Ben Witherington III, "Hearing the Hum in a Wired World: Preliminary Musings on Virtual Reality and Evangelical Education," in *Critical Thinking and the Bible in the Age of New Media*, ed., C. M. Ess. (Lanham: University Press of America, 2004), 201.

106. Citton, *L'avenir des humanités*, 45f.

107. Citton, *L'avenir des humanités*, 74.

societies appear to be satisfied with knowing about the world; what matters for interpretation cultures is to transform it."[108] That is the very mission the Church has received for the world.

THE DEMISE OF THE PRINTED PAGE

The wind of the digital revolution blows on the muffled world of literature carefully categorized in libraries, sacred temples where the faithful reader respects religiously the law of silence. Each book is shelved at the assigned spot in accordance with the "canon" of classification set up by Melvil Dewey.[109] Changed into media libraries, it is the law of demand that imposes the shelving for what is on offer. Far from being ergonomic, trying to facilitate the act of reading which the codex and the printing press had established, the digital world has made the choice of going down the economic road, making the reader into "an actor of consumerism"[110] since the book is no longer an object that we own but a service that we have access to. For the doctor of psychology Claire Bélisle, "Western societies are becoming service provider societies, more and more based on information: a multimedia, multilingual and multicultural information system."[111]

Reading the Bible is not like reading an eighteenth century novel; readers choose extracts according to their circumstances. Linear reading was a constraint imposed by the format of the *volumen*, which had to be unwound.[112] The invention of the page enabled the text to be freed from the continuous, linear way of reading a scroll. For Christian Vanderdope, the page has made the book "tabular." [113] In other words, "A book is said to be tabular when it can be spread out in order to display various items simultaneously in order to help the reader identify the links and find as quickly as possible relevant pieces of information."[114]

Hypertext links are the outcome in the virtual world of the improvement brought about by the book compared to the scroll. Nevertheless, reading in the hypermedia space is more like navigating than weaving: we now speak of surfing on the web.[115] We no longer turn the page; rather, the page disappears with

108. Citton, *L'avenir des humanités*, 134.

109. Inventor of the decimal classification of books, taken up and improved by the Universal Decimal Classification.

110. Ch.Longhi and S. Rocchia, "'Ceci tuera cela'? Dynamique des changements dans l'industrie du livre, *Revue d'économie industrielle* 145(2014): 121–154.

111. Cl. Bélisle, ed., *Lire dans un monde numérique* (Paris: Presse de l'ENSSIB, 2011), 31.

112. The Latin verb *explicare* means "to unwind."

113. Vanderdorpe, *Du papyrus à l'hypertexte*, 53.

114. Vanderdorpe, *Du papyrus à l'hypertexte*, 65.

115. Vanderdorpe, *Du papyrus à l'hypertexte*, 208.

every click, leaving no trace. The trace had been the material representation of the spoken word by writing, ensuring its transmission, just as human beings followed a path to discover their surroundings leaving a trace that had the specific character of "being drawn *before* and to subsist *after* the walker had made use of it. It's because of its material nature that it can be defined not as a trail but as a path, a repeatable and reversible trace which can be followed in both directions."[116] Digital navigation no longer offers this possibility of going back and forth as we can do with a paper book. In the labyrinth of virtual reading, only the hypertext link can be used like the golden thread of Greek mythology, but it can be broken at any moment. Paradoxically, digital reading brings us back to the practice of reading from a *volumen*.[117] The menus and screens scroll down, revealing only the "page" (meaning the column) of the papyrus. The sequential reading of the codex had enabled one to follow the pattern of the story of salvation through the different Bible texts and to see the links between them as a collection. Thanks to the book format, a concrete and palpable reality gave depth to the overall narrative running through the whole of the Bible, enabling Scripture to interpret Scripture since the reader and the author shared the same horizon.[118] Virtual linearity has lost sight of this horizon by shifting to a vertical approach of the text: instead of reading continuously horizontally, the eye now reads the text from top to bottom with "fleeting horizontal glimpses" providing an *F* pattern scheme of reading, useful when researching information but useless for acquiring knowledge.[119] According to Régis Debray, going back to this older medium has a very direct consequence: he considers that the twenty-first century is a reversal of the sixteenth century: "The Reformation was the insurrection of the sign against the image: of the insurrection of the sacred word against the statues of saints. Of the insurrection of holy reading by the family or the individual against the holy communion. Today we are experiencing a Counter Reformation of the image against the sign, of music against reading, of audio-visual media against blackboards."[120] Digital reading has reinstated the image at the expense of writing,[121] establishing a new way of reading similar to virtual surfing.[122]

116. Régis Debray, *Transmettre* (Paris: Odile Jacob, 1997), 139, emphasis original.

117. Régis Debray, *Transmettre*, 165; Cavallo and Chartier, eds., *Histoire de la lecture dans le monde occidental*, 36.

118. Siker, *Liquid Scripture*, 68.

119. Bélisle, ed., *Lire dans un monde numérique*, *passim*.

120. Debray, *Cours de médiologie générale*, 365.

121. Jacques Ellul, *Parole humiliée* (Paris: Seuil, 1981), *passim*.

122. Ch. Vanderdorpe, "Quelques questions clés que pose la lecture sur écran," in *Lire dans un monde numérique*, 55.

REMEMBERING THE PAST

Virtuality is an operating mode of the human brain that is capable of projecting a know-how into a tool enabling it to transfer what has been acquired. "The way we relate to virtual objects via screens extends the relationship we have with our virtual psychic selves, just as mechanical tools extend what we can do with our hands and writing with our memory."[123] The transfer of knowledge goes along with digitization of the medium, right from the beginning of writing. The basic materials have become lighter and smaller by getting rid of stone and using clay, papyrus, skin, paper, and then the virtual page. It is the same with writing, which has seen the number of its characters being reduced first with picture writing, then syllabic symbols, and eventually alphabetical characters before being encrypted in binary code. This digitization has enabled writing to become more abundantly mobile and autonomous and to end up evaporating into the *cloud* of the digital space, with the new motto *volant scripta*. The content has become so independent from the receptacle that it is possible to start reading a text on one medium and to continue reading it on another one somewhere else. This process of digitization characterizes our society in which what is intangible controls access to knowledge and transforms the buyer into a user.[124] This change can also be seen in churches where the use of the overhead projector and then the video projector have made hymnals disappear, and the smartphone has caused the paper Bible to be put in storage and to replace it with an application navigating between Scylla and Charybdis.

Régis Debray, in his course on mediology, feared that in the twenty-first century the finger pointing to the moon would be more important than the moon itself.[125] The smartphone screen, by showing only a limited number of verses, hides the forest of books contained in the Bible. The codex, which had been the case enclosing inspired Scriptures, is reduced to a screen, a skylight window looking out on a space with no frame or limits. In other words, without a frame such as context or paratext, the reader cannot situate the extract being read. Web pages are just like the pages of the medieval[126] *Biblia pauperum* (a book containing biblical pictures that are commented upon, often in vernacular language). In both cases, the image provides the context enabling the interpretation of the text. Roger Chartier sums up the situation by declaring:

123. S. Tisseron, *Rêver, fantasmer, virtualiser. Du virtuel psychique au virtuel numérique* (Paris: Dunod, 2012), 12.

124. A. Gorz, *L'Immatériel. Connaissance, valeur et capital* (Paris: Galilée, 2003), 60.

125. Debray, *Cours de médiologie générale*, 33.

126. Adam, "Interpreting the Bible at the Horizon of Virtual New Worlds," 172.

"In the digital world, all textual entities are like databases which offer units of text without any reference to the overall picture within a piece of work or of the corpus it comes from."[127] Copyright, hard won in regard to the printing press, is devalued with the web, and so the authority of the written word fritters away due to the defragmentation of texts posted online, unravelling what the codex had weaved.

THE BOOK AS A SIGN

Several decades were necessary before the impact of the codex and the printing press produced a change in society. But within only a few years the digital revolution has transformed western society by rehabilitating a new orality that had progressively disappeared while disparaging writing. Since its invention, writing had never succeeded in catching up with the immediacy of speech, which it came from, in spite of the constant progress of materials and of writing. "While science makes quick progress, the printing press is not capable (in spite of all the processes that have been set up to reduce its "slowness") of reporting developments in knowledge within a reasonable (i.e. short) time-scale."[128] The rapidity of the digital world seems to be able to close the gap by rehabilitating the sort of orality that Walter Ong calls a "second" wave.[129] The new reading habits seem therefore to be bringing us back to the initial practices of reading as Jeffrey Siker points out: "The digitization of the Bible reminds us that the words were not always written, that the message of the Bible has always been delivered in oral form for an aural experience."[130] Back in 1958, after emphasising the oral dimension of twelfth-century literature, Lucien Febvre wrote: "It seems . . . that today these new means of unwritten dissemination of thought such as films, and especially radio broadcasting, should help us to better understand what the transmission of works and ideas which are not following the usual pattern of the written text can mean for millions of individuals."[131]

As a conclusion, we should remember that what unites biblical texts together is not the book. Our Bible is just the reconfiguration of a text from which come families of papyri, codices, translations, and quotations that were copied and

127. R. Chartier, "La mort du livre?," *Communication and Languages* 159, no. 1 (2009): 62.

128. Waquet, Parler comme un livre, 366.

129. Ong, *Orality and Literacy*, 3; R. M. Fowler, "Why Everything We Know about the Bible Is Wrong," in *The Bible in Ancient and Modern Media*, 14.

130. Siker, *Liquid Scripture*, 245.

131. L. Febvre and H.-J Martin, *L'apparition du livre* (Paris: Albin Michel, 1971), 54.

transmitted by the church through the centuries before becoming a fixed form via the printing press.[132] What unites biblical texts is Christ, "the Word made flesh" (John 1).[133] The medium used by God to spread his Word was the incarnation (Heb 1:1–2). After the ascension, the Word continued to be passed on using the principle of mediation. The Word was translated into the language understood by the listener. This was how the church was born on the day of Pentecost when the cosmopolitan crowd heard for the first time the message of salvation in keeping with the diversity of mother tongues present (Acts 2). It was also in this way that the church could be reformed in the sixteenth century when the Bible was transcribed into the vernacular languages of the emerging nations. Jesus is the preferential medium, he alone maintains the unity of the books of the Bible. "The first Christian writers, and the New Testament itself, saw that the unity of the Bible was to be founded on the uniqueness of the 'referent.'"[134] Christ is the common denominator of the law and the prophets (Luke 24:25–27; Acts 8:34–35). As referent, he is also the one who explains that the Scriptures refer to him; he imparts their full meaning on the Scriptures (Luke 4:18–21). The semiologist Louis Panier states: "Christ is the *reference* and the *reader* of the Scriptures in that he 'incarnates' the word that the letter of the Scriptures preserves."[135]

The printed book, a legacy of the codex, makes this unity tangible. Just as water holds symbolic value[136] for baptism and the bread and the wine for communion, a copy of the Scriptures makes visible the invisible reality to which it refers: the Word of God. After the invention of the printing press, the Reformation set the pulpit above the communion table, highlighting the centrality of the Word. On this communion table was placed an open Bible embodying immediate access to the Word. Treatises on homiletics still stress today the importance for the preacher to have a printed copy available while delivering a sermon.[137] To transmit and to assert its identity, a service in the synagogue maintains the use of hand-written scrolls when reading the Torah. It is therefore possible to preserve the use of an obsolete medium in spite of the supremacy of a trendy medium. To set itself apart from Judaism, early Christianity copied the scrolls of

132. Siker, *Liquid Scripture*, 138; Fowler, "Why Everything We Know about the Bible Is Wrong," 11.

133. Adam, "Interpreting the Bible at the Horizon of Virtual New Worlds," 164.

134. L. Panier, "De la sacralisation à la lecture: une approche énonciative de la Bible," *Topicos des Seminario. Revista de semiotica* 22 (2009): 53–74.

135. Panier, "De la sacralisation à la lecture: une approche énonciative de la Bible," 9.

136. P. Zumthor, *Performance, réception, lecture* (Longueuil: Le Préambule, 1990).

137. For professor Quentin Craddock, "The Bible is more than a string of words written on pages, it's a symbol of authority and inspiration. Reading Scripture passages from a piece of paper, even if the quotation is perfectly correct, does not have the same impact on the listener." Craddock, *Prêcher* (Genève: Labor et Fides, 1991), 215.

the First Testament on to codices.[138] In a digital, paperless world,[139] which is continually preaching in favour of dematerialisation, keeping and using a copy of the Scriptures in the format handed down from the codex will have the same value as identity papers, reminding us that the Word was made flesh and that we follow in the footsteps of those who have transmitted it over the centuries.

FOR FURTHER READING

Botha, Pieter J. J. *Orality and Literacy in Early Christianity*. Eugene, OR: Cascade, 2012.

Citton Yves. *L'avenir des humanités. Économie de la connaissance ou cultures de l'interprétation?* Paris: La Découverte, 2010.

Debray, Régis. *Media Manifestos: On the Technological Transmission of Cultural Forms*. Translated by Eric Rauth. London: Verso, 1996.

Ellul, Jacques. *The Humiliation of the Word*. Eugene, OR: Wipf and Stock, 2021.

Gamble, Harry Y. *Books and Readers in the Early Church: A History of Early Christian Texts*. New Haven, CT: Yale University Press, 1995.

Hearon, Holly E. and Philip Ruge-Jones, eds. *The Bible in Ancient and Modern Media*. Eugene, OR: Cascade, 2009.

Hurtado, Larry W. *The Earliest Christian Artifacts. Manuscripts and Christian Origins*. Grand Rapids: Eerdmans, 2006.

Ong, Walter J. *The Presence of the Word: Some Prolegomena for Cultural and Religious History*. New Haven, CT: Yale University Press, 1967.

Ong, W. J. *Orality and Literacy: The Technologizing of the Word*. New York: Routledge, 1982.

Siker, Jeffrey S. *Liquid Scripture: The Bible in a Digital World*. Minneapolis: Fortress, 2017.

Soukup, Paul A. and Robert Hodgson, eds. *From one Medium to Another: Basis Issues for Communicating the Scriptures in New Media*. Kansas City: Sheed & Ward, 1997.

Vanderdorpe, Christian. *Du papyrus à l'hypertexte: essai sur les mutations du texte et de la lecture*. Paris: La Découverte, 1999.

Wolton, Dominique. *Informer n'est pas communiquer*. Paris: CNRS éditions, 2009.

Young, Frances. *Biblical Exegesis and the Formation of Christian Culture*. Peabody, MA: Hendrickson, 2002.

---

138. Roberts and Skeat, *The Birth of the Codex*, 45.

139. Claudine Dardie, in her article, "L'identité papier," writes, "Recording in writing is not just a metaphor. If your name isn't on the paper, you are 'marginal' – a status which is specific to written culture which defines margins and deprives of their very existence anyone who is on the margins of society. Each one of us has to daily prove their existence by their 'papers'" (*Cahiers de médiologie* 4, Pouvoirs du papier [1997]: 226).

CHAPTER 13

Reading the Bible in the Context of Christianity Worldwide

Benno van den Toren

The twentieth and early twenty-first century has seen a dramatic shift of the point of gravity of Christianity to the Global South. In 1900, 82 percent of the world's Christians lived in Europe and North America; in 2020, 67 percent of the world's Christians live in Africa, Latin America, and Asia. The shift is projected to continue. The Center for the Study of Global Christianity at Gordon-Conwell Theological Seminary estimates that by the middle of this century only 22 percent of the world's Christians will live in Europe and North America.[1] This shift is not only numerical in nature, but it has also changed the most characteristic expressions of Christianity. One might say that Christianity in the global north has for centuries been struggling either to adapt or react to the Enlightenment and modernity, either by modernizing the religion, by maintaining traditional enclaves, or by combining modern expressions with traditional theology. In the global south, cultures have not been influenced in the same way by Western modernity and are lived in contexts where often the supernatural world is experienced as a powerful reality. Churches are charismatic and vibrant. The challenges of these Christian communities are not primarily about how to find a place in a secularizing world. Churches in the global south are often more concerned with how to relate the Christian faith to poverty and corruption,

1. G. A. Zurlo, T. M. Johnson, and P. F. Crossing, 'World Christianity and Mission 2020: Ongoing Shift to the Global South," *International Bulletin of Mission Research* 44, no. 1 (2020): 8–19.

to illness and demon possession, to traditional cultural and religious practices, and to other religious communities such as Islam and Hinduism.[2] As Europe became post-Christian, Christianity became post-Western.[3]

These changes in the makeup of Christianity worldwide have also changed how the Bible is interpreted. The Bible has of course always been interpreted in different contexts and traditions. The difference between Eastern Orthodox and Roman Catholic interpretations of the Bible are at least in part related to the different cultural contexts in which they arose. Yet in the self-understanding of both traditions, such differences were not related to context and were rather seen as mutually exclusive formulations of eternal theological truth. Communities in different traditions were often too far away to present a serious intellectual challenge to the culturally homogenous community. Theologians in Africa, Asia, and Latin America in churches that were established by Western mission churches related, however, in a different way to their "mother" churches in the West. They inherited European styles of interpreting the Bible but did not find these appropriate to their own contexts. In their experience, such Western interpretations read the Bible in individualistic and spiritualized ways that did not appropriately respond to the challenges of their contexts of oppression, poverty, and political struggles. They approach the Bible with different questions that arise from their own cultural context. Theirs is not a disenchanted world as in the West but a world in need of healing and deliverance from spiritual oppression. In the West, the fact that the Bible is a Western book originating from a distant past and from the Middle East is often seen as a problem for interpretation, a problem that needs to be overcome by interpretative procedures that bridge this chasm and allow the Bible to be brought into the modern world. In contrast, many Christian communities in the South experience the Bible as a book that speaks directly into their contexts. Various aspects of the culture of biblical times resemble their world more than the West: communication through proverbs and stories, a social life shaped by kinship relations and food laws, experiences of oppression and of illnesses caused by demons. Reading the Bible in the context of these new expressions of Christianity has also permitted new insights into the nature of the Bible as a book that can speak into different social and cultural contexts. Cultural variety and distance are not merely seen as a problem that needs to

2. See, e.g., Philip Jenkins, *The Next Christendom: The Coming of Global Christianity* (New York: Oxford University Press, 2002).

3. The expression is from Andrew F. Walls, *Crossing Cultural Frontiers: Studies in the History of World Christianity*, ed. Mark R. Gornik (Maryknoll, NY: Orbis, 2017), 263.

be overcome. According to Christians, part of the nature of what the Bible is and how God speaks through it is that it can incarnate again and again in new cultural contexts and garbs.

In this chapter, we will explore how the reading of the Bible in these new contexts of Christianity worldwide has contributed to understanding the Bible, what it is, and how it speaks. We will start with an exploration of Bible translation. Bible translation is in fact the fundamental form of cross-cultural interpretation of the Bible, a form that has been present from the very beginning of the history of the church. In the middle section, we will give an overview of a range of interpretative methods that over the last decades have been developed in Christian communities across the globe. In the final section, we will draw some lessons for what this means for the role of the Bible today in the context of a global Christianity and in view of the many particular contexts in which people live with this book. In the process, Western biblical interpretation needs to be recognised as a culturally located phenomenon shaped by the particular context of Western modernity and later modernity. Western interpretation can no longer be considered the norm to help everyone everywhere. That recognition can also help Westerners like myself, for it relativizes some of the problems with which the Western church since the beginning of modernity has been struggling with in its reading of the Bible.

BIBLE TRANSLATION

BIBLE TRANSLATION AS INTERPRETATION

The growing recognition in the twentieth century of the great cultural variety of expressions of Christianity has made us more aware how the interpretation of the Bible is always coloured by the different cultural and social contexts in which the Bible is read. This cultural variety is however not a new phenomenon, but has been a reality in the Christian community from its earliest beginnings. One area in which this has been visible is Bible translation. The New Testament itself is already written in Hellenistic Greek, different from the Galilean Aramaic dialect that Jesus of Nazareth spoke, and it often uses the Septuagint translation when referring to the Hebrew Bible. In the early centuries of the church, Christian travellers and missionaries crossed many cultural and linguistic boundaries, and in the process, they produced new translations in, for example, Syriac, Latin, Coptic, and Armenian.

Theologians like Andrew Walls and Kwame Bediako have therefore called the history both of Christianity and of mission a continuous translation process.[4] With this expression, they not only refer to the activity of translating from one language to another. The process of linguistic translation is seen as both an example of and metaphor for the wider inculturation process. Each time the message is translated in a new language, it takes on a new cultural colour, and each time Christianity is introduced in new cultural contexts, it takes on new forms beyond this change in language: new liturgical expressions, new ways of organizing community life, new ways of understanding the meaning of Jesus.[5]

Lamin Sanneh, a Gambian theologian, has pointed to the New Testament story of Pentecost as both the starting point, symbolic expression and theological justification of this ongoing translation process.[6] According to Acts of the Apostles, seven weeks after the death and resurrection of Jesus Christ, his followers were together on the Jewish feast of Pentecost. On that day they received the gift of the Holy Spirit as the powerful and renewing presence of God himself, one of the gifts the Hebrew Bible promised for the time at the end of history. One of the signs of the presence of this Spirit was a linguistic phenomenon. Under the influence of the Holy Spirit, the followers of Jesus started proclaiming what God had done through Jesus Christ to save humanity. The many pilgrims who had come to Jerusalem from different regions of the known world all heard the followers of Jesus speak in their own languages. It was not the case that they could all miraculously understand the same language, be it Aramaic or Greek. Instead, they heard the message in the languages of the various regions in which they lived. This was not necessary for understanding what was going on. As travellers, they would have been able to understand the trade-languages of the time: Greek, Aramaic, or both. It was therefore a symbolic event, expressing that from now on, the message of and about Jesus Christ could be communicated in every language and that in the process it could therefore be expressed in ever new cultural forms.

THREE DYNAMICS IN THE TRANSLATION PROCESS

As indicated, biblical translation can be seen as an example and model for the cross-cultural movement of the Christian message and for cross-cultural

4. Andrew F. Walls, *The Missionary Movement in Christian History: Studies in the Transmission of Faith* (Maryknoll, NY: Orbis, 1996), 26–42; Kwame Bediako, *Christianity in Africa: The Renewal of a Non-Western Religion* (Maryknoll, NY: Orbis, 1995), 109–25.

5. See for the use of translation as a model for contextualisation and contextual interpretation: Stephen B. Bevans, *Models of Contextual Theology* (Maryknoll, NY: Orbis, 1992), 37–53. Note, however, that Bevans uses *translation* for a more restricted understanding of the contextualisation process than Walls, Bediako, and others; see Benno van den Toren and Liz Hoare, "Evangelicals and Contextual Theology: Lessons from Missiology for Theological Reflection," *Practical Theology* 8, no. 2 (2015): 90–91 [77–98].

6. Lamin O. Sanneh, *Translating the Message: The Missionary Impact on Culture* (Maryknoll, NY: Orbis, 1989), 211–38.

biblical interpretation. Translation is a complex process, and there are at least three different dynamics that each throw light on what this process contributes to the understanding of the nature of the Bible and its interpretation.

The first dynamic is that as the Bible is translated, the message itself takes on new meanings. This movement is already visible in the New Testament itself. In the earliest Christian communities, Jesus of Nazareth was understood to be the *Messiah*, the anointed king and liberator promised in the Hebrew Bible. For the Greek speaking readers of the New Testament, the word *Messiah* did not however have the same existential weight and might not even have been understood. *Messiah*, or the Greek translation *Christos*, therefore, virtually becomes a second name for Jesus, and the title *Kurios*, or Lord, becomes more prominent. Though this term also appears in the Septuagint translation of the Hebrew Bible, it takes on different meanings related to the connotations and expectations attached to the title in the Hellenistic world. Now Jesus as *kurios* is compared to and also becomes a competitor of the Roman emperor who also claimed the same title. The message of Jesus challenged the existing power of the Roman empire in a way it could never have done if it would only have been proclaimed in a minority language using the title *Messiah*, which for many would have been virtually meaningless.[7]

In the translation process, many questions of interpretation become unavoidable. When one, for example, needs to translate the word *theos*, or God, one needs to ask if a term in the receptor language and culture has significant overlap with the biblical term. In European languages of Northern Europe, translators have often used generic terms for *God* such as *theos* as translation of the Hebrew *Elohim*, and other terms like *deus*, or *Gott*. In African languages, translators have often not chosen generic names but the proper name of the high God, such as *Komba*, *Imana*, or *Akongo*.[8] In China, the question of how to translate the word *God* has deeply divided Christian communities based on different appreciations of existing Chinese religions.[9] In Malaysia, the question has become politically charged as a Muslim government forbid the use of the word *Allah* in translations of the Christian Bible because it was supposed to refer to the God of the Qur'an only.

---

7. Daniel Allmen, "The Birth of Theology: Contextualization as the Dynamic Element in the Formation of New Testament Theology," *International Review of Mission* 64, no. 253 (1975): 37–55; cf. Kwame Bediako, "How Is Jesus Christ Lord? Aspects of an Evangelical Christian Apologetics in the Context of African Religious Pluralism," *Exchange* 25, no. 1 (1996): 27–42.

8. Kwame Bediako, *Theology and Identity: The Impact of Culture upon Christian Thought in the Second Century and in Modern Africa* (Oxford: Regnum, 1992), 291.

9. Cf. Archie C. C. Lee, "Scriptural Translations and Cross-Textual Hermeneutics," in *The Oxford Handbook of Christianity in Asia*, ed. Felix Wilfred (New York: Oxford University Press, 2014), 121–33.

In the translation process, the biblical words therefore take on new connotations that are linked to the words in the receptor languages and cultures. There is, however, also a second reverse dynamic that the meaning of the words in the receptor language is changed in relation to the realities they are now used to describe. When Jesus was called *kurios* in Greek, the term took on new meanings because Jesus now became the model of true lordship. My family lived for eight years in the Central African Republic, where the biblical title *kurios* was in turn translated into Sango, the national trade language, as *kota gbia*, or "great chief." In the first dynamic described above, this meant that Jesus was understood in terms of what people expected from a traditional chief. But in the reverse direction of the second dynamic, *kota gbia* took on new meanings when applied to Jesus. Before that no one could have imagined a chief that would be so powerful that he could conquer death. Neither could one imagine a chief who would conquer through the acceptance of a shameful death for his people. The interpretation of the Bible in a new language therefore also leads to changes in how this receptor language functions and leads to new understandings in the receptor culture. It brings to light that the greatest chiefs still had important limitations compared to the lordship of Jesus Christ. It also brings to light that their authority was exercised through overpowering others, which might at the same time be a sign of their weakness when compared to a Lord reigning from the cross.

A third dynamic in the translation process is that in the process the meaning of Christ actually grows. In the words of Andrew Walls:

> The process [of cross-cultural transmission of the Gospel from its Jewish origins to a Greek context] was hugely enriching; it proved to be a discovery of Christ. As Paul and his fellow missionaries explain and translate the significance of the Christ in a world that is Gentile and Hellenistic, that significance is seen to be greater than anyone had realized before. It is as though Christ himself actually grows through the work of mission. . . . It is surely right to see the process as being repeated in subsequent transmissions of the faith across cultural lines.[10]

Where the first dynamic points to that fact that in the translation process, the Christian message takes on different meanings, this third dynamic states that through the processes of translation, the meaning of Christ *grows* because what God has done through him is explained in ever new contexts and

10. Walls, *The Missionary Movement in Christian History*, xvii.

situations. Christ is understood to be not only Messiah but also lord, *heliand*, *sadguru*, elder brother, proto-ancestor, and whatever locally appropriate terms have been used to translate his meaning in new contexts. *This* may be thought of as an accumulation of new meanings that are *given to* the story of Jesus of Nazareth. Christians themselves, however, believe that in Jesus of Nazareth God himself was active for the salvation of humanity and the world. If so, in the process new aspects of what this salvation entails come to the fore. New meanings are therefore not only attributed to Christ; new meanings are also *discovered*.

TRANSLATION AND THE NATURE OF THE BIBLE AS WORD OF GOD

In the first contribution to this volume, Kevin Vanhoozer argues that the nature of the Bible as the Word of God should not in the first place be decided on the basis of a general understanding of the holy books of different religious traditions. To understand what the Bible is, one needs to look into the self-understanding of the Bible and into the place the Bible has in the Christian faith.[11] In this line of thought, the translation of the words of Jesus in the New Testament and the continuing history of Christian mission as a history of translation also point to specific characteristics of the Christian understandings of the Word of God in comparison to other religious traditions.

Sanneh, himself a former Muslim, has pointed out that the translatability of the Christian Bible contrasts with the Qur'an. In traditional Islam, the Arabic Qur'an is understood to have been eternally with God. It is the Word of God only in Arabic and needs to be read and recited in that language. Translations of the Qur'an can no longer be considered the Word of God but are only aids to its interpretation. In practice Islam also takes on different shapes in different receptor cultures so that we now have not only Arabic Islam but also Turkish, Urdu, Indonesian, and many other expressions of Islam. In principle, however, Islamisation according to Sanneh always needs to lead to Arabization of the receptor cultures. This means that the message does not so much incarnate itself in new cultural forms but that it assimilates new cultural communities to itself. This is different from the Christian understanding of the Word of God that can take on ever new cultural forms.[12] Because of this characteristic of Christianity, Sanneh also believes that mission in Africa was not only a Western colonizing movement. By translating the Bible in local African languages, it allowed these cultures to develop their proper languages, their proper identities and their

11. See Kevin Vanhoozer, "The Bible – Word of God?" which is chapter 1 in this volume.
12. Sanneh, *Translating the Message*, 211–16.

proper interpretations of Christianity as alternatives for the western culture and Christianity imported by the colonizers.[13]

Walls points to a contrasting difference with scriptures in oriental religions such as Hinduism. In Hinduism, the divine is in principle mysterious and ineffable. Christianity does not share the same notion of the incomprehensibility of God. It understands the incomprehensibility of God primarily as a characteristic of God's greatness that can never be captured by the human mind. Yet this does not prevent God from making himself truly known in God's revelation in Jesus Christ, which allows trustworthy human knowledge of God, even if this knowledge is far from exhaustive. If God remains in principle completely mysterious to the human mind, as in Hinduism, then all linguistic expressions remain symbolic and point to a reality that never can be expressed adequately. In this case, the translation of such words does not need to be given careful attention because the words themselves do not contribute in a real way to understanding the divine.[14]

The Christian Scriptures therefore understand the idea of the Bible as the Word of God in a way that is different from how Islam on the one hand and Hinduism on the other understand the notion of "sacred scriptures." In comparison to Hindu scriptures, the Christian Bible testifies to a revelation that allows human beings to understand God in human language. Yet the words of the Bible are the Word of God in a secondary sense because they point to God's decisive and primary revelation in Christ. In comparison to the words of the Qur'an, the words of the Bible are not eternal and before time. That is only true of the identity of Jesus as the eternal Son of God. God is believed to speak in the words of the Bible, but with the help of ordinary human words. The Word of God in the Bible is not intrinsically bound to the linguistic forms of a specific language and culture.

CONTEXTUAL HERMENEUTICS

FROM CONTEXTUAL INTERPRETATION TO CONTEXTUAL HERMENEUTICS

The translation process that has characterized the history of the church from its inception shows that the Bible has always been interpreted in relation to a variety of contexts. The dynamics that were part of this process were, however, not themselves part of critical theological reflection. The presupposition often was that how the Bible was read in one's own community is how it should be

13. Sanneh, *Translating the Message*, 232–34.

14. Walls, *The Missionary Movement in Christian History*, 26.

read by everyone, without awareness of the reader's social and cultural location. The awareness of the role of varying cultural locations in interpreting the Bible started developing in the context of mission enterprises in the early modern era. For example, the debates surrounding Jesuit missions in China and India in the late sixteenth and early seventeenth centuries placed the question on the agenda of the church of how far local theological language and church practices could be adapted to fit these cultural contexts.[15]

When the question came up again in the second half of the twentieth century, it took on new dimensions. The question was not merely whether peripheral matters of faith and practice could be "indigenised" or "adapted" to local contexts, while leaving the kernel of the faith intact. The question asked by a new generation of theologians from Latin America, Africa, and Asia was whether one should not recognize that all Christian practice and all readings of the Bible are inevitably shaped by particular social and cultural contexts. If this is the case, the question was not whether a universally normative European reading could be adapted to other cultures that needed a stepping stone before they could fully grasp the normative readings of Thomas Aquinas, Martin Luther, or John Calvin. The European readings were equally local readings. These local readings may even need to be studied with a degree of suspicion: it needed to be asked whether such European readings were themselves shaped and potentially distorted by their specific social and cultural contexts.[16] From now on, cultural and social contexts were no longer allowed to play an undetected and implicit role, as in the translation process that accompanied the church from its inception. The role of context became a focus of critical hermeneutical reflection.

Various contextual hermeneutical approaches are characterized by two different but related features. Each focuses first on a particular aspect of the context that it considers most important. This then corresponds to a second feature: each hermeneutical approach concentrates in its reading of the Bible on a specific aspect of its content.[17] In the early years of contextual theology and hermeneutics, a tension played out between two main approaches that came up regularly in the earlier meetings of the Ecumenical Association of Third World Theologians (EATWOT) in the 1970s and 1980s. On the one hand a group of

---

15. Klaus Koschorke et al., *A History of Christianity in Asia, Africa, and Latin America, 1450–1990: A Documentary Sourcebook* (Grand Rapids: Eerdmans, 2007), 33–38.

16. David Jacobus Bosch, *Transforming Mission: Paradigm Shifts in Theology of Mission* (Maryknoll, NY: Orbis, 1991), 423.

17. I take these two features from Gerald West, who in fact points out three features, with certain corresponding theological or ideological convictions or presuppositions as the third feature. Gerald West, "Biblical Hermeneutics in Africa," in *African Theology on the Way: Current Conversations*, ed. Diane B. Stinton (London: SPCK, 2010), 22. We will discuss this third feature in the concluding section.

theologians focussed on sociopolitical aspects of the context and on the biblical message as a message of liberation. Another stream focussed on cultural and religious aspects of the contexts and sought for the inculturation of the message of the Bible that itself was much more understood in religious and cultural terms.[18]

This early opposition between liberation theologies and intercultural theologies in the circles of the World Council of Churches has later been nuanced with many readings of Scripture trying to integrate elements of each. After all, as the Cameroonian priest Engelbert Mveng remarked, "anthropological poverty" or "cultural poverty" of communities whose cultures are repressed by colonial powers is also a form of poverty, a notion which was later picked up by EATWOT.[19] On the other hand, cultures themselves can have both liberating and oppressive features and what counts as one or the other will itself depend on cultural and religious values. Though these two hermeneutic approaches have been building bridges towards one another, an overview of a great variety of positions suggests that it still is valid to say that one finds, on the one hand, a range of positions that start with a focus on sociopolitical analysis of the context and the Bible and often read cultural and religious issues through this lens. On the other hand, one finds a range of positions that start with cultural and religious differences and that understand sociopolitical differences as an aspect of this broader cultural and religious analysis of both context and the scriptural message.

SOCIOPOLITICAL READINGS

Though the themes circling around liberation had been around for some time in theological discussions, the expression "theology of liberation" was, according to the Peruvian priest and theologian Gustavo Gutiérrez, one of its main representatives, coined in 1968.[20] This theology was shaped by the context of poverty and oppression in Latin America and focussed particularly on stories of liberation within the Bible. The so-called exodus story of Israel's liberation from slavery in Egypt became the central biblical story and the cross and resurrection of Christ was seen as the culmination of this history.[21] From its earliest inception,

---

18. See for e.g., Volker Küster, *Einführung in die Interkulturelle Theologie* (Stuttgart: UTB, 2011), 157f.

19. Engelbert Mveng, "Impoverishment and Liberation: A Theological Approach for Africa and the Third World," in *Paths of African Theology*, ed. Rosino Gibellini (Maryknoll, NY: Orbis, 1994), 154–65; Virginia Fabella and Sergio Torres, eds., 'The Irruption of the Third World: Challenge to Theology – Final Statement of the Fifth EATWOT Conference, New Delhi, August 17–29, 1981," in *Irruption of the Third World: Challenge to Theology; Papers from the Fifth International Conference of the Ecumenical Association of Third World Theologians, August 17–29, 1981, New Delhi, India* (Maryknoll, NY: Orbis, 1983), xl.

20. Gustavo Gutiérrez, *A Theology of Liberation: History, Politics, and Salvation*, 15th anniversary ed. (Maryknoll, NY: Orbis, 1988), xviii.

21. Gilberto da Silva Gorgulho, "Biblical Hermeneutics," in *Mysterium Liberationis: Fundamental Concepts of Liberation Theology*, ed. Ignacio Ellacuría and Jon Sobrino (Maryknoll, NY: Orbis, 1993), 123–50.

liberation theology was not only a theological proposal concerning the content of the Christian message but also a hermeneutical proposal on how the Christian Scriptures should be understood. The Bible needs to be read in the context of the struggle of the poor for their liberation. Action and reflection cannot be separated but need to be dialectically related in a continuing cycle. The main dialogue partners for the understanding of the Bible are no longer philosophy and, with it, the educated critical interlocutor, as in Europe. Amongst the sciences, liberation theologians now prefer the social sciences that allow for a critical understanding of structures of oppression. Amongst the readers the poor are the preferred interlocutors because of God's "preferential option for the poor."

In the process, academic western biblical hermeneutics are also exposed as socially located. These are the readings of academics with generally stable and well-paid positions in society, who are therefore not well placed to understand the revolutionary impact of the biblical message. These are the readings of a church that too often compromises with the powerful and that therefore prefers spiritualized readings of its message. By not challenging the powerful, such academic readings limited to historical questions concerning the origins of the Bible and such spiritual messages of the soul and eternity, are effectively condoning oppression.

Since it originated in Latin America, liberation hermeneutics has been used in many different contexts. Because the analysis of the socio-political contexts plays a major role in this form of biblical interpretation, different varieties read the Bible in relation to these different contexts. So we have Black theology and Hispanic theology in North America, another variety of Black theology in the context of South African apartheid, *Minjung* theology in South Korea, and Dalit theology in India. Feminist readings of the Bible also fall in this broader category because these readings of the Bible also address specific forms of oppression. Feminist thinkers from the South add their own sets of questions. African women, for example, will experience multiple forms of oppression at once, being both African and women. They also have an ambivalent relationship with the inculturation theologies that will be discussed in the next section. The call for the respect for traditional cultural values can after all also be used to maintain traditional patriarchal hierarchies.[22]

The so-called theology and hermeneutics of reconstruction is a specifically African development within the larger stream of liberation theology. After the end of the apartheid era in South Africa and in the light of the realisation that the colonial era in other parts of Africa had already ended for some time, theologians like Jesse Mugambi (Kenya), Kä Mana (Democratic Republic of Congo),

22. See, e.g., Musimbi R. A. Kanyoro, "Reading the Bible from an African Perspective," *Ecumenical Review* 15, no. 1 (1999): 18–24.

and Charles Villa-Vincencio (South Africa) argued that our readings of the Bible now need to move from a focus on liberation to reconstruction. Rather than the story of the Exodus from Egypt, Mugambi uses the biblical stories of Ezra and Nehemiah related to the rebuilding of the nation Israel and the temple of Jerusalem after the Babylonian exile as the biblical paradigm for rebuilding nations and communities today.[23]

Postcolonial hermeneutics has its origin in broader postcolonial literary theory associated with theorists such as Edward Said and Gayatri Spivac. It shares the interest in politics and power with liberation theology, but the focus is less on liberating action motivated by the Bible and more on a critical reading of the Bible itself. These readers see the Bible as a "site of struggle" in which one finds not only resources for the struggle for liberation but also the voices of the powerful that legitimate oppression. The task of hermeneutics is therefore both to unmask such oppressive messages and to unearth the so-called "sub-altern voices" that propose alternative visions of life.[24]

CULTURAL AND INTERRELIGIOUS READINGS

Where liberation hermeneutics and related approaches focus on the sociopolitical aspects both in the context and in the message of the Christian Bible, inculturation hermeneutics focus in context and content on the cultural and religious aspects. Some of the most influential representatives of this approach have developed in Africa south of the Sahara and north of the Limpopo river (the boundary river of South Africa).[25] In this region, the negation of African culture was often experienced as the more pressing issue for biblical interpretation. African Christians and theologians felt that the ways of reading the Bible imported with the missionaries from the North Atlantic world did not fit their cultural framework or their needs. They took a particular issue with the so-called "demythologisation" hermeneutics that claimed that the biblical framework of a world filled with spiritual powers and miracles was mythical and no longer acceptable in the modern world and therefore needed to be "demythologised." The radical form of this approach was associated with the twentieth

---

23. E.g., Jesse N. K. Mugambi, "The Future of the Church and the Church of the Future," in *The Church of Africa: Towards a Theology of Reconstruction*, ed. J. B. Chipenda (Nairobi: All Africa Conference of Churches, 1991), 29–50.

24. E.g., Rasiah S. Sugirtharajah, *Postcolonial Reconfigurations: An Alternative Way of Reading the Bible and Doing Theology* (London: SCM, 2003). For a critical engagement of postcolonial theology, see Benno van den Toren, "The Significance of Postcolonial Thinking for Mission Theology," *Interkulturelle Theologie. Zeitschrift für Missionswissenschaft* 45, no. 2–3 (2019): 210–28.

25. See, e.g., Justin S. Ukpong, "Inculturation Hermeneutics: An African Approach to Biblical Interpretation," in *The Bible in a World Context: An Experiment in Contextual Hermeneutics*, ed. Walter Dietrich and Ulrich Luz (Grand Rapids: Eerdmans, 2002), 17–32.

century German New Testament scholar Rudolph Bultmann.[26] Yet from an African perspective, many other readings of the Bible, be they more orthodox or more liberal, were in fact seen to suffer from the same fault. These Western readings would sometimes explicitly deny, often reinterpret, and often simply neglect the spirit world in the Bible and its many references to supernatural healing and exorcisms, elements that were highly relevant to the African context. This led to a more general interest in the role of culture in biblical interpretation, and a range of studies was produced in which aspects of the biblical message were compared and related to aspects of the African religious and cultural heritage.[27] A number of inculturation-type hermeneutics explicitly establish a link to Bible translation as a paradigm of inculturation. They may use detailed studies of the translation of biblical terms in vernacular languages as a tool for exploring how the biblical message relates to local understandings.[28] Other approaches develop "translation" as a metaphor for the total inculturation process.[29]

A major incentive behind the development of this inculturation hermeneutics was the rise of the so-called African Initiated Churches (AICs) – or parallel developments in other regions of the world such as the Indian Initiated Churches. These were churches started by local church prophets and healers that attracted a significant following because their understanding of the Bible with its focus on spiritual power, healing, and deliverance related more effectively to the worldview and felt needs of the African population.[30] The same can be argued for Pentecostal and neo-Pentecostal churches that are much more critical of African religious traditions than AICs but also express the Christian message in a way much closer to the traditional African worldview than earlier missionaries.[31] A number of the earlier explorations into inculturation hermeneutics were inspired by Bible reading practices in these AICs,[32] not just because they

26. Rudolf Bultmann, "New Testament and Mythology: The Mythological Element in the Message of the New Testament and the Problem of Its Re-Interpretation," in *Kerygma and Myth: A Theological Debate*, ed. Hans Werner Bartsch, trans. Reginald H. Fuller (New York: Harper & Row, 1961), 1–44.

27. E.g., John S. Mbiti, *New Testament Eschatology in an African Background: A Study of the Encounter between New Testament Theology and African Traditional Concepts* (New York: Oxford University Press, 1971).

28. J. E. T. Kuwornu-Adjaottor, "Mother-Tongue Biblical Hermeneutics: A Current Trend in Biblical Studies in Ghana," *Journal of Emerging Trends in Educational Research and Policy Studies* 3, no. 4 (2012): 575–79.

29. E.g., Charles H. Kraft, *Christianity in Culture: A Study in Dynamic Biblical Theologizing in Cross Cultural Perspective*, 25th anniversary ed. (Maryknoll, NY: Orbis, 2005).

30. Allan H. Anderson, "The Hermeneutical Processes of Pentecostal-Type African Initiated Churches in South Africa," *Missionalia* 24, no. 2 (1996): 171–85.

31. So Cephas Omenyo, "Charismatic Churches in Ghana and Contextualization," *Exchange* 31, no. 3 (2002): 252–77.

32. For an early source, see Harold W. Turner, *Profile through Preaching: A Study of the Sermon Texts Used in a West African Independent Church* (London: Edinburgh House Press, 1965); and for its theological

were seen as a challenge to the mission initiated churches that needed a response, but also and primarily because they were seen to point to an inherent weakness of Bible readings inherited from Europe.

The influence of AICs and varieties of Pentecostalism points to a specific characteristic of many types of hermeneutics across the globe: the role of the so-called ordinary reader. In the North Atlantic world, biblical interpretation in general gave great authority to the academic scholar of the Bible; scholarly interpretation was subsequently shared through biblical commentaries with pastors and with the wider Christian community through preaching from the pulpit. Hermeneutical approaches from the global south have in general given more attention to readings of Bible at the grass-roots level. This has been a feature of liberation theology given the privileged epistemological position of the poor as exemplified in the influential stories of shared readings of the priest Ernesto Cardenal from Nicaragua with the poor in Solentiname.[33] This has also led to the development of new forms of contextual Bible reading that consciously bring in a variety of ordinary readers in the process.[34] In AICs and Pentecostal churches, the charismatic leadership take the lead in biblical interpretation with no reference to inherited scholarly interpretations from either Europe or their own regions. This then subsequently raises the question of whether such non-scholarly readings can or should be taken into account in the scholarly reflection on the hermeneutics of the Bible.

WHAT DOES THIS MEAN FOR THE READING OF THE BIBLE?

The worldwide church is rich with a great variety of expressions, and any overview in a few pages will automatically flatten complex and nuanced positions and exclude crucial voices and themes. One major theme left out from this overview is the question of how the Christian Bible is read in contexts where other religious scriptures are also granted authority.[35] Yet it is not the purpose of this contribution to give an exhaustive overview but rather to indicate some of the

---

use John S. Mbiti, "Some African Concepts of Christology," *Christ and the Younger Churches*, ed. Georg F. Vicedom, (London: SPCK, 1972), 51–62.

33. Ernesto Cardenal, *The Gospel in Solentiname*, vol. 1–4 (Maryknoll, NY: Orbis, 1976).

34. E.g., Gerald O. West, "Locating 'Contextual Bible Study' within Biblical Liberation Hermeneutics and Intercultural Biblical Hermeneutics: Original Research," *HTS: Theological Studies* 70, no. 1 (2014): 1–10.

35. R. S. Sugirtharajah, "Inter-Faith Hermeneutics: An Example and Some Implications," in *Voices from the Margin: Interpreting the Bible in the Third World*, ed. R. S. Sugirtharajah (Maryknoll, NY: Orbis, 1991), 352–63; Lee, "Scriptural Translations and Cross-Textual Hermeneutics."

important hermeneutical perspectives on the reading of the Bible that have been developed in Christian communities worldwide in order to explore what this means for the understanding of the Bible in a globalizing world. In this final section, we will draw some more general conclusions from these explorations.

Even this relatively limited overview has shown clearly that different ways of reading the Bible are influenced by contextual differences. We can be more specific and note that they are shaped by a range of different types of contextual factors. The understanding of the Bible is shaped by the language in which the Bible is read, by the sociopolitical context, by power dynamics, by gender, by culturally shaped worldviews, by the presence of other religions and religious texts, and by the institutional context. It is often said that culture is to human beings what water is to a fish: because our life is so intricately bound up with our culture, it is hard to become aware of it. This is equally true for the question of *what* aspect readers of the Bible foreground in their contextual readings: Will they focus on language and culture or on sociopolitical aspects and power dynamics? This is partly contextually shaped: in 1970s Latin America, social inequality felt most pressing, in sub-Saharan Africa the negation of African cultures in a westernized church, and in India the presence of other religions with their own scriptures.

The globalization of biblical hermeneutics has made Bible readers much more aware of the contextual location of their reading. Yet at the same time we need to recognize that much Bible reading, both academic and ordinary, does still have little awareness of what this means for its own understanding of the Bible. This is partly because we all are like the fish in the water: we are so used to the dominant reading habits in our context that we cannot easily distance ourselves from the way they shape us. If Bible readers are working in an academic context, the whole institutional system surrounding them breathes the idea that (Western) academic readings are superior. This is no different when people read the Bible in a globally southern neo-Pentecostal church and believe that academic study has nothing to offer because the Spirit is already given to them. Particularly, if people read the Bible from a position of power (because they belong to a dominant culture, a learned class, the right race and gender), they may easily miss how their position shapes their reading and how they may be both questioned and enriched by other readings. That is why we need to give particular attention to readings of the Bible by people who are more aware of their own context. One can, for example, think of readers who are bi- or multilingual and can move between different languages or even language families, other readers who are bicultural because they have been raised in such environments or because they have extensive life and work experience in different cultural contexts, readers who because of their life experience can more easily develop a sensitivity for the influence of power structures on their reading, or readers who are able to move between the academy and communities of "ordinary readers" and appreciate the specific contributions of both. Such movements between contexts, such intercultural readings, allow people to become aware of their own "ghetto position"[36] and to be enriched by others.

In this overview, we have seen how different hermeneutical approaches first focus on different aspects of the context and how they second and correspondingly draw on different strands of scriptural content and therefore also construct the authority of Bible in different ways. These choices are partly shaped by contextual pressures as we saw above. In some contexts social relations are simply more pressing, while in others cultural diversity, interreligious relations, or academic credibility in a secular university demand most attention. Gerald West points to a third factor that shapes different hermeneutical approaches: what he calls the "ideo-theological orientation" of the reader.[37] This overview shows that fundamental ideological and theological positions indeed shape hermeneutical approaches. Inculturation and liberationist/Black hermeneutics not only differ with regards to the question what aspects of the context are considered to be most pressing. The difference is also determined by a difference in the theological understanding of the nature of the human condition and salvation: Is the human condition primarily determined by a fundamental religious orientation that also has social consequences? Or is the prime issue social and political oppression from which humanity needs to be liberated? Similarly, postcolonial and Pentecostal readings of the Bible are shaped by contrasting appreciations of power: Is power always a negative force that leads to oppression so that the prime task of the reader is to detect how oppressive powers have shaped the text? Or is there a stronger healing and liberating power of God, and is the task of the reader of the Bible therefore to open oneself to the power of the Spirit? Similarly, different hermeneutical approaches in the Western academy are shaped by ideological presuppositions that at times are themselves hotly debated but at other times remain hidden: Should the Bible be studied in the academy just as any other literary document following the secular principle that all public academic endeavour is done – *etsi deus non daretur* ("as if there is no God")? Or does this presupposition itself make it impossible to do justice to this particular document? Should the Bible be studied from a neutral standpoint, or can it only be

36. I have borrowed this term from: Hans de Wit, "Through the Eyes of Another: Objectives and Backgrounds," in *Through the Eyes of Another: Intercultural Reading of the Bible*, ed. Hans de Wit et al. (Elkhart, IN: Institute of Mennonite Studies, 2004), 10, 481.

37. West, "Biblical Hermeneutics in Africa," 22.

properly understood if the reader is fully committed to the struggle for a better world and/or to love God with all one's mind?

In the North Atlantic world, the awareness that the reading of the Bible is shaped by theological and ideological presuppositions can easily lead to the conclusion that the way someone reads the Bible is therefore, in the end, merely a matter of personal choice, taste, historical influences, or environmental pressures. The author of this article does, however, not agree with the idea that the "shape" that the readers perceive in the Bible "is not inherent to scripture, it is ideo-theologically constructed."[38] Both personal choice and environmental pressure play a significant role in shaping how people read the Bible. One can indeed draw on certain phenomena if one wants to argue that the theological meaning people give to the Bible is given by the readers rather than drawn from the text itself. The study of contextual Bible readings does of course provide much material to support this thesis. Bible readings from the church worldwide point, however, also in a different direction. I would want to venture the thesis that most of the ways of reading the Bible in the global south – and equally among most "ordinary readers" in the north – presuppose that in reading the Bible the reader encounters a God who speaks, who addresses the reader. This message is experienced as an authoritative divine address that is able to break through human preconceptions about who God is and how God acts and saves. This is also how the Bible presents itself to the reader. It is also presupposed in most of the hermeneutical proposals from the worldwide church discussed above. In an intercultural conversation, the question needs to be asked: Which cultural pressures may have led to the specifically Western approach that excludes the theological and ideological positions themselves that shape the readings of the Bible and the theological content of the Bible from critical conversation? Historical studies do indeed suggest that specific historical and cultural pressures in Western modernity have led scholars to see theological positions as entirely subjective, belonging to the private sphere rather than public debate and as outside the proper realm of the secular university.[39] Intercultural comparisons of ways of reading the Bible across the globe therefore also relativize the Western tendency that relativizes every theological position as a private matter of personal taste. It invites us to take the idea that the Bible might be a book that contains a message that speaks with authority in a variety of cultural settings much more seriously than seems plausible from a Western perspective.

Our overview of biblical interpretation and hermeneutics has revealed

38. West, "Locating 'Contextual Bible Study,'" 6.

39. See, e.g., Brad S. Gregory, *The Unintended Reformation: How a Religious Revolution Secularized Society* (Cambridge, MA: Belknap, 2012).

the crucial role of the context in the hermeneutical enterprise. The interaction between different cultural positions, as it is exemplified in this chapter, underlines the fact that readers are never completely imprisoned in their context and contextual readings but can critically engage with readings from other contexts. This suggests that intercultural interaction with other reading communities across the globe is a value that needs to be nurtured so that readers can be enriched by readings from other contexts and can also be helped to become critically aware of how their own cultural location is not only an asset but a hindrance to understanding the specific message of this book. In reading the Bible as a European with Central African friends, we all became more deeply aware how deeply our cultural preunderstandings shaped our readings. Yet in the process the Bible could also begin to speak in new ways. I discovered much more about the important value of communal existence in the Bible, and in the same exchange, my friends could be pointed to the fact that the Bible itself is at the origin of the great respect for the individual, who is placed before God even if this sets her apart from the community to which she belongs.

De Wit therefore rightly presents "nonexclusion" and "willingness to interact" as two normative criteria for the reading of the Bible in a globalizing environment.[40] In the words of Robert Schreiter, we need to develop a "new catholicity." The theological term *catholicity* does not merely point to the Roman Catholic church. It is a qualitative term describing the nature of the Christian church: that the gospel of Jesus Christ represents the truth for all humanity and that the church therefore intends to share its message to all. If, as we have seen, context is such a decisive factor in the reading of the Bible, readings can only claim to be catholic and universal in scope if they are in principle open to draw on insights from the great cultural variety of the church worldwide.

Beyond de Wit's criteria and beyond the need to read to each other, readers will also need to be attentive to the message of the Bible itself. Using an image from the cognitive sciences, we can speak of the need for "joint attention."[41] Together we are attentive to the Bible. Listening to one another in a worldwide community of readers, we can become more aware of the particular nature of this book and its message, both in its specificity and in the inexhaustible variety of meanings it contains and of the many ways it speaks to humanity. If reading in the church worldwide is characterized by such "joint attention," this may also help to give the Bible itself a voice. Next to what we might call the "catholic principle," we need what may be called the "canonical principle" that allows the

40. De Wit, "Intercultural Bible Reading and Hermeneutics," 477–79.

41. Cf. Benno van den Toren, "Intercultural Theology as a Three-Way Conversation: Beyond the Western Dominance of Intercultural Theology," *Exchange* 44 (2015): 142.

Bible to speak for itself. This principle is given with the content of the Bible that presents the story of Jesus Christ as the story that once and for all changed the course of human history.[42] Precisely because of that characteristic, it speaks to and into every culture and context throughout time and space.

FOR FURTHER READING

Anderson, Allan H. "The Hermeneutical Processes of Pentecostal-Type African Initiated Churches in South Africa." *Missionalia* 24, no. 2 (1996): 171–85.

Gorgulho, Gilberto da Silva. "Biblical Hermeneutics." In *Mysterium Liberationis: Fundamental Concepts of Liberation Theology*, edited by Ignacio Ellacuría and Jon Sobrino, 123–50. Maryknoll, NY: Orbis, 1993.

Sanneh, Lamin O. *Translating the Message: The Missionary Impact on Culture*. Maryknoll, NY: Orbis, 1989.

Sugirtharajah, Rasiah S. *Postcolonial Reconfigurations: An Alternative Way of Reading the Bible and Doing Theology*. London: SCM, 2003.

Ukpong, Justin S. "Inculturation Hermeneutics: An African Approach to Biblical Interpretation." In *The Bible in a World Context: An Experiment in Contextual Hermeneutics*, edited by Walter Dietrich and Ulrich Luz, 17–32. Grand Rapids: Eerdmans, 2002.

van den Toren, Benno, Elizabeth W. Mburu, and Samuel K. Bussey. "Biblical Hermeneutics." In *The Bibliographical Encyclopaedia of African Theology*, January 2021. https://african.theologyworldwide.com/encyclopaedia-bible-in-africa/biblical-hermeneutics.

Walls, Andrew F. "The Translation Principle in Christian History." In *The Missionary Movement in Christian History: Studies in the Transmission of Faith*, 26–42. Maryknoll, NY: Orbis, 1996.

42. Kevin J. Vanhoozer, '"One Rule to Rule Them All?" Theological Method in an Era of World Christianity', in *Globalizing Theology: Belief and Practice in an Era of World Christianity*, ed. Craig Ott and Harold A. Netland (Grand Rapids, Michigan: Baker Academic, 2007), 112f.

Postscript

Craig G. Bartholomew

This volume is the third in KLC's new Scripture Collective Series with Zondervan Academic. The first two are *The Scripture and Hermeneutics Seminar: Retrospect and Prospect* and *Divine Action in Hebrews*. The first was published on the occasion of the twenty-fifth anniversary of the Scripture and Hermeneutics Seminar in 2022 and reminds us that this series and the work it embodies have a history.

Some twenty-five years ago now, we convened, in partnership with British and Foreign Bible Society, a consultation of scholars in Cheltenham, UK, to discuss the relationship between speech act theory and biblical interpretation. Three of the authors in this volume were present at that event – namely, Anthony Thiselton, Kevin Vanhoozer, and Craig Bartholomew. At the end of the consultation, we held a discussion on what needed to be attended to if our work was to contribute towards a renewal of biblical interpretation. We identified eight areas calling for attention and mapped out an eight-year process with an international consultation to be held each year. The result of this rich process, drawing in many of the top Christian scholars in the world, resulted in our eight volume Scripture and Hermeneutics Series, published by Paternoster and Zondervan Academic. The series is as follows:

- Vol. 1: *Renewing Biblical Interpretation* (2000)
- Vol. 2: *After Pentecost: Language and Biblical Interpretation* (2001)
- Vol. 3: *A Royal Priesthood? The Use of the Bible Ethically and Politically: A Dialogue with Oliver O'Donovan* (2002)
- Vol. 4: *"Behind" the Text: History and Biblical Interpretation* (2003)
- Vol. 5: *Out of Egypt: Biblical Theology and Biblical Interpretation* (2004)
- Vol. 6: *Reading Luke: Interpretation, Reflection, Formation* (2005)

- Vol. 7: *Canon and Biblical Interpretation* (2006)
- Vol. 8: *The Bible and the University* (2007)

This original series remains in print with Zondervan Academic, and one of our goals with the new series is to continue to promote the ongoing reception of the rich content in the eight volumes. After the conclusion of our nine-year process of consultations, the Scripture and Hermeneutics Seminar continued to meet each year around the annual Society of Biblical Literature meeting. We continued to publish, namely Craig G. Bartholomew and David J. H. Beldman, eds., *Hearing the Old Testament: Listening for God's Address* (Grand Rapids: Eerdmans, 2012), and Craig G. Bartholomew and Heath A. Thomas, eds., *A Manifesto for Theological Interpretation* (Grand Rapids: Baker Academic 2016).[1]

Over time, the Scripture and Hermeneutics Seminar (SAHS) differentiated into four seminars, namely SAHS, the Scripture and Doctrine Seminar – out of whose work emerged *Divine Action in Hebrews*, the Scripture and Church Seminar (practical theology), and the Scripture and University Seminar. With the establishment of the Kirby Laing Centre in 2021, all four seminars became an integral and central part of our work under the name of our Scripture Collective, now directed by David Larsen (https://kirbylaingcentre.co.uk/scripture-collective/).

Renewing biblical interpretation is an ongoing and immense challenge, and our new Scripture Collective Series with Zondervan Academic is a marvellous opportunity in this respect. Lydia has written eloquently in the preface about the Bible as the bestseller of all time and the myriad languages into which it has been translated. Translation is one huge thing,[2] deep engagement with the Bible another. In relation to the latter, during our original nine consultations, Philip Jenkins was busy publishing his seminal works on the shift in the centre of Christianity to the majority world.[3] We recognise in *The Scripture and Hermeneutics Seminar: Retrospect and Prospect*, that this is a development we need to take far more seriously, and it is the topic addressed by Benno van den Toren in his chapter in this volume.

Reading the Bible with the global church is easier said than done. When

---

1. The actual manifesto can be found online here: https://kirbylaingcentre.co.uk/wp-content/uploads/2021/09/BartholomewThomas_ManifestoInterpretation_Ch1Manifesto.pdf.

2. See Lamin Sanneh, *Translating the Message: The Missionary Impact on Culture*, 2nd ed. (Maryknoll, NY: Orbis, 2009).

3. Philip Jenkins, *The Next Christendom: The Coming of Global Christianity*, 3rd ed. (Oxford: Oxford University Press, 2011); *The New Faces of Christianity: Believing the Bible in the Global South* (New York: Oxford University Press, 2006).

I returned to Cambridge from some fifteen years in North America, I discovered in my research that there were books published by UK authors that I was unaware of, and in the UK we were often unaware of books published in North America. And this despite the imperialism of English in which both contexts shared. Here in the UK, Europe with its vast academic riches and traditions is right on our doorstep, and yet far too often we remain unengaged with one another. Language is a barrier but a poor excuse when European scholars, unlike so many of us English scholars, are commonly fluent in several languages including English. Surely an important way to begin reading the Bible with the global church is to start with one's geographical neighbours. I have long been aware of the depth and rigour of European scholarship, and thus it is a delight to have as our third volume in this series an updated version of a book originally published in French. It includes prominent American and British authors, but most of the authors are European, mainly French speaking, and thus the volume provides a wonderful window into the rigour and riches of French European scholarship.

Régis Debray, a French author to whom I was delightfully introduced by Philipe de Pol's profound chapter in this book, notes: "A civilization also means windows and ventilators, missionaries and merchants. Marco Polo, taking the silk Road, blew a little Italian air into the Mongol Empire, and a little of the air of Asia into Pisa *intra muros*."[4] A renewal of biblical interpretation requires just such windows and ventilators, and in this volume one gets a taste of how helpful it is for some French air to blow into the English world of biblical interpretation! KLC is deeply committed to building relationships across Europe, and our hope is that this volume is a signpost on that journey.

Each era presents its opportunities and challenges for biblical interpretation. During our original nine years of consultations, for example, postmodernism spread like wildfire in the academy, and one simply could not – and should not – ignore it. In her preface, Lydia foregrounds the centrality of *epistemological* questions in the planning of this volume. She is right to do so. Whereas in the Middle Ages, ontology – the nature of reality – generally took precedence over epistemology, in modernity epistemology has moved front and centre, not least because of modernity's stress on human autonomy. As an example of this, it seems appropriate to invoke the French philosopher René Descartes. In his quest for certainty he sought to doubt everything until he found – or so he thought – solid ground on *cogito ergo sum* (I think, therefore I am). Descartes seeks to (re)build his philosophy from this epistemological point.

---

4. Régis Debray, *Civilization: How We All Became American*, trans. David Fernbach (London: Verso, 2019), 1.

I define epistemology as *how to go about knowing something so that we can trust the results of the knowing process*. Clearly, all academic interpretation of the Bible will assume some epistemology, albeit unconsciously. And we know that in our modern era epistemological issues are complex and contested. They yield a huge variety of challenges for biblical interpretation, and the genius of this volume is to show in a variety of ways the challenges and how we might understand and respond to them.

In a postscript of this nature, I cannot begin to engage with all the chapters in this volume. Suffice it to foreground some key issues and their connection with the work of our Scripture Collective. Communication is at the heart of the Bible. In a fascinating book, *The Invention of Hebrew*, Seth Sandres claims, "The [Hebrew] Bible is the first text to address people as a public. It is this call that the Bible's audiences have been answering for more than two thousand years."[5] According to Sanders we find in the Hebrew Bible / Old Testament texts of unique communicative power in their ancient Near Eastern context.[6] However, modernity has worked to mute this acoustic, and we might say that postmodernism has questioned whether we can ever hear such a text truthfully – let alone as the Word of God – *the* epistemological question.

The philosophy of language – think of Derrida's deconstruction of Saussure – has been at the heart of postmodernism, raising questions about the (im) possibility of truthful interpretation. In different ways, Kevin Vanhoozer and Olivier Riaudel leverage speech-act theory and its development in pragmatics to tackle the view of Scripture as human and inspired (Vanhoozer) as well as to nuance a proper understanding of *sola scriptura* (Riaudel) lest it be viewed as a licence for the final authority of each individual reader.[7] Henri Blocher explores with nuance what we might mean when we describe the Bible as inspired and thus inerrant. Pragmatics, as a discipline in linguistics that further develops speech act theory and includes *nonverbal* aspects, backs us into the role of the body – think, for example, of facial expressions – in interpretation, a topic that has recently been foregrounded as of importance.[8] In these and many other ways, certain developments in philosophy of language help us to see how we might together read the Bible truthfully and to hear God's address today. Vanhoozer

---

5. Seth L. Sanders, *The Invention of Hebrew* (Urbana: University of Illinois Press, 2009), 1.

6. See my discussion of this in Craig G. Bartholomew, *The Old Testament and God*, Old Testament Origins and the Question of God (Grand Rapids: Baker Academic, 2022).

7. On language and biblical interpretation see vol. 2 of the SAHS, namely *After Pentecost: Language and Biblical Interpretation*.

8. Richard Kearney and Brian Treanor, eds., *Carnal Hermeneutics* (New York: Fordham University Press, 2015).

rightly notes that such an approach only makes sense in the context of a nexus of beliefs.

The normative use of the Bible in ethics cries out for attention. It is a topic we addressed in volume 3, *A Royal Priesthood? The Use of the Bible Ethically and Politically: A Dialogue with Oliver O'Donovan* (2002). However, Karsten Lehmkühler's chapter is a wonderful overview of the issues at stake and the main philosophical approaches. It is a chapter that professor and student alike will find very helpful.

In recent decades the reception history of the Bible has come to be seen as important for biblical interpretation. Anthony Thiselton (1937–2023) provides a masterful overview of the challenges of interpretation of the Bible down through the centuries. This is one of Anthony's last written pieces before his death in 2023. He was deeply involved in the Scripture and Hermeneutics seminars and is sorely missed. Emmanuel Durand's foray into the influential interpretation of Augustine and Aquinas takes us onto the terrain of reception history, but so too do Jeremiah Unterman's overview of Jewish biblical interpretation,[9] Armin D. Baum's assessment of the historical-critical method,[10] Karen Swallow Prior's exploration of literature and the Bible, and the chapters on reading with the global church and the new media of transmission of the Bible. At the heart of hermeneutics, inevitable since the historical turn in philosophy, is the understanding that not just the biblical texts but also we the readers are embedded in history and particular cultures. In the best sense of hermeneutics, these chapters call us to attention to both contexts. Henk van den Belt's chapter on the Spirit and interpretation creatively addresses an area of reception of the Bible that has often been ignored but is starting to receive greater attention.[11]

If the Bible is a communicative book par excellence, then we do well to remember that we are amidst a communications revolution, on par with the invention of the codex and the printing press. In a fascinating chapter Philipe de Pol explores what the digital revolution might mean for biblical interpretation today. Even as so many Christians leap onto the technological bandwagon unthinkingly, de Pol alerts us to the media that made the Bible possible, the influence of the printing press, and the effect of the many new media today. There is so much here that needs sustained exploration, and my hope is that we

9. KLC has a vested interest in Jewish interpretation. When Jeremiah Unterman's creative, *Justice for All: How the Jewish Bible Revolutionized Ethics* (Philadelphia: Jewish Publication Society, 2017) released, we cohosted an event with him on his book at Society of Biblical Literature.

10. Cf. Craig Bartholomew's chapter in vol. 1 of *Renewing Biblical Interpretation*.

11. See, e.g., Ronald Herms, John R. Levison, and Archie T. Wright, eds., *The Spirit Says: Inspiration and Interpretation in Israelite, Jewish and Early Christian Texts* (Berlin: De Gruyter, 2021).

might use de Pol's chapter to spark a volume in this series devoted to this topic. Let me end where de Pol himself does, reminding us that the Bible is important because it bears authoritative witness to the living Word, Jesus Christ.

We are very grateful to Lydia for all her work in bringing this volume together and overseeing the translation. A feast awaits, and we invite you, the reader, to tuck in!

List of Contributors

Craig G. Bartholomew is the director of the Kirby Laing Centre for Public Theology in Cambridge, UK, having been the H. Evan Runner Professor of Philosophy at Redeemer University College (Ontario, Canada) from 2004 to 2017. He has edited and published numerous books, most recently *The Old Testament and God*; *Listening to Scripture: An Introduction to Interpreting the Bible*; and, coauthored with Heath Thomas, *The Minor Prophets: A Theological Introduction*.

Armin D. Baum is professor of New Testament at the Freie Theologische Hochschule Giessen (Gießen School of Theology, Germany) and associate professor in the PhD program of the Evangelische Theologische Faculteit Leuven (Evangelical Theological Faculty Leuven, Belgium). He has published several monographs, the first volume of a major introduction to the New Testament (Gospels and Acts), and many articles in peer-reviewed journals. His fields of research are ancient and early Christian historiography, ancient and early Christian pseudepigraphy, gender roles in antiquity and the New Testament, interdisciplinary approaches to the synoptic problem, and biblical hermeneutics.

Henri Blocher held the chair of systematic theology at the Faculté Libre de Théologie Evangélique, Vaux-sur-Seine, from 1965 to 2003, and the Gunther Knoedler Chair at Wheaton College Graduate School from 2003 to 2008. His books and articles cover various fields of systematic theology. He was a member of the team responsible for the *Nouvelle Bible Segond* and was vice-president of the United Bible Societies from 1988 to 1996. His books include *In the Beginning: The Opening Chapters of Genesis*; *Evil and the Cross: An Analytical Look at the Problem of Pain*; *Original Sin: Illuminating the Riddle*; *La Bible au microscope: exégèse et théologie biblique*; *Dieu et sa Parole*; and his forthcoming Kantzer Lectures, *God, Evil and Possibility*.

Emmanuel Durand taught theology in Paris (2001–14), in Ottawa (2015–19), and in Rome (2019–20), before joining Fribourg University in Switzerland. His doctoral thesis (Paris/Leuven, 2004) and his habilitation thesis (Fribourg, 2007) have contributed to the renewal of French-speaking Trinitarian theology. Emmanuel Durand has published monographs and scientific articles in the fields of Trinitarian theology, Christology, and Christian anthropology. He is currently engaged in research on the theology of hope, addressing the crisis in representations of the future and salvation. His last book is *Divine Speech in Human Words: Thomistic Engagements with Scripture.*

Lydia Jaeger is professor and academic advisor at the Institut Biblique de Nogent-sur-Marne (France). She is the author of various books and articles on the relationship between Christianity and science. She is research associate at St. Edmund's College, University of Cambridge. Her research interests include the natural order, the epistemological and ethical implications of the doctrine of creation, the theology of science, and our understanding of human persons in the light of evolutionary biology, neuroscience, and philosophy.

Karsten Lehmkühler is professor of systematic theology and ethics at the Faculté de théologie protestante de Strasbourg and member of the advisory board on ethical issues of the Community of Protestant Churches in Europe (CPCE). His research work focuses on several themes: theological anthropology, bioethics, comparative theology of religions, Dietrich Bonhoeffer's theology, truth and truthfulness. His books include *Inhabitatio: Die Einwohnung Gottes im Menschen* and *Accompagnement spirituel des personnes en fin de vie: Témoignages et réflexions* (coeditor).

Philippe de Pol is pastor of the Union des églises évangéliques libres (Union of Evangelical Free Churches), working as chaplain at the Fondation John Bost, translating and explaining the Bible using the five senses for people with disabilities. He previously created French language resources for the Marble Project of the United Bible Societies. Marble is negotiating the transition from print to digital, to facilitate translators' access to the resources they need (translations, commentaries, lexicons, dictionaries, etc.) through Paratext software (in partnership with SIL International). In addition, Marble is developing an application for the public, which brings together most of the resources for translators.

Karen Swallow Prior earned her PhD in English at the State University of New York at Buffalo. Currently a writer and speaker and a columnist for Religion

New Service, she served for years as professor of English at Liberty University and later as research professor of English and Christianity and Culture at Southeastern Baptist Theological Seminary. She is a senior fellow at the Trinity Forum. Her writing has appeared in the *New York Times*, *The Atlantic*, *Vox*, the *Washington Post*, *Christianity Today*, and many other places. Her most recent book is *The Evangelical Imagination: How Stories, Images, and Metaphors Created a Culture in Crisis*.

Olivier Riaudel is professor at the Faculty of Theology of the Université Catholique de Louvain-la-Neuve (Belgium). His research focuses on the problems and trends of contemporary systematic theology, particularly Protestant theology, with a special interest in Wolfhart Pannenberg, and the analysis of religious and theological language and the rationality of the Christian faith. He is the editor of Karl Rahner's *Complete Works* in French.

Anthony C. Thiselton (1937–2023) was emeritus professor of Christian theology and former head of department in the University of Nottingham (from 1992). He was formerly principal of St John's College, University of Durham (1988–92). He was ordained in the Church of England (from 1960), canon theologian of Leicester and Southwell and Nottingham, and vice-chairman of the Church of England Doctrine Commission. He published thirty-three books (mostly on hermeneutics, New Testament, and doctrine) and eighty-five research articles and taught all over the world.

Jeremiah Unterman is the academic editor of The Koren Tanakh of the Land of Israel series and a resident scholar at the Herzl Institute in Jerusalem. Author of two books (*Justice for All: How the Jewish Bible Revolutionized Ethics* and *From Repentance to Redemption: Jeremiah's Thought in Transition*), as well as over one hundred scholarly articles, he has taught at Yeshiva University, Dartmouth College, Northwestern University, University of California–Irvine, and other universities. He received his PhD from the University of California, Berkeley, in the Judaica Program of the Near Eastern Studies Department. He is an ordained Orthodox rabbi.

Henk van den Belt (PhD, Leiden University) is professor of systematic theology at the Vrije Universiteit (Free University), Amsterdam, and professor of dogmatics at the Theological University of Apeldoorn. He is ordained as a pastor in the Protestant Church in the Netherlands and previously taught at the universities of Utrecht and Groningen in the Netherlands. He is the editor of one of the volumes of the critical edition of the Leiden *Synopsis of Purer Theology* and the author of *The Authority of Scripture in Reformed Theology: Truth and Trust* and many articles on Reformed Orthodoxy and on neo-Calvinism.

Benno van den Toren is professor of intercultural theology at the Protestant Theological University in Groningen. He arrived in Groningen after eight years of teaching in French-speaking Africa followed by eight years at Wycliffe Hall, University of Oxford. The experience of teaching theology in a social and cultural environment deeply influenced by African Traditional Religion and Islam and marked by poverty and injustice has profoundly shaped his theological understanding and approach. It has deepened his confidence in the vibrancy, power, and relevance of the Christian faith.

Kevin Vanhoozer (PhD, Cambridge University) is research professor of systematic theology at Trinity Evangelical Divinity School (TEDS) in Deerfield, Illinois. Previously, he taught at the University of Edinburgh and the Wheaton College Graduate School. He is the author or editor of twenty books, including *Is There a Meaning in This Text?*, *The Drama of Doctrine*, and, most recently, *Mere Christian Hermeneutics: Transfiguring What it Means to Read the Bible Theologically*. He serves as theological mentor of the Augustine Fellowship, one of six groups associated with the Center for Pastor Theologians.

Acknowledgments

This book would not have been possible without the help and contribution of many people. The original idea for a multiperspective volume on biblical interpretation focusing on methodological questions and adapted for a nonspecialist audience came from Roger Pouivet. Bernard Reber read the complete (French) manuscript and made helpful comments. Chapter 2 was translated from French into English by David Brown, chapter 9 by David McIlroy, and chapter 12 by Véronique de Pol, revised by David Brown. Rachel Vaughan provided administrative assistance and Eliette Gaiblet worked hard on harmonizing reference style and formatting for the English edition. We are grateful to the editors on both sides of the Atlantic for welcoming this bilingual project: to the French Bible Society and Katie Badie for publishing the French edition and to Zondervan Academic, Katya Covrett, and David McNutt for publishing the English edition. My special gratitude goes to the leadership of the Institut Biblique de Nogent-sur-Marne (France), and in particular to its principal Etienne Lhermeneult, for having encouraged me to go forward with this project. After getting Anthony Thiselton on board and writing a chapter for the French edition, Craig Bartholomew played an ever-increasing part in the English edition, so that we decided to share the editorial responsibility for this volume. We the editors are grateful to be able to work within intellectually stimulating and spiritually nurturing research communities: the Kirby Laing Centre for Public Theology in Cambridge (England) and the Francophone Center for Interdisciplinary Research and Training (CERIF), based at the Institut Biblique de Nogent. It is a special privilege to have a piece written by Anthony C. Thiselton, which he was able to complete before the Lord called him home.

APPENDIX A

Centre d'Enseignement et de Recherche Interdisciplinaire Francophone en Sciences, Culture et Théologie in Nogent-sur-Marne, France

The Institut Biblique de Nogent-sur-Marne is an interdenominational Bible college near Paris, which trains pastors, missionaries, and evangelical leaders for France and the French-speaking world. Since its foundation in 1921 by the pastor and evangelist Ruben Saillens, an important figure in France's evangelical movement, the institute's motto has been "The whole Christ in the whole Bible for the whole world." The institute is well-known in French evangelical circles and trusted both for the clarity of its theological convictions and its desire for unity among evangelicals. It played a significant role in fostering relationships between evangelical denominations which led to the creation of the CNEF (Conseil National des Evangéliques de France) in 2010. The CNEF is a member of the European Evangelical Alliance and accounts for 75 percent of French evangelical churches.

For over a decade, the Institut Biblique de Nogent has been working in partnership with the Groupes Bibliques Universitaires et Lycéens (French branch of IFES) on a series of projects on the interactions between science, philosophy, and theology. These projects have culminated in the creation of a new Francophone Center for interdisciplinary research and training in sciences, culture and theology (CERIF), based at the Institut Biblique de Nogent and generously supported by the Templeton Religion Trust.

The aim of CERIF is to centralize resources for people of all ages and backgrounds, providing a hub for research and training on issues at the intersection of contemporary culture and Christianity. This volume aligns with our ethos, as it seeks to equip Christians to integrate current scientific, philosophical, and theological research into their worldview. It is particularly fitting that this volume includes a chapter on biblical inerrancy, a subject at the heart of CERIF, written by theologian Henri Blocher, a key contributor to many of our resources.

CERIF is a new and exciting venture, and we are keen to develop international partnerships. If you want to find out more about CERIF, visit www.cerif.org or contact Lydia Jaeger.

APPENDIX B

Kirby Laing Centre for Public Theology in Cambridge, UK

The Kirby Laing Centre (KLC) became a fully independent UK charity on 1 January 2021. We are a research centre in *public theology*, with the latter understood as Christian research across the disciplines oriented towards the question, "How then should we live?" Our delightful office is at Chesterton Mill, near the centre of Cambridge. KLC is an Associate Member of the Cambridge Theological Federation.

Our ethos is distinctive. Central to KLC is intellectual community and we seek to ground this in Christian spirituality. Our desire is to do work for the glory of God and in the service of the church and the world.

In our view the Bible is central to public theology. This is reflected in our Scripture Collective, directed by Dr David Larsen. The Scripture Collective now houses four Seminars: The Scripture and Hermeneutics Seminar, the Scripture and Doctrine Seminar, the Scripture and Church Seminar (practical theology), and the Scripture and University Seminar. Each Seminar has its own committee and chair/s.

The origins of our Scripture Collective are found in the Scripture and Hermeneutics Seminar, which, in 2022, celebrated its 25th anniversary. We are delighted to have a formal publishing partnership with Zondervan Academic, and it is a joy to see this third volume in the series in partnership with Lydia Jaeger and our French colleagues, go to print.

KLC is a growing community, and we invite you to become part of it. You can sign up for our emails and see who we are and what we are up to on our website at www.kirbylaingcentre.co.uk.

Rev Dr Craig G. Bartholomew
Director, Kirby Laing Centre, October 2023

APPENDIX C

British and Foreign Bible Society

The British and Foreign Bible Society (BFBS) was founded in 1804 by Thomas Charles, William Wilberforce, and other members of the Clapham Sect. We exist to promote the widest possible distribution and use of the Bible throughout the world. We do this through translation, publishing, distribution, literacy, Bible engagement, and advocacy throughout all spheres of society. We work with all Christian traditions.

Throughout the nineteenth century BFBS helped establish a worldwide Bible Society network. Over 150 societies now operate in over 200 territories under the umbrella of United Bible Societies (UBS). BFBS continues to operate worldwide in partnership with members of UBS.

We believe that the global church faces a crisis of Bible confidence in the midst of a growing opportunity and openness to the Bible in multiple contexts. Our vision is to see Christians confident in the Bible in all aspects of life, to see a changed conversation about the Bible in wider society, and as a result to see the transformation that the Bible brings when it is embodied in our lives, relationships, and communities.

We seek to work with the highest possible standards of academic and research excellence both with respect to the Bible and with respect to societies and cultures. This requires an attitude of deep listening both to Scripture and to our varied and distinctive audiences. Our interventions always seek to help people and communities engage the Bible more deeply for themselves and experience the reality of Jesus to which the Scripture leads.

We are delighted to continue our association with the Scripture and Hermeneutics Seminar through an ongoing partnership with the Kirby Laing Centre for Public Theology. KLC are now administering our research grant programme, intended to support research into the relationship between the Bible and contemporary life. For further information on Bible Society's work see www.biblesociety.org.uk.

Professor Paul S. Williams
Chief Executive, British and Foreign Bible Society